The Immortal Games

of

CAPABLANCA

—

FRED REINFELD

DOVER PUBLICATIONS, INC.
NEW YORK

Published in Canada by General Publishing Company, Ltd., 30 Lesmill Road, Don Mills, Toronto, Ontario.
Published in the United Kingdom by Constable and Company, Ltd.

This Dover edition, first published in 1990, is an unabridged and unaltered republication of the work first published by Horowitz & Harkness, New York, in 1942.

Manufactured in the United States of America
Dover Publications, Inc., 31 East 2nd Street, Mineola, N.Y. 11501

Library of Congress Cataloging-in-Publication Data

Capablanca, José Raúl, 1888–1942.
    The immortal games of Capablanca / [selected and annotated by] Fred Reinfeld.
        p.   cm.
    Reprint. Originally published: New York : Horowitz and Harkness, 1942.
    Includes index.
    ISBN 0-486-26333-9
    1. Capablanca, José Raúl, 1888–1942. 2. Chess—Collections of games.
I. Reinfeld, Fred, 1910–1964.   II. Title.
[GV1439.C3A3   1990]
794.1′5—dc20   90-36483
                                                                        CIP

Contents

Part I
THE BOY PRODIGY BECOMES A MASTER. 1902-1909.

Part II
GRANDMASTER. 1910-1914.

Part III
CHALLENGER. 1914-1920.

Part IV
WORLD CHAMPION. 1921-1927.

Part V

EX-CHAMPION. 1927-1942.

José Raoul Capablanca

Biography of
José Raoul Capablanca

The February 1909 issue of THE AMERICAN CHESS BUL-LETIN began with this remarkable "advertisement": "Wanted: a youth with the genius of Morphy, the memory of Pillsbury and the determination of Steinitz." A few months later, the assignment was filled by a 20-year-old Columbia junior. This young man proved himself one of the outstanding masters of the day by defeating Frank Marshall by the amazing score of 8—1. Two years later, the young man proved that his first success was no fluke, by carrying off the first prize in one of the strongest international tourneys ever held (San Sebastian 1911).

The young man was now considered the outstanding con-tender for the World Championship. He was the darling of the gods. Everything came to him easily, effortlessly. What others achieved after years of study and toil, he attained with no trouble to speak of. He never bothered to study the game systematically, because he did not need to. His admirers called this self-reliance, his detractors termed it laziness.

Eventually he achieved his ambition and became World Champion. And now the story takes a tragic turn. The fam-ous accuracy begins to sag, fighting spirit dims, boredom sets in, and we hear ominous announcements that the game is played out, that it is too simple. After only seven years, he loses the title; he fights manfully, but all his art and all his skill are not enough. From this point on, the road is down-ward. This player, who was once the world's greatest light-ning-chess wizard, now frequently suffers from grueling time-pressure. Once he appraised positions with staggeringly rapid intuition; now he finds it difficult to concentrate, he is content to take the easiest way. Once he got along famously on his lack of book knowledge; today there are others who flourish on the same quality—worse yet, there are others who combine great ability with thorough book knowledge. The same player who was previously considered a combinative genius, becomes the symbol in certain quarters for a dry, unimaginative type of play. He frequently used the style for which Flohr has been execrated so often—the policy of defeating the also-rans and drawing with most of the prize-winners. This explains, by the way, why he won so relatively few first prizes. There was a brief flickering of the old genius at the Moscow and Nottingham tournaments of 1936; but the decline continued, and reached its nadir in the Avro tournament of 1938.

That player was Jose R. Capablanca. His career was a tragic one, not only because he died so prematurely, but because he had long ago taken the downward path. There is obvious tragedy in the lives of great men (such dissimilar types, for example, as Lincoln and Mozart) who were cut off in the plenitude of their powers, just as they were on the verge of what would have been their greatest achievements. Yet such a fate is not so bitter as that of men like Capablanca (or Napoleon), who have reached the heights, have been dislodged from them, and have made vain efforts to recover the lost position.

To those who observed Capablanca's sensational climb to fame, he was an inspiration; their faith in him never wavered. To those who belonged to a later generation, Capablanca was by no means the same impressive figure. This was due to the fact that he had not only entered a period of decline, but that interested parties indulged in systematic detraction of Capablanca. As I have no personal axe to grind, I do not care to engage in these polemics; but it is my conviction that in the years to come, Capablanca's reputation as a great master will be steadily on the upgrade. Partisan wrangles will disappear, and the games will speak for themselves.

One interesting indication of Capablanca's greatness is that to non-chess-players his name was better known than the names of all other chess masters put together! This was due partly to his engaging personality and distinguished appearance: he was one of those exceptional people who at once stand out in a crowd. Wherever he went, he was a goodwill ambassador for Latin America and for chess.

There is a certain significance in the fact that Jose Raoul Capablanca was born in Havana in 1888. At that time, and throughout the second half of the nineteenth century, Havana was one of the outstanding chess centers of the world.

Attracted by the city's charm, the lavish hospitality, the more than generous remuneration and the keen and sympathetic interest of the Cuban amateurs, many of the greatest masters of the age made the trip to Havana: Steinitz, Dr. Lasker, Pillsbury, Tchigorin, Blackburne, Mackenzie and others. Even the great Morphy had sojourned there a while during the terrible days of the Civil War.

This was the atmosphere, redolent of chess and chess events, into which Capablanca was born. No wonder, some will say, that he became a chess prodigy; for intense preoccupation with a given field in a given era will generally culminate in the appearance of stupendous genius in that field. This was true of the Italian Renaissance as it has been true of the tremendous strides of medical research in more recent times. And yet the fact remains, after all allowances have been made for these historical conditioning influences, that it was precisely an individual named Capablanca, and not someone else, who emerged a chess genius.

The early stages of his progress are well known; how he learned the moves at the age of four by watching his father play; how, with very little study or further play, he developed to the point where he was able to win the Championship of Cuba at the age of 12 in a set match with Juan Corzo.

Many years later, as a mature man, Capablanca described this match in his book MY CHESS CAREER, now out of print, in the following words:

"I began to play with the conviction that my adversary was superior to me; he knew all the openings, and I knew none; he knew many games of the great masters by heart, things of which I had no knowledge whatever; besides, he had played many a match and had the experience and all the tricks that go along with it, while I was a novice.

"The first two games were quickly won by him, but something in the third, which was a draw, showed me that he had his weaknesses and gave me the necessary courage and confidence. From there on, he did not win a game, but only scored five more draws before I won the four required."

The really decisive turn to Capablanca's career occurred when he came to this country to prepare himself for entrance into Columbia University. Although the studies of the teen-age youngster came first, he was now able to give more time to chess, and to join the Manhattan Chess Club, where he made many friendships which were to endure for the rest of his life. In the match with Corzo, Capablanca had revealed his capabilities as a match-game player; in view of his tender years, virtual absence of experience and ignorance of the book lines of the openings, it is clear that nothing but pure natural ability was the source of his success. And this aspect of his play became more dazzling than ever when he began to astound his fellow-members of the Manhattan Chess Club with his phenomenal rapid-transit play.

This type of play is peculiarly the domain of the naturally gifted player, and thus the young college student began to acquire a sensational reputation which was soon enhanced by his amazingly successful results in simultaneous play. So rapidly did the news of young Capablanca's achievements in simultaneous play become known to players all over the country that an extensive transcontinental tour was soon arranged. This tour in turn was completed in such a bravura style that an exhibition match was arranged with the American Champion, Frank J. Marshall.

A great deal of nonsense has been written about this match. It is true that the twenty-year-old Cuban won the contest by the magnificent score of 8—1; yet to insist, as did all the contemporary critics, that the chief factor in the result had been Marshall's miserable play, is to do scant justice to either player. Rather than to insist that Marshall had played badly, it would be more to the point to remember that Capablanca had played wonderfully; to remember that Marshall had made no preparation for the match; to remember that no one had realized beforehand that Capablanca had the slightest chance. How could Marshall, or anyone else for that matter, have foreseen that the chess world was about to witness the definitive appearance of one of its most celebrated geniuses?

Whatever the attendant circumstances, the fact was now clear: at the age of 20, Capablanca had become one of the select handful of outstanding masters.

The vital question which now agitated European chess circles was: had Cuba really produced a great chess master, or was Capablanca's victory over Marshall just a flash in the pan? Naturally the young master received an invitation to the next important tourney, at Hamburg in 1910. It goes without saying that Capa gladly accepted the invitation, but he subsequently found that his second United States tour (during the winter of 1909-1910) had been so extensive and so tiring that the state of his health made it inadvisable for him to take part in an international tournament without more rest. Immediately sneers were heard in Europe about the young man's health, although his easy victory in the 1910 New York State Championship, ahead of Marshall and Jaffe, should have sufficed to smother such insinuations.

The following year, Capablanca undertook still another tour, and after its conclusion at Indianapolis took the train to New York and on the very morning of his arrival, began play in the National Tournament. As was to be expected, he did badly in the first part of the contest. Subsequently his play improved, but ultimately he came in second to Marshall, who was in superb form. Nevertheless, Capablanca's recovery had been good enough to put him only half a point behind Marshall. Another week passed, and Capa was on his way to Europe to take part in the great tournament at San Sebastian. This contest had a basic condition which automatically produced a first-class entry: no one was admitted unless he had won at least two third prizes in a very strong tournament. The result was that all the great players of the day, with the exception of the World Champion, participated. A special exception had to be made to secure the entry of Capablanca, and as may be readily imagined, many of the masters looked askance at him.

Two of the most loquacious objectors were Bernstein and Nimzovich, so that it must have given the young Cuban deep satisfaction to smash both of them, which is just what he did. The more level-headed observers felt that Capablanca would make a good score, but in view of the formidable entry, nothing sensational was expected of the 22-year-old making his first appearance in international competition—and what competition!

In the first round Capablanca was paired with Bernstein, who, evidently brimful of over-confidence, took matters too easily and eventually succumbed in a game which is one of the most famous in chess history. In the second round Capa drew warily with Marshall, but in the third, he added the scalp of Amos Burn, England's Grand Old Man. This game was simplicity itself, and one may imagine Burn's feelings on losing so effortlessly to a youngster about one-third of his age. In the fourth round came a hard-fought draw with Tarrasch in which both players were evidently out for blood. The "experts" were beginning to wonder, but at last it seemed that the Cuban was getting his come-uppance, for Janowski outplayed him practically all the way in a superb battle; after adjournment, however, Janowski missed a clear win and allowed Capablanca to conclude with a problem-like win. In the sixth round, Capa won a difficult ending against Leonhardt and the following day he drew rather a dull affair with Duras.

After these exertions, the neophyte was bunched at the top with Schlechter (who had recently drawn a match for the World Championship), Marshall and Tarrasch. Rubinstein, something of a disappointment so far, had drawn his first six games! But now the pace became hotter, for Rubinstein won his next three games, while Capablanca took full advantage of Nimzovich's unaccountably feeble play, and drew readily with Schlechter and Maroczy. In his next game Capablanca was very lucky to win from Spielmann, who had outplayed him but lost his grip at the decisive moment. Nevertheless the Cuban had by this time built up a comfortable lead, so that even his loss to Rubinstein in a sensational encounter still left him in first place. There followed what the Tournament Book describes as a "leathery" draw with Teichmann, and when the last round arrived, the leading scores were Capablanca and Rubinstein 9, Vidmar 8½—but with Rubinstein having a bye, and the other two leaders paired with each other! Thus Capa needed only a half-point to clinch first prize. At first he appeared to be in difficulties, but he soon squirmed out of them dexterously, making the draw obvious and thus gaining the coveted first prize.

How hard-fought the tournament was, may be seen from the even gradation of the scores: Capablanca 9½, Rubinstein and Vidmar 9, Marshall 8½, Nimzovich, Schlechter and Tarrasch 7½, Bernstein and Spielmann 7, Teichmann 6½, Janowski and Maroczy 6, Burn and Duras 5 and Leonhardt 4.

The European critics greeted Capablanca's victory with something less than enthusiasm. They pointed out sourly that he had been lucky and that his style was not very enterprising. In reply to these charges, it may be admitted that every tournament victor has a certain amount of luck, which, however, seems to stand out disproportionately because of his prominent position. As to his alleged lack of fighting spirit, it should be mentioned that Capablanca had less draws than the next six players in the score-table! In any event, a certain amount of timidity was inevitable in so inexperienced a player, especially if he was taking his rivals at their own high valuation! Granted that his play was a bit spotty, that of his opponents was still more imperfect; his performance still remains a very fine one, and small wonder that from this time on, he was definitely considered as being of World Championship caliber.

At any rate, Capablanca was constantly in the public eye. Taking advantage of this interest, he toured Europe during

March and April, Argentina and Uruguay in May and June, then back to Europe in September, October, November. Everywhere he was greeted with the greatest enthusiasm and everywhere he achieved splendid results: Paris, Frankfort, Nuremberg, Munich, Berlin, Hamburg, Cologne, Rotterdam, Hague, Amsterdam, Breslau, Prague, Budapest, Vienna and London. He did not travel to Russia during these trips.

In 1913 he took part in three tournaments; although they were not of first-rate importance, they were valuable in guiding him to maturity and deepening his grasp of the game. In the Second American National Tournament in 1913, he came a half-point ahead of Marshall; in the Havana Tournament, a little later, their respective roles were reversed. This was a great disappointment for the young Cuban, as his native land had arranged the tournament for the specific purpose of honoring its illustrious son. The outcome of the tournament hinged on the individual contest between Capablanca and Marshall—a game in which both players were terribly nervous and neither was seen at his best. Capablanca soon established a clear superiority, but Marshall fought back hard and eventually, when Capablanca weakened badly, actually succeeded in winning.

Several months later, Capa played in a tournament organized by the Rice Chess Club, winning all thirteen games—an achievement comparable to that of Lasker in the New York 1893 tourney. To facilitate his participation in the coming tournament at St. Petersburg, Capablanca was appointed to a position in the Cuban diplomatic service, with the understanding that he was to proceed to his duties at St. Petersburg! His second trip to Europe was vastly different from the preceding one. This time he came with the reputation of a first-rate master, and was accepted everywhere with enthusiasm or at least wholesome respect. He continued to display his marvelous talent for simultaneous play, but a more impressive demonstration of his powers was seen in the series of exhibition games he played during this trip with some of the world's leading masters. Reti and Tartakover in Vienna, Mieses and Teichmann in Berlin, Alekhine, Znosko-Borovsky and Dus-Chotimirsky in St. Petersburg, Bernstein in Moscow and Nimzovich in Riga—all were defeated convincingly. These games were among Capablanca's finest to date, revealing a new confidence, a new depth in his play. All this augured well for his showing in the great tournament soon to take place at St. Petersburg.

This magnificent contest occupies a prominent place in chess history for several reasons: it was the first tournament in which both Lasker and Capablanca took part, and the interest in their meeting was at fever heat; the entry, as at San Sebastian, had been assembled under rigorous standards; and finally, it was the last great chess event before the outbreak of the first World War. It was also destined to be the tournament in which 22-year-old Alekhine was to attain grand mastership, after barely managing to draw a tie-match with Nimzovich on being bracketed with him in the most recent All-Russian Championship.

The tournament was run on rather a peculiar basis. There were eleven masters, who were to play a round-robin tournament, after which the last six players were to be dropped, and the first five would proceed to play a double-round tournament among themselves. The verdict of experience on this type of contest is that it has always proved unsatisfactory, partly because an early loss suffices to ruin a player's chances, partly because there is always the problem of whether the scores should be carried over from the initial tournament (clearly, some of these points, having been gained against weaker players, have less qualitative value than those gained in the finals).

Capablanca started off rather uncertainly, losing a Pawn in the opening against Nimzovich and Rubinstein and scoring a point and a half from these two games! Thereafter he played in his best form, and aided by an unlucky loss by Lasker to Bernstein, the Cuban reached the finals with the tremendous lead of one and a half points. His ultimate victory seemed assured, all the more so since the Champion's form seemed rather uneven because of lack of practice. The finalists, in addition to Capablanca and Lasker, were Alekhine, Tarrasch and Marshall. All went well for Capa for the first four rounds, although Lasker's play had greatly improved, and he was now fighting with all the tenacity and resourcefulness for which he was famous. The first encounter between the two great rivals in the finals produced a battle royal in which the younger player secured a marked advantage right in the opening. Fighting like a lion, continually hovering on the brink of defeat, Lasker managed to draw in a hundred-move struggle!

The second meeting in the finals between Lasker and Capablanca has since been known as one of the most famous and most decisive battles ever waged over the chessboard. In this game, one of his very finest, Lasker made his young opponent look pitiable; he trussed him up and left him in a helpless state, winding up with a neat combination. Visibly shaken by this catastrophe, Capablanca left a piece *en prise* the next day against Tarrasch. Although he fought on for hours, Capablanca had to surrender eventually, ultimately coming out half a point behind Lasker.

Once more the great Lasker had displayed his wizardry, and it was clear to everyone that his poise and his superb fighting spirit were equalled by no man. Yet Capablanca's showing had demonstrated with like clarity that he too was "super-class," that he was Lasker's worthiest rival. Despite his tragic failure, Capablanca had come out of the dramatic struggle with a heightened reputation.

In July of 1914 Capablanca left Europe to fulfill a series of engagements in South America. Before the ship arrived at Buenos Aires, the World War had broken out. The result was (if one may mention so trifling a matter in the midst of so great a catastrophe) that Capablanca's hopes of getting a match for the title were dashed, if not permanently, at least for years to come. In addition, international chess was to come to a standstill. Yet this period had its value for Capablanca. He played in a number of tournaments in the United States, easily taking first prize each time.

The chief tournaments in which he competed were the Rice Memorial Tournament of 1915, where his victory was certain long before the end; the Manhattan Chess Club Tournament of 1918, which had a very respectable entry, including Kostich, Marshall and Janowski; and the Hastings Victory Tournament of 1919. This last was anything but formidable, but it was notable for being the first international tourney held under Allied auspices, and for being the first of the illustrious series of Hastings Tournaments. Describing this event in his entertaining book CHESS AND ITS STARS (Out of print— Ed.) Brian Harley writes:

"It is probable that no chess player, past or present, has ever been the object of so much hero-worship. All through the fortnight of the Tourney it was impossible to get near Capablanca's board, unless one belonged to the camp-stool brigade. Otherwise one obtained merely a back-view of a throng of worshippers sitting at the shrine of 'Capa.' These devotees did not so much watch his play as himself. When, as often happened, the champion took a constitutional down the roped-in track, their eyes followed him adoringly. I noticed one small boy, who had been honored with the sacred autograph, standing stock-still for a full five minutes, with a look of ineffable bliss upon his face."

In 1919 Capablanca also played his second important match, with the Serbian master Kostich. However, five straight wins by Capablanca soon led to the inevitable conclusion that Kostich's reputation had outrun his ability.

Once more, the match with Lasker was a burning problem. "I hope the match will come," wrote Capablanca in MY CHESS CAREER in 1920, "the sooner the better, as I don't want to play an old man, but a master in the plenitude of his powers."

In 1920, Lasker offered to resign the title, but this did not satisfy Capablanca. Asked what he would do if Lasker refused to play, the Cuban replied that he would then be justified in claiming the title and that he would be willing to accept a challenge from the Russian master, Rubinstein.

In 1921 the chess world at last had its wish come true, and the long-awaited Championship Match took place. But alas! like many another consummation devoutly to be wished, the actual performance was a disappointing one. The fault was not Capablanca's but Lasker's. None of that grand resourcefulness and superb fighting spirit which had marked his play for thirty years were to be seen; truly this veteran of a hundred heroic fights played like a "tired old man" and not like "a master in the plenitude of his powers."

Many explanations have been advanced for Lasker's poor showing, but it still remains a vexing problem—all the more so when we remember that for years to come, he was to resist the ravages of old age, always figuring high up in the prize list of every tournament in which he participated, always lending an added touch of glamor to every contest in which he took part. Some commentators have suggested that the Havana climate affected him adversely, while others have asserted equally strongly that the climate played no significant role. The more profound reason is undoubtedly of a personal character: Lasker had lost all his savings in the war, and agreed to the match primarily to recoup his losses. In addition, the war and its aftermath had undoubtedly had a depressing effect on him; add to this the premonitions of an elderly man pursued by a young and ambitious rival, and then the strangely listless moves of a man who plays without conviction from the very first move are no longer puzzling. A tragic business this, the dethronement of a Titan!

Capablanca had at last reached the heights, and had achieved all that a chess master can hope to accomplish. But this result, instead of spurring his ambition, only caused it to slacken. In his first tournament after gaining the title (London 1922), he won first prize in superior style, and earned his prize on the basis of a fine performance. But his next tournament, the great double-round tourney at New York in 1924, was a disappointment. He got off to a sensationally bad start, four nondescript draws and then a bad drubbing from Reti which has remained proverbial to this day. That game made more propaganda for the Hypermoderns than a ton of articles on the Hypermodern School and its theories. Capablanca then pulled himself together and rose steadily in the score table, but it was too late to overtake Lasker, once more playing in the great form of his earlier days. Moscow 1925 repeated the same dismal story: two bad losses in the early rounds, the first to Iljin-Ghenevsky, who scored magnificently with a well-conducted attack, and the second to Werlinsky, who succeeded in winning Capablanca's Queen for only two minor pieces before fifteen moves had been made! Again Capablanca began a splendid series of victories, but again it was too late to rise to first place. Two bad results in two years! Not that these results were bad in an absolute sense; but the chess world expects only the best from its champions.

At Lake Hopatcong the following year, Capablanca scored an easy victory, and then came the great test: the sextangular tournament at New York. It is not generally known that Capablanca entered the tournament with the greatest misgivings, but this is readily apparent from an article he wrote for the *New York Times* on the eve of the first round.

"We have now considered all our competitors. It remains only to discuss the writer's chances. It would be rank hypocrisy to say that we do not consider ourselves a contender for one of the first three places. Were we merely to consider the past records and the results of our previous encounters with every one of the masters involved, there could be only one conclusion. It is also self-evident that the possessor of the world's title must have some qualifications not easily found among every one of his competitors. We are aware, however, that such conditions are not permanent and that we may now be somewhat weaker than when at our best ten years ago. In the writer's opinion, he was at his best in Havana when playing Kostich the match which Kostich lost in five straight games. On the other hand, some of our competitors, if not all

of them, are now stronger than ever. How much of a difference our loss and their gain combined will make the result
alone will show. It might be interesting to compare the past
with the present. At San Sebastian, in 1911, in our first international encounter, we did not have much confidence of carrying the chief prize, but we had plenty of ambition, and having
been favored by the goddess of chance, we succeeded in winning the honor.

"Today we have plenty of confidence, the confidence which
only years of continuous success can give, but most of the
ambition is gone and the fickle lady has not been kind of late.
Then we were practically ignorant of our opponent's qualities,
but we had a tremendous capacity for work. Today we know
our opponents thoroughly, but alas! our capacity for work
is not the same. Then we were very nervous and easily upset.
Today we are cool and collected and nothing short of an
earthquake will ruffle us. We have now more experience, but
less power. Can some of the power come back? What will
happen? We shall soon see. The stage is set, the curtain is
about to rise on what should be one of the most memorable
struggles in the history of chess."

The tense attitude revealed in his admirably objective pas-
sage may have arisen from the understanding that the second-
prize winner (in the event that Capablanca came first) would
be recognized as official challenger for the title; or if Capablanca did not win the tournament, then the first-prize winner
would be recognized as challenger.

As the tournament actually took its course, Capablanca's
forebodings turned out to be groundless. He took an early
lead and won the contest with points to spare. He defeated
Alekhine, Vidmar and Spielmann once, Nimzovich twice and
Marshall three times. In fact, he could have turned at least
two draws into wins had he needed the extra half-points. It
was a magnificent triumph, the pinnacle of the great Cuban's
career. And yet, even in the very act of achieving this splendid victory, he had revealed weak points in his armor which
were to prove his undoing before the year was out.

Before the 1927 match for the title took place, not a single
commentator considered the possibility that Capablanca could
lose the match. Some speculated that Alekhine might win a
game or two, but that was the limit of their expectations. After
all, the Russian had never managed to come out victorious in
one single encounter with Capablanca, and had five losses to

show for his pains. It is therefore easy to imagine the sensation created by Capablanca's loss of the title.

And yet, as one looks back at the match, what else could have been the result? The challenger was at least as equally gifted as the champion in respect of ability. But as regards ambition, willingness to study, capacity for concentration, intensity of love for the game, Alekhine was unrivalled. For years Capablanca had not bothered to prepare for even the most serious tests; he had always shirked the chore of studying the fine points of opening theory; what did not come easily to him, did not come to him at all. And so he was to discover, in the bitter phrase of Anderssen after his match with Morphy, that one cannot keep chess ability intact in a glass case.

With the loss of the title, Capablanca's best years were over. He was now a master like the other masters, one of many fighting for glory. He had ups and downs, periods in which he approached the play of his best years, and at other times there were lapses that left him unrecognizable. Thus in the great tournament at Carlsbad in 1929, he turned out masterpieces with almost mass-production frequency; yet he put a piece *en prise* against Saemisch on the ninth move! He scored some notable successes during this period, it is true: at Berlin in 1928, when he achieved an easy victory in a double round tourney with Nimzovich, Spielmann, Rubinstein, Reti, Tartakover and Marshall; again at Moscow in 1936 in a similar tournament, where he had the pleasure of coming ahead of Botvinnik and Dr. Lasker among others; and most pleasing triumph of all, when he divided first prize in the great Nottingham Tournament with Botvinnik, ahead of three World Champions and a flock of contenders!

What is important for the rest of us, however, is that Capablanca at all times remained a master of the first rank, and that he produced many fine games which will continue to delight chess players for generations to come. In such books as the present one, old rivalries and controversies fade into their true perspectives of unimportance as we study the life-work of a great artist and a great chess master like Jose Raoul Capablanca.

FRED REINFELD

New York, October 4, 1942

Capablanca's Tournament and Match Record

Tournaments

	Rank	Won	Lost	Drawn	Total
New York State, 1910	1	7	0	0	7
New York, 1911	2	8	1	3	12
San Sebastian, 1911	1	6	1	7	14
New York, 1913	1	10	1	2	13
Havana, 1913	2	8	2	4	14
New York, 1913	1	13	0	0	13
St. Petersburg, 1914	2	10	2	6	18
New York, 1915	1	12	0	2	14
New York, 1916	1	12	1	4	17
New York, 1918	1	9	0	3	12
Hastings, 1919	1	10	0	1	11
London, 1922	1	11	0	4	15
New York, 1924	2	10	1	9	20
Moscow, 1925	3	9	2	9	20
Lake Hopatcong, 1926	1	4	0	4	8
New York, 1927	1	8	0	12	20
Bad Kissingen, 1928	2	4	1	6	11
Berlin, 1928	1	5	0	7	12
Budapest, 1928	1	5	0	4	9
Carlsbad, 1929	2-3	10	2	9	21
Ramsgate, 1929	1	4	0	3	7
Barcelona, 1929	1	13	0	1	14
Budapest, 1929	1	8	0	5	13
Hastings, 1930-31	2	5	1	3	9
New York, 1931	1	9	0	2	11
Hastings, 1934-35	4	4	2	3	9
Moscow, 1935	4	7	2	10	19
Margate, 1935	2	6	1	2	9
Margate, 1936	2	5	0	4	9
Moscow, 1936	1	8	0	10	18
Nottingham, 1936	1-2	7	1	6	14
Semmering, 1937	3-4	2	1	11	14
Paris, 1938	1	6	0	4	10
Avro, 1938	7	2	4	8	14
Margate, 1939	2-3	4	0	5	9
Buenos Aires, 1939	–	6	0	5	11
		267	26	178	471

Matches

		Won	Lost	Drawn	Total
Corzo, 1902		4	2	6	12
Marshall, 1909		8	1	14	23
Kostich, 1919		5	0	0	5
Dr. Lasker, 1921		4	0	14	18
Alekhine, 1927		3	6	25	34
Euwe, 1932		2	0	8	10
		26	9	67	102

14

Part I
The Boy Prodigy Becomes A Master
1902-1909

A detailed study of the opening play of any great master is always rewarding, not only for the additions to one's store of knowledge, but also for the insight it gives us into that master's style, his methods and his ideas. Like his great rival Lasker, Capablanca attached no great value to exhaustive opening knowledge and was content to be a member of the "rough and ready" school throughout his career. This tendency is particularly marked during his early years, in which he lacked not only knowledge but experience as well.

Capablanca followed the general pattern by starting out as a 1 P—K4 specialist. In Games no. 4 and 5 he produced two classics with the Ruy Lopez though the opening play was not particularly distinguished. The first of these games is one of his finest, universally praised by admirers and rivals alike; yet the restrained and timid opening bespeaks the neophyte sailing through uncharted seas. Game no. 5, on the other hand, is handled admirably from the very first move and shows a splendid understanding of how to play the opening with a view to an advantageous middle game.

The single Queen Pawn Opening adopted by the 13-year-old player in Game no. 2 was obviously played with the intention of steering clear of the open-game complexities in which Corzo was so well versed. The later unfolding of the game is so fine and is topped off so neatly by a well-calculated Queen sacrifice, that it is perhaps the most impressive game in this section.

With the black pieces, Capablanca always had the problem, during this early period, of coping with prepared variations. Game no. 1 gives us an idea of the difficulties the young player encountered, and how admirably he met them. The opening is a tricky variation of the King's Gambit in which the most experienced masters have been known to go astray. In Game no. 3, Capablanca adopts what was to be his favorite defense against the Ruy Lopez for almost two de-

cades. The way in which the youthful master easily disposes
of one of the ranking American players in this game is quite
striking.

In Game 2a, Capablanca relies on the French Defense,
presumably to avoid a gambit attack. This game is of the
coffee-house variety, but it is featured by a very fine combination which left an indelible impression on the players who
witnessed it.

As can well be imagined, close games like the Queen's
Gambit were something of a mystery to the young master.
Yet in the two examples we have here, he acquits himself very
creditably. In Game no. 6 he is called upon to endure one of
Marshall's proverbially ingenious and endlessly resourceful
attacks. Only iron nerves could hold out against such an
onslaught. In Game no. 7 he adopts, on the spur of the moment, a line of play in the Tarrasch Defense shown him by a
friend who had seen it in the paper; observe how casual all
this is, far removed from the midnight-oil school! From beginning to end Capablanca plays with extraordinary precision,
never giving his opponent the slightest loophole. Truly a
game that foreshadows a coming World Champion!

1. Match, 1902

KING'S GAMBIT

In this match, Corzo adopted little-known lines in order to take advantage of his 12-year-old opponent's lack of book knowledge. However, Capablanca's use of sturdy common sense proved adequate to the situation — as it so often did throughout his career.

J. Corzo	J. R. Capablanca
White	Black
1 P—K4	P—K4
2 Kt—QB3	Kt—QB3
3 P—B4	P x P
4 Kt—B3	P—KKt4
5 P—KR4	P—Kt5
6 Kt—KKt5	P—KR3
7 KtxP	KxKt

It is not apparent that White has adequate compensation for the piece; but the idea of the gambit is to develop rapidly and thus take advantage of the exposed state of Black's King.

8 P—Q4	P—Q4
9 P x P	....

In line with the previous note, B x P would be stronger.

9	Q—K2ch
10 K—B2	P—Kt6ch
11 K—Kt1	....

White's King now finds himself in a situation which is even worse than that of his colleague. The manner in which the youthful player of the black pieces utilizes this circumstance is most impressive.

Capablanca

Corzo

11	Kt x P!
12 Q x Kt	Q—B4

The point. If now 13 Q x Q?? B x Qch and mate follows. The unfortunate position of White's King now plays a decisive role.

13 Kt—K2	Q—Kt3!

Forcing the exchange of Queens by the threat of . . . B—QB4, and thus bringing his QR into the game.

14 Q x Q	RP x Q
15 Kt—Q4	B—QB4
16 P—B3	R—R5!

Threatening . . . R x Kt! If now 17 P—Kt4, R x KtP!

17 B—K2	B x Ktch
18 P x B	R x QP
19 P—Kt3	Kt—B3
20 B—Kt2	R—Q7

Naturally not 20 . . . R x P? 21 B—B4.

17

21 B—R5ch   . . . .

The resource on which White has relied, but it leads to a snappy finish.

21 . . . .   Kt x B!
22 B x R   P—B6
23 P x P   Kt—B5
24 B—K5   . . . .

Against 24 R—K1 there are various winning methods, as for example 24 . . . B—R6; 25 B—K5 (if 25 R x B, Kt x Rch and the KKtP queens), R—Kt7ch; 26 K—B1, R—K7ch; 27 R x B, P—Kt7ch; 28 K—Kt1, R x Rch etc.

24 . . . .   R—Kt7ch
25 K—B1   R—B7ch

If now 26 K—Kt1, Kt—K7 mate.

26 K—K1   Kt—Q6ch

White resigns; a remarkable game for a youngster.

---

2.   Match, 1902

QUEEN'S PAWN OPENING

This game is perhaps the most remarkable of Capablanca's career: the arduous jockeying for position in the middle game, the delightful and carefully calculated Queen sacrifice and the ensuing accurate endgame play—all are worked out with a skill which is astounding in one so young.

J. R. CAPABLANCA   J. CORZO

White   Black

1 P—Q4   P—Q4
2 Kt—KB3   P—QB4
3 P—K3   Kt—QB3
4 P—QKt3   P—K3
5 B—Kt2   Kt—B3
6 QKt—Q2   P x P?

Poor play, which gives White

more freedom by clearing the K file for him. The proper procedure for Black was demonstrated many years later by Capablanca himself in one of the classic games of his mature period. (See Game No. 49.)

7 P x P   B—Q3
8 B—Q3   O—O
9 O—O   Kt—KR4
10 P—Kt3   P—B4
11 Kt—K5   Kt—B3

The last three moves have had little value aside from solidifying Black's game. But the prospects for his QB are dreary indeed!

12 P—KB4   . . . .

This is a move which a more experienced player would avoid, as it allows Black to barricade the position with a subsequent . . . Kt—K5. 12 P—QR3 (preventing . . . Kt—QKt5) would have been preferable.

12 . . . .   B x Kt
13 BP x B   Kt—KKt5

As this Knight will be unable to find a good post for the remainder of the game, . . . Kt—K5 was more logical.

14 Q—K2   Q—Kt3
15 Kt—B3   B—Q2

This "developing" move should have been postponed in favor of . . . Kt—QKt5, leading to Bishops of opposite color and the removal of one of White's most useful pieces.

16 P—QR3   K—R1
17 P—R3   Kt—R3
18 Q—B2   Kt—B2
19 K—Kt2   P—Kt4

One can understand Black's desire for counterplay, but this move creates a disquietingly loose position on the long diagonal. True, this vital line is closed for the time being.

20 P—KKt4!   . . . .

Well played. Black can never push by with . . . P—B5, for then P—KR4! will follow with crushing effect. Hence the exchange of Pawns will eventually bring about the first break in the center leading to the opening of the long diagonal.

20	Kt—K2
21 Q—K3	R—KKt1
22 QR—K1	Kt—Kt3
23 P x P	Kt—B5ch
24 K—R2	Kt x B

Now parting with this Bishop no longer matters because the opening of the long diagonal is much more important.

| 25 Q x Kt | P x P |
| 26 P—B4! | . . . . |

Forcing the opening of the long diagonal. White's pieces are all placed to the best advantage for getting the most out of this thrust.

26	Q—K3
27 P x P	Q x P
28 P—K6	B—Kt4

Of course if 28 . . . B x P; 29 R x B etc.

Corzo

Capablanca

29 Q x B!!?   . . . .

One cannot blame the youthful master for being carried away by the combinative possibilities of this interesting position; but there is a much simpler win with 29 Q—Q2, B x R; 30 P x Kt, Q x BP (if 30 . . . Q x Kt; 31 P—Q5ch! R—Kt2; 32 R—K8ch and wins); 31 P—Q5ch, R—Kt2; 32 Kt x P, Q—Kt3; 33 R—K7, R—KKt1; 34 Kt—B7ch winning easily.

29	Q x Q
30 P—Q5ch	R—Kt2
31 P x Kt	P—KR3

Black is helpless in the grip of the pressure on the terrible diagonal. If 31 . . . R—KB1; 32 Kt—Q4, Q x QP; 33 R—K8, Q x BP; 34 R x Rch, Q x R; 35 Kt x P and wins.

32 Kt—Q4   Q x R

He has little choice. Against 32 . . . Q—Q2 Capablanca indicates the neat win 33 Kt x P, Q x BP; 34 B x Rch, K—R2; 35 R—K7 winning the Queen (if 35 . . . Q x P; 36 B—K5ch, K—Kt3; 37 R—Kt7ch, K—R4; 38 Kt—Kt3ch, K—R5; 39 R—B4ch, P x R; 40 R—Kt4 mate!).

33 R x Q	R x P
34 R x P	R x R
35 Kt x Rch	K—R2
36 Kt—K7!	. . . .

The fireworks are over and the rest requires only moderate care; nevertheless White plays the final phase with a precision rarely seen in young players. The text keeps Black's King out of play, thus preparing for the victorious advance of the QP.

36	R—KB1
37 K—Kt2	P—KR4
38 P—Q6	P—Kt5
39 P x P	P x P
40 B—K5	K—R3
41 P—Q7	R—Q1
42 Kt—Kt8ch!	R x Kt

Or 42 . . . K—Kt3; 43 Kt—B6, K—B2; 44 B—B7.

43 B—B6	K—Kt3
44 P—Q8(Q)	R x Q
45 B x R	P—Kt4
46 K—B2	K—B4
47 K—K3	K—K4
48 K—Q3	K—Q4

He plays on in vague hope that his inexperienced opponent will allow a stalemate.

49 K—B3	P—Kt6
50 B—R4	P—Kt7
51 B—B2	P—R4
52 P—Kt4	K—K5

If now 53 P x P? K—Q4 and White cannot win!

53 B—Kt6	K—Q4
54 K—Q3	K—B3
55 B—Kt1	K—Q4
56 B—R2	K—B3
57 K—Q4	P—R5
58 K—K5	K—Kt3
59 K—Q5	K—R3

Hoping for 60 K—B6? P—Kt8(Q) and draws!

| 60 K—B5! | Resigns |

2a. Havana, 1902
FRENCH DEFENSE

This game was discovered just as the book was going to press. The beautiful combination makes it well worthy of inclusion in a collection of Capablanca's finest games.

E. CORZO   J. R. CAPABLANCA

White	Black
1 P—K4	P—K3
2 P—Q4	P—Q4
3 Kt—QB3	P x P
4 Kt x P	B—Q2

An unusual continuation which has the drawback of blocking the QBP when the Bishop goes to QB3. But the young player's prime object was doubtless to avoid the pitfalls of a gambit.

5 Kt—KB3	B—B3
6 B—Q3	Kt—Q2
7 O—O	KKt—B3
8 B—KKt5	. . . .

Simply Kt—Kt3 (avoiding exchanges) was best.

| 8 . . . . | B—K2 |
| 9 Kt x Ktch | . . . . |

Again the Knight should have retreated. The exchange only helps Black.

9	B x Kt
10 B—K3	O—O
11 P—B3	P—QKt3

Not 11 . . . P—K4? 12 Kt x P, Kt x Kt; 13 P x Kt, B x KP; 14 B x Pch etc.

| 12 Q—B2 | K—R1 |

Trappy. If 13 B x P? B x Kt! 14 P x B, P—Kt3; 15 B x P, P x B; 16 Q x P, KR—Kt1. (!)

| 13 Kt—Q2 | R—K1 |

Again provoking the sacrifice of the Bishop for three Pawns. The invitation shows a good understanding of the position, as Black's piece will outweigh the Pawns. White's best course was 14 P—KB4.

14 B x P	P—Kt3
15 B x P	P x B
16 Q x P	Q—K2
17 P—KB4	Q—R2

. . . R—KKt1, gaining a tempo, was more exact.

| 18 Q x Qch | K x Q |
| 19 Kt—B3 | . . . . |

White can expect nothing from such dawdling. The more energetic P—KKt4 was called for.

19	R—KKt1
20 QR—K1	R—Kt3
21 B—Q2	B—Q4
22 P—QKt3	R—KB1
23 K—R1	P—B4

Black's pieces are all in good play, and the value of White's Pawns is negligible.

24 P x P	Kt x P
25 P—B4	B—QR1
26 B—Kt4	QR—KKt1
27 B x Kt?	. . . .

A blunder but how many players could prove it?! R—K2 had to be tried.

Capablanca

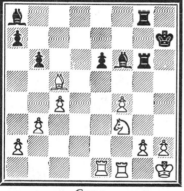

Corzo

| 27 . . . . | R x P!! |

Truly magnificent play from a thirteen-year old! If now 28 B—R3, R—Kt8ch! leads to mate; or if 28 B—Kt1, R x Bch! If 28 R x P, P x B; 29 R x B (or 29 R—K3, B—Q5; 30 R—Q3, R—Kt8ch; 31 R x R, R x R mate), B x Kt and mate follows.

| 28 B—K3 | B—R5! |

Decisive, for if Black is allowed to capture the Rook, White will be unable to retake. On other moves, Black's next leaves his opponent defenseless.

29 R—Q1	B—B7!
30 R—Q7ch	K—R3
31 R—Q5	. . . .

Desperation.

31	B x B
32 Kt—Kt5	R(7) x Kt!
33 P x Ktch	R x P
34 R—B6ch	K—R4
35 R x P	B x Rch

And mate next move. Very snappy!

---

3. New York, 1906
(Team Match)

RUY LOPEZ

It is curious that despite its rather low repute, the Steinitz Defense in this opening was the favorite of three successive World Champions: Steinitz, Lasker and Capablanca. The excellent results they achieved with it may, however, be attributed to their ability rather than to its merits.

A. W. FOX   J. R. CAPABLANCA

(Manhattan Chess Club)   *(Columbia University)*

White	Black
1 P—K4	P—K4
2 Kt—KB3	Kt—QB3
3 B—Kt5	Kt—B3
4 O—O	B—K2
5 R—K1	P—Q3
6 P—Q4	P x P
7 Kt x P	B—Q2
8 Kt—QB3	O—O
9 Kt(4)—K2	. . . .

In view of the cramped character of Black's game, it had come to be felt that White ought to avoid exchanges. However, this is more effectively accomplished with 9 B—B1 rather than with the text.

9	R—K1
10 Kt—Kt3	Kt—K4
11 B x B	Q x B
12 P—B4	Kt—Kt3
13 Kt—B5	. . . .

White's position still seems quite good; but the fact is that he has forfeited most of his opening advantage, as will soon be made clear by Capablanca's energetic play.

| 13 . . . . | B—B1 |
| 14 Q—Q3 | QR—Q1 |

Avoiding the trap 14 . . . Kt x KP? 15 R x Kt, Q x Kt; 16 R x R, Q x Q; 17 R x Bch!

| 15 B—Q2 | P—Q4! |

Whenever Black can satisfactorily advance this Pawn in the Steinitz Defense, there has been something wrong with his opponent's play.

| 16 P—K5 | B—B4ch |

Black's pieces come to life. 17 B—K3 would be refuted by . . . Kt x BP.

| 17 K—R1 | Kt—Kt5 |
| 18 Kt—Q1 | P—KB3! |

Smashing up White's imposing center formation.

Capablanca

Fox

19 P—KR3   . . . .

On 19 P x P, Kt x P(B5); 20 Kt—K7ch (or 20 R x Rch, R x R; 21 Q—QB3, Q x Kt; 22 Q x B, Kt—K7 and wins), Capablanca intended 20 . . . R x R(Q)ch; 21 P x R, Kt x Q; 22 P x R(Q)ch, Q x Q; 23 P x Kt, Q—R5; 24 P—KR3, Q—Kt6 and mate follows.

19	Kt—B7ch
20 Kt x Kt	B x Kt
21 R—K2	P x P!

Establishing a won position.

22 R x B	P—K5
23 Kt—R6ch	P x Kt
24 Q—Q4	Q—Kt2
25 Q x RP?	. . . .

B—B3 would have held out longer. Black wins now without any trouble.

25	Q x P
26 R—K1	P—Q5!
27 P—B5	P—K6
28 R(2)—K2	Kt—B5
29 B—B1	Q—Kt3
30 Q—R4	Kt x R
31 Q—B4ch	K—R1
32 R x Kt	Q—R3
33 Q—Q3	Q x Q
34 P x Q	P—B4!
35 P—Kt4	P—B5

White resigns. An impressive victory by the youthful master.

---

4.   Match, 1909
(6th Game)
RUY LOPEZ

Despite Capablanca's inferior treatment of the opening, this is one of the finest games of his whole career. It was this game which first impressed the chess world at large with Capablanca's phenomenal ability.

J. R. CAPABLANCA F. J. MARSHALL

White	Black
1 P—K4	P—K4
2 Kt—KB3	Kt—QB3
3 B—Kt5	P—Q3
4 P—B3	. . . .

An unusual and unnecessary move. The immediate P—Q4 is in order.

4 . . . .   B—Kt5

And this reply is also somewhat questionable, as the Bishop may be embarrassed later on with P—KR3. Black would do better, very likely, with . . . P—KKt3.

5 P—Q3   . . . .

Again rather conservative; P—Q4 is logical.

5	B—K2
6 QKt—Q2	Kt—B3
7 O—O	O—O
8 R—K1	P—KR3

The plan initiated with this move deserved a better fate than it had in the actual play. Even better, however, seems Tarrasch's suggestion 8 . . . P—QR3; 9 B—R4, P—QKt4; 10 B—Kt3, P—Q4 and Black has freed himself—the logical result of White's fourth and fifth moves. In that event the sequel might be 11 P x P, Kt x P; 12 P—KR3, B—R4; 13 P—Kt4, B—Kt3; 14 Kt x P, Kt x Kt; 15 R x Kt, Kt—B5 recovering the Pawn advantageously.

| 9 Kt—B1 | Kt—R2 |
| 10 Kt—K3 | . . . . |

Now the dubious aspect of 4 . . . B—Kt5 comes to the fore.

10 . . . .   B—R4

Some annotators have recom-

mended 10 . . . P—B4 here, but this introduces Pawn weaknesses which will prove disastrous for Black. For example, Capablanca indicates the line 10 . . . P—B4; 11 P x P, B x P; 12 Kt x B, R x Kt; 13 P—Q4! P x P (if 13 . . . B—B3; 14 B—Q3 wins the exchange); 14 B x Kt, P x B; 15 Kt x P and wins.

| 11 P—KKt4 | B—Kt3 |
| 12 Kt—B5 | . . . . |

Not only is the Knight powerfully posted here, but it cannot very well be captured because of the resulting opening of the KKt file.

12 . . . .   P—KR4?

But this weak move robs Black's eighth move of all value. Dr. Lasker has pointed out that the proper continuation 12 . . . Kt—Kt4; 13 K—Kt2, Kt x Kt; 14 Q x Kt, B—Kt4; 15 R—R1, B x B; 16 QR x B, Kt—K2; 17 P—KR4, P—KB3 would have given Black far better prospects.

13 P—KR3   P x P??

Worse and worse. The opening of the KR file should have been avoided, because only White can make use of it. From now on Capablanca handles the game in irreproachable style.

14 P x P	B—Kt4
15 Kt x B	Kt x Kt
16 K—Kt2	P—Q4

Naturally striving to free himself, but even this attempt turns out to White's advantage.

| 17 Q—K2 | R—K1 |
| 18 R—R1 | . . . . |

What is Black to do against the coming doubling of White's Rooks on the KR file? 18 . . . P x P would relieve him of his later embarrassment about the protection of the QP, but after 19 P x P the resulting open lines would only be available to White.

18 . . . .   R—K3?!

As Marshall has been positionally outplayed, he has recourse to a tactical swindle: he hopes for 19 B x KKt, Q x B; 20 P x P, B x Kt; 21 P x R, B x KtP with a Pawn for the exchange, in addition to attacking chances and a free position. But now comes the finest move of the game:

19 Q—K3!!   . . . .

Black's reply is forced, for if 19 . . . Kt—R2; 20 Q—R3 with the murderous threat of Kt—R4.

19 . . . .   P—B3

Capablanca has now created a serious weakness in Black's position on the diagonal leading to his King. His next two moves exploit that weakness.

20 B—R4!   Kt—K2
21 B—Kt3   P—B3
22 Q—Kt3   . . . .

Making room for the development of the QB, which in turn prepares for the ultimately decisive doubling of the Rooks on the KR file.

22 . . . .   P—R4

Preparing a defense along the second rank, and incidentally hoping to drive White's KB off the terrible diagonal.

23 P—R4   Kt—B2
24 B—K3   P—Kt3
25 R—R4   K—B1
26 QR—R1   Kt—Kt1

White's pieces are all beautifully posted, while Black's forces have wretchedly small scope. Nevertheless Black's position gives an appearance of defensive solidity which is rudely dispelled by the following fine move:

27 Q—B3!   . . . .

Marshall

Capablanca

27 . . . .   B x Kt

This soon proves fatal because the presence of the Bishop was vital to the defense of the white squares on the King-side; but how else was Black to guard the QP? If 27 . . . P x P; 28 P x P, R—K1; 29 Q—R3 and the sacrifice of the exchange by R—R8 will win quickly.

28 KtP x B   R—Q3
29 Q—R5   R—R2

This move, intended to bolster the other wing, only facilitates his downfall. But there was no defense against the infiltration of White's heavy pieces.

30 Q—Kt6   Kt(2)—R3

A despairing attempt to prevent R—R7. If 30 . . . Kt—K2; 31 R—R8ch, Kt x R; 32 R x Ktch, Kt—Kt1; 33 Q—R7, K—B2; 34 B x KtP! wins. Now comes a crisp finish.

31 R x Kt!   P x R

On 31 . . . Kt x R White wins easily with either 32 B x Kt or 32 R x Kt.

32 B x Pch   K—K2

If 32 . . . Kt x B; 33 R x Kt and

Black is helpless against R—R8ch.

33	Q—Kt7ch	K—K1
34	Q x Ktch	K—Q2
35	Q—R7ch!	Q—K2
36	B—B8!	Q x Q
37	R x Qch	K—K1
38	R x R	Resigns

A masterpiece.

---

5.   Match, 1909
(8th Game)
RUY LOPEZ

This charming game deserves to be better known. It illustrates one of the most important accomplishments of the first-rate master—that of being able to slash his way through the tactical complications which often follow the attainment of a positional advantage.

J. R. CAPABLANCA	F. J. MARSHALL
White	Black
1 P—K4	P—K4
2 Kt—KB3	Kt—QB3
3 B—Kt5	P—Q3
4 O—O	P—QR3

In later years this defense was to become fashionable in the more precise form 3 . . . P—QR3; 4 B—R4, P—Q3. Capablanca counters with what is currently considered the best reply.

| 5 B x Ktch | P x B |
| 6 P—Q4 | P x P |

This is not best, as it gives White's Pieces too much scope and leaves Black with a lifeless game, despite his two Bishops. Preferable is 6 . . . P—B3, a move to which Capablanca was himself partial in later years (see for example Game No. 104). However, Marshall's dislike for such close positions is proverbial.

| 7 Kt x P | B—Q2 |
| 8 R—K1 | P—QB4 |

It is irksome to have the QB tied to the defense of the QBP, but the text does not help matters, as it weakens the Pawn structure and leaves Black's Q4 accessible to White's pieces.

| 9 Kt—KB3 | B—K2 |
| 10 Kt—B3 | P—QB3 |

Partly because he wishes to avoid an eventual Kt—Q5, and partly because in reply to . . . Kt—B3 he fears P—K5; but the text has the drawback of weakening the QP.

11 B—B4	B—K3
12 Q—Q3	Kt—B3
13 QR—Q1	P—Q4

Forced; but it creates new weaknesses on the Queen-side; incidentally, White has all his forces in play whereas Black's game has remained undeveloped.

| 14 Kt—KKt5 | P—Q5 |

A difficult position for Black; if 14 . . . P x P; 15 Q—K3! leaves him with a very bad game.

| 15 Kt x B | P x Kt |
| 16 Kt—R4! | . . . . |

Ordinarily a Knight is badly posted at the side of the board; but in the present position, the Knight has excellent prospects. The immediate threat is Q—B4 winning a Pawn.

| 16 . . . . | Q—R4 |

Practically forced, but the Queen is badly placed here. One difficulty leads to another.

| 17 P—QKt3 | R—Q1 |
| 18 Kt—Kt2! | Kt—R4 |

Not 18 . . . Q x P?? 19 Kt—B4 and the Queen is lost!

| 19 B—K5 | O—O |

| 20 Kt—B4 | Q—Kt5 |
| 21 Q—R3 | . . . . |

This not only wins a Pawn; it leads to a devastating attack.

| 21 . . . . | P—Kt3 |

If 21 . . . Kt—B3; 22 Q x KPch, R—B2; 23 B—B7 followed by Kt—K5 and wins.

| 22 Q x Pch | R—B2 |
| 23 P—Kt4! | . . . . |

Decisive! But the remaining play requires great accuracy.

| 23 . . . . | B—R5 |

A desperate bid for counterplay —not that he has any choice. For if 23 . . . Kt—Kt2; 24 B x Kt, K x B; 25 Kt—K5 and wins; or 23 . . . Kt—B3; 24 B x Kt, B x B; 25 Kt—Q6 etc.

| 24 P x Kt | B x Pch |
| 25 K—R1 | Q—B6 |

Or 25 . . . B x R; 26 P x P, P x P; 27 Q x Pch, K—B1; 28 Kt—Q6, R—B8ch; 29 K—Kt2 and wins.

Marshall

Capablanca

| 26 R—K3!! | Q x BP |

There is no satisfactory reply to the pretty Rook move. If 26 . . .

B x R; 27 P x P, P x P; 28 Q x Pch, K—B1; 29 Kt—Q6, R(1)—Q2; 30 B—Kt7ch! or still more simply Kt x R) and wins.

27 R(3)—Q3	Q—K7
28 Kt—Q6	R x Kt
29 B x R	B—K8

Threatening mate; but White's attack comes first.

| 30 Q—K8ch | K—Kt2 |
| 31 P—R6ch! | Resigns |

White's economical utilization of his forces has been most impressive.

---

6. Match, 1909
(11th Game)

QUEEN'S GAMBIT DECLINED

While neither player's moves were wholly free from mistakes, this game was Capablanca's most arduous and perhaps most impressive victory of the match. To survive one of Marshall's most ingenious attacks is a feat even for the mature master; how much more creditable is it in the case of a young, inexperienced player.

F. J. MARSHALL	J. R. CAPABLANCA
White	Black
1 P—Q4	P—Q4
2 P—QB4	P—K3
3 Kt—QB3	Kt—KB3
4 B—Kt5	B—K2
5 P—K3	Kt—K5

Capablanca never played this defense again after the match, though he relied on it almost exclusively during this contest, for a number of reasons: because Lasker had had such striking success with it in his match with Marshall two years earlier, because the simplifying character of the variation tends to lighten Black's problems and because Capablanca wished to avoid the customary lines of play, with which he had only a hazy acquaintance at best.

6 B x B   Q x B
7 B—Q3   . . . .

After this Black has an easy game. The standard move is 7 P x P (as in Game No. 9), giving Black far greater difficulties.

7 . . . .   Kt x Kt
8 P x Kt   P x P

An important move, despite the apparently strong center which it permits White: Black is now able to post his Bishop to good effect.

9 B x BP   P—QKt3
10 Q—B3   . . . .

A nervous attacking move which gives the clue to Marshall's mood.

10 . . . .   P—QB3
11 Kt—K2   B—Kt2
12 O—O   O—O
13 P—QR4   . . . .

Not only loss of time, but the Pawn soon becomes a serious weakness. P—K4 has been recommended, with a view to answering . . . P—QB4 with P—Q5.

13 . . . .   P—QB4
14 Q—Kt3   Kt—B3
15 Kt—B4   QR—B1
16 B—R2   . . . .

The Bishop was menaced by the threat of . . . P x P followed by . . . Kt x P. But now the weakness of the QRP becomes noticeable.

16 . . . .   KR—Q1
17 KR—K1   Kt—R4
18 QR—Q1   . . . .

As the QRP cannot be defended very well, White makes a virtue of necessity, leaving the Pawn to its fate and playing for the attack.

18 . . . .   B—B3
19 Q—Kt4   . . . .

Now the game begins to be exciting. 19 . . . B x RP is to be answered by 20 Kt x P!

19 . . . .   P—B5
20 P—Q5   . . . .

Edward Lasker suggests 20 P—K4, B x RP; 21 Kt—R5, P—Kt3; 22 P—K5, B x R; 23 R x B with a strong threat of Kt—B6ch followed by Q—R4.

20 . . . .   B x RP

A greedy capture which involves Black in serious difficulties, with both minor pieces out of play. The simple positional course was 20 . . . P x P; 21 Kt x P, B x Kt; 22 R x B, R x R; 23 Q x Rch, R—Q1; 24 Q—B5, P—Kt3; 25 Q—B2, Q—Q3 followed by . . . Q—Q7 with a winning position.

21 R—Q2   P—K4
22 Kt—R5   P—Kt3
23 P—Q6!   . . . .

Marshall is now in his element. The position has become very difficult for Black.

23 . . . .   Q—K3
24 Q—Kt5   . . . .

Not 24 Q x Q, P x Q; 25 Kt—B6ch, K—Kt2; 26 Kt—Kt4, R—B3; 27 P—Q7 (or 27 Kt x P, R(3)x P; 28 R x R, R x R; 29 Kt x BP, Kt x Kt; 30 B x Kt, R—B3; 31 B—R2, R x P and Black's Queen-side Pawns win easily), R—B4 and wins.

24 . . . .   K—R1

If 24 . . . R x P?? 25 R x R, Q x R; 26 Q—R6 and Black can resign.

25 Kt—B6   R x P
26 R x R   Q x R
27 B—Kt1   Kt—B3
28 B—B5!   R—Q1

And not 28 . . . P x B; 29 Q—R6 and wins.

Capablanca

Marshall

29 P—R4?!   . . . .

Although this move creates dangerous threats, it is not so strong as 29 B—Q7! Q—B1! (White threatened Kt—K8 winning the exchange. If 29 . . . R x B? 30 Q—R6! forces mate!) and White can draw: 30 Q—R4, K—Kt2 (if 30 . . . P—KR3; 31 Q x P and wins); 31 Kt—R5ch! P x Kt; 32 Q—Kt5ch, K—R1; 33 B x Kt, B x B; 34 Q—B6ch with perpetual check.

29 . . . .   Kt—K2

At last Black's minor pieces are taking part in the defense.

30	Kt—K4	Q—B2
31	Q—B6ch	K—Kt1
32	B—K6?!	. . . .

Trying a swindle which comes within an ace of winning, but with two Pawns down, it was too late for a more tranquil continuation.

| 32 | . . . . | P x B |
| 33 | Q x KPch | . . . . |

If 33 Kt—Kt5, Kt—Q4 is a satisfactory defense.

33 . . . .   K—B1

| 34 | Kt—Kt5 | Kt—Kt1 |
| 35 | P—B4 | R—K1 |

An inexactitude which fans White's flagging hopes. . . . B—K1 was better.

36 P x P!   R—K2

Obviously . . . R x Q? loses, and meanwhile R—B1ch threatens to be deadly. The text is forced.

| 37 | R—B1ch | K—Kt2 |
| 38 | P—R5 | B—K1 |

At last Black is fully consolidated; but White still has some shots left.

39 P—R6ch!   K—R1

If 39 . . . Kt x P?? 40 Q—B6ch and mate next move. If 39 . . . K x P? 40 Q—Kt4, K—Kt2 (else Q—R4ch); 41 Kt—K6ch etc.

40 Q—Q6   Q—B4!

Not 40 . . . Q x Q? 41 P x Q and the mating position is deadly: 41 . . . R x P; 42 P—Q7! B x P; 43 Kt—B7 mate! Or 41 . . . R—Q2; 42 R—B8, R—Q1; 43 R x B!

41 Q—Q4   . . . .

After the game, Capablanca disposed of the alternative 41 Q x Q as follows: 41 . . . P x Q; 42 R—B8, R x P; 43 Kt—B3, R x P; 44 Kt—Kt5, R—K4; 45 Kt—B3, R—K2; 46 Kt—Kt5, B—B3; 47 Kt—B7 ch, R x Kt; 48 R x R, Kt x P; 49 R x P, B—Q4 and wins.

| 41 | . . . . | R x P |
| 42 | Q—Q7 | . . . . |

White is determined to die like a hero. Against 42 R—B7 Capablanca had prepared 42 . . . Kt x P; 43 R—B8ch, Kt—Kt1; 44 R—B7, Kt—B3; 45 R x Kt, Q x Q; 46 KP x Q, R x Kt; 47 R—B8ch, K—Kt2; 48 R x B, R—Kt6 and wins.

42 . . . .   R—K2

43 R—B7   B x Q

White resigns. A battle royal!

---

7. Match, 1909
(23rd and Last Game)

QUEEN'S GAMBIT DECLINED

With the score hopelessly against him, Marshall's spirits were at a low ebb, and his play was correspondingly lifeless. Nevertheless contemporary connoisseurs thought highly of Capablanca's handling of this game; Dr. Lasker commented, for example: "His play is an example of how slight advantages should be utilized."

F. J. MARSHALL	J. R. CAPABLANCA
White	Black
1 P—Q4	P—Q4
2 P—QB4	P—K3
3 Kt—QB3	P—QB4
4 BP x P	KP x P
5 Kt—B3	Kt—QB3

This is one of the very few instances of Capablanca's adoption of the Tarrasch Defense, which he never used after 1911. The isolated QP and accompanying weaknesses must have been repellent to so accomplished a master of position play.

6 P—KKt3	B—K3
7 B—Kt2	B—K2
8 O—O	Kt—B3
9 B—Kt5	. . . .

Not the best, as Black's reply proves. The modern continuation 9 P x P! B x P; 10 Kt—QR4, B—K2; 11 B—K3 leaves Black with a poor game.

9 . . . .   Kt—K5!

An admirable equalizing move which enables Black to shake off the difficulties of the opening.

10 B x B   Q x B

As 11 P x P, Kt x Kt; 12 P x Kt, Q x P is quite satisfactory for Black, Marshall decides to embark on complications.

11 Kt—K5   Kt x QP

Better than the seemingly attractive 11 . . . KKt x Kt; 12 P x Kt, Kt x Kt; 13 P x Kt, Q—Q2; 14 P—KB4, O—O; 15 Q—B2 and White has excellent prospects.

12 Kt x Kt	P x Kt
13 P—K3	. . . .

Not 13 B x P? B—R6 etc.

13	Kt—B6ch
14 Kt x Kt	. . . .

Better than 14 B x Kt, P x B; 15 Q—R4ch (recommended by some critics), K—B1! (naturally not the spineless 15 . . . B—Q2, which gives White an easy game after 16 Kt x B, Q x Kt; 17 Q—K4ch) followed by . . . P—B3 and . . . K—B2 and artificial castling, with an admirable game for Black.

14	P x Kt
15 Q x P	O—O

Naturally Black would be quite satisfied with 16 Q x P, Q x Q; 17 B x Q, QR—Kt1 followed by . . . R x P with a fairly certain win.

16 KR—B1?   . . . .

A wasted move at best, and in any event it shows that Marshall has not appraised the position correctly. His best counter against Black's Queen-side majority is not **passive resistance**, but **active counterplay** in the form of P—K4, Q—K3, P—B4 etc. This procedure, which was still available a move later, would have led to attacks on opposite wings with interesting complications and about level chances. As the game goes, there is no fight in White's play at all.

16 . . . .   QR—Kt1

| 17 Q—K4? | Q—B2 |
| 18 R—B3 | .... |

Another pointless move, as it ensures Black's later command of the Q file. Capablanca is now ready to make the Queen-side Pawns tell.

| 18 .... | P—QKt4 |
| 19 P—QR3 | P—B5 |

Tempting White to play 20 P—Kt3, which would be answered advantageously with . . . Q—R4. White's best chance of holding the position was now 20 R(3)—B1 so as to answer . . . KR—Q1 with R—Q1.

| 20 B—B3? | KR—Q1 |

"Capablanca points out all his opponent's inexactitudes to him; first he gets the Queen-side majority in motion, and now he takes command of the Q file" (Tarrasch).

21 R—Q1	R x Rch
22 B x R	R—Q1
23 B—B3	....

Capablanca

Marshall

| 23 .... | P—Kt3! |

A many-sided move. It frees the Black Rook from the last rank (for example 23 . . . R—Q7; 24 R—B2, B—Q4?? 25 Q—K8 mate) and it threatens to win White's Bishop

in rather a subtle manner (24 . . . B—Q4; 25 Q—Kt4, P—KR4). In addition, it prevents R—B2 as a defense against . . . R—Q7, because of the possibility . . . B—B4.

| 24 Q—B6 | Q—K4! |
| 25 Q—K4 | Q x Q |

Exchanging Queens a move earlier would have left his QKtP exposed to attack.

| 26 B x Q | R—Q8ch |

An important interpolation to prevent the helpful defensive maneuver K—B1—K2.

| 27 K—Kt2 | P—QR4 |

The advance of the Queen-side Pawns, in conjunction with the dominating position of Black's pieces, assures an easy win.

28 R—B2	P—Kt5
29 P x P	P x P
30 B—B3	....

White's King cannot be used for the defense, for if 30 K—B3, P—Kt6; 31 R—K2, P—B4; 32 B—B6, R—Q3 followed by . . . R—Kt3 and . . . P—B6 winning easily.

| 30 .... | R—Kt8 |
| 31 B—K2 | .... |

If 31 B—K4, P—B4 wins.

| 31 .... | P—Kt6 |

Decisive; if 32 R—B3, R x P; 33 B x P, R—B7 and wins.

| 32 R—Q2 | R—QB8 |

The threat of . . . R—B7 now wins a piece.

33 B—Q1	P—B6
34 P x P	P—Kt7
35 R x P	R x B
36 R—B2	B—B4
37 R—Kt2	R—QB8
38 R—Kt3	B—K5ch

Black handles the final phase in good style. If now 39 P—B3, R—B7ch wins the KBP.

39	K—R3	R—B7
40	P—KB4	P—R4

Threatening . . . B—B4ch and leaving White without any hope whatever.

41	P—Kt4	P x Pch
42	K x P	R x RP

43	R—Kt4	P—B4ch
44	K—Kt3	R—K7
45	R—B4	R x Pch
46	K—R4	K—Kt2
47	R—B7ch	K—B3
48	R—Q7	B—Kt7
49	R—Q6ch	K—Kt2

White resigns. Young Capablanca's play has been characterized by extraordinary precision throughout the game.

Part II
Grandmaster

1910-1914

In this period Capablanca's opening play is characterized by greater sophistication; but it is interesting to note that he gets much better results with the white pieces than with black, suggesting that he has difficulty in obtaining the initiative as second player. His outstanding weapon in this period is the Ruy Lopez, described by Tarrasch at the time as the chief milch cow of tournament play!

In Games no. 10 and 11, Capablanca has no squeamishness in fighting against his own favorite Steinitz Defense; he concludes the first game with a charming combination, and in the latter game, his first encounter in an international tournament, he brings off several far-sighted sacrifices which eventually net him the brilliancy prize. Game no. 13 illustrates the interesting positional theme of exerting pressure on a backward Pawn in the then fashionable Tarrasch Defense, while in Game no. 18 a poor defense by Chajes is refuted relentlessly. Game no. 22 is of considerable theoretical importance, and is interesting later on because of the fine series of forcing moves by means of which the Cuban master demolishes Dus-Chotimirsky's seemingly excellent position. Finally, Game no. 29 illustrates Capablanca's style to perfection. Adopting the famous Exchange Variation, he reduces Janowski to helplessness with a few simple strokes. Can chess be that easy?!

An opening Capablanca played a great deal at this time —The Four Knights' Game—is seen in Game no. 17 against Janowski. It concludes with one of Capablanca's finest endings—a masterpiece in the field of Rook and Pawn endings.

Although his play in the opening is a bit shaky in Game no. 16, Capablanca's handling of the middle game is exemplary, taking advantage of one of Black's chronic weaknesses in the French Defense: the undeveloped QB.

As his play matures, the young master branches out into the openings beginning with 1 P—Q4. There are two Ortho-

33

dox Defenses: the so-called Old-orthodox, with eventual . . .
P—QKt3 (Game no. 21 against Teichmann) in which Capablanca produces another masterly ending—this time with
Bishops of opposite color; and in Game no. 28, Bernstein tries
the Orthodox Defense in its modern form (. . . P—QB3).
However, he treats the opening in a superficial and provoca-
tive manner, receiving a trouncing from Capablanca which
nets him another brilliancy prize.

In Game no. 9 Capablanca is called upon to face the
Lasker Defense which he had used to such good advantage
against Marshall. Capablanca takes the initiative and winds
up an exciting contest with a neat Rook sacrifice. During
this period, the Slav Defense began to achieve some prom-
inence. However, in the two examples given here, both Jaffe
(Game no. 8) and Alekhine (Game no. 23) succumb inglor-
iously; the former is crushed by a brilliant attack, the latter
is smothered by first-rate positional play. In Game no. 12
Capablanca adopts the indifferent symmetrical variation
(strongly recommended by Tarrasch), lets the initiative slip
out of his hands, and is finally subjected to a murderous attack. The clever way in which he escapes and concludes the
game with an exquisitely artistic combination, makes a suit-
able finish to this thrilling game.

Pre-war chess had relatively few "irregular" defenses,
and when Capablanca encountered them, he disposed of them
with common-sense continuations. Thus in Game no. 14, he
refutes the Stonewall Variation with one of chess history's
outstanding combinations; while in Game no. 20, his mastery
of the black squares ruins Mieses' Benoni Counter Gambit
in short order.

With the black pieces, the selection of games is smaller
but no less distinguished. Capablanca's favorite Steinitz Defense is again used with telling effect to defeat Alekhine in
short order (Game no. 27). An unorthodox Giuoco Piano
with Nimzovich (Game no. 25) eventually leads to a classic
win with Bishops of opposite colors—a game of which Capablanca was very proud. In Game no. 19 Capablanca falters
at the crucial point of a very unusual opening line (Center
Game), loses the exchange—and then stages a magnificent
recovery. A perfect example of the difference between a
good player and a very good one! The French Defense is
used by Capablanca in one of his most famous exhibition

Games (no. 26), and again he produces a masterly ending. By this time the strength of his endgame play has become proverbial. One of Capablanca's rare excursions into the field of openings which involve a positional weakness is seen in Game no. 24, against Bernstein. The game concludes with Capablanca's most famous "swindle!" With Game no. 15, Capablanca won still another brilliancy prize, this time against his old rival Juan Corzo. A very pretty game, but the variations which didn't happen are the best part of the game! The defense used here by Capablanca was the King's Indian, of which he was one of the pioneers.

8. New York State Championship, 1910
(Tie-match)

QUEEN'S GAMBIT DECLINED

This is not the kind of game usually associated with Capablanca's style. The manner in which Black's sadly weakened King-side is smashed up is quite striking.

J. R. CAPABLANCA	C. JAFFE
White	Black
1 P—Q4	P—Q4
2 Kt—KB3	Kt—KB3
3 P—K3	P—B3
4 P—B4	P—K3

Leads to an unpromisingly cramped game; . . . B—B4 is preferable.

5 Kt—B3	QKt—Q2
6 B—Q3	B—Q3
7 O—O	O—O
8 P—K4	P x KP
9 Kt x P	Kt x Kt
10 B x Kt	Kt—B3

. . . P—QB4 could be tried here; the text has no great value.

11 B—B2	P—KR3

Black must guard against Q—Q3 followed by B—Kt5.

12 P—QKt3	. . . .

Preparing to renew the threat against the Knight in a different way; the QB is formidable on the long diagonal.

12	P—QKt3

13 B—Kt2	B—Kt2

. . . This Bishop, on the other hand, never manages to play a worthy role.

14 Q—Q3	P—Kt3

Not a pretty move, but it is intended to guard against the threat of P—Q5 followed by B x Kt.

Likewise inadequate would have been 14 . . . Q—B2; 15 P—B5! B—K2; 16 P—Q5, KR—Q1; 17 P—Q6, P x P; 18 B x Kt, B x B; 19 Q—R7 ch and mate next move.

. . . R—K1 would have been preferable, but Black's position would have continued to be inferior.

15 QR—K1	. . . .

At once concentrating on the new weakness. The threat is R x P!

15	Kt—R4

This loses quickly. . . . Q—K2 would have prolonged his resistance.

16 B—B1!	K—Kt2

Realizing that the intended 16 . . . B—B5 (not 16 . . . Kt—B5; 17 B x Kt, B x B; 18 R x P and wins) is refuted by 17 R x P! B x B; 18 R x R, P x R; 19 Q x Pch, Kt—Kt2; 20 Q—R7ch, K—B2; 21 Kt—K5ch and wins.

White is now ready for the final attack.

(see diagram next page)

17 R x P	Kt—B3
18 Kt—K5!	P—B4

Or 18 . . . P x R; 19 Q x Pch, K—R1; 20 Q x Pch, K—Kt1; 21 Q—

Jaffe

Capablanca

Kt6ch, K—R1; 22 R—K1, Q—K1;
23 Q—R6ch, K—Kt1; 24 R—K3
and wins.
Only . . . B x Kt would have held
out for a while.

| 19 B x Pch! | K x B |
| 20 Kt x Pch! | Resigns |

All four Black Pawns on the
King-side were shot away by sacrifices!

---

9. Philadelphia, 1910
(Team Match)

QUEEN'S GAMBIT DECLINED

This game speaks well for the
youthful Capablanca's mastery of
the problem of switching from
strategical jockeying for position
to outwitting the opponent in critical tactical play where one slip
can be fatal. There is a touch of
young genius in this little-known
game which makes it most attractive.

J. R. CAPABLANCA	H. G. VOIGHT
(Manhattan C. C.)	*(Franklin C. C.)*
White	Black
1 P—Q4	P—Q4

2 P—QB4	P—K3
3 Kt—QB3	Kt—KB3
4 B—Kt5	B—K2
5 P—K3	Kt—K5

This time Capablanca has to con-
tend with the defense he made
famous in his match with Marshall.
He adopts the best line.

6 B x B	Q x B
7 P x P	Kt x Kt
8 P x Kt	P x P
9 Q—Kt3	P—QB3

. . . Q—Q3 is favored nowadays,
QB3 being reserved for the later
development of the Knight.

10 Kt—B3	Kt—Q2
11 P—B4	P x P
12 B x P	Kt Kt3
13 O—O	O—O
14 P QR4	Kt x B
15 Q x Kt	B—K3

Black has developed in a fairly
satisfactory manner, and aside
from some possible difficulty later
on with his Queen-side Pawns, the
position is about even.

16 Q—B3	B—Q4
17 Kt—K5	P—B3
18 Kt—Q3	Q—K5
19 Kt—B4	KR—K1
20 QR—Kt1	QR—Kt1
21 Q—R5	B—B5

The alternative move 21 . . . B—
B2 could be answered by 22 KR—
K1 with a view to P—B3. This is
much stronger than 22 Q x P, P—
KKt4; 23 Kt—R3, B—Q4; 24 P—B3,
Q x Pch etc.

| 22 KR—B1 | P—QKt4?! |

Giving up a Pawn for a strong
but unsound attack. However, if
22 . . . B—R3; 23 P—Q5! with advantage (23 . . . P—KKt4; 24 Kt—
R5).

| 23 P x P | P x P |

| 24 Q x RP | R—R1 |
| 25 Q—B5 | R—R7 |

Threatening . . . R x P! White must have his wits about him in the following play.

| 26 P—Q5! | R—Q7 |
| 27 R—R1! | . . . . |

White will make good use of the open file. His opponent does not care for 27 . . . B x P; 28 Q x P, which would leave him without compensation for the Pawn down. He therefore attempts to force matters with the following daring advance.

27	P—Kt4?!
28 Kt—R5	Q—Kt5
29 P—Kt4!	K—R1

If 29 . . . B x P; 30 Q—B3 wins; likewise, if 29 . . . R x QP; 30 Q—B6 threatens R x B and also Q x KR ch and Kt x P ch. The game has taken an extraordinarily interesting turn.

Voight

Capablanca

30 R x B!   . . . .

In return for the exchange, White gets two Pawns (one of them the formidable QP) and a mating attack based on the strong position of the Knight at R5 and the Rook at R7.

30	P x R
31 Q x P	R—Kt7
32 R—R7!	Q—Kt8ch

There is no satisfactory defense: I 32 . . . R—KB1; 33 Q—Q4, Q—B7; 34 Q x P ch and mate follows. II 32 . . . R—Kt8ch; 33 K—Kt2, Q—K5ch? 34 Q x Q, R x Q; 35 R—R8ch and mate next move.

| 33 K—Kt2 | R—Kt5 |

Black seems to have devised a flourishing counterattack.

| 34 R x P ch!! | Q x R |

Not 34 . . . K x R; 35 Q—B7ch forcing mate.

35 Q x R	Q—KB2
36 Q—Q4	R—K4
37 P—K4	Q—K2
38 P—Q6	Resigns

---

10.   New York, 1910?

RUY LOPEZ

While Capablanca had the reputation of dryness, it is interesting to note that throughout most of his career he had a knack of dealing drastically with complications once they did arise.

J. R. CAPABLANCA	TANEROW
White	Black
1 P—K4	P—K4
2 Kt—KB3	Kt—QB3
3 B—Kt5	Kt—B3
4 O—O	P—Q3

Black's order of moves is a well-known finesse to avoid White's Queen-side castling, which often leads to a dangerous attack difficult for Black to parry. (The old line was 3 . . . P—Q3; 4 P—Q4, B—Q2; 5 Kt—B3, Kt—B3; 6 B x Kt, B x B; 7 Q—Q3, P x P; 8 Kt x P,

B—Q2;	9 B—Kt5,	B—K2; 10
O—O—O! etc.)		

5 P—Q4	B—Q2
6 Kt—B3	B—K2
7 R—K1	P x P
8 Kt x P	Kt x Kt

He hopes to free his somewhat cramped game by simplification.

9 Q x Kt	B x B
10 Kt x B	O—O
11 Q—B3!	. . . .

White avoids the somewhat colorless B—Kt5, which only leads to further simplification, and defers the development of the Bishop to a later date, when it may be more effective.

11	P—B3

If instead 11 . . . P—Q4; 12 P—K5, Kt—K1; 13 Kt—Q4, P—QB4; 14 Kt—B5 with a strong position for White. The latter's last move is explained by his desire to plant the Knight on the strong square KD5. This will now have the ad ditional virtue of menacing the weakened QP.

12 Kt—Q4	Kt—Q2
13 Kt—B5	B—B3
14 Q—KKt3	Kt—K4
15 B—B4	. . . .

See the note to White's 11th move. The Bishop is very well placed here.

15	Q—B2

White threatened to win the QP with QR—Q1.

16 QR—Q1	QR—Q1

. . . KR—Q1, at the cost of a Pawn would have prevented the combination which follows; but that was surely difficult to foresee at this moment.

17 R x P!	R x R

18 B x Kt	R—Q8?!

Pretty but inadequate. 18 . . . Q—R4; 19 B—B3, B x B; 20 P x B, R—Kt3; 21 Kt—K7ch, K—R1; 22 Kt x Rch, RP x Kt was better.

19 R x R	B x B

If 19 . . . Q x B; 20 Kt—R6ch still wins.

20 Kt—R6ch!	K—R1
21 Q x B!	Q x Q
22 Kt x Pch	Resigns

Tanerow

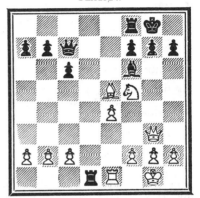

Capablanca

---

11. San Sebastian, 1911

(First Brilliancy Prize)

RUY LOPEZ

There is an interesting story behind this game. The freely expressed scorn of the other masters goaded Capablanca to do his very best, and as this game was played in the first round, it is obvious that Bernstein was a victim of his underestimation of the Cuban master!

J. CAPABLANCA   O. BERNSTEIN

White	Black
1 P—K4	P—K4
2 Kt—KB3	Kt—QB3
3 B—Kt5	Kt—B3
4 O—O	B—K2
5 Kt—B3	P—Q3
6 B x Ktch	P x B
7 P—Q4	P x P

Also possible is Tchigorin's . . . Kt—Q2; but after 8 P x P, P x P Black has a development and Pawn configuration which are none too inviting.

8 Kt x P	B—Q2
9 B—Kt5	. . . .

The opening has proceeded on conventional lines. This last move is however probably less promising than 9 P—QKt3 and 10 B—Kt2 or 9 Q—B3, as it gives Black opportunities for simplification.

9	O—O

"Threatening" 10 . . . Kt x P; 11 B x B, Kt x Kt with far-reaching simplification. White's most promising reply is 11 Q—Q3 to be followed by QR—K1 and P—B4 with a markedly freer game.

10 R—K1	P—KR3
11 B—R4	Kt—R2
12 B x B	Q x B
13 Q—Q3	QR—Kt1
14 P—QKt3	Kt—Kt4

The more usual disposition of this Knight is (after . . . KR—K1) . . . Kt—B1—Kt3. The text has the drawback that sooner or later the Knight will go to K3, giving White the opportunity of planting one of his Knights very strongly at KB5. It must be admitted, however, that it is difficult to find a good spot for this Knight even under the best circumstances —one of the defects of Black's rather cramped position in this variation.

15 QR—Q1	. . . .

Tarrasch rightly recommends the sharper 15 P—B4, Kt—K3; 16 Kt—B5, Q—B3; 17 P—K5! and Black's game is extremely uncomfortable (17 . . . Kt x P? 18 P x Q, Kt x Q; 19 Kt—K7ch winning a piece).

15	Q—K4
16 Q—K3	Kt—K3
17 Kt(3)—K2	Q—QR4

This is where Black starts on the downward path — psychologically but not objectively. The threat of Kt x Kt followed by Q x QRP could have been met in at least two satisfactory ways: 17 . . . Kt x Kt; 18 Kt x Kt, KR—K1 (Lasker) or 17 . . . Kt—B4; 18 Kt—Kt3, KR—K1 (Tarrasch).

It will be noted that either of these methods keeps Black's Queen in good (centralized) play and prevents a White Knight from reaching KB5. It is precisely these two points about which the coming play will revolve.

18 Kt—B5!	Kt—B4

On 18 . . . Q x P Capablanca intended 19 Q—QB3! (threatening to win the Queen), Q—R3; 20 Kt—B4, P—B3; 21 Q—Kt3, P—Kt4; 22 Kt—Kt6! R—B2 (if 22 . . . KR—K1; 23 Q—R3!); 23 Kt x Pch, K—Kt2; 24 Kt x R, K x Kt (3); 25 Kt x QP, P x Kt; 26 R x P, R—Kt2; 27 P—K5 or 24 . . . K x Kt(2); 25 P—KB4— in either case with a winning game.

19 Kt(2)—Q4	K—R2

Guarding against the threat of 20 Kt x BP, B x Kt; 21 Kt—K7ch and 22 Kt x B. It goes without saying that 19 . . . Q x P?? would have lost the Queen by 20 R—R1, Q—Kt7; 21 KR—Kt1; but Black is biding his time.

20 P—KKt4	QR—K1
21 P—KB3	Kt—K3
22 Kt—K2!?	. . . .

Giving Black the choice of gobbling up two Pawns or heading in-

to a somewhat inferior ending with
22 . . . Q—Kt3. The sacrifice of
the two Pawns is a most original
conception, and evidently calculated with his 28th move in view.

22 . . . .   Q x P

He decides to see it through.

23 Kt(2)—Kt3   Q x BP

Even this capture, risky though
it is, is feasible. The real flaw in
Black's reasoning is that he is
creating a situation which will be
difficult to handle in over-the-board
play.

After the more conservative 23
. . . P—B3; 24 Kt—R5, R—B2 the
outcome would still be difficult to
forecast, as the extra Pawn would
play a minor role.

24 R—QB1   Q—Kt7
25 Kt—R5   R—KR1

. . . P—Kt4 was indicated by
Capablanca as a better defense,
but the position is still tenable.
Less good, however, would be 25
. . . P—Kt3; 26 Q x Pch, K—Kt1;
27 P—K5! P x Kt(R4); 28 KtP x P
and White wins on the KKt file.

26 R—K2   Q—K4
27 P—B4   Q—Kt4

Bernstein

Capablanca

28 Kt(B5) x KtP!   Kt—B4?

Black loses his head . . . and the
game. It is true that the obstrep-
erous Knight cannot be captured
(28 . . . Kt x Kt; 29 Kt—B6ch, K—
Kt3; 30 Kt x B (threatening 31 P—
B5ch, K—R2; 32 Kt—B6 mate!),
P—B3; 31 P—K5, K—B2; 32 Kt x P,
R—K2; 33 Kt—K4, P x P; 34 P x P
and Black's position is fatally
smashed up.

Correct was 28 . . . R—Q1; 29
P—B5, Kt—B1 (not 29 . . . Kt x
Kt?? 30 Kt—B6 mate!); 30 P—Kt5,
Q—Kt3; 31 P x P, Q x Qch; 32 R x Q
and the outcome is still unclear!

29 Kt x R   B x Kt
30 Q—QB3!   P—B3

Black's position is in ruins, and
he might well resign.

31 Kt x Pch   K—Kt3
32 Kt—R5   R—Kt1
33 P—B5ch   K—Kt4
34 Q—K3ch   K—R5
35 Q—Kt3ch   Resigns

It is mate next move. With this
imperfect but fascinating game,
Capablanca fully convinced his col-
leagues!

---

12. San Sebastian, 1911

QUEEN'S GAMBIT DECLINED

An exceptionally interesting and
arduous game all the way. The
problem-like series of forcing
moves adopted by Capablanca after Janowski's tragic slip on move
53, is particularly deserving of
careful study.

J. R. CAPABLANCA   D. JANOWSKI

White	Black
1 P—Q4	P—Q4
2 P—K3	Kt—KB3
3 Kt—KB3	P—B4
4 P—B4	P—K3

5 Kt—B3	B—K2

Janowski is doubtless anxious to avoid symmetry and consequent drawing possibilities, but the text looks somewhat questionable because it loses a tempo. A good alternative is 5 . . . Kt—B3; 6 P—QR3, Kt—K5! (Janowski-Marshall, Cambridge Springs, 1904).

6 QP x P	O—O
7 P—QR3	B x P
8 P—QKt4	B—K2
9 B—Kt2	P—QR4

There has been a great deal of controversy over this move. On the whole, its effect seems good, as it forces White's Queen-side Pawns into a somewhat disjointed position, and gives Black's pieces access to his QB4.

10 P—Kt5	P—QKt3?

But this is dubious, as it weakens Black's Queen-side without any compelling reason. Simply . . . P x P followed by . . . QKt—Q2 was in order.

11 P x P	P x P
12 Kt—Q4	. . . .

White is proceeding in orthodox fashion against the QP, but Black has compensation in his command and occupation of strong points in the center.

12	B—Q3
13 B—K2	. . . .

Capablanca sees in this move the cause of his later difficulties; he believes that P—Kt3 and B—Kt2 were in order, menacing the QP and interrupting the important attacking diagonal. However, in that case, Black would have had complete control of White's QB4—a circumstance which would have cancelled much of Black's positional inferiority.

Such positions, in which both players have weak and strong points, are very difficult to judge accurately, especially in the heat of battle.

13	B—K3
14 B—B3	R—R2
15 O—O	R—B2
16 Q—Kt3	. . . .

Simply R—B1 was in order. White is too anxious to augment the pressure on the isolated QP, and he is evidently under the impression that the Queen move prevents . . . QKt—Q2.

16	QKt—Q2!

For neither Kt—B6 nor Kt x P is feasible:

I 17 Kt—B6, R x Kt! 18 P x R, P—Q5; 19 Kt—Q5, B x Kt; 20 B x B, Kt—B4; 21 Q—R2, Kt x B; 22 Q x Kt, B x Pch etc.

II 17 Kt x P, B x Kt; 18 B x B, Kt—B4 winning as above.

This is one line of play which would have been ruled out by White's fianchetto on move 13!

17 KR—Q1	Kt—K4
18 B—K2	Q—K2
19 QR—B1	KR—B1

Janowski has built up a splendid position and has good prospects on either wing or in the center. Capablanca therefore decides to ease the pressure by simplifying.

20 Kt—R4	R x R
21 R x R	R x Rch
22 B x R	Kt—K5
23 B—Kt2	. . . .

Reconciling himself to the combination which follows. 23 P—B3 was the alternative (but not 23 Kt x P? Q—B2 etc.).

23	Kt—B5
24 B x Kt	B x Pch!

Quite right. Black is always sure of a draw, and all the winning chances are on his side.

25 K x B	Q—R5ch

26 K—Kt1	Q x Pch
27 K—R2	Q—Kt6ch
28 K—Kt1	. . . .

Avoiding 28 K—R1? B—R6; 29 B—KB1, Kt—B7ch; 30 K—Kt1, Kt—Kt5 and wins.

28	P x B
29 Q—B2	Q x KPch
30 K—R2	Q—Kt6ch
31 K—Kt1	Q—K8ch
32 K—R2	Q—Kt6ch
33 K—Kt1	Q—K8ch
34 K—R2	Kt—B3!

Having gained considerable time on the clock, Black has devised a new and dangerous form of the attack.

35 Kt x B	Q R5ch
36 K—Kt1	Q—K8ch
37 K—R2	Q R5ch
38 K—Kt1	Kt—Kt5
39 Q—Q2!	. . . .

Forced: if 39 Q—B3? Q—B7ch and mate next move; if 39 B—B3, Q—R7ch winning the Queen three moves later.

39	Q—R7ch
40 K—B1	Q—R8ch
41 K—K2	Q x Pch
42 K—Q1	Kt—B7ch
43 K—B2	Q—Kt3ch
44 K—B1	Q—Kt8ch
45 K—B2	Q—Kt3ch
46 K—B1	Kt—Q6ch
47 K—Kt1	P x Kt
48 Q—QB2?	. . . .

K—R2 would have saved a priceless tempo by at once threatening Kt x P. Capablanca considers that 48 K—R2 would have given him at least a draw and would thus have vindicated the hotly disputed moves 20 Kt—R4 and 23 B—Kt2.

48	P—R4
49 B—Q4	P—R5
50 B x QKtP	. . . .

Now White has a strong passed Pawn as well, and the coming phase promises to be very exciting.

50	P—R6
51 B—B7	P—K4
52 P—Kt6	. . . .

White could remove the advanced RP with 52 Q x Pch, K—B1; 53 B—Q6ch, Q x B; 54 Q—B8ch, K—B2; 55 Q x P; but this would not suffice to save the game.

52	Q—K5!

This should have been the winning move.

53 B x P	. . . .

Desperation, for if 53 Kt—B3, P—R7! 54 Q x P, Q—K8ch and White can resign.

Janowski

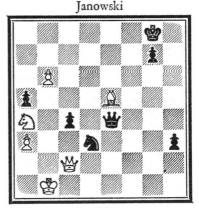

Capablanca

53	Q—K8ch??

Throwing away the fruit of all his hard work. 53 . . . Q—R8ch (preventing the further advance of White's KtP) followed by . . . Kt x B would have left White helpless.

54 K—R2	Kt x B?

There was still a draw with 54 . . . Kt—B8ch; but who could foresee that the text leaves White with a forced win?!

55 P—Kt7	Kt—Q2
56 Kt—B5!	Kt—Kt1
57 Q x Pch	K—R1

Not 57 . . . K—B1? 58 Q—B4ch and wins. Now comes a very fine centralizing move which is the key to the winning manoeuvre.

| 58 Kt—K4!! | K—R2 |

White was threatening to win the Queen, for example 58 . . .P—R7; 59 Q—B8ch, K—R2; 60 Q—R3ch, K—Kt1 (if 60 . . . K—Kt3; 61 Q—K6ch followed by Kt—B6 ch); 61 Q—K6ch, K—R1 (if 61 . . . K—B1; 62 Q—Q6ch or 61 . . . K—R2; 62 Kt—Kt5ch): 62 Q—K8 ch, K—R2; 63 Kt—Kt5ch etc. (Schlechter)

| 59 Q—Q3!! | P—Kt3 |

If 59 . . . Q—R5; 60 Kt—Kt5ch, K—R3; 61 Kt—B7ch, K—R4; 62 Q—B5ch, P—Kt4; 63 Kt—K5 and wins.
Or 59 . . . P—R7; 60 Kt—Kt5ch, K—R3! 61 Kt—B7ch, K—R4; 62 Q—B5ch, K—R5; 63 Q—B4ch, K—R6; 64 Kt—Kt5ch, K—Kt7; 65 Q—B3ch, K—Kt8; 66 Kt—R3 mate! (Schlechter)

| 60 Q x Pch | K—Kt2 |
| 61 Q—KB3! | Q—QB8 |

Threatening perpetual check if given the opportunity. Other moves are no better, for example 61 . . . Q—R5; 62 Q—B3ch; or 61 . . . Kt—Q2; 62 Q—Q3 etc.

| 62 Q—B6ch | K—R2 |

62 . . . K—Kt1; 63 Q—K6ch leads to the same position. The rest is silence.

63 Q—B7ch	K—R3
64 Q—B8ch	K—R4
65 Q—R8ch	K—Kt5
66 Q—B8ch	Resigns

This subtle and artistic ending was a suitably dramatic conclusion to a magnificent struggle.

---

13. Lodz, 1911
(Consultation Game)
RUY LOPEZ

An instructive example of the pressure on an open file against a backward Pawn.

J. R. CAPABLANCA	ALLIES
White	Black
1 P—K4	P—K4
2 Kt—KB3	Kt—QB3
3 B—Kt5	P—QR3
4 B—R4	Kt—B3
5 O—O	Kt x P
6 P—Q4	P—QKt4
7 B—Kt3	P—Q4
8 P x P	B—K3
9 P—B3	B—K2
10 QKt—Q2	Kt—B4
11 B—B2	B—Kt5

So far all book. The threat of 12 . . . Kt x P is parried easily enough; however, the plausible 11 . . . P—Q5 was subsequently refuted by Capablanca with 12 Kt—K4, P x P; 13 Kt x Kt, B x Kt; 14 B—K4, Q—Q2; 15 P x P, leaving Black with a palpably inferior position.
The further progress of the present game bears out the reputation of this variation for giving Black a free game at the expense of certain Pawn weaknesses.

12 P—KR3	B—R4
13 R—K1	B—Kt3
14 Kt—Q4!	Kt x Kt

This creates the weakness on the QB file which gives the rest of the game its theme; the alternative 14 . . . Q—Q2 could be answered by 15 P—KB4 with unpleasant possibilities for Black.

15 P x Kt	Kt—K3
16 Kt—Kt3!	B—Kt4
17 P—Kt3	KB x B
18 R x B	O—O
19 P—B4	B x B

Practically compulsory, as . . .
P—KB4 would hem in the Bishop
permanently.

20 R x B	P—Kt3
21 Kt—B5!	R—K1
22 Q—Q3	Kt x Kt
23 R x Kt	Q—Q2

White has simplified down to the
proper position. He is free to exercise all possible pressure against
the QBP, while Black is limited
to purely passive measures. White
can vary his procedure with minor
tactical threats, and with an attempt to gain ground on the King-
side (P—KKt4 followed by P—B5).
Black will gradually be reduced to
helplessness.

24 P—KKt4	P—QB3
25 KR—QB1	QR—B1
26 Q—QB3	R—K3
27 K—R2	K—R1
28 Q—R3	. . . .

P—B5 would also have been very
strong, but Capablanca prefers to
maintain the pressure.

28	Q—Kt2
29 Q—KKt3	P—B4

In order to banish the possibility
of P—B5. White maneuvers cleverly now to force . . . P x P, which
will strengthen his position still
more and renew the menace of
P—B5.

30 Q—KB3	Q—Q2

Q x P was threatened.

31 K—Kt3	R—B1
32 Q—R3	R—R1
33 Q—QB3	R—QB1
34 Q—B2	K—Kt1

Allies

Capablanca

Of course if now 35 P x P, P x P;
36 Q x P?? R—Kt3ch wins. But
Capablanca's next move creates a
situation in which Black cannot
simultaneously defend both BPs.

35 K—B3!	P x Pch
36 P x P	Q—KB2
37 K—K3	R—B1
38 R—B1	Q—Q2
39 Q—Kt2	Q—K2

In order to answer P—B5 with
. . . Q—Kt4ch. However, Black's
struggles are futile, for White will
eventually find the proper setup
for P—B5.

40 R(1)—B1	R(3)—B3
41 R—B1	K—R1
42 Q—QB2	Q—K1
43 Q—R2	Q—K2
44 R—KB3	R—K3
45 K—B2	P—QR4

White's last three moves have
brought about the desired position.

46 P—B5	P x P
47 P x P	Q—Kt4!?

A last attempt, as normal moves
must lose quickly. If now 48 P x R,
Q—Q7ch; 49 K—Kt1 (if 49 K—Kt3,
R—Kt1ch; 50 K—R3, Q—R3 mate),

Q—Q8ch; 50 K—B2, Q x Rch; 51
K—Kt1, Q—B8 mate. Or 51 K—
K1, Q—B8ch winning the Queen.

48 Q—B4!   R x BP

The exchange of Queens would
of course be quite hopeless.

49 Q x R   Q—Q7ch
50 K—B1   R—Kt3
51 Q—KB8ch   R—Kt1
52 Q—B6ch   R—Kt2
53 R—Kt3   Resigns

He has nothing left but a few
checks: 53 . . . Q—Q8ch; 54 K—
Kt2, Q—K7ch; 55 Q—B2, Q—K5ch;
56 Q—B3 etc. The Allies were
made up of a team of the six best
players of Lodz, including Salwe.

---

14. Havana, 1912

QUEEN'S GAMBIT DECLINED
(In effect)

This game deserves to be known
more widely because it contains
one of the immortal combinations.
Such moves could have been produced only by an artist of very
fine sensibilities.

J. R. CAPABLANCA	AMATEUR
White	Black
1 P—Q4	P—Q4
2 P—K3	P—K3

There is no compelling reason
for aping White's old-fashioned
move. Excellent alternatives are:
2 . . . P—QB4; 2 . . . B—B4; 2 . . .
Kt—KB3 followed by . . . P—KKt3.

3 B—Q3	P—QB3
4 Kt—KB3	B—Q3
5 QKt—Q2	P—KB4

The logical corollary of the previous moves; he sets up the "Stone-

wall" formation, which weakens
the black squares and also hems
in the QB (note the Pawn formation!); on the other hand, it leads
to a close game in which it is not
easy for White to break through.

6 P—B4	Q—B3
7 P—QKt3	Kt—KR3
8 B—Kt2	O—O
9 Q—B2	Kt—Q2
10 P—KR3!	. . . .

Note that Capablanca has avoided the hackneyed O—O; he has
decided that the seemingly more
risky O—O—O will give him better prospects of smoking out
Black's carefully guarded King.
The text, for example, threatens
P—KKt4! Black parries the menace at once, but by so doing he
creates a weakness which soon
receives Capablanca's most searching attention.

10	P—KKt3
11 O—O—O	P—K4

Black loses patience and makes
a forcible attempt to free himself.
This plan is unsound, but it requires play of the highest order
to demonstrate its inadequacy.

12 QP x P	Kt x P
13 P x P	P x P

White's last move actually seems
quite inferior, as Black now threatens an attack with . . . B—K3 and
. . . R—B1. But now comes the
first astounding move of a remarkable combination.

14 Kt—B4!!   P x Kt

The object of the Knight sacrifice is to force open the attacking lines: the two diagonals bearing down on the Black King, and
the Q file as well. Euwe shows
that there is no really satisfactory
alternative to the capture:
I 14 . . . Kt x Bch; 15 Q x Kt,
Q—K2; 16 Kt x B, Q x Kt; 17 Q—
Q4 and wins.

II 14 . . . Kt(3)—B2; 15 Kt x B, Q x Kt; 16 Q—B3, Q—QB3; 17 B—Kt5! with a winning positional advantage.

15 B x Pch	Kt(3)—B2
16 R x B!	Q x R
17 Kt x Kt	B—K3

Practically forced, as White was threatening a quick win with Q—B3 (always this same motif of menace on the weakened diagonal). After the text, the attack requires more fuel.

| 18 R—Q1 | Q—K2 |

Amateur

Capablanca

19 R—Q7!!   . . . .

The second surprise, even finer than the first. The Greek gift cannot be declined, for example 19 . . . Q—K1; 20 Kt x Kt, R x Kt; 21 Q—B3, R x R; 22 Q—R8ch, K—B2; 23 Q—Kt7 mate.

| 19 . . . . | B x R |
| 20 Kt x B | KR—B1 |

Black pins his faith to the removal of one of the terrible Bishops, realizing that if 20 . . . Q x Kt; 21 Q—B3 decides; and that if he does not take the Knight, he must guard against the amusing threat 21 Kt—B6ch, K—Kt2; 22 Kt—Kt4 ch, K—Kt1; 23 Kt—R6 mate!

21 Q—B3   . . . .

At last!

| 21 . . . . | R x B |
| 22 P x R | Resigns |

For he now perceives that after 22 . . . Kt—Q3; 23 Q—R8ch leads to a decisive gain of material. Euwe's final comment: "Such an achievement in the realm of combinative chess can only be described as superb."

---

15.   Havana, 1913
(First Brilliancy Prize)
INDIAN DEFENSE

This is one of Capablanca's most brilliant games, and is characterized throughout by originality quite out of the ordinary. A striking feature of the game is that although the KKt file is never opened, the possibility plays a dominant role in the notes!

J. Corzo   J. R. Capablanca

White	Black
1 P—Q4	Kt—KB3
2 P—QB4	P—Q3

It is not generally known that Capablanca was one of the pioneers of this defense. Popular opinion of the day is reflected in the chess column of T. F. Lawrence, then one of the leading English players: "Although adopted successfully by Capablanca . . . this is not a defense to be ventured on lightly by ordinary mortals."

3 Kt—QB3	QKt—Q2
4 P—K4	P—K4
5 P—B4?	. . . .

As so often happens, Black's conservative development tempts White to adopt an apparently aggressive but really weakening continuation. Today P—KKt3 or Kt—B3 is the approved move.

5 . . . .   P x QP

If the weakness of White's center is to be demonstrated, this must be played at once.

6 Q x P   Kt—B4
7 B—K3   Q—K2!

Doubtless an unexpected move, and its sequel is even more astonishing. White's reply is virtually forced, for if 8 B—Q3?? Kt—K3 wins the Queen, or if 8 P—K5, Kt—Kt5 with advantage.

8 Kt—Q5   Kt x Kt
9 KP x Kt   B—B4
10 Kt—B3   . . . .

If White had had an inkling of the troubles in store for him, he would have castled. Now comes a most unexpected reply.

10 . . . .   P—KKt3!!

Developing the KB very powerfully without loss of time. If now 11 Q x R, Q x Bch; 12 K—Q1, Kt—K5 and wins.

11 K—B2   . . . .

It would have been somewhat better to play 11 O—O—O, despite the fact that Black would have a promising game after the reply 11 . . . B—Kt2.

11 . . . .   KR—Kt1
12 R—K1   B—Kt2
13 Q—Q1   Kt—K5ch
14 K—Kt1   . . . .

White's KR is hemmed in and in fact it never moves throughout the game—an important factor in making possible Black's coming sacrifices.

14 . . . .   K—B1!

The King is safer here than after the more orthodox . . . O—O—O.

15 B—Q4   . . . .

Capablanca

Corzo

White seems to be on the way to consolidating his position, but the following ingenious move revives the attack.

15 . . . .   P—KKt4!!

Capablanca shows that the following possible replies would now be inadequate:

I   16 Kt x P, B x Bch; 17 Q x B, Kt x Kt! 18 R x Q, Kt—R6 mate.

II   16 P x P, Kt x P; 17 R x Q, Kt—R6ch; 18 P x Kt, B x B mate!

III   16 P x P, Kt x P; 17 Kt x Kt, B x Bch; 18 Q x B, Q x R.

IV   16 P x P, Kt x P; 17 B x Bch, R x B; 18 Kt x Kt, Q x Kt with advantage.

16 B x Bch   R x B
17 Kt—Q4   B—Q2
18 P—KB5   . . . .

White would have been well-advised to adopt the more prudent line 18 B—Q3, P—B4; 19 B x Kt, P x B; 20 P—KB5. The text soon leads to a new crisis.

18 . . . .   Q—K4
19 Q—Q3   R—K1
20 Kt—K6ch!?   P x Kt
21 BP x P   R x P!!

A resource that had been prepared several moves ago.

22 P x R   B-B3
23 Q—B3ch   Q—B5!

Black's pieces are posted so powerfully that paradoxically enough,
the exchange of Queens would give
him an overwhelming attack: 24
Q x Qch, P x Q; 25 P—KR4 (or 25
B—Q3, Kt—B4; 26 B—B1, P—B6
and White cannot avoid a serious
loss of material: 27 P—KKt3, P—
B7ch etc.), P—B6; 26 R—Q1, P—
B7ch; 27 K—R2, Kt—Kt6; 28
R—Q2, Kt x R; 29 K x Kt, R x P!
and wins.

24 Q—K3   K—K2
25 P—QKt4   P—Kt3
26 P—Kt5   B—Kt2
27 P—Kt3   Kt—Q7!

Against this pretty move the
only chance was 28 B—Kt2 (not
28 P x Q, P x Pch; 29 Q—Kt3, P x Q
and wins), Q x Qch; 29 R x Q, B x B;
30 K x B, Kt x P; 31 R—QB3, P—
Q4 with very good winning chances
for Black.

28 Q—QB3?   Kt—B6ch
29 K—B2   Q—B1!

Decisive. White cannot save
both Rooks, and makes a last desperate attempt.

30 P—B5   Kt—K4ch
31 K—Kt1   Kt—B6ch
32 K—B2   KtP x P
33 Q—R5   Kt—K4ch
34 K—Kt1   Q—B6
35 Q x Pch   K—B3
36 Q x QP   Q x Rch
37 K—B2   Q x Pch
   Resigns

---

16. Havana, 1913

FRENCH DEFENSE

The distinguished critic Hans
Kmoch comments: "A very beautiful game, played by Capablanca
with impeccable precision and
economy." This praise is well-
deserved, with the exception of
some inexact opening play. Particularly instructive is the exploitation of the sadly weakened black
squares by powerful Queen moves.

J. R. CAPABLANCA   R. BLANCO
   White   Black

1 P—K4   P—K3
2 P—Q4   P—Q4
3 Kt—QB3   P x P

A weak line of play which gives
White too great a command of the
board.

4 Kt x P   Kt—Q2
5 Kt—KB3   KKt—B3
6 Kt x Ktch   Kt x Kt
7 Kt—K5?!   . . . .

This highly praised move is played to prevent . . . P—QKt3, which
is to be answered by B—Kt5ch.
However, the normal course B—Q3
etc. would have been preferable.

7 . . . .   B—Q3!

A reply which has been severely
criticized, although it is quite good
if followed up correctly. The immediate purpose is to threaten to
win a Pawn with 8 . . . B x Kt;
9 P x B, Q x Qch; 10 K x Q, Kt—
Kt5. The text also has the additional object of undermining the
position of the advanced Knight.

8 Q—B3   P—B3?

Too timid. He should have been
consistent by playing 8 . . . P—B4!
White would then have been in
difficulties, for example 9 P—B3,
P x P; 10 P x P, B x Kt; 11 P x B,
Q—R4ch winning a Pawn; or 9
B—Kt5ch, K—B1 threatening . . .
Q—R4ch in addition to . . . P x P.

9 P—B3   . . . .

Now all is well. If instead 9
Kt x QBP, Q—B2 regains the Pawn
advantageously.

9 . . . .   O—O

| 10 B—KKt5 | B—K2 |
| 11 B—Q3 | Kt—K1 |

Black is already in serious difficulties, as White was threatening 12 Q—R3, forcing a weakening Pawn advance.

12 Q—R3!   P—KB4

Burdening himself with a weak KP which soon has to bear the brunt of powerful hostile pressure. However, if 12 . . . P—KR3; 13 B x P yields a winning attack; or 12 . . . P—KKt3; 13 B—KR6 and the outlook for Black's game is bad.

13 B x B	Q x B
14 O—O	R—B3
15 KR—K1!	. . . .

Putting his finger on the weak point. Black's position is cramped, his Bishop has no scope and he is permanently burdened with a weak Pawn on an open file. **He has a strategically lost game.**

15	Kt—Q3
16 R—K2	B—Q2
17 QR—K1	R—K1
18 P—QB4!	Kt—B2

Tempting White to play for the immediate win of a Pawn, thus: 19 Kt x B, Q x Kt; 20 B x P, Kt—Kt4; 21 Q—Kt4, R x B; 22 P—KR4, P—KR4! 23 Q x R, P x Q; 24 R x R ch, K—R2; 25 P x Kt, Q x P and White's advantage has disappeared. In such positions, one must not undertake seemingly decisive action unless all the necessary preliminary steps have been completed.

19 P—Q5!   Kt x Kt

There was no satisfactory continuation; for example, if 19 . . . BP x P (not 19 . . . KP x P?? 20 Kt x B); 20 P x P, B—B1; 21 B—B4! maintaining the pressure.

20 R x Kt   P—KKt3

This weakens Black's position still more; hence a better defense

against the threatened B x P would have been 20 . . . Q—B2.

21 Q—R4!   K—Kt2

Giving the KR additional protection; White threatened P—Q6!

22 Q—Q4!   . . . .

Powerful centralization, incidentally creating a new pin.

| 22 . . . . | P—B4 |
| 23 Q—B3 | P—Kt3 |

He could have prolonged his resistance somewhat with . . . Q—Q3.

24 P x P   B—B1

Obviously Black cannot recapture; but he hopes to consolidate his position and pick off the KP later. However, Capablanca maintains the advantage with a very fine maneuver.

Blanco

Capablanca

25 B—K2   B x P

On other moves White continues B—B3—Q5, gradually r e d u c i n g Black to a state of complete helplessness.

26 B—B3   K—B2

The pin will be fatal, but the

attempt to remove it by 26 . . .
Q—Q2 is refuted by 27 B—Q5, B—
B2; 28 R x R, B x R; 29 R—K6,
Q—Q1; 30 Q—K5, B moves; 31
R—K7 (Kmoch).

| 27 B—Q5 | Q—Q3 |
| 28 Q—K3 | R—K2 |

Against 28 . . . P—B5 Capablanca had prepared 29 Q—KR3,
P—KR4; 30 Q—R4, R—K2; 31
Q—Kt5, K—Kt2; 32 P—KR4, Q—
Q2; 33 P—KKt3, P x P; 34 P—B4
and in due course P—B5 will be
decisive.

| 29 Q—R6! | K—Kt1 |
| 30 P—KR4! | P—R3 |

Black is helpless to prevent the
creation of the final weakness
which will topple the whole rickety
structure of his position.

| 31 P—R5 | P—B5 |
| 32 P x P | P x P |

Or 32 . . . R x P; 33 R x B!

| 33 R x B! | Resigns |

If 33 . . . R(2) x R; 34 R x R,
R x R; 35 Q x Pch.

---

17. New York, 1913
(National Tournament)

FOUR KNIGHTS' GAME

This is the kind of game which
usually bores the amateur because
it proceeds in so quiet a vein that
he fails to realize what the struggle
is all about. In reality, however, it
is intensely interesting to see how
Capablanca creates a very slight
positional advantage, and how he
brings it to fruition.

J. R. CAPABLANCA	D. JANOWSKI
White	Black
1 P—K4	P—K4
2 Kt—KB3	Kt—QB3

| 3 Kt—B3 | Kt—B3 |
| 4 B—Kt5 | . . . . |

Although this opening was quite
a favorite with the Cuban in the
early part of his career (doubtless
because it required little book
knowledge), he virtually discarded
it about a year after this game
was played.

4	P—QR3?
5 B x Kt	QP x B
6 O—O	. . . .

A more forceful method of exploiting Black's inferior 4th move
is 6 Kt x P, Kt x P; 7 Kt x Kt, Q—
Q5; 8 O—O, Q x Kt(4); 9 R—K1,
B—K3; 10 P—Q4, Q—KB4; 11 B—
Kt5! B—Q3; 12 P—KKt4! Q—Kt3;
13 P—KB4 (Znosko-Borovsky-Ru-
binstein, Ostend, 1907) with a quick
win in sight for White.

| 6 . . . . | B—KKt5 |

If 6 . . . B—Q3; 7 P—Q4 is very
powerful.

| 7 P—KR3 | B—R4 |

Janowski often courted trouble
by trying to maintain the two Bishops . . . B x Kt was better.

8 Q—K2	B—Q3
9 P—Q3	Q—K2
10 Kt—Q1	O—O—O

Stubbornly continuing his policy.
Dr. Lasker recommends the preferable course 10 . . . Kt—Q2; 11
Kt—K3, B x Kt; 12 Q x B, P—KKt3;
with chances of counterplay.

| 11 Kt—K3 | B—Kt3? |

Since this Bishop will be exchanged later under more unfavorable conditions, Black should now
have played 11 . . . B x Kt; 12 Q x B,
P—KKt3 and if 13 Kt—B4, P—R3.

12 Kt—R4	KR—Kt1
13 Kt(3)—B5	Q—K3
14 P—KB4!	. . . .

In contrast to his opponent, Capablanca has proceeded with simple and clear moves, and has now secured a definite positional advantage. The threat is now Kt x Bch followed by P—B5.

14	. . . .	B x Kt
15	Kt x B	P x P
16	B x P	B—B4ch
17	B—K3	B—B1
18	Q—B2!	R—Q2
19	B—B5!	B x B
20	Q x B	K—Kt1

Q—R7 was threatened. White has reached the stage of welcoming exchanges, for he realizes that the Pawn position is much in his favor. Whereas Black's Queen-side Pawns are in a state which makes it difficult to turn them to account, White has promising endgame prospects if he can induce . . . P—B3. Once that move is made, he can advance P—KKt4—5, eliminating the KBP and thus creating a passed KP. The first part of this plan requires pressure on the KB file; the second part of the plan demands the exchange of Queens before the KKtP can be thrust forward.

21	R—B2	Kt—K1
22	QR—KB1	P—B3

If 22 . . . Q x P; 23 Kt—K7, R—R1; 24 R x P regains the Pawn with a quick win in sight. The text was inevitable, and now that the Pawn is on the third rank, White is ready for the exchange of Queens.

23	P—QKt3	Kt—Q3
24	R—B4	Kt x Kt

This and the following exchange only hasten the end, but Black had little to hope for in any event.

25	Q x Kt	Q x Q
26	R x Q	R—K1

Janowski

Capablanca

27	P—KKt4!	. . . .

The key to the ending! As already explained, White will eventually play this Pawn to Kt5, obtaining a passed KP. However, White is in no hurry to do this, as he must also paralyze Black's counterplay on the Queen-side, and in addition bring his King to K3 to support the KP in preparation for its subsequent advance.

27	. . . .	P—QKt3

Striving for . . . P—B4, which Capablanca at once prevents.

28	P—Kt4!	K—Kt2

As Black's attempts to make headway on the Queen-side are doomed to be frustrated, Black should have played the King to the other side, where it might have fulfilled a valuable defensive function. This criticism applies to later moves as well.

29	K—B2	P—QKt4

Hoping for . . . P—QR4, but White gets there first.

30	P—QR4!	R—Q5
31	R—QKt1	R—K4
32	K—K3	R—Q2

If 32 . . . R x R; 33 KtP x R, R—Q2; 34 P—Q4 with a winning end-game.

33 P—R5!   R—K3

Now that the Queen-side Pawns are fixed, White can turn all his attention to the other wing.

34 R(1)—KB1   R(2)—K2

Or 34 . . . P—R3; 35 P—R4 and the game proceeds in much the same way.

35 P—Kt5   P x P
36 R x P   . . . .

White has achieved his goal: he has a strongly supported passed KP, he has pressure on the KKtP and he holds the only open file.

36 . . . .   R—R3
37 R—Kt3   R(3)—K3
38 P—R4   P—Kt3
39 R—Kt5   P—R3

Creating another weakness; but if he sits tight, P—R5 also leaves him with another weak Pawn.

40 R—Kt4   R—Kt2

Now the KP is ready to advance; there is no hope for Black.

41 P—Q4   K—B1
42 R—B8ch   K—Kt2

42 . . . K—Q2; 43 R—QR8 is equally bad.

43 P—K5   P—Kt4
44 K—K4   R(3)—K2
45 P x P   P x P
46 R—B5   K—B1
47 R(4) x P   R—R2
48 R—R5   K—Q2
49 R x R   R x R
50 R—B8   R—R5ch
51 K—Q3   R—R6ch
52 K—Q2   P—B4

Much too late!

53 KtP x P   R—R6
54 P—Q5   Resigns

If 54 . . . R x P; 55 R—B7ch wins easily. "White's play was irreproachable and he executed his plan in a very able manner" (Dr. Lasker).

---

18. New York, 1913
(Rice Chess Club Tournament)
RUY LOPEZ

Capablanca follows up his superior opening play with his splendid handling of the middle game.

J. R. CAPABLANCA	O. CHAJES
White	Black
1 P—K4	P—K4
2 Kt—KB3	Kt—QB3
3 B—Kt5	P—QR3
4 B—R4	Kt—B3
5 O—O	P—QKt4
6 B—Kt3	B—K2
7 P—Q4	. . . .

Taking advantage of the unusual order of Black's last two moves. But the interpolation of P—QR4 would be even more energetic.

7	P—Q3
8 P—B3	B—Kt5
9 B—K3	. . . .

If now 9 . . . Kt x KP; 10 B—Q5, Q—Q2; 11 P x P! with considerable advantage. But it may well be that 9 P—Q5 was stronger.

| 9 . . . . | O—O |
| 10 QKt—Q2 | Kt—QR4? |

Feeble. 10 . . . P—Q4! would have given Black a beautiful game. After this lapse, Capablanca gives his opponent not a moment's peace.

| 11 B—B2 | R—K1 |

In view of the reply to this, it

would have been better to play 11
. . . P—B4, despite the fact that
12 P—KR3 would have forced . . .
B x Kt.

| 12 P—Kt4! | P x P |

Practically forced, although the
resulting powerful center and open
QB file are decisive weapons in
White's hands. However, if 12 . . .
Kt—B5; 13 Kt x Kt, P x Kt; 14
P x P, B x Kt forced; 15 Q x B,
P x P; 16 Q—K2 and the advanced
Pawn goes; or 12 . . . Kt—Kt2;
13 P—QR4 with a strong Queen-side
initiative and leaving the QKt badly
out of play; or finally 12 . . . Kt—
B3; 13 P—Q5, Kt—Kt1; 14 P—QR4
and the previous comment still
applies.

13 P x P	Kt—B3
14 P—QR3	B—KB1
15 R—B1	Kt—K2

Black's desire to remove this unfortunate Knight from the line of
fire and use it to bolster the King-
side is quite natural; but since
he should have postponed the following advance as long as possible,
. . . Q—Q2 would have been preferable.

| 16 P—K5 | P x P |
| 17 P x P | B x Kt |

Not 17 . . . Kt—Q2? 18 B x Pch,
K x B; 19 Kt—Kt5ch. White's attacking chances are gradually
shaping up.

18 Q x B	Kt—Q2
19 Q—R3	Kt—KKt3
20 P—B4	Kt—Kt3
21 Kt—B3	Kt—B5

Just as Black congratulates himself on having secured a good
square for this Knight, the final
storm breaks over his hapless
King!

| 22 Kt—Kt5 | P—R3 |

Chajes

Capablanca

| 23 Kt x P! | K x Kt |

The idea of the sacrifice is obvious enough, but it has to be followed up accurately. White's mon-
opoly of the attacking lines is the
decisive factor.

24 Q—B5ch	K—Kt1
25 Q x Kt	Kt x B
26 Q—R7ch	K—B2
27 B—Kt3ch	Kt—B5

Or 27 . . . K—K2; 28 Q—Kt6
and wins:
I 28 . . . Q—Q2; 29 KR—K1, K—
Q1 (if 29 . . . Kt—B5; 30 QR—Q1
wins); 30 R x Kt etc. (Tarrasch)
II 28 . . . Kt—B5; 29 KR—Q1,
Q—Kt1; 30 P—K6, Q—Kt3ch; 31
K—B1, Kt—Q3; 32 R x Kt, Q x R;
33 Q—B7ch, K—Q1; 34 R—Q1, B—
K2; 35 Q x P and wins. (Capa-
blanca)

28 KR—Q1	Q—Kt1
29 R x Kt!	P x R
30 B x Pch	K—K2
31 Q—B5	Q—Kt3ch
32 K—B1	Resigns

Note that Black's Rooks and
Bishop played no part in the game:
a heritage of the misplayed opening.

19. Berlin, 1913
(Exhibition Game)
CENTER GAME

This game is far from the conventional conception of a masterpiece, for both players commit mistakes. Nevertheless the game is an outstanding one, for it shows how the greatest masters rise above adverse conditions to defeat less able opponents who lack the ability to turn their advantage to account.

J. MIESES	J. R. CAPABLANCA
White	Black
1 P—K4	P—K4
2 P—Q4	P x P
3 Q x P	Kt—QB3
4 Q—K3	Kt—B3
5 Kt—QB3	B—Kt5
6 B—Q2	O—O
7 O—O—O	R—K1

Black has an excellent development and now menaces the KP. Instead of troubling to guard this Pawn, Mieses selects the characteristic course of surrendering it at once and playing for complications.

8 Q—Kt3?!	Kt x P
9 Kt x Kt	R x Kt
10 B—KB4	Q—B3

Likewise in aggressive mood. After the obvious 10 . . . P—Q3 there follows 11 B—Q3, R—K1; 12 Kt—B3 and White's rapid development gives him good prospects.

11 Kt—R3 . . . .

Mieses naturally does not care for the continuation 11 B x P, P—Q3; 12 B x P, Q—R3ch; 13 K—Kt1, Q—Q7!

11 . . . . P—Q3

Now this move threatens to win a piece.

12 B—Q3 Kt—Q5!

The complications increase at every move. The Rook is immune, nor can White play to win a piece with 13 P—QB3 because of 13 . . . Kt—K7ch; 14 B x Kt, R x B; 15 Q—Q3, B x Kt etc.

13 B—K3 . . . .

Capablanca

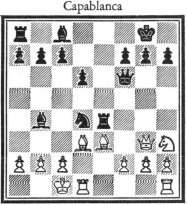

Mieses

13 . . . . B—Kt5?

But in creating greater complications Capablanca overreaches himself. He subsequently pointed out that the proper continuation was 13 . . . R—Kt5!; 14 B x Kt, R x B; 15 P—QB3, B x P; 16 P x B, R—KKt5; 17 Q—K3, Q x Pch; 18 B—B2, Q x Q; 19 P x Q, R x P and with four Pawns for the piece and with White's Pawn position in so ragged a state, Black has a winning position.

14 Kt—Kt5! R x B

The loss of the exchange is forced.

15 Q x B!	Kt—K7ch
16 B x Kt	R x B
17 Kt—K4!	R x Kt
18 Q x R	Q—Kt4ch

Black has a Pawn for the exchange — inadequate compensation with proper play on White's part. But Mieses handles the remaining part of the game in an inexplicably feeble manner.

19 P—B4	Q—Kt4
20 P—B3	B—B4
21 KR—K1	Q—B3
22 R—Q5	. . . .

The exchange of Queens would lead to a winning endgame, but White wants to win in a more "interesting" way.

22	Q—Q2
23 P—B5	. . . .

23 R—R5, forcing a weakness in the Black King's position, would have been more exact. The idea of the Pawn storm is not a bad one, but White carries it out in a very ineffectual manner.

23	P—QB3
24 R—Q2	P—Q4
25 Q—B3?	. . . .

Very superficial, as it allows Black to work his Bishop around to the fine square B3. The proper move was P—KKt4, as the Queen was not really attacked.

25	B—K2
26 R(2)—K2	B—B3

Taking advantage of every opportunity, Capablanca has improved his position considerably; and the idea of advancing the Pawns against White's King begins to take shape.

27 Q—R5?	. . . .

Intending P—KKt4—5, but again he plays in a slovenly manner. Correct was P—KKt4 followed by Q—Kt3.

27	P—KR3!
28 P—KKt4	K—R2

If now 29 P—KR4?? P—KKt3! wins the Queen. White is obliged to retreat and admit that the expedition was a failure.

29 K—Kt1	R—Q1

30 R—Q1	P—B4
31 Q—R3	Q—R5!

Very strong. The Queen is placed aggressively for the attack, and still maintains contact with the other wing.

32 R(2)—Q2	Q—K5ch
33 K—R1	P—QKt4
34 Q—Kt2	Q—R5

This cannot be answered by 35 R x P?? because of . . . Q x Rch!

35 K—Kt1	P—Kt5
36 P x P?	. . . .

This is the decisive mistake, as White's position becomes too vulnerable for adequate defense. Since White will be helpless because of the deadly pressure against his QKt2, he should have played 36 P—B4, forcing . . . P—Q5. Evidently the idea of winning the QP has a fatal attraction for him.

36	Q x P

Intending to answer 37 R x P with . . . R x R; 38 R x R, B x P! with a winning attack.

37 P—QR3	Q—R5
38 R x P	R—QKt1

Black has given up the extra Pawn gladly, as he now has a decisive attack.

39 R(1)—Q2	P—B5
40 Q—Kt3	R—Kt6
41 Q—Q6	P—B6

A quicker way was 41 . . . B x P! 42 R x B, P—B6! and wins.

42 R—QB2	P x P
43 R—Q3	Q—K5!

Absolutely decisive.

44 R—Q1	. . . .

Or 44 R(2)—Q2, R—B6! 45 R—Q1, B—Kt4! 46 K x P, R—B3 followed by . . . R—Kt3ch with a winning attack.

44 . . . .   R—QB6

White resigns, for if 45 Q—Q2,
R x P etc.   A most instructive
game.

---

20. Berlin, 1913
(Exhibition Game)

BENONI COUNTER GAMBIT

Both Capablanca and Lasker had
a habit of expressing themselves
rather contemptuously about the
hypermodern theories. This led
to a widespread assumption that
both of them stood aloof from these
theories. The fact is, however,
that they were quite familiar with
these concepts, and made frequent
use of them. Here, for example,
we are given an opportunity to
admire Capablanca's mastery of
the process of exploiting weak col-
or complexes.

J. R. CAPABLANCA	J. MIESES
White	Black
1 P—Q4	Kt—KB3
2 Kt—KB3	P—B4

As will be seen, this leads to a
dreary, unpromising game for
Black.

3 P—Q5	P—Q3
4 P—B4	P—KKt3
5 Kt—B3	B—Kt2
6 P—K4	O—O
7 B—K2	P—K3
8 O—O	P x P?

Very poor play, as it only hands
over the K file to White, with no
compensation for Black. 8 . . . P—
K4 was much better (eventual
goal: . . . P—B4), but the development of Black's Queen-side would
still have constituted a serious
problem.

9 KP x P	Kt—K1

Black should be thinking about
mobilizing the Queen-side. The
text accomplishes nothing.

10 R—K1!	B—Kt5
11 Kt—KKt5!	. . . .

A move that shows a fine grasp
of the situation. Capablanca avoids
. . . QB x Kt and courts the exchange of Bishops, for his KKt
can be of more service than his KB.

The text presents Black with
a further problem: if he now
retreats his QB, he has lost time
and the problem of developing his
Queen-side becomes more troublesome than ever. If he exchanges
Bishops, he assures White's control of the K file.

There is still another instructive
aspect of the text: Capablanca
does not fear Black's following
move, because he realizes that the
ensuing weakness of Black's black
squares will be far more serious
than the rather academic weakness
of White's Queen-side.

11	B x Kt?
12 P x B	B x B
13 Q x B	Kt-Kt2

This has to be played sooner
or later, but it only creates a new
target for White.

Mieses

Capablanca

14 Kt—K4!   . . . .

Well-played! White threatens to exploit the feeble black squares with the deadly move B—Kt5.

14 . . . .　　　　　P—B3

Parrying the threat (not 14 . . . R—K1? 15 B—Kt5! winning the exchange), but creating a new weakness.

15 B—B4!　　　　. . . .

Another fine move. He gains a whole tempo as compared to the immediate 15 B—R6.

15 . . . .　　　　Kt—K1
16　B—R6　　　　Kt—Kt2

He has no choice, for if 16 . . . R—B2? 17 Kt—Kt5! wins.

17 QR—Q1　　　　Kt—R3
18 R—Q3　　　　　. . . .

Threatening either R—K3 or R—R3 according to circumstances. Rendered desperate by this possibility, Black hastens the end with his next move.

18 . . . .　　　　　P—B4
19 Kt—Kt5　　　　Kt—B2
20 Q—K7!　　　　. . . .

Absolutely decisive. Black might well resign.

20 . . . .　　　　　Q x Q
21 R x Q　　　　Kt(B2)—K1
22 R—R3　　　　　P—B5
23 B x Kt　　　　　Kt x B
24 R x RP　　　　Kt—B4
25 R—K6　　　　　KR—K1
26 R x Pch　　　　Resigns

There is a quick mate in the offing. Not a flashy game, but a most impressive one.

21.　Berlin, 1913
(Exhibition Game)

QUEEN'S GAMBIT DECLINED

Although this game is one of Capablanca's finest achievements, it has remained one of his most obscure efforts. The subtlety and delicacy of his endgame play have rarely been seen in a more attractive light. Note once more Capablanca's deadly work on the black squares!

J. R. CAPABLANCA　R. TEICHMANN

White	Black
1　P—Q4	P—Q4
2　Kt—KB3	Kt—KB3
3　P—B4	P—K3
4　B—Kt5	B—K2
5　Kt—B3	QKt—Q2
6　P—K3	O—O
7　R—B1	P—QKt3
8　P x P	P x P
9　B—Kt5!	. . . .

Regarding this variation, see also Game No. 24. The text is a new move introduced by Capablanca in this game, its object being to exert pressure on the Queen-side.

9　. . . .	B—Kt2
10　O—O	P—QR3
11　B—QR4	R—B1

Black's position is difficult. If 11 . . . P—B4; 12 B x QKt! Q x B; 13 P x P, P x P; 14 Kt—QR4 with marked advantage.

12　Q—K2	P—B4
13　P x P	Kt x P

After 13 . . . P x P; 14 KR—Q1 Black would have had a difficult game because of the constant menace against his center Pawns; but after the text, with its resulting isolated Pawn, the situation is even worse.

| 14 KR—Q1 | Kt x B |

Teichmann evidently hopes to compensate for the weakness of the QP by securing two Bishops. The alternative 14 . . . P—Kt4; 15 B—B2, P—Kt5; 16 Kt—QR4, Kt(4) —K5 suggested by Capablanca, looks more promising, but Black's weaknesses would eventually come to light.

15	Kt x Kt	P—Kt4
16	R x R	Q x R
17	Kt—B3	Q—B5
18	Kt—Q4	Q x Q
19	Kt(3) x Q	. . . .

Teichmann

Capablanca

If Black hoped to utilize his Bishops in the ending, he is soon undeceived. The salient factors of the position are these: (1) Black's QP has to be guarded by pieces, which condemns Black to an eternally passive position; (2) with all but one of Black's Pawns on white squares, his QB has virtually no scope, with concomitant weaknesses on the black squares; (3) due to the ineffectual position of the Bishops, White's Knights have great striking power; (4) White's Q4 is an admirable base for the White pieces throughout the ending.

19 . . . .   R—B1

19 . . . P—Kt3 would have prevented White's next move, but af-

ter 20 R—QB1, R—B1; 21 RxRch, B x R; 22 Kt—B6, K—B1; 23 Kt—B4, B—Kt2; 24 Kt x B, K x Kt; 25 P—B3 White would threaten to bring his King to K5, forcing Black to give up a Pawn with . . . P—R3 in order to extricate himself from the terrible pin.

20 Kt—B5!   K—B1

What else? If 20 . . . B—Q1 (or 20 . . . B—B1; 21 B x Kt and Black's Pawn position is shot to pieces); 21 Kt—Q6, R—B2; 22 Kt x B, R x Kt; 23 B x Kt, B x B; 24 R x P, R—B2; 25 R—Q2 (Capablanca) and White has won a Pawn.

21 Kt x B   K x Kt
22 Kt—Q4   P—Kt3

A new but unavoidable weakness: he cannot allow Kt—B5ch. But now the precarious state of his Knight forces the loss of a Pawn.

23 P—B3!   . . . .

Threatening, in due course, the invasion K—D2—Kt3—D4—K5! Black must remove the pin.

23 . . . .   P—R3
24 B x P   Kt—Q2
25 P—KR4   Kt—B4

Eventually White will establish an outside passed Pawn with P—KKt4 and P—R5, but Black can do nothing about it; if 25 . . . R—KR1; 26 B—B4 and the RP cannot be captured.

26 B—B4   Kt—K3

Relying on the Bishops of opposite color; but Capablanca has already foreseen that this hope is futile.

27 Kt x Kt   K x Kt

Or 27 . . . P x Kt; 28 B—K5! (always the black squares!) with a winning position.

28 R—Q2   R—KR1

Capablanca considers that Black could have prolonged his resistance with 28 . . . P—Kt5; 29 K—B2, P—R4; 30 P—Kt4, B—R3.

29 R—QB2!	R—QB1

He cannot permit R—B7.

30 R x R	B x R
31 K—B2!	P—Q5

Sad but necessary, else the White King comes to Q4 (note once more the great strategic importance of this square) and Black must allow' an invasion via QB5 or K5, with fatal results in either event.

32 P x P	K—Q4
33 K—K3	B—K3
34 K—Q3	K—B3
35 P—R3	B—B5ch
36 K—K3	B—K3
37 B—R6!	. . . .

The placement of the Bishop at Kt7 is more exact than 37 P—KKt4, which could be answered by . . . P—B4.

37	K—Q4
38 B—Kt7	Resigns

If 38 . . . K—B5; 39 P—Kt4, K—Kt6; 40 K—B4 and wins. Or 38 . . . B—B4; 39 K—B4 (threatening P—R5!), B—Q6; 40 K—Kt5, K—K3; 41 P—KKt4, B—B7; 42 P—B4, B—Q6; 43 P—B5ch! P x P; 44 P x Pch and Black cannot play 44 . . . B x P because of 45 P—Q5ch. A very beautiful game.

---

22. St. Petersburg, 1913

(Exhibition Game)

RUY LOPEZ

This is one of Capablanca's finest games. Only a superlative tactician could have evolved the sudden attack which begins with his 25th move.

J. R. CAPABLANCA

F. J. DUS-CHOTIMIRSKY

White	Black
1 P—K4	P—K4
2 Kt—KB3	Kt—QB3
3 B—Kt5	P—QR3
4 B—R4	Kt—B3
5 O—O	B—K2
6 R—K1	P—QKt4
7 B—Kt3	P—Q3
8 P—B3	Kt—QR4
9 B—B2	P—B4
10 P—Q4	Q—B2
11 QKt—Q2	. . . .

In modern master play, it is customary to play P—KR3 here, or even a move earlier, in order to rule out any inconvenience from . . . B—Kt5.

11	Kt—B3
12 Kt—B1	. . . .

A speculative Pawn sacrifice which was fashionable at the time, but is rarely seen nowadays, P—Q5 being preferred.

12	BP x P
13 P x P	B—Kt5

Chotimirsky declines the Pawn after all, following his natural inclination for attack.

14 P—Q5	Kt—Q5
15 B—Q3	O—O

The more aggressive line 15 . . . Kt—R4! followed by . . . Kt x Ktch was adopted in a game Yates-Thomas, B. C. F. Championship, 1921.

16 B—K3	QR—B1

Black had two better moves at his disposal here. One was . . . Kt x Ktch, avoiding the weak QP which results from the text. The other preferable continuation was 16 . . . KR—B1, with his Rooks on both open files after move 19.

17	B x Kt	P x B
18	P—QR4!	Q—Kt3

Practically forced.

19	P x P	P x P
20	P—R3!	. . . .

Just at the right moment. If Black retreats to Q2, he takes that square away from the Knight, and also leaves the QP to its fate.

20	. . . .	B x Kt
21	Q x B	Kt—Q2
22	KR—B1	Kt—B4
23	P—QKt4!	Kt—R5?

Black is led astray by the attractive idea of planting the Knight at B6. Relatively best was 23 . . . Kt x B; 24 Q x Kt, B—B3 with difficult and interesting possibilities. The text virtually gives White a forced win, which is however made up of clever and far from obvious moves.

24	R x R	R x R

Dus-Chotimirsky

Capablanca

25	P—K5!	P—Kt3

It is clear that Chotimirsky has not foreseen his opponent's last move. If 25 . . . P x P? 26 Q—B5 wins at once.

26	P—K6!	R—B1

Or 26 . . . P x P; 27 Q—Kt4 etc.

27	Kt—Kt3!	Q—Kt2

If 27 . . . P x P; 28 Q—Kt4, P—K4; 29 B x KKtP, P x B; 30 Q x Pch, K—R1; 31 Kt—R5 and wins. Or 27 . . . P—B4; 28 Kt—K2 with advantage.

28	Kt—B5!	. . . .

Whereas Black's Knight has remained out of play, White's Knight enters the game with a bang. 28 . . . P x Kt obviously leads to a quick mate, and in other lines, Black's Pawn weaknesses prove fatal.

28	. . . .	P x P

Or 28 . . . K—R1; 29 Q—K4 winning easily. The text leads to rapid deterioration of Black's position.

29	P x P	Q—B2

Of course not 29 . . . Q x Q? 30 Kt x Bch winning a piece. If 29 . . . Q—R2; 30 Kt x Bch, Q x Kt; 31 Q—Q5 with an easy win.

30	Q—B6!	Q—Q1

The loss of the exchange is forced after this, but he had no choice; if 30 . . . R—B1? 31 Kt x Bch, or if 30 . . . B—Q1; 31 Q x Q, B x Q; 32 P—K7, R—Kt1; 33 B x P etc.

31	Kt x Bch	Q x Kt
32	B x QKtP	Kt—B6
33	Q—Q7!	Q x Q
34	B x Q	R—Kt1

There is no good defense: 34 . . . Kt—Q4; 35 R—Q1, R—B5; 36 P—Kt3, R—K5; 37 B—B6, R—K4; 38 R x P, Kt—K2; 39 R x P (Capablanca); or 34 . . . P—Q6; 35 P—K7, P—Q7; 36 P x R(Q)ch; 37 B—Kt4 etc.

35	P—K7	K—B2
36	R—K1	R—K1
37	B x Rch	K x B

38 R—K6	P—Q4

Black should have resigned here or at move 44, but there's no accounting for tastes.

39 K—B1	Kt—Kt4
40 K—K2	Kt—B2
41 R—K5	Kt—R3
42 P—Kt5	Kt—Kt5
43 P—Kt6	P—Q6ch
44 K—Q2	K—Q2

A continuation that requires psychoanalysis rather than chess analysis.

45 P—K8(Q)ch	K—Q3
46 Q—K7ch	K—B3
47 Q x Kt	Resigns

---

23.   St. Petersburg, 1913
(Exhibition Game)

QUEEN'S GAMBIT DECLINED

This appears to have been the first encounter between the two future World Champions. Alekhine makes a very poor impression, and one gathers that he had a bad attack of "Capablanca fright."

J. R. CAPABLANCA	A. ALEKHINE
White	Black
1 P—Q4	P—Q4
2 P—QB4	P—QB3
3 P—K3	Kt—B3
4 Kt—KB3	P—K3
5 QKt—Q2	....

One of Capablanca's innovations. The main idea is to answer an eventual . . . P x P with Kt x P, avoiding loss of time by the KB and at the same time reserving a powerful post for the QKt at K5. Capablanca later adopted the same idea in the Orthodox Defense, as for example in Game No. 37.

5	QKt—Q2

Rather colorless. Either . . . P—B4 or . . . Kt—K5 would offer better chances.

6 B—Q3	B—K2

If 6 . . . B—Q3; 7 P—K4 leads to the same advantageous type of play as seen in Game No. 8.

7 O—O	O—O
8 Q—B2	....

White has quite a choice of good moves. In addition to the text, P—K4 or P—QKt3 yields an excellent game.

8	P x P
9 Kt x P	P—B4
10 QKt—K5	P x P
11 P x P	Kt—Kt3

White has attained his objective (a strong Knight on K5), but Black appears to have counterplay in his occupation of Q4 and potential pressure on the isolated QP. Capablanca therefore forces a weakness in the hostile position with:

12 Kt—Kt5!	P—Kt3

An ugly move, but he has no choice (12 . . . P—KR3?? 13 B—R7ch forcing mate!).

13 Kt(Kt5)—B3!	K—Kt2

The retreat of the Knight involved no loss of time, as White threatened 14 B—KR6, R—K1; 15 Kt—Kt5.

14 B—KKt5	QKt—Q4
15 QR—B1	B—Q2

If 15 . . . Kt—QKt5; 16 Q—Q2 and there is no time for . . . Kt x B because of the threatened B—R6ch. On the other hand, if 15 . . . P—KR3 (so that if 16 B—R4, Kt—QKt5) White continues with 16 B x P! RP x B; 17 B x P! with a winning attack. The weakness created on move 12 makes itself felt!

16 Q—Q2	Kt—Kt1

17 B x B	Q x B
18 B—K4	. . . .

A much admired move, not least of all by Capablanca himself. **As the game goes, it proves to be the winning move.**

Alekhine

Capablanca

18	B—Kt4
19 KR—K1	Q—Q3?

But this is tantamount to resignation. 19 . . . Kt.(1)—B3 would still have made a fight of it (20 B x Kt, Kt x B; 21 Kt—Kt4, P—B3).

20 B x Kt	P x B

Of course not 20 . . . Q x B? 21 R—B5. The disastrous results of the foregoing exchange are now clear: the removal of the valuable Knight at Q4 makes possible an invasion of the QB file, particularly the vulnerable seventh rank. Black's game crumbles now in short order.

21 Q—R5	P—QR3
22 Q—B7!	Q x Q
23 R x Q	P—R3

Or 23 . . . QR—Kt1; 24 Kt—Kt5 threatening the BP as well as Kt—K6ch.

24 R x P	QR—B1
25 P—QKt3	R—B7

26 P—QR4	B—K7

Leaving his Q2 unguarded, but it cannot be said that . . . B—K1 is an inviting alternative.

27 Kt—R4	P—KR4

If 27 . . . K—B3; 28 Kt—Q7ch or if 27 . . . P—Kt4; 28 Kt—B5ch. Black might have spared himself the rest.

28 Kt(4) x P	R—K1
29 R x Pch	K—R3
30 P—B4	P—R4
31 Kt—R4	R x Kt
32 BP x R	K—Kt4
33 P—Kt3	K—Kt5
34 R—Kt7ch	K—R6
35 Kt—Kt2!	Resigns

---

24. Moscow, 1914
(Exhibition Game)

QUEEN'S GAMBIT DECLINED

Although somewhat marred by Bernstein's feeble play, this is a noteworthy game because of the originality displayed by Capablanca, culminating in a famous finish which has endeared itself to chess players the world over.

O. BERNSTEIN J. R. CAPABLANCA

White	Black
1 P—Q4	P—Q4
2 P—QB4	P—K3
3 Kt—QB3	Kt—KB3
4 Kt—B3	B—K2
5 B—Kt5	O—O
6 P—K3	QKt—Q2
7 R—B1	P—QKt3

Capablanca must have played this move for experimental purposes, for as a rule he had a strong dislike for lines of play which were likely to involve organic weaknesses.

8 P x P	P x P
9 Q—R4	. . . .

The object of this move (introduced into master play by Duras) is to create a serious weakness in Black's Queen-side formation by exchanging Bishops. Capablanca's move 9 B—Kt5 first played a few months earlier in Game No. 21) is more effective, as Black could now secure a good game, despite the loss of a Pawn involved, by means of 9 . . . P—B4! 10 Q—B6, R—Kt1; 11 Kt x P, B—Kt2 etc.

9	B—Kt2
10 B—R6	B x B
11 Q x B	P—B4
12 B x Kt?	. . . .

A pointless exchange which only releases some of the pressure on Black's position. Simply 12 P x P was in order, followed, in the event of 12 . . . Kt x P by 13 Q—K2, or if 12 . . . P x P; 13 O—O and 14 KR—Q1. Without the foregoing exchange, the mobility of Black's pieces would have been seriously hampered.

12	Kt x B
13 P x P	P x P
14 O—O	Q—Kt3
15 Q—K2	P—B5!

A deep and original move. Black decides that in return for the pressure on his "Hanging Pawns," he will maintain a counter-threat on the QKtP. It is true that the text yields Q4 for the White Knights, but as Capablanca comments, the occupation of this square blocks the pressure on the QP.

16 KR—Q1	. . . .

Bernstein is still in an optimistic mood; else he would give the game a drawish turn with 16 P—K4.

16	KR—Q1
17 Kt—Q4	B—Kt5!

Even with best play on White's

part, this will lead to a relaxation of the pressure on the QP.

18 P—QKt3	QR—B1
19 P x P	. . . .

This unfortunate idea is part of a psychological duel: White thinks that the QBP will be weak; Black relies on the fact that it is a passed Pawn.

19	P x P

At last Black is rid of the sickly QP!

20 R—B2	B x Kt
21 R x B	Kt—Q4

As White dare not play 22 R x P? because of 22 . . . Kt—B6, Black gains time for the further advance of the QBP. The psychological duel continues: White thinks that the Pawn is weakened by its further advance.

22 R—B2	P—B6
23 KR—QB1	R—B4

Black could have played . . . R—Q2 preparatory to doubling on the QB file; instead, he plays to entice his opponent into an unusually subtle trap.

24 Kt—Kt3	R—B3
25 Kt—Q4	R—B2
26 Kt—Kt5	R—B4

Black's peculiar order of moves has misled Bernstein; instead of going back to Q4, which might have brought about a quick draw by repetition of moves or else an exciting fight for the QBP, he snaps at the bait.

(see diagram next page)

27 Kt x BP?	Kt x Kt
28 R x Kt	R x R
29 R x R	Q—Kt7!

White resigns, as he must lose at least the Rook. A remarkable conclusion.

Capablanca

Bernstein

25. Riga, 1914

(Exhibition Game)

GIUOCO PIANO

Since the winning possibilities which are frequently present in endings with Bishops of opposite color were rarely recognized at this time, it is remarkable that Capablanca won this game and the one with Teichmann (Game No. 21) within the short space of a few months.

A. NIMZOVICH   J. R. CAPABLANCA

White	Black
1 P—K4	P—K4
2 Kt—KB3	Kt—QB3
3 Kt—B3	Kt—B3
4 B—B4	. . . .

The previous encounter between these two masters (at San Sebastian) had begun with the moves 1 P—K4, P—K3; 2 P—Q3, P—Q4; 3 Kt—Q2. Evidently chastened by the resulting catastrophe, Nimzovich has decided to proceed in more orthodox fashion.

| 4 . . . . | B—B4 |
| 5 P—Q3 | P—Q3 |

| 6 B—KKt5 | B—K3 |

. . . Kt—QR4 is also good. With reasonably exact play, Black has little to fear in this variation.

| 7 B—Kt5 | P—KR3 |
| 8 B—KR4 | B—QKt5 |

Imitating White in order to take the sting out of his intended P—Q4.

| 9 P—Q4 | B—Q2 |
| 10 O—O | B x Kt! |

Beginning a seemingly hazardous but well thought out line of play. Black exposes himself to what looks like a dangerous attack, knowing full well that he can virtually force White to lead into an ending in which the doubled and isolated QBPs may become a fatal weakness.

| 11 P x B | P—Kt4! |

Capablanca tells us that the spectators raised their eyebrows over this and his next move, not perceiving the ultimate drift.

| 12 B—Kt3 | Kt x KP! |
| 13 B x Kt | . . . . |

Q—Q3 has been recommended as more aggressive, but after 13 . . . Kt x B; 14 RP x Kt, O—O! Black has little to fear.

13	B x B
14 P x P	P x P
15 B x P	Q x Q
16 QR x Q	P—B3!

White must now come to a decision with the Bishop. If 17 B x QBP, Kt x QBP with advantage to Black.

| 17 B—Q4 | K—B2 |
| 18 Kt—Q2 | KR—K1 |

Capablanca is quite willing to indulge his opponent's passion for simplification, for he realizes that the Bishops of opposite color do not automatically ensure a draw.

| 19 P—B3 | Kt x Kt |

| 20 R x Kt | QR—Q1 |
| 21 P—Kt4? | . . . . |

To fix Pawns on the vulnerable white color is only tempting fate.

| 21 . . . . | B—Kt4 |
| 22 R—Kt1 | B—R3 |

Now White cannot play 22 K—B2? because of 22 . . . P—QB4; 23 B—K3, R x Rch; 24 B x R, R—K7ch etc.

| 23 R(1)—Q1 | R—K7! |

Threatening to double Rooks, forcing White's reply and leading to a sharp skirmish that concludes unfavorably for White.

24 R x R	B x R
25 R—K1	B x P
26 R—KB1	P—QB4!

Capablanca

Nimzovich

27 B x KBP   . . . .

Had Nimzovich been less obsessed by his faith in the Bishop ending, he would have tried 27 R x B, P x B; 28 R—Q3, R—QB1; 29 R x P, R x P; 30 R—Q7ch, K—Kt3; 31 R x P, R—QR6; 32 P—B4 with excellent prospects of a draw.

| 27 . . . . | R—Q8! |
| 28 B—K5 | R x Rch |

| 29 K x R | B x P |

Black has come out a Pawn to the good, and as will be seen, has a forced win. The weakness of White's Queen-side proves his undoing.

30 P—QR4?   . . . .

After this faulty move, Black has an easy although most instructive win, based on the fact that he cannot be prevented from securing a passed QRP, tying up White's forces with fatal effect.

However, Fine has demonstrated in his **Basic Chess Endings** that the ending is untenable in any event, suggesting the following alternative line: 30 K—K1, B—B4; 31 K—Q2, P—B5! (it is important to prevent P—B4); 32 B—Kt8, P—R3; 33 K—K3 (if the King remains at Q2, Black advances his King to support the advance of his Kingside Pawns), B x P; 34 K—Q4, P—Kt4; 35 K—B5, K—K3; 36 K—Kt6, K—Q4! 37 K x P, B—R5 (threatening . . . P—QKt5); 38 P—QR3, P—R4; 39 B—B7, P—KKt5; 40 B—Kt3, K—K5; 41 K—Kt6, K—Q6!! (wins a valuable tempo); 42 B—K5 (or 42 B—K1, P—R5!), P—R5; 43 K—B5, K—K5; 44 B—Kt8, K—B6; 45 K—Q4, P—Kt6; 46 P x P, P x P! 47 B—R7, P—Kt7; 48 K—K5, K—K7 and wins.

| 30 . . . . | K—K3 |
| 31 B—Kt8 | P—QR4! |

Threatening above all . . . P—Kt4!

32 K—K1	K—Q4
33 K—Q2	B—Q2
34 B—B7	K—B3

For if 34 B x P? P—Kt3 traps the Bishop. Black has the win well in hand now, as the QRP is doomed.

35 B—Q8	P—Kt3
36 P—B4	K—Kt2
37 K—B3	B x P

Now White will have to confront

simultaneous threats of advancing Pawns on both wings, creating an impossible defensive burden.

38	K—Kt2	B—Q2
39	K—Kt3	B—K3
40	K—B3	P—R5
41	K—Q3	K—B3
42	K—B3	P—Kt5
43	B—R4	P—R4
44	B—Kt3	P—R6
45	K—Kt3	B x Pch!

For if 46 K x B, P—R7; 47 B—K5, P—R5; 48 K—Kt3, P—Kt6; 49 P x P, P—R6 and one of the Pawns must queen.

| 46 | K x P | P—Kt4 |
| 47 | P—B3 | K—Q4 |

Now the King takes an active hand. In short order Black will have a new passed Pawn on the Queen-side.

48	B—B2	B—K7
49	K—Kt3	B—Q8ch
50	K—Kt2	K—B5

The neatness and inexorability of Black's play make the ending most enjoyable.

51	K—B1	B—B6
52	K—Q2	P—Kt5
53	P x P	P x P
54	B—R4	B—K5
55	B—B6	B—Kt3
56	B—R4	P—QKt6

Beginning the final phase. The advance of the Pawns is calculated to a nicety.

57	B—B6	P—R5!
58	K—K3	P—Kt6!
59	P x P	P—R6
60	K—B2	B—B4

Now it is all over.

61	P—Kt4	B x P
62	K—Kt3	K—Q6
63	K—R2	K—B7

White resigns. This superb ending is one of the finest in the whole range of chess literature.

---

26. Vienna, 1914
(Consultation Game)
FRENCH DEFENSE

Reti tells us that during this game he obtained a very enlightening insight into Capablanca's theories, which were really part of the Hypermodern ideas that ruled chess thought in the turbulent postwar period. The admirable play following the exchange of Queens is full of instructive features.

H. FAEHNDRICH   J. R. CAPABLANCA
DR. A. KAUFMANN   R. RETI

White	Black
1 P—K4	P—K3
2 P—Q4	P—Q4
3 Kt—QB3	Kt—KB3
4 P x P	P x P
5 B—Q3	P—B4

Black wants to steer clear of the deadening symmetry of the Exchange Variation, even at the cost of creating a permanent weakness in the form of the isolated QP.

6 P x P	B x P
7 Kt—B3	O—O
8 O—O	Kt—B3
9 B—KKt5	B—K3
10 Kt—K2	. . . .

A weak move which only loses time. Q—Q2 would have been far better.

| 10 . . . . | P—KR3! |
| 11 B—R4 | B—KKt5 |

As a result of Black's 10th move, neither Kt—Kt3 nor Kt—B4 is now feasible.

| 12 Kt—B3 | Kt—Q5 |
| 13 B—K2 | Kt x Bch |

14 Q x Kt   . . . .

Black has played well in the last few moves, but two difficulties—the isolated QP and the annoying pin—still plague him.

14 . . . .   B—Q5!

Beginning a profoundly thought out manoeuvre which gets rid of one difficulty.

15 Q—Q3   B x QKt
16 Q x B   Kt—K5!

White cannot very well go in for the exchange of Queens: 17 B x Q, Kt x Q; 18 B—R4, Kt—K7ch; 19 K—R1, B x Kt; 20 P x B, Kt—Q5 and Black has the advantage.

17 Q—Q4   P—KKt4
18 Kt—K5   . . . .

White does not care for the prosaic B—Kt3, as Black's rather open King-side invites an attack.

18 . . . .   B—B4
19 P—KB3   . . . .

The previous note applies here as well. A more or less level position could have been reached with Capablanca's suggestion 19 B—Kt3, Kt x B; 20 BP x Kt, B x P; 21 Kt—Kt4, P—B4; 22 Kt—K3, B—K5; 23 QR—Q1, Q—Kt3; 24 Kt x QP, B x Kt; 25 Q x Q, P x Q; 26 R x B, R x P etc.

19 . . . .   P x B
20 P x Kt   B x P

Although this Bishop makes only one more move, 23 moves later, and for the purpose of being exchanged, it plays an important role from now on, **because of its powerfully centralized position.**

21 R—B2   . . . .

Kt—Kt4 looks dangerous for Black, but there is an adequate reply in . . . P—B4!

21 . . . .   P—R6!

Well played. This "extra" Pawn is useless to Black, and its advance subsequently proves highly advantageous.

22 R—K1   P—B4

If 21 . . . B x KtP; 22 R—K3 with a strong attack.

23 P x P   . . . .

Giving Black a passed KBP which later proves the basic factor in the winning process. However, 23 P—KKt3 would reduce White's mobility and leave a strong sentinel at his KR3, not to mention the later possibility of . . . P—KR4-5 etc.

23 . . . .   Q—B3

An inexactitude, based on the view that Black has a win after 24 R x B, QP x R; 25 R—Kt2ch, K—R1; 26 R—Kt6, R—KKt1; 27 Kt—B7ch, K—R2; 28 Q x Q, R x Rch; 29 Kt—Kt5ch, R x Ktch; 30 K—B2. Actually Black can make no headway, and the game should end in a draw.
23 . . . K—R2 was therefore correct.

24 Kt—B3   K—R2
25 Q x Q   R x Q
26 R—K3   R—Kt3

If now 27 P—B3, P—B5! 28 R—K1, R—Kt1ch; 29 K—R1, R x P! etc.

27 P—Kt3   R—QB1
28 Kt—Q4   R—KB3
29 R—B4   K—Kt3
30 P—B3   K—Kt4
31 Kt—K2   R—R3!

Preparing a decisive breakthrough.

32 P—R4ch   K—B3
33 P—R4   . . . .

Capablanca
Reti

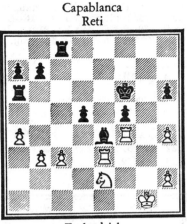

Faehndrich
Kaufmann

33 . . . .   P—Kt4!

The winning move. Black has in
mind the kind of position obtained
eight moves later, with his King
on K4 and a Rook on the seventh
rank, and all defensive possibilities
for White exhausted.

34 P x P   R—R8ch

If now 35 K—B2, K—K4, with
the embarrassing threat of . . . R—
R7 and . . . R x Ktch.

35 R—B1	R x Rch
36 K x R	K—K4
37 Kt—Q4	P—B5
38 R—R3	. . . .

A highly unfortunate post for
the Rook, but there is nothing else
available.

38 . . . .   R—KKt1

Now Black gains the seventh
rank after all.

39 K—K1	R—Kt8ch
40 K—K2	R—Kt7ch
41 K—B1	R—Kt7
42 K—K1	P—KR4!

The desired position. White

cannot play Kt—B6ch, for this
would allow . . . K—B4—Kt5. On
42 P—Kt4, Black wins as in the
text.

43 K—Q1   B—B4!

Exceedingly simple, but highly
effective!

| 44 Kt x B | K x Kt |
| 45 P—B4 | . . . . |

An alternative indicated by Capa-
blanca is 45 R—Q3, K—K5; 46
R—Q4ch, K—K6; 47 R x QP, P—
B6; 48 R—K5ch, K—B5; 49 R—K7,
P—B7; 50 R—B7ch, K—K6; White
must give up his Rook.

45 . . . .   K—K5

If now 46 P x P, P—B6; 47 P—
Q6, K—K6; 48 P—Q7, P—B7
wins; or 46 P—B5, P—B6; 47
P—B6, P—B7 etc.

| 46 R—QB3 | P—B6 |
| 47 K—K1 | P—Q5 |

White resigns. A masterly
ending.

———————

27. St. Petersburg, 1914

RUY LOPEZ

In this somewhat imperfect game,
there is reflected some of the ex-
citement which reigned in one of
the greatest tournaments of chess
history. Nevertheless, it was a victory which must have given Capablanca considerable satisfaction in
later years.

A. ALEKHINE   J. R. CAPABLANCA

White	Black
1 P—K4	P—K4
2 Kt—KB3	Kt—QB3
3 B—Kt5	P—Q3

As already indicated, Capablanca's favorite defense to the
Lopez in the early part of his ca-

reer; but Alekhine soon adopts a poor move against it.

4 P—Q4	P x P
5 Kt x P	B—Q2
6 Kt—QB3	Kt—B3
7 O—O	B—K2
8 Kt—B5	. . . .

This is questionable, as it leads to a weak Pawn formation and enables Black to free his game without loss of time. P—QKt3 or R—K1 is better.

8	B x Kt
9 P x B	O—O
10 R—K1	. . . .

White's 8th move **stands or falls by the advance of the KKtP,** and if Alekhine was reluctant to adopt this aggressive line, he should have avoided 8 Kt—B5.

10	Kt—Q2
11 Kt—Q5	B—B3
12 P—QB3	Kt—Kt3

The Knight is not too well placed here, but Capablanca r i g h t l y judges that removing the dominating White Knight is the lesser evil. Besides, Black's Queen gets into good play now, making way meanwhile for the occupation of the open K file by his Rooks.

13 Kt x Bch	Q x Kt
14 B x Kt	P x B
15 Q—B3	KR—K1
16 B—K3	P—B4

Else the Bishop gets too good a square at Q4.

17 R—K2	R—K4
18 QR—K1	QR—K1!

There is nothing to be gained from 18 . . . Q x P (not 18 . . . R x P?? 19 B—Kt5); 19 Q x Q, R x Q; 20 B x P etc.

19 Q—Kt7	. . . .

This fishing trip turns out badly,

but 19 P—KKt4 would be dangerously weakening, and 19 B—B1, R x R; 20 R x R, R x R; 21 Q x R, P—KR3 does not look inviting.

19	Q x P
20 Q x BP	Q—K3

Black could save time with . . . Kt—Q4 at once.

21 Q x RP	Kt—Q4
22 K—B1	Kt—B5
23 R—Q2	. . . .

Capablanca

Alekhine

23	Kt x P!?

This is perfectly sound, but Tarrasch indicates the following as more conclusive: 23 . . . Q—Kt5; 24 P—B3 (the interpolation of 24 Q—Kt7, P—Q4 makes no essential difference), Q—K3; 25 B x Kt, R x Rch; 26 K—B2, R—B8ch! 27 K—Kt3, P—Kt4! 28 B x P, Q—Kt3; 29 K—R4 (if 29 K—B4, R—K5ch etc.), R—K4; 30 P—B4, R x P ch! and wins.

24 K x Kt	Q—Kt5ch

Leaving White little choice, for if 25 K—R1, R—Kt4; 26 Q—Kt7, P—Q4 and wins.

25 K—B1	Q—R6ch

Again forcing White's hand, for if 26 K—Kt1? R—Kt4ch and mate follows.

26 K—K2   R x Bch!
27 P x R   Q x KPch
28 K—Q1   Q x Rch
29 K—B2   Q—K5ch
30 K—Kt3?   Q—B3?

Time pressure on both sides. After 30 . . . P—B5ch! 31 K—Kt4, Q—B3 (threatening . . . R—R1) White can resign.

31 P—QR4   . . . .

P—QR3 or P—B4 holds out longer.

31 . . . .   P—Q4
32 P—R5   . . . .

This only hastens the end. Here or on move 35, he should have tried R—KB2, which would have held out a bit longer.

32 . . . .   Q—Kt4ch
33 K—R3   . . . .

On 33 K—B2 (if 33 K—R2, Q—R5ch; 34 K—Kt1, R—K8ch) Black has a mate in six: 33 . . . Q—R5ch; 34 P—Kt3, Q—R7ch; 35 K—Q3, Q—Kt8ch; 36 R—B2, Q—B8ch etc.

33 . . . .   R—Kt1
34 K—R2   P—R3

Freeing his Rook for active duty.

35 P—R6   Q—Kt6ch

White resigns, for if 36 K—Kt1, R—K1; 37 R—QB2, R—K8ch; 38 R—B1, R—K7 forcing mate.

---

28. St. Petersburg, 1914
(First Brilliancy Prize)

QUEEN'S GAMBIT DECLINED

This game is notable for the incisive manner in which Bernstein's unsatisfactory handling of the opening is refuted. The combination has some charming features, although the fact that so many roads lead to Rome detracts somewhat from its luster.

J. R. CAPABLANCA   O. BERNSTEIN

White   Black

1 P—Q4   P—Q4
2 Kt—KB3   Kt—KB3
3 P—B4   P—K3
4 Kt—B3   QKt—Q2
5 B—Kt5   B—K2
6 P—K3   P—B3

Black commits himself too soon; . . . O—O is indicated. It is symptomatic of Black's ill-considered play in this game that he never gets around to castling.

7 B—Q3   P x P
8 B x BP   P—Kt4?

Following a preconceived but inferior plan. . . . Kt—Q4 is a more reasonable freeing method.

9 B—Q3   P—QR3
10 P—K4   P—K4?

Relatively better was 10 . . . P—B4, despite the formidable appearance of White's position after 11 P—K5. With the bold text Black only succeeds in overreaching himself.

11 P x P   Kt—Kt5
12 B—KB4   B—B4
13 O—O   Q—B2

While Black concentrates on recovering the Pawn, Capablanca gains time for further strengthening his position. 13 . . . Q—K2 would be answered advantageously by 14 P—K6! P x P (not 14 . . . Q x P? 15 Kt—Kt5); 15 Kt—Kt5, KKt—B3; 16 P—K5 with a strong game.

14 R—B1   . . . .

White's QR and Black's Queen

on the same file—an ominous portent for Black!

14 . . . .   P—B3

As Tarrasch observes, immediate capture of the Pawn would lose some material: 14 . . . KKt x KP; 15 Kt x Kt, Kt x Kt; 16 Q—R5, B—Q3; 17 Kt—Q5, Q—Kt1; 18 B x Kt etc.

15 B—Kt3   P x P

. . . KKt x KP was somewhat better, in order to rescue the stranded Knight from its insecure position.

16 P—Kt4!   B—R2

Black is paying the penalty for t h e weaknesses so carelessly created in the opening. If 16 . . . B—K2; 17 Kt—Q5 is much in White's favor, while if 16 . . . B—Q3; 17 B x KtP and Black cannot retake. Finally, if 16 . . . B x P; 17 Kt—Q5, Q—Q3; 18 Kt x B, Q x Kt; 19 R x P and Black cannot parry the numerous threats, such as P—KR3 followed by the win of the KP, or B—B2—Kt3 in conjunction with Kt—Kt5.

The text is no better, for White's **quantitatively and qualitatively superior development** allows him to exploit his advantage with great energy.

Bernstein

Capablanca

17 B x KtP!   RP x B
18 Kt x KtP   Q—Q1
19 Kt—Q6ch   . . . .

Even 19 R x P was good enough, as White would be bound to win at least the KP. If Black tries 19 . . . O—O there follows 20 Q—Q5ch, K—R1; 21 P—KR3 followed by 22 R x Kt and 23 Q x R. Or 19 . . . B—Kt1; 20 Q—Q5, B—Kt2; 21 R—K6ch, K—B2; 22 Kt—Kt5ch and wins.

19 . . . .   K—B1
20 R x P   Kt—Kt3

White could now simply capture the KP, but he prefers to continue "in the grand manner."

21 B—R4   Q—Q2

After 21 . . . Kt—B3 there would be many ways to win: simply 22 Kt x P, or 22 Kt x B, R x Kt; 23 Q x Qch, R x Q; 24 R x Ktch, P x R; 25 B x P, K—B2; 26 B x KR, R x B; 27 Kt x Pch etc.

22 Kt x B!   Q x R

Not 22 . . . R x Kt; 23 Q x Q, Kt x Q; 24 R x Rch and wins. Or 22 . . . Q x Q; 23 R x Q and the coming R—Q8ch is murderous. Black is now a Rook ahead, but he must lose by force!

23 Q—Q8ch?!   . . . .

This is part of a highly elegant winning method, but 23 B—K7ch! would have decided more rapidly: I 23 . . . K—B2; 24 Kt—Kt5ch, K—Kt3; 25 Q x Kt, Q x Kt; 26 Kt—K6ch, K—B2; 27 Q x Pch, K x Kt; 28 R—Q1, Kt—Q4; 29 P x Ktch, K—Q2; 30 B—B6ch, K—Q3; 31 B x P mate!

II 23 . . . K—K1; 24 Q—Q8ch, K—B2; 25 Kt—Kt5ch, K—Kt3; 26 Q x R, Kt—B3; 27 B x Kt! Q x B; 28 P—KR4, K—R4; 29 Q x Pch, Q—R3; 30 Q—B5, K x P; 31 Kt—B3 mate!

23 . . . .   Q—K1

If 23 . . . K—B2; 24 Kt—Q6ch wins the Queen.

| 24 B—K7ch | K—B2 |
| 25 Kt—Q6ch | K—Kt3 |

A delicious position would result from 25 . . . K—K3?? 26 Kt—Kt5 mate!

| 26 Kt—R4ch | K—R4 |

Not 26 . . . K—R3? 27 Kt(6)—B5 ch, K—R4; 28 Kt—Kt3ch, K—R3; 29 B—Kt5 mate.

27 Kt x Q	R x Q
28 Kt x Pch	K—R3
29 Kt(7)—B5ch	K—R4

Black still has a Rook for four Pawns . . . and he is still making forced moves! But now comes a quiet little move which regains the sacrificed material with interest.

| 30 P—KR3!! | Kt—B1 |

Incomprehensible at first sight; but he cannot play 30 . . . Kt—R3 because of 31 Kt—Kt7 mate; and meanwhile White was threatening mate in three with 31 P x Ktch, K x P; 32 P—B3ch etc. The text is played to unmask the Bishop and thus prevent a move by the BP.

31 P x Ktch	K x P
32 B x R	R x B
33 P—Kt3	R—Q7
34 K—Kt2	R—K7

Or 34 . . . R x P; 35 Kt—B3 etc.

35 P—R4	Kt—Kt3
36 Kt—K3ch	K—R4
37 P—R5	Kt—Q2
38 Kt(4)—B5	Kt—B3
39 P—Kt5	B—Q5

Black should resign.

40 K—B3	R—R7
41 P—R6	B—R2
42 R—B1	R—Kt7
43 P—Kt4ch	K—Kt4
44 R—B7	R x Pch

| 45 K x R | Kt x KtPch |
| 46 K—B3 | Resigns |

---

29. St. Petersburg, 1914
RUY LOPEZ

The amateur often has occasion to wonder how a perfectly harmless opening variation, met by superficially satisfactory moves, can lead to a rapid win. The fact is that this can happen only after moves which despite their plausible appearance are really mistakes.

J. R. CAPABLANCA   D. JANOWSKI

White	Black
1 P—K4	P—K4
2 Kt—KB3	Kt—QB3
3 B—Kt5	P—QR3
4 B x Kt	QP x B
5 Kt—B3	B—QB4

The reader will recall that Janowski met with difficulties in a similar position in Game No. 17. The modern masters prefer 5 . . . P—B3 here, before committing themselves to any deployment of the Bishops.

| 6 P—Q3 | B—KKt5 |
| 7 B—K3 | B x B |

Giving White a useful open file and a strong Pawn center. . . . Q—Q3 or Q—K2 would be preferable.

| 8 P x B | Q—K2 |
| 9 O—O | O—O—O |

Out of place, for whatever attacking possibilities which will arise from this position will be at White's disposal. He should have played out the Knight and then castled on the other wing.

| 10 Q—K1 | Kt—R3 |

A Knight is generally poorly posted at the edge of the board, and here we have an instance of that general rule. Kt—B3 was better.

11 R—Kt1!   . . . .

A most effective move, but by no means obvious. White wants to advance his QKtP and QRP for two reasons: (1) direct attack against the King; (2) elimination of the Black Pawn at QB3, making it possible to plant the QKt very powerfully at Q5. Note that the absence of Black's Knight from the normal square KB3 leaves the vital central squares without sufficient protection.

11 . . . .   P—B3
12 P—Kt4   Kt—B2
13 P—QR4   B x Kt

The further advance of the KtP could have been prevented by . . . P—QKt4, but this would have left White with an easy initiative on the Queen-side. Janowski evidently hopes to ease the pressure with this simplifying exchange, but it would have been better to preserve the Bishop for an eventual retreat to K3, guarding his Q4.

14 R x B   P—QKt3
15 P—Kt5   BP x P
16 P x P   P—QR4

Black has prevented the opening of a file, but his Q4 is now ripe for occupation.

17 Kt—Q5   Q—B4
18 P—B4!   . . . .

Capablanca's plan is simple but irresistible. He intends P—Q4 followed by P—B5 (after due preparation) with crushing effect.

18 . . . .   Kt—Kt4
19 R—B2!   . . . .

This is better than KR—B1, for it prevents a subsequent propitiatory sacrifice of the exchange by Black.

19 . . . .   Kt—K3
20 Q—B3   . . . .

Had White played 19 KR—B1, Black could now continue with . . . R x Kt and . . . Q x Pch.

20 . . . .   R—Q2
21 R—Q1   K—Kt2

This loses quickly, because it later enhances the power of the advancing QBP. However, the only reasonable alternative, . . . K—Q1 followed by the flight of the King to the other side, would only have prolonged his resistance without changing the result.

Janowski

Capablanca

22 P—Q4   Q—Q3

Or 22 . . . Q—B1; 23 R—B2, P x P; 24 P x P, Q—K1; 25 P—B5, R—Q1; 26 P x P, P x P; 27 Q—B6 ch and wins.

23 R—B2   P x P
24 P x P   Kt—B5
25 P—B5   Kt x Kt

Loss of a piece was unavoidable.

26 P x Kt   Q x QP
27 P—B6ch   K—Kt1
28 P x R   Q x P (2)
29 P—Q5   R—K1
30 P—Q6   P x P
31 Q—B6   Resigns

Janowski's bad judgment has made Capablanca's clarity stand out all the more favorably.

Part III
Challenger
1914-1920

During this period, Capablanca was winning everything in sight, and his games reflect this state of affairs. In Game no. 36 he is called upon to repulse a prepared variation which Marshall had thoughtfully saved up for him for a good many years. Very few masters can come through such an ordeal successfully. Game no. 39 is a good example of a still currently fashionable variation of the Ruy Lopez. The weaknesses on the white squares which Yates carelessly creates are destined to plague him for the rest of the game.

Game no. 31 begins with a King's Gambit Declined and continues in a style worthy of the opening, ending with a long-distance combination which reveals extraordinary poise and foresight.

In Games no. 34 and 37 Capablanca produces brilliancy prize games against the Orthodox Defense. The first is particularly striking, because of the way Capablanca harries the hostile King to QKt3 and then stalemates the hostile Queen! Against the Slav Defense in Game no. 30, Capablanca begins very tamely, as in his earliest days; but soon he is offering his Queen! Then comes a tranquil interlude, and finally the Queen is sacrificed after all!

This period was one of experimentation for Capablanca, as regards his defenses against the Queen's Gambit. Thus, in Game no. 38, he plays what later became the model game of the Orthodox Defense, being widely copied for many years thereafter. Against Edward Lasker he experiments with still another defense which was to become popular some fifteen years later. And in Game no. 35, he tries the Slav Defense against Janowski with good results. In all three games, Capablanca presents us with magnificent specimens of his superb endgame play. Game no. 40 illustrates the advantage of a lasting initiative, even in those cases where an objectively valid defense is possible. Kostich finally breaks down under the strain.

30. Buenos Aires, 1914

(Exhibition Game)

QUEEN'S GAMBIT DECLINED

A simple but subtle positional game of the highest order. How the achievement of strategical goals is facilitated by clever tactical play, is effectively illustrated by the magnificent Queen sacrifice on move 18.

J. R. CAPABLANCA	B. VILLEGAS
White	Black
1 P—Q4	P—Q4
2 Kt—KB3	Kt—KB3
3 P—K3	P—B3
4 B—Q3	B—Kt5

Black's last two moves are unorthodox but quite feasible. Capablanca makes no attempt to refute them, but is content to build up his position quietly.

5 P—B4	P—K3
6 QKt—Q2	QKt—Q2
7 O—O	B—K2

. . . B—Q3 was preferable; the text is unnecessarily passive.

8 Q—B2	B—R4

As this Bishop is not likely to be very useful, Black welcomes the opportunity to exchange it.

9 P—QKt3	B—Kt3
10 B—Kt2	B x B
11 Q x B	O—O
12 QR—K1	Q—B2
13 P—K4	. . . .

Utilizing his somewhat more active development to open up the game in a favorable manner.

13	P x KP
14 Kt x P	Kt x Kt
15 R x Kt!	. . . .

Much stronger than Q x Kt, as will be seen.

15	B—B3
16 Q—K3!	P—B4

The move Black relied on; but it suffers a brilliant refutation.

17 Kt—K5	P x P

Banking on 18 B x P, Kt x Kt; 19 B x Kt, B x B; 20 R x B, KR—Q1 and Black's command of the Q file gives him an excellent position.

Villegas

Capablanca

18 Kt x Kt!!	Q x Kt

Realizing that 18 . . . P x Q would not do because of 19 Kt x Bch, K—

R1 (not 19 . . . P x Kt? 20 R—Kt4 ch and mate next move); 20 R—R4, P—KR3 forced; 21 R x Pch! P x R; 22 Kt—K8ch and wins. An exquisite variation!

19	B x P	B x B
20	R x B	. . . .

Now we see the importance of White's 15th move.

20	. . . .	Q—B2
21	KR—Q1	KR—Q1

Black's game is most difficult, as he has no compensation for his opponent's possession of the Queen-side majority. The uncanny speed with which Capablanca makes this advantage tell, is most impressive.

22	P—QKt4!	R x R
23	Q x R	P—QKt3

This Pawn advance should have been avoided, as it greatly facilitated the utilization of White's Queen-side majority; . . . P—QR3 was in order.

| 24 | P—Kt3 | . . . . |

In endings with these pieces, it is always wise to guard against surprise attacks on the first rank.

24	. . . .	R—QB1
25	R—QB1	R—Q1
26	Q—K3	K—B1

Evidently with some vague hope of getting the King to the Queen-side and thus helping to guard that sector.

27	P—B5	P x P
28	Q—K4!	. . . .

Finely played. He prevents . . . Q—B3, enabling the advance of the passed Pawn to B6, where it is manifestly more dangerous than on B5.

28	. . . .	R—Q4
29	P x P	P—Kt3

Of course not 29 . . . R x P? 40 Q—QKt4 and wins.

30	P—B6	K—Kt2
31	P—QR4!	. . . .

Black is now defenseless against the threat of Q—QKt4—Kt7 (the text cuts off Black's Rook from QKt4 in the event of . . . Q x Q in answer to Q—Kt7).

| 31 | . . . . | R—Q3 |

Loses neatly; however, Black has nothing to reproach himself for, since 31 . . . P—QR4; 32 Q—QB4 followed by Q—R6—Kt7 is equally hopeless. The text leads to brisk removal of the blockader of the passed Pawn.

| 32 | Q—K5ch | Resigns |

For 33 Q x R is fatal. There is an unobtrusive elegance about this game which is most impressive.

---

31.   Buenos Aires, 1914
(Consultation Game)

KING'S GAMBIT DECLINED

This game is characterized by some unusually fine combinative play, including some moves that must have been uncommonly difficult to discover. It is easy to foresee the brutal sacrifices and their sequel, but to make a sacrifice intuitively and follow it up unconcernedly with quiet waiting moves whose cumulative force finally crushes the enemy—that is consummate chess artistry.

J. R. CAPABLANCA	L. MOLINA E. RUIZ
White	Black
1 P—K4	P—K4

2 P—KB4	....

Indicating from the start that he wants lively chess.

2	B—B4

It would have been interesting to see which of the gambits Capablanca would have adopted after 2 ... P x P.

3 Kt—KB3	P—Q3
4 Kt—B3	Kt—QB3
5 Kt—QR4!	....

An unusual move, but one of real excellence. It makes early castling feasible, secures the two Bishops (and what noble work they perform later!) and makes P—B3 possible (preventing ... Kt—Q5) in the event of ... B—KKt5.

5	B—Kt3
6 B—Kt5	B—Q2
7 Kt x B	RP x Kt
8 P—Q3	KKt—K2

At first sight unduly conservative, but in reply to ... Kt—B3 Black evidently fears a subsequent P x P followed by B—Kt5, with a rather virulent pin because of the open KB file.

9 O—O	O—O
10 P—B5	....

Renouncing the idea of opening the KB file in favor of cramping Black's game and possibly initiating a storming advance with the King-side Pawns (P—KKt4 etc.).

10	P—B3

Angling for the liberating ... P—Q4 which if played at once would lose a Pawn.

11 B—B4ch	K—R1
12 P—QR3	....

Preserving the Bishop against ... Kt—R4.

12	B—K1
13 B—K6	B—R4
14 Q—K1	Q—K1

... B—B2 was better, although White would retain the initiative and attacking chances.

15 Q—R4	Kt—Q1
16 B—R2	B—B2
17 P—B4!?	P—B4?

White's last move was played to avoid exchanges at all cost, but the text is a poor reply. ... P—QKt4 was much better.

18 P—KKt4	Kt—Kt1
19 B—Q2	P—QKt4
20 P—Kt5	BP x P

Forced by the threat of P—Kt6.

21 Kt x KtP	Kt—KB3

... P—R3 here or next move was better, but Black would still have had to reckon with the attack on the KKt file.

22 R—B3	P x P
23 Kt x P!	....

A very fine sacrifice which eventually leads to a remarkable zugzwang position.

23	Kt x Kt
24 R—R3	B—Kt1
25 B x P	R—B2

That Black should offer the exchange comes as a surprise, but Capablanca shows the following fine continuation against the more obvious 25 ... Kt—B2: 26 P—B6! P—KKt4; 27 Q—R5, Kt—Q1; 28 Q—R6, R—B2; 29 B x P, Q—B1; 30 K—R1, Q x Q; 31 B x Q, R x P; 32 R—KKt1! and wins.

26 K—R1	P—QKt4

Since White's QR is about to join the attack, Black wants to bolster the defense by utilizing his QR. The way in which Capablanca later exploits this move is very striking.

27 B—Q5	QR—R2
28 R—KKt1	R—B3
29 B—Kt5	QR—KB2

Black has set up what he considers an impregnable position, although actually he has maneuvered himself into a peculiar **zugzwang** position, giving White the opportunity to take advantage of his helplessness in a highly original manner.

Allies

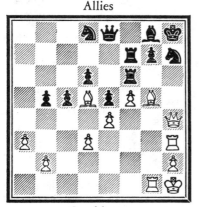

Capablanca

30 P—Kt3!	Q—B1

The QR dare not move. If 30 . . . R—B1; 31 B x B or if 30 . . . R—R2; 31 B x R etc.

31 P—R4	P x P
32 P x P	Q—K1

He cannot hold back the passed Pawn. If 32 . . . Kt—Kt2; 33 QB x R, P x B; 34 B x R, Q x B; 35 R(3)—Kt3 and wins. Or 32 . . . R—R2; 33 B x B, Q x B; 34 B x R and wins.

33 P—R5	Kt—B3
34 P—R6	Kt—Kt5

Although White is still a piece down, he is now ready for the grand simplification. The passed RP is of course the secret of his winning method.

35 QB x R	Kt x B

If 35 . . . R x B; 36 Q x R, P x Q; 37 R x Bch, Q x R; 38 B x Q, K x B; 39 P—R7 and wins. Or 35 . . . P x B; 36 R x Bch! Q x R; 37 B x R, Q x B; 38 Q x Kt ch! and wins.

36 B x Pch!	R x B
37 R x R	K x R
38 Q—R6ch	K—R1

On 38 . . . K—B2 Capablanca intended 39 R—Kt3, K—K2; 40 R—Kt7ch, B—B2; 41 Q—K6ch, K—B1; 42 R x Bch, Q x R; 43 Q x Qch, K x Q; 44 P x Kt and wins.

39 Q x P! and wins	

There is no satisfactory defense: 39 . . . Q—B2 (if 39 . . . Q—K2; 40 Q x Q, Kt x Q; 41 P—R7. Or 39 . . . Kt moves; 40 Q—B6 mate); 40 Q x Pch, Kt—B3 forced; 41 P—R7, Q x P; 42 Q x Ktch with an easy win.

---

32.   New York, 1915

QUEEN'S GAMBIT DECLINED

After an original opening there ensues a short but sharp middle game, culminating in an instructive ending in which Capablanca outplays his opponent.

E. LASKER	J. R. CAPABLANCA
White	Black
1 P—Q4	P—Q4

2 Kt—KB3	Kt—KB3
3 P—B4	P—K3
4 Kt—B3	QKt—Q2
5 B—Kt5	B—Kt5

An experiment. For the continuation 6 P x P, P x P; 7 Q—R4 see Game No. 62.

| 6 P—K3 | P—B4 |
| 7 B—Q3 | . . . . |

White's game is already somewhat difficult. If 7 Q—B2, Q—R4; 8 BP x P (hoping for 8 . . . KP x P; 9 B Q3, P—B5; 10 B—D5) Dlack replies 8 . . . Kt x P! 9 R—B1, Q x P etc.

| 7 . . . . | Q—R4 |

Harking back to the Cambridge Springs motif of direct attack on the Queen-side plus indirect attack on the QB.

| 8 Q—Kt3 | Kt—K5 |

Black can win a piece for three Pawns here with 8 . . . P—Kt4! 9 P x KtP, P—B5; 10 B x BP, P x B; 11 Q x P, B—Kt2 leaving him with a winning game. Evidently Capablanca found the simpler text more to his taste.

| 9 O—O | . . . . |

There is little choice. If 9 B x Kt? P x B; 10 Kt—Q2 (or 10 Kt—K5, P—B3; 11 Kt x Kt, QB x Kt; 12 B—B4, B—R5), BP x P winning a piece.

| 9 . . . . | Kt x B |

Much superior to . . . Kt x Kt.

| 10 Kt x Kt | BP x P |

Threatening to win a piece with . . . P x BP and thus leaving White no choice.

| 11 Kt—Kt5 | Kt—B4 |
| 12 Q—B2 | . . . . |

Perhaps White should have tried the more complicated 12 Kt—Q6ch, although Black would come out with two pieces for a Rook: 12 . . . K—K2; 13 Q—B2, Kt x B!

| 12 . . . . | Kt x B |
| 13 Q x Kt | P—QR3 |

But this is not the best. Capablanca later pointed out that he could have maintained the advantage with 13 . . . B—K2; 14 Kt—KB3, P x KP; 15 P x KP, P x P; 16 Q x BP, O—O etc. White would have no compensation for the Pawn minus.

| 14 Kt x QP | P x P |
| 15 Q x BP | B—Q2 |

Threatening to win a piece with 16 . . . QR—B1, for there would be no point to 17 Q—Kt3 because of . . . B—R5.

| 16 Kt—Kt3 | . . . . |

Kt—K4 was doubtless better. Although the text has the merit of doing away with Black's Bishop-pair, it has the disadvantage of leaving White with a rather ineffectual Knight against a wide-ranging Bishop.

16	Q x Kt
17 Q x B	B—B3
18 P—K4	P—QR4
19 Q—Q2	. . . .

Entering an inferior ending, but there is little choice: 19 Q—K1, Q—K4 winning a Pawn, and if 20 P—B3, Q x KtP; 21 Kt x P?? Q—Kt3ch.

| 19 . . . . | Q x Q |
| 20 Kt x Q | O—O—O! |

Gaining a great many tempi (as compared to . . . O—O) by having the King in the center and developing the QR at once.

| 21 Kt—B4 | . . . . |

Or 21 KR—Q1, R—Q5! 22 Kt—Kt3 (else . . . KR—Q1), R x Rch; 23 R x R, B x P; 24 Kt x P, B—Q4 with much the same kind of ending as in the text.

21	B x P
22 KR—B1	K—Kt1
23 P—B3	. . . .

This move has been criticized, but White is really helpless. Thus if 23 Kt x P, B—Q4; 24 Kt—B4, B x Kt; 25 R x B, R—Q7 and Black will succeed in doubling Rooks on the seventh rank with a won game.

| 23 . . . . | B—Q4 |
| 24 Kt x P | R—QB1 |

Angling for the following favorable simplifications. Black's plan is to leave his opponent **with a worthless Pawn majority on the Queen-side, whilst turning his own majority to account on the other wing.**

| 25 P—QKt3 | . . . . |

The QRP was threatened, and if 25 Kt—Kt3, B x Kt leaves White with a devaluated Queen-side majority.

25	R x Rch
26 R x R	R—QB1
27 R x Rch	K x R

All according to plan.

28 K—B2	K—B2
29 K—K3	K—Kt3
30 Kt—B4ch	B x Kt
31 P x B	K—B4

The desired position, which Capablanca must have had in mind when he exchanged Queens.

(see diagram next column)

| 32 K—Q3 | P—K4 |

Black's plan is clear. While White is tied to the defense of the QBP, Black plays to secure a

Capablanca

Lasker

passed Pawn on the King-side. Eventually White runs out of waiting moves, and the rest is a matter of counting.

| 33 P—Kt4 | P—B3 |

Not 33 . . . P—KKt3? 34 P—Kt5.

| 34 P—KR4 | P—Kt3 |
| 35 K—K4 | . . . . |

If 35 K—B3, P—B4; 36 K—Q3, K—Kt5 etc.

| 35 . . . . | K—Q3 |

Simpler than 35 . . . K x P; 36 P—Kt5, P x P which, however, also wins for Black.

| 36 P—B4 | . . . . |

Or 36 P—R5, K—K3 followed by . . . P—B4ch and . . . K—Q3—B4.

36	P x P
37 K x P	K—B4
38 P—R5	K x P
39 K—K4	P—QKt4
40 P—R3	K—Kt6

White resigns. An interesting ending, nicely played by Capablanca.

33. New York, 1915

RUY LOPEZ

One of the most difficult aspects of tournament chess is the phase that ensues when a player with a cramped position gives up some material to free his game. The whole character of the position undergoes so rapid and violent a change that very often the player who has the advantage lets it slip through his hands because he cannot accommodate h i m s e l f to changed circumstances. In the following game, Capablanca handles this problem admirably.

J. R. CAPABLANCA   A. B. HODGES

White	Black
1 P—K4	P—K4
2 Kt—KB3	Kt—QB3
3 B—Kt5	Kt—B3
4 O—O	B—K2
5 Kt—B3	P—Q3
6 P—Q4	B—Q2
7 R—K1	P x P
8 Kt x P	O—O

Regarding this line of play, see also Game No. 3. White's task is to prevent his opponent from extricating himself from his cramped position.

9 B—B1!	Kt x Kt
10 Q x Kt	B—B3
11 P—QKt4!	. . . .

A many-sided move. It prevents the contemplated maneuver . . . Kt—Q2 followed by . . . B—B3, and it provides for the fianchetto development of White's QB.

| 11 . . . . | K—R1 |
| 12 B—Kt2 | Kt—Kt1 |

This unimpressive retreat is m e r e l y another indication of Black's inability to develop his forces effectively. He is restricted to passive defense.

| 13 Kt—Q5 | P—B3 |

Black is unwilling to give his opponent the two Bishops with . . . B—B3, but the text likewise has its dubious qualities, in view of the hole created at K3.

| 14 Kt—B4 | . . . . |

But this is somewhat premature and leads to nothing tangible. Far more forcing would have been R—K3 and QR—K1 before proceeding to the attack.

| 14 . . . . | Q—B1 |
| 15 R—K3 | Q—Kt5 |

Forestalling R—KKt3 by practically forcing White's next move.

| 16 P—Kt3 | Q—B1 |

White threatened to win the exchange by 17 B—R3, Q—Kt4; 18 Kt—K6.

17 B—B4	B—Q2
18 Q—Q5	P—B3
19 Q—KR5	Q—K1
20 Q—Q1	Kt—R3
21 Kt—K6	B x Kt
22 B x B	Q—Kt3

Obviously White has not accomplished a great deal in the last six moves, but he still has a much freer game and the two Bishops. Black is naturally anxious to free himself and therefore decides to give up a Pawn for a promising counterattack.

23 K—Kt2	B—Q1?!
24 Q x P	B—Kt3
25 R—K2	P—KB4

Forcing the opening of the KB file, as 26 P—K5? would lose after 26 . . . QR—Q1.

| 26 P x P | Kt x P |
| 27 Q—Q3! | . . . . |

Hodges

Capablanca

The position has begun to look dangerous, but White has a satisfactory defense:

I 27 . . . Kt—K6ch?! 28 R x Kt, B x R; 29 Q x B (not 29 Q x Q, R x P ch), QR—K1; 30 R—K1, R—K2 (with a view to . . . KR—K1); 31 Q—Q4!! KR—K1; 32 B—B5! Q x B; 33 Q x Pch and mate follows (Schlechter).

II 27 . . . QR—Q1; 28 B x Kt! R x B; 29 QR—K1! P—KR3; 30 R—K8ch and the attack evaporates.

28 K—R1!   . . . .

Stronger than 28 K—B1. White returns the extra Pawn, but he has a compensating continuation in mind.

28	. . . .	R x P
29	R x R	B x R
30	Q x Q!	Kt x Q
31	R—KB1!	. . . .

31 R—Q1 is less forcing because of . . . Kt—B1. The text is best answered by 31 . . . R—K1; 32 R x B, R x B; 33 R—B7, R—K2; 34 B x Pch, K—Kt1; 35 R x R and White has a won ending.

| 31 | . . . . | R—KB1? |
| 32 | R—Q1! | Resigns |

Black has no way of preventing the absolutely decisive move R— Q7. A curiously abrupt finish!

---

34. New York, 1916
(Rice Memorial Tournament)
(Second Brilliancy Prize)

QUEEN'S GAMBIT DECLINED

Capablanca had a great knack of trussing up his opponents in tragicomic zugzwang situations. Here is a good example of the genre.

J. R. CAPABLANCA   A. SCHROEDER

White	Black
1 P—Q4	P—Q4
2 Kt—KB3	P—K3
3 P—B4	Kt—KB3
4 Kt—B3	QKt—Q2
5 B—Kt5	B—K2
6 P—K3	O—O
7 R—B1	P—QR3

As the plan which Black has in mind has serious drawbacks, it would be better to play . . . P—B3.

8 Q—B2!	R—K1
9 B—Q3	P x P
10 B x P	P—Kt4
11 B—Q3	B—Kt2
12 P—QR4	. . . .

Black is not allowed to continue comfortably with . . . P—B4.

12	. . . .	P—Kt5
13	B x Kt	Kt x B
14	Kt—K4	. . . .

The flaw in Black's calculations is now apparent. The QBP is backward on an open file.

| 14 | . . . . | Kt x Kt |
| 15 | B x Kt | B x B |

The interpolation of 15 . . . P— Kt6 would not help, as there would

follow 16 B x Pch, K—R1; 17 Q—
Q3, P—Kt3; 18 B x P, P x B; 19
Q x KKtP with a winning attack.

16 Q x B   P—QB4

Black cannot wait until the pressure is further intensified with R—
B6 or Kt—K5.

17 P x P   Q—R4
18 P—QKt3   B x P

Thus he has removed what
threatened to be a fatal weakness,
at the cost of exposing himself to
attack on the unguarded King-side.

19 Kt—Kt5   P—R3

19 . . . P—Kt3 was a better defense, although after Capablanca's
intended 20 Q B3! he would have
maintained considerable pressure.

20 Q—R7ch   K—B1

Schroeder

Capablanca

21 Q—R8ch!   . . . .

The beginning of a far-sighted
combination which has a pleasing
effect because it operates by rendering the opponent helpless rather
than by bludgeoning him into submission.
Capablanca points out that the
more obvious 21 Kt—K4 would

have been less good because of
the continuation 21 . . . B—Kt3;
22 Q—R8ch, K—K2; 23 Q x KtP,
Q—KB4; 24 Kt—Kt3, Q—Q6.

21 . . . .   K—K2
22 Q x KtP   P x Kt
23 Q x KtPch   K—Q3
24 K—K2!   . . . .

By thus threatening to bring the
KR into the game, White forces
the hostile King to QKt3, thus preventing the re-entry of Black's
Queen into active play.

24 . . . .   QR B1
25 R—B4   K—B3
26 KR—QB1   K—Kt3

Now that Black is helpless, Capablanca plays his last trump: the
KRP.

27 P—R4!   P—B4

The fitting continuation would
have been the following, indicated
by Capablanca: 27 . . . R—B2; 28
P—R5, KR—QB1; 29 P—R6, B—
Q3; 30 Q x Qch, K x Q; 31 R x R,
R x R (if 31 . . . B x R; 32 R—B6!
wins); 32 R x R, B x R; 33 P—B4,
B—Q1; 34 P—Kt4, B—B3; 35 P—
Kt5, B—R1; 36 P—K4, K—Kt3; 37
P—B5, P x P; 38 P x P, K—B4; 39
P—Kt6, P x P; 40 P x P. What a
pity that this delightful variation
did not occur in the game!

28 Q—Kt7   R—K2
29 Q—K5   . . . .

White's Queen is ideally situated here, as it menaces the Bishop and commands the Queening
square of the KRP.

29 . . . .   R—B3

Loses at once. He should have
tried 29 . . . R(2)—QB2, although
the position could not be held very
long in any event.

30 R x B!   Resigns

If 30 . . . R x R; 31 Q—Q6ch etc.

35. New York, 1916

(Rice Memorial Tournament)

QUEEN'S GAMBIT DECLINED

This game is an ideal example of the famous doctrine of "accumulation of small advantages." Committing only some harmless inexactitudes, and making no overt blunders, Janowski is inexorably forced into a losing position. Thus the game reveals Capablanca's genius in a very impressive light.

D. JANOWSKI   J. R. CAPABLANCA

White	Black
1 P—Q4	Kt—KB3
2 Kt—KB3	P—Q4
3 P—B4	P—B3
4 Kt—B3	B—B4
5 Q—Kt3	. . . .

Not the best. 5 P x P and if . . . P x P; 6 Q—Kt3 is decidedly stronger.

5	Q—Kt3
6 Q x Q	P x Q
7 P x P	Kt x P
8 Kt x Kt	P x Kt

The position is about even. Black has the open QR file at the cost of being left with weak Queen-side Pawns. However, he has already evolved a plan to rid himself of this weakness.

9 P—K3	Kt—B3
10 B—Q2	B—Q2!

Very few players would hit on this fine move, which deliberately retreats this Bishop with the prospect of blocking it with . . . P—K3. But this retreat is useful in a number of respects: (a) after the routine 10 . . . P—K3 White would reply 11 Kt—R4 securing the two Bishops; (b) it supports the contemplated advance of the QKtP, which is part of Black's plan.

11 B—K2	. . . .

Black's intention is to continue with . . . Kt—R4, . . . P—QKt4 and . . . Kt—B5, establishing a fine position on the Queen-side. This possibility could have been ruled out or at least hampered by B—Kt5, here or on the next few moves. But Janowski misses the point.

11	P—K3
12 O—O	B—Q3
13 KR—B1	K—K2

The King is perfectly safe here, and valuable time is saved by having the King in the center for the ending.

14 B—B3	KR—QB1

Here is the last chance for White to play B—Kt5.

15 P—QR3	Kt—R4

Now Black is well on the road toward carrying out his plan; it is true that White can play 16 B x Kt, but after . . . P x B Black's Pawn position is straightened out and he has all the advantages accruing from a two-Bishop game.

16 Kt—Q2	P—B4
17 P—KKt3	P—QKt4

Further progress with his plan.

18 P—B3	Kt—B5

Success! The Knight is too strong here, and will have to be removed—but how? If 19 Kt x Kt, KtP x Kt both White Bishops are hemmed in and P—K4 is impossible, at least for a long time to come.

19 B x Kt	. . . .

It must have cost Janowski quite a pang to part with one of his beloved Bishops, but he must have considered that the Knight would be more useful in this barricaded position, and that P—K4 would offer some relief. Both speculations prove to be faulty; worse yet, White is left with his inferior Bishop, which after three moves, is completely hemmed in by his own Pawns and plays a sorry role throughout the remainder of the game.

19 . . . .   KtP x B

The sickly QKtP is gone, and White must always reckon with the possibility of . . . P—QKt4—5.

20 P—K4   K—B2
21 P—K5   B—K2
22 P—B4   . . . .

One would think that White has gained ground with his last two moves, but this is far from being the case. Actually he has created a new target for Black, for now the duly prepared . . . P—KKt4 will open a file on the King-side. Thus Black is now enabled to attack on both wings.

22 . . . .   P—QKt4

Should White attempt to eliminate the potential threat of . . . P—Kt5 by playing 23 B—Kt4, there simply follows 23 . . . B x B; 24 P x B, R—R5; 25 R x R, P x R and . . . R—QKt1 wins a Pawn.

23 K—B2   R—R5
24 K—K3   KR—QR1

Threatens . . . P—Kt5; but he really has his eye on the other wing.

25 QR—Kt1   P—R3!
26 Kt—B3   P—Kt4
27 Kt—K1   . . . .

Or 27 P x P, P x P followed by . . . R—R1 etc.

27 . . . .   R—KKt1
28 K—B3   P x P
29 P x P   R(5)—R1
30 Kt—Kt2   . . . .

Kt—B2 would have permanently

ruled out . . . P—Kt5, but would have left the King-side without adequate protection. Thus we see how effectively Black's attack on both wings has worked out.

30 . . . .   R—Kt5
31 R—Kt1   QR—KKt1
32 B—K1   . . . .

Capablanca

Janowski

Now matters come to a head. Still applying the principle of attacking on both wings, Capablanca gets the hitherto inactive QB into the game.

32 . . . .   P—Kt5!
33 P x P   . . . .

33 B x P, B x B; 34 P x B, R—Kt1 likewise loses for White.

33 . . . .   B—QR5!

For if 34 QR—B1, R x P ch! wins. Thus the QB reaches the deadly square K5 (as in Game No. 26).

34 R—QR1   B—B7
35 B—Kt3   B—K5ch
36 K—B2   P—R4!

Absolutely decisive, 37 Kt—K3 being answered by . . . P—R5.

37 R—R7   B x Kt
38 R x B   P—R5

39 B x P	R x Rch
40 K—B3	R x RP
41 B x B	. . . .

R x Bch is no better.

41	R—R6ch
42 K—B2	R—QKt6
43 B—Kt5ch	K—Kt3
44 R—K7	R x Pch
45 K—B3	R—QR1

With a mating threat that forces White's capitulation.

| 46 R x Pch | K—R2 |
| Resigns | |

---

36. New York, 1918

RUY LOPEZ

This is probably the most sensational game of Capablanca's career. To meet a prepared variation of this dangerous character without any previous inkling of its existence, and to resist the efforts of one of the most ingenious masters of attacking play in the history of the game—that is a feat of which only a few great players have been capable.

J. R. CAPABLANCA	F. J. MARSHALL
White	Black
1 P—K4	P—K4
2 Kt—KB3	Kt—QB3

A surprise for Capablanca, this being the first time since the 1909 match that Marshall had not replied 2 . . . Kt—KB3.

3 B—Kt5	P—QR3
4 B—R4	Kt—B3
5 O—O	B—K2
6 R—K1	P—QKt4
7 B—Kt3	O—O

Another surprise, 7 . . . P—Q3 being customary. As 8 B—Q5 would

lead to nothing after 8 . . . Kt x B; 9 P x Kt, Kt—Kt5 etc. Capablanca decides to continue in orthodox fashion.

| 8 P—B3 | P—Q4!? |

The third surprise, and the real object of Marshall's play. Capablanca at once realized that acceptance of the Pawn sacrifice would lead to a tremendous onslaught, but he felt that to decline the offer would be a pusillanimous course, unworthy of the players and of the occasion.

9 P x P	Kt x P
10 Kt x P	Kt x Kt
11 R x Kt	Kt—B3
12 R—K1	B—Q3

Now Black's plan is revealed. He is ready for a quick concentrated attack, and White's defense is rendered all the more difficult by the fact that he cannot expect any assistance from his Queen-side pieces for a long time to come.

| 13 P—KR3 | Kt—Kt5! |

To capture this Knight would be fatal: 14 P x Kt, Q—R5 (threatening 15 . . . Q—R7ch; 16 K—B1, Q—R8ch; 17 K—K2, B x Pch and wins); 15 Q—B3 (if 15 P—KKt3, KB x P; 16 P x B, Q x Pch and 17 . . . B x P), Q—R7ch; 16 K—B1, B x P! 17 Q x B, Q—R8ch; 18 K—K2, QR—K1ch etc.

| 14 Q—B3! | Q—R5 |
| 15 P—Q4 | . . . . |

Again the best, for if 15 R—K8, Black gets a winning game with 15 . . . B—Kt2! 16 R x Rch, R x R; 17 Q x Kt, R—K1! 18 K—B1, Q—K2; 19 Q—Q1 (or 19 B—K6, B—Q4!), Q—K5; 20 P—B3, Q—K4; 21 P—Q4, Q—R7 with a winning position.
Or 15 R—K4, P—KR4; 16 P—Q4, B—Kt2; 17 R x Kt, P x R; 18 Q x B, QR—K1; 19 Kt—Q2 (if 19 B—Q2, R—K7), R—K8ch; 20 Kt—B1, P x P and wins (Tartakover).

15 . . . .   Kt x P!

Marshall

Capablanca

White appears to be lost now, for if 16 Q x Kt, B—R7ch! (not 16 . . . B—Kt6?? 17 Q x Pch! forcing mate); 17 K—B1, B—Kt6; 18 Q—K2, B x P! 19 P x B, QR—K1 and wins: 20 B—K3, B x R; 21 Q x B, Q x Pch; 22 K—B2, Q—R5ch; 23 K—B1, Q x Qch; 24 K x Q, R x B ch; 25 K—B2, KR—K1 etc.

16 R—K2!   B—KKt5

According to Tartakover, 16 . . . Kt—Kt5! is best, with the following possibilities:

I 17 Q x R (or 17 P x Kt, B x P and wins), Q—Kt6; 18 P x Kt, Q—R7ch; 19 K—B1, B—Kt6; 20 B—K3, Q—R8ch; 21 B—Kt1, B—R7; 22 K—K1, Q x Bch and wins.

II 17 B—KB4, B—Kt2! 18 P—Q5! Kt—B3; 19 B x B, P x B; 20 Kt—Q2, QR—K1; 21 QR—K1, Q x Rch; 22 R x Q, R x Rch; 23 K—R2, KR—K1 with advantage to Black.

III 17 R—K8! Kt—B3; 18 R x R ch, K x R; 19 Kt—Q2! R—Kt1; 20 Kt—B1, B—Kt2; 21 Q—B2 with about an even game, thus justifying Capablanca's faith in the defensive powers of his position.

17 P x B   . . . .

Not 17 Q x Kt, B—Kt6; 18 Q—

B1, B x R; 19 Q x B, QR—K1 and wins.

17 . . . .   B—R7ch

Best, for if 17 . . . Kt x P? 18 B—KB4!

18 K—B1   B—Kt6

After 18 . . . Kt—R8; 19 B—K3 is an adequate defense. White is defending himself with magnificent coolness.

19 R x Kt   Q—R8ch
20 K—K2   B x R

On 20 . . . Q x B Tartakover gives the following as best: 21 Q x B, Q x Pch; 22 K—Q3, Q x R; 23 K—B2, P—Kt5; 24 P—Kt5! P x P; 25 Q x P(B3), Q x Qch; 26 Kt x Q and White wins the ending.

21 B—Q2   B—R5
22 Q—R3   QR—K1ch
23 K—Q3   Q—B8ch

The attack still looks dangerous, but White has survived the worst.

24 K—B2   B—B7
25 Q—B3   Q—Kt8

Capablanca points out that Black's best chance was 25 . . . R—K7; 26 Kt—R3! R x Bch; 27 K x R, Q x R; 28 Q x B, Q x Pch; 29 Kt—B2, P—B4; 30 B—Q5 and White has a difficult win on his hands.

26 B—Q5!   P—B4
27 P x P   B x P
28 P—Kt4   B—Q3
29 P—R4   P—QR4

Allowing White a strong passed Pawn, but other moves permit White to make good use of the QR file.

30 RP x P   P x P
31 R—R6   P x P
32 Kt x P   B—Kt5

And now Black's game collapses with kaleidoscopic rapidity.

33 P—Kt6	B x Kt
34 B x B	P—R3
35 P—Kt7	R—K6

Capablanca announced mate in five: 36 B x Pch, R x B; 37 P—Kt8 (Q)ch, K—R2; 38 R x Pch, K x R; 39 Q—R8ch, K any; 40 Q(8)—R5 mate.
Marshall's ferocious attack and Capablanca's masterly defense have produced a tense and thrilling game, highly creditable to both masters!

___

37. New York, 1918
(Second Brilliancy Prize)
QUEEN'S GAMBIT DECLINED

An impressive game because of the implacable manner in which Black is punished for one seemingly slight lapse.

J. R. CAPABLANCA   D. JANOWSKI

White	Black
1 P—Q4	P—Q4
2 Kt—KB3	Kt—KB3
3 P—B4	P—K3
4 B—Kt5	QKt—Q2

Also possible here is 4 . . . P—KR3.

| 5 P—K3 | P—B3 |
| 6 QKt—Q2 | . . . . |

This move has the double object of avoiding the Cambridge Springs Defense and also of answering the natural freeing move . . . P x P (which may be expected a little later), with Kt x P with crushing command of the vital square K5. The move has a drawback which will be indicated later.

| 6 . . . . | B—K2 |
| 7 B—Q3 | P x P? |

A mistake which plagues Black for the balance of the game. Because the QKt has less scope at

Q2 than on its normal square QB3, Black should permanently refrain from the text in order to keep the Knight at Q2.
The proper course was . . . O—O and . . . P—B4 followed by . . . P—QKt3 and . . . B—Kt2, with satisfactory prospects for Black.

8 Kt x P	O—O
9 O—O	P—B4
10 R—B1	P—QKt3
11 Q—K2	B—Kt2
12 KR—Q1	Kt—Q4

Apparently the logical freeing course, but he is due for an unpleasant jolt.

| 13 Kt—Q6! | B—QB3 |

The QB is very insecure here; but if instead 13 . . . B x B; 14 Kt x QB, Q—K2; 15 Kt x B, Q x Kt; 16 P x P with a Pawn ahead an easy win.

| 14 Kt—K4 | P—B4? |

A violent attempt to extricate himself. Although it soon leads to disaster, it is evidently motivated by the consideration that after 14 . . . B x B; 15 Kt(3) x B, P—KR3; 16 Kt—KB3, Q—K2; 17 P x P Black has a strategically lost game.

| 15 B x B | Q x B |
| 16 Kt(4)—Q2 | . . . . |

Now the Knight is back to its original point of departure, but it threatens to go to K5, with permanent occupation of the hole created by Black's unfortunate 14th move.

| 16 . . . . | P—K4 |

It is a case of now or never, but the cure is worse than the disease.

17 P x KP	QKt x P
18 Kt x Kt	Q x Kt
19 Kt—B3	Q—K2

No better was 19 . . . Q—B3 (protecting the Bishop); 20 B—B4,

QR—Q1; 21 P—K4, P x P; 22 Q x P,
Q—B4; 23 Q x Q, R x Q; 24 R—Q2,
K—R1; 25 R(1)—Q1, P—QKt4; 26
B—Q3 followed by B—K4 and wins.
The fatal pin plays a part in the
following play as well.

Janowski

Capablanca

20 Kt—Q4!   . . . .

At last the remarkable wanderings of the Knight come to an end,
but White now has a clear win
in sight.

20 . . . .   P x Kt
21 R x B   Kt—Kt5

He has no time to save his Pawn
because of the threat of B—B4;
and if 21 . . . K—R1; 22 P x P,
Q x Q; 23 B x Q, Kt—Kt5; 24 R—
B4 and the QRP is immune.

22 B—B4ch   K—R1
23 R—K6   P—Q6

His game is hopeless.

24 R x P   Q—B4
25 R—Q4   P—QKt4

. . . QR—Q1 would have lasted
a little longer.

26 B x P   Kt x P
27 B—B4   Kt—Kt5
28 Q—R5   P—Kt3

Else R—R4 is decisive in short
order. If 28 . . . QR—Q1; 29 R x R,
R x R; 30 R—K8ch etc.

29 R x P   QR—Q1
30 R—Kt7!   Resigns

If 30 . . . K x R; 31 Q—Kt5ch,
K—R1; 32 R x R and Black cannot
meet the threat of Q—B6 mate. A
classic game by reason of White's
masterly simplicity.

---

38. New York, 1918

QUEEN'S GAMBIT DECLINED

This game is one of the milestones in the history of this opening, so much so that the system
of defense used here by Capablanca has often been named after
him. Aside from that, it is intensely interesting to observe the
effect of Capablanca's speculative
positional sacrifice on move 18.

F. J. MARSHALL   J. R. CAPABLANCA

White	Black
1 P—Q4	P—Q4
2 Kt—KB3	Kt—KB3
3 P—B4	P—K3
4 Kt—B3	QKt—Q2
5 B—Kt5	B—K2
6 P—K3	O—O
7 R—B1	P—B3
8 Q—B2	P x P

In later years, after this line of
play had undergone considerable
investigation, it became customary
to interpolate waiting moves (such
as . . . P—QR3 or . . . R—K1) in
order to defer this capture until
White had spent a tempo with
B—Q3.

9 B x P   Kt—Q4

This is the move which Capablanca popularized. Black's intention is of course to free his rather
cramped game by exchanges.

10 B x B	Q x B
11 O—O	Kt x Kt
12 Q x Kt	P—QKt3

Since the alternative method . . . P—K4 is not available for freeing the Bishop, Black resorts to the fianchetto. White's problem is now to nullify as far as possible his opponent's efforts at emancipation.

13 P—K4	B—Kt2
14 KR—K1	KR—Q1

The crisis. Black intends to continue with . . . Kt—B3, . . . QR—B1 and finally the thematic freeing move . . . P—QB4. Marshall therefore strikes out boldly in an attempt to maintain the initiative.

15 P—Q5	Kt—B4!

In an earlier round of the same tournament Capablanca had played . . . Kt—B1, which is too passive. The more aggressive text threatens . . . Kt x P! above all.

16 P x KP	Kt x P(3)
17 B x Kt	Q x B

This looks most promising, and yet . . . P x B was better, despite the fact that it yields K4 to the enemy. It protects the squares KB4 and Q4 in Black's camp and opens the KB file for him, so that the addition of . . . P—QB4 gives him a fine game.

18 Kt—Q4!	. . . .

Ignoring the attack on the RP, for if 18 . . . Q x RP?? 19 R—R1 wins the Queen. Black is in trouble, for if 18 . . . Q—Q2; 19 Kt—B5 or 18 . . . Q—B3; 19 P—K5! or 18 . . . Q—K2; 19 Kt x P. Capablanca finds the only correct move.

18	Q—K4!
19 Kt x P	Q x Q
20 R x Q	R—Q7!
21 R—Kt1?	. . . .

An error of judgment, resulting

from Marshall's failure to realize the power of Black's Bishop and the Rook on the seventh rank. White would have done better to play for a draw as indicated by Capablanca: 21 Kt—K7ch, K—B1; 22 R—B7, R—K1! 23 R x B, R x Kt; 24 R—Kt8ch etc.

21	R—K1!

Very strong. 22 P—B3 would hardly do because of 22 . . . P—B4! leaving White embarrassed for a good move (23 P x P, QR—K7).

22 P—K5	P—KKt4!

Excellent. This not only creates a flight square for the King (threatening . . . B x Kt followed by . . . R x P), but also prevents P—B4.

23 P—KR4	. . . .

The idea of disrupting Black's Pawns in this manner looks good at first glance, but after Black's reply, he threatens . . . R—K3—Kt3 and . . . P—R6.

23	P x P
24 R—K1	. . . .

Waste of time, but there is no good move. Black could go after the QKtP now, but he continues the pressure inflexibly.

24	R—K3!

If now 25 Kt x P, R—Kt3; White would have no defense.

25 R(1)—QB1	K—Kt2

Necessary preparation for . . . R—Kt3. The manner in which Black's pieces cooperate is nothing short of magnificent.

26 P—QKt4	P—Kt4!

Preventing P—Kt5, which would free White's Rooks from their disagreeable defensive task.

27 P—R3	R—Kt3
28 K—B1	R—R7!

Completing the tieup of White's pieces.

29 K—Kt1   . . . .

P—K6 might hold out longer, but the position is not attractive in any event.

29 . . . .   P—R6
30 P—Kt3   P—QR3

Now White must give up some material.

31 P—K6   R x KP

The Knight still dare not move (32 Kt—Q4? P—R7ch; 33 K x P, R—R3ch; 34 K—Kt1, R—R8 mate).

32 P—Kt4   R—R3

Capablanca

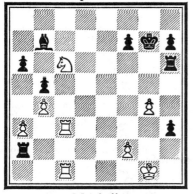

Marshall

With the terrible threat of 33 . . . P—R7ch; 34 K—R1 (if 34 K—Kt2, B x Ktch; 35 R x B, P—R8(Q)ch wins), R x BP and Black wins as he pleases.

Marshall avoids this by closing the Bishop's terrible diagonal, but in so doing he opens up the equally terrible second rank.

33 P—B3   R—Q3!
34 Kt—K7   R(3)—Q7
35 Kt—B5ch   K—B3
36 Kt—R4   K—Kt4

37 Kt—B5   R—Kt7ch
38 K—B1   P—R7
39 P—B4ch   K x BP

White resigns. A highly enjoyable game, played in admirable style by Capablanca.

———

39. Hastings Victory Tournament, 1919

RUY LOPEZ

This tournament proved to be the genesis of the celebrated series of Christmas Tournaments. The opposition was not too exacting, but the tournament was important in that it marked the resumption of international chess after a long lull.

J. R. CAPABLANCA   F. D. YATES

White	Black
1 P—K4	P—K4
2 Kt—KB3	Kt—QB3
3 B—Kt5	P—QR3
4 B—R4	Kt—KB3
5 O—O	B—K2
6 R—K1	P—QKt4
7 B—Kt3	P—Q3
8 P—B3	Kt—QR4
9 B—B2	P—B4
10 P—Q4	Q—B2
11 QKt—Q2	B—Kt5

This has little to recommend it. 11 . . . Kt—B3 or 11 . . . BP x P; 12 P x P, Kt—B3 is preferable.

12 P—Q5   P—Kt4?

A bad move on several counts. White has not created a "target" with P—KR3, hence the text is futile for attacking purposes; worse yet, it robs Black of his chances for a normal development, as he cannot very well castle, and furthermore, he weakens his KB4 very seriously.

| 13 Kt—B1 | P—R3 |
| 14 Kt—Kt3 | R—Q1? |

Another mistake, as White's reply at once demonstrates.

| 15 P—QR4! | P—Kt5 |

A sad choice. He avoids the opening of the QR file, but thereby permits the opening of the QB file, on which White soon trains his guns.

In addition, White gets a magnificent square for a Knight at QB4, and his opponent's Queen-side Pawns are deplorably weak.

16 P x P	P x P
17 B—Q3	B—QB1
18 B—K3	Kt—Kt5
19 QR—B1	Q—Kt1

It has already become evident that White has gained considerable ground on the Queen-side.

20 B—Q2	Q—Kt3
21 Q—K2	Kt—Kt6
22 R—B6	Q—R4
23 B x RP!	B—Q2

Yates

Capablanca

By means of the following well thought out positional sacrifice of the exchange, Capablanca gains **complete mastery of the white squares.**

24 B—Kt5!	B x R
25 B x Bch	K—B1
26 Q—B4	. . . .

Going after the QKtP, which is so weak that its fall can only be a question of time.

26	Kt x B
27 Kt x Kt	Q—R2
28 Q—K2	P—R4
29 Kt—B5	B—B3

A necessary preliminary to . . . Kt—R3, which will have to be played to get rid of the annoying Knight.

30 Kt—B4	Q—B4
31 P—QKt3	Kt—R3
32 Kt x Kt	R x Kt

Despite his formal material advantage, Black has a lost game because his pieces are placed so badly. The coming exchange of Queens will make matters still worse.

| 33 Q—K3! | R—B1 |
| 34 R—QB1 | B—Q1 |

Black is at a loss for a good move. After 34 . . . Q x Q; 35 Kt x Q, B—Q1; 36 R—B4, B—R4; 37 Kt—B2, R—Kt1; 38 B—Kt5 winning the QKtP, there can be no doubt about the outcome.

35 Q x Q	P x Q
36 Kt x P	K—K2
37 R x P	P—B4

Giving White a mighty center, but there was no good move.

38 R—B4	B—R4
39 B—Kt5!	R x R
40 Kt x R	B—B2
41 P—K5	B—Kt1
42 Kt—K3	. . . .

Winning more material. Black should resign.

| 42 . . . . | R—R2 |

43 Kt x Pch	K—B2
44 P—K6ch	K—B3
45 P—K7	R x P
46 Kt x R	K x Kt

And Black resigned 15 moves later, the remaining play being of no interest. A highly instructive example of good positional chess.

---

40. Match, 1919

QUEEN'S PAWN OPENING

Capablanca's play here shows some similarity to that in Game No. 35. White defends well up to the crucial point, where he excusably falters and succumbs to the pressure.

B. KOSTICH   J. R. CAPABLANCA

White	Black
1 P—Q4	Kt—KB3
2 Kt—KB3	P—K3
3 B—Kt5	. . . .

A continuation rarely seen nowadays because it allows Black to equalize without much trouble.

3	P—B4
4 P—K3	Kt—B3
5 P—B3	Q—Kt3
6 Q—Kt3	P—Q4
7 QKt—Q2	B—Q2

Each player waits for his opponent to exchange Queens, in order to have the advantage of the open QR file.

8 B—K2	P x P

This is probably best answered by 9 Q x Q, P x Q; 10 Kt x P, Kt x Kt (else the Knight goes to Kt5); 11 KP x Kt with about an even game

9 KP x P	B—Q3
10 O—O	P—KR3!

As a result of White's inexac-

titude on his previous move, Black is now able to secure two Bishops.

11 B—R4	Kt—KR4
12 Q x Q	P x Q
13 KR—K1	P—KKt4
14 B—Kt3	. . . .

He has no choice, as the attempt to avoid this line by 14 Kt—K5? loses a Pawn after 14 . . . B x Kt; 15 P x B (not 15 B x Kt? B—B5), Kt—B5 etc.

14	Kt x B
15 RP x Kt	P—B3
16 P—KKt4	. . . .

Preventing . . . P—R4 for a long time to come. As Black has the two Bishops and the initiative, White has to play very carefully to keep his head above water. From now on Kostich handles the defense very ably . . . up to a point.

16	K—B2
17 Kt—R2	Kt—R4
18 Kt(R2)—B1	P—Kt4
19 P—R3	Kt—B5

This Knight must be removed, as it is too strongly posted.

20 Kt x Kt	KtP x Kt
21 Kt—K3	R—R3
22 P—KKt3	. . . .

Preventing a subsequent . . . B—B5 when the move might be inconvenient.

22	R—Kt3
23 R—R2	. . . .

This looks unnatural, but after 23 QR—Kt1 Black would threaten to work his QB to KKt3 with fatal effect.

23	R—R1
24 B—B3	. . . .

Making room for the Rook at K2 and also discouraging an eventual . . . P—K4.

24	R—R4
25 K—Kt2	R(4)—Kt4
26 R—K2	B—K1
27 R—Q2	K—Kt2
28 B—Q1	B—Kt3
29 B—R4	R—R4
30 B—B2	B x B
31 R x B	K—Kt3
32 R—K2	R(4)—Kt4
33 Kt—Q1	B—B1

After White's last move it is futile to seek anything more on the Queen-side; hence Capablanca turns to the other wing.

34 R—R1	P—R4
35 P—B3	P x P
36 P x P	P—B4
37 P x Pch	. . . .

Hoping to obtain play on the K file; but Black gets more playing space as well.

37	P x P
38 R—B1	R—KB3
39 R(1)—B2	B—Q3
40 R—K8	K—B2
41 R—K1	P—B5
42 P—KKt4	P—B6ch!

Just in time to forestall K—B3.

43 K—B2	R—R3!
44 K x P	R—R6ch
45 K—K2	R—R7ch
46 Kt—B2	B—Kt6

(see diagram next column)

This is the kind of position in which the obvious "forced" move loses, whereas the "obviously bad" move draws!
White has a draw now with 47 K—B1! R x Ktch; 48 R x Rch,

Capablanca

Kostich

B x R; 49 K x B, R x Pch; 50 R—K2, R—Kt6 (the exchange of Rooks draws); 51 R—K5, R x BP; 52 R x QP, R x P; 53 R—B5 drawing easily (Selesnieff).

| 47 R—KB1? | R—Kt3 |

White is lost, as he cannot extricate the Knight from the unfortunate pin.

48 K—B3	B—R5
49 K—K2	R—KB3
50 K—K3	P—Kt4!

If White continues to see-saw, Black brings his King to QR4 and then exchanges all the pieces, winning with . . . K—R5—Kt6.

| 51 R—Q2 | K—K2 |
| 52 P—Kt4 | . . . . |

A last feeble hope.

| 52 . . . . | P x P e.p.! |
| 53 Kt—Q3 | R(7) x R |

White resigns, as he must lose a piece. An effective finish.

Part IV
World Champion
1921-1927

As bespeaks the status of World Champion, Capablanca displays a new depth and sureness in his play. Also interesting is the fact that the King Pawn openings virtually disappear from his play with the white pieces. There is only one game in this section with 1 P—K4—a Ruy Lopez in which the Champion has a difficult assignment on his hands against one of the most illustrious members of the Hypermodern School (Game no. 44).

We find two fascinating examples of the acceptance of the Queen's Gambit, which had begun to have a certain vogue at this time. Game no. 54 nets the Cuban another first brilliancy prize, while the next game ends in a satisfying triumph over the first-prize winner, after running the whole gamut of combinative possibilities! In both examples of the Orthodox Defense, Capablanca produces convincing refutations of inadequate lines of play. The first of these, from the World Championship Match of 1921, is a particularly impressive example of relentless pressure against a cramped position (Game no. 42). In the other game (no. 44), some amusing variations arise from the positional sacrifice of two Pawns! The Cambridge Springs Defense undergoes a simple but thoroughgoing refutation in Game no. 56, while a related variation is refuted even more drastically in Game no. 62, yielding another first brilliancy prize. The solitary specimen of the Slav Defense occurs in one of the titanic struggles between Capablanca and Dr. Lasker, and again a brilliancy prize game is produced. Against Tartakover's Dutch Defense (Game no. 47), Capablanca proceeds indifferently in the opening, but he makes amends with the classic ending. Game no. 48 is one of Capablanca's most original games, one which shows him at the height of his powers. From the very beginning, he gives the play against the King's Indian Defense a most unusual stamp. Reti's Opening is adopted in Game no. 53 primarily for the purpose of exploiting Marshall's unfamiliarity with its basic ideas—and that is just how the game unfolds.

During this time, Capablanca begins to adopt the Caro-Kann Defense. In Games no. 45 and 63 he takes exemplary advantage of the weaknesses on the white squares created in the opening by Atkins and Nimzovich. The latter of these games winds up with a notable *Zugzwang* process which richly earns the prize for the best-played game. Still another example of this defense is seen in Game no. 58, in which a surprising Rook sacrifice throws Maroczy off balance. Capablanca answers 1 P—K4 with . . . P—K4 only once in this section, leading to an amusing King's Gambit with Tartakover (Game no. 51).

The Queen Pawn games are extremely interesting. For example, Game no. 41 was studied the world over after the publication of Breyer's sensational analysis. Although his claim does not appear to be correct, the game is of exceptional interest throughout its length. In Game no. 60 Capablanca has an easy time of it against Nimzovich's timid opening line, with some clever play on the seventh rank later on. In Games no. 49 and 59 Bogolyubov and Lasker likewise play the opening without any ambition, and Capablanca is consequently able to take the initiative to good effect. The Dutch Defense by transposition in Game no. 57 is exceedingly interesting because of the way that Capablanca hides his true objectives from Kupchik, leading to a surprise finish. The King's Indian Defense, once a favorite with Capablanca, is now adopted sparingly; but there is a fascinating specimen of it in Game no. 52, involving the positional sacrifice of two Pawns, a conception which was awarded a brilliancy prize. We have two examples of the Queen's Indian Defense: Game no. 43, one of Capablanca's most exciting games, with its best parts in the notes; and Game no. 61, in which Capablanca administers an overwhelming drubbing to Alekhine. In all these fine games there is little portent that Capablanca is to topple from his pedestal so soon.

41. World Championship Match, 1921

(Tenth Game)

QUEEN'S GAMBIT DECLINED

This is generally considered the finest game of the match, and the one most characteristic of Capablanca's style. It was Lasker who said, with commendable objectivity, that the logic of the Cuban's play from the 24th move on, was enchanting.

	Dr. E. Lasker	J. R. Capablanca
	White	Black
1	P—Q4	P—Q4
2	P—QB4	P—K3
3	Kt—QB3	Kt—KB3
4	B—Kt5	B—K2
5	P—K3	O—O
6	Kt—B3	QKt—Q2
7	Q—B2	P—B4

While this move appears to free Black's game, it leads to new difficulties. It is therefore likely that the more conservative . . . P—B3 is preferable.

8 R—Q1 . . . .

The older continuation. For the modern 8 BP x P see Game No. 97.

8	. . . .	Q—R4
9	B—Q3	P—KR3

White threatened B x Pch. However, this Pawn advance may turn out to be weakening later on.

10	B—R4	BP x P
11	KP x P	P x P
12	B x P	Kt—Kt3

13	B—Kt3	B—Q2

Black seems to have developed most effectively, as he has no organic weaknesses (with the possible exception of the advanced KRP) and may soon be able to exert pressure on the isolated QP. However, White's position is so much freer and more aggressive that the latter must be conceded the better prospects.

14	O—O	QR—B1

In a later game with Stahlberg at Moscow, 1935, Capablanca attempted an improvement with 14 . . . B—B3; but after 15 Kt—K5, B—Q4? (better . . . QR—B1); 16 Kt x B, QKt x B; 17 Q—K2, QR—Q1; 18 P—B4! Kt—K1; 19 B x B, Kt x B; 20 P—B5! Kt x P; 21 Kt x P! White had a winning attack.

15	Kt—K5	B—Kt4

This much-admired move is actually an inexactitude, as it loses a precious tempo in a critical situation, driving the KR to a good square. . . . B—B3 at once was better.

16	KR—K1	QKt—Q4!

(see diagram next page)

Here is the famous position which has appeared all over the world because of Breyer's sensational analysis giving White the better game. Bogolyubov has subjected this analysis to searching scrutiny, however, and shown that Black can still escape with an even game: 17 QB x Kt, B x Kt! (not 17 . . . Kt x Kt; 18 Kt—Kt6! followed by R x P!); 18 B x Kt! P x B. I 19 Q—B5, B—B3; 20 Kt—Kt4

Capablanca

Lasker

(if 20 Kt—Q7, B x Kt; 21 Q x B, KR—Q1! 22 Q—B5! R—B5! 23 Kt x P, Q x Kt; 24 R—K8ch, R x R; 25 Q x Q, R x P; 26 Q—B3, R—Q7! and White has no winning chances), B—KKt4; 21 P—B4, P—KKt3; 22 Q—K5, QR—K1 with even chances. II 19 Kt—Kt4, B—Kt4; 20 P—B4, B x P; 21 Q—B5, B—Kt4! (Lasker refutes 21 . . . B—B2? with 22 Kt x P); 22 Q x P (if 22 Kt x P, Q—R3), P—R3; 23 P—QR4, QR—Q1; 24 Q x P, B x P! 25 P—Kt4! Q—KB4; 26 Kt x Pch, B x Kt; 27 Kt x B, Q—B7; 28 Kt—B5, B—K6 ch; 29 K—R1, B x P; 30 Q x P! B x Kt with a drawn position. III 19 Kt—Kt4, B—Kt4; 20 P—B4, B—KR5; 21 P—KKt3, B—Q1; 22 Q—B5, R x Kt! 23 P x R, Q x BP; 24 Q x P (else . . . B—Kt3), B—QB3; 25 Q—Kt3, Q—B6 or . . . Q x Q regaining the exchange.

A position which requires such a magnificent analysis to demonstrate its worth is, however, not likely to inspire confidence!

17 KB x Kt	Kt x B
18 B x B	Kt x B
19 Q—Kt3	B—B3

. . . B—R3 might have been tried here. However, Capablanca realizes that despite appearances to the contrary, White's QP will be weaker than Black's QBP.

20 Kt x B	P x Kt
21 R—K5	. . . .

If 21 Kt—R4 (the natural move), KR—Q1 (threatens . . . R x P); 22 R—K5, R—Q4 and Black has the better game.

21	Q—Kt3
22 Q—B2	. . . .

Exchanging Queens would eliminate Black's Pawn weakness, while White's would remain.

23	KR—Q1

If now 23 Kt—R4 Bogolyubov suggests 23 . . . Q—Kt1; 24 R—QB5, Kt—B4! 25 Q—B3, Q—B5; 26 R—B4, P—K4! with advantage.

23 Kt—K2	R—Q4!

R—K3 has been suggested in reply as best, but then 24 . . . Kt—B4; 25 R—QKt3, Q—Q1; 26 R—Kt4, Q—Q2 (Bogolyubov) threatens either . . . P—K4 or . . . QR—Q1. Lasker therefore exchanges Rooks, blocking a frontal attack on the weak Pawn but ironing out Black's Pawn structure and giving him the QB file.

24 R x R	BP x R
25 Q—Q2	Kt—B4
26 P—QKt3	P—KR4

A bit hasty, as it gives White the opportunity for a simplifying exchange by Kt—Kt3, with the resulting likelihood that the Queen and Rook ending can be drawn.

27 P—KR3?	P—R5!

Black is constantly striving to improve the position of his pieces, and trying to limit White's mobility at the same time.

28 Q—Q3	R—B3
29 K—B1	P—Kt3
30 Q—Kt1?	. . . .

Allowing the following infiltration, and thus losing more ground. Q—Q2 was better.

30	Q—Kt5!
31 K—Kt1?	. . . .

Another weak move, which should have been replaced by 31 Q—Kt2 and if 31 . . . P—R4; 32 Q—Q2. But Black would have maintained the advantage in any event.

31	P—R4!

This will result in Black's being in a position to menace the QP and the QKtP simultaneously.

32 Q—Kt2	P—R5
33 Q—Q2	Q x Q
34 R x Q	P x P
35 P x P	R—Kt3!

Forcing the penetration of the Rook to the seventh rank, for if 36 R Kt2, R Kt5 wins a Pawn.

36 R—Q3	R—R3
37 P—KKt4	P x P e.p.
38 P x P	. . . .

Or 38 Kt x P, R—R8ch; 39 K—Kt2, Kt—Q3 followed by . . . R—Kt8. White will soon have to part with a Pawn.

38	R—R7
39 Kt—B3	R—QB7

Threatening . . . Kt x P.

40 Kt—Q1	Kt—K2

If now 41 P—QKt4, R—B8 followed by . . . R—Kt8 and the QKtP falls.

41 Kt—K3	R—B8ch
42 K—B2	Kt—B3
43 Kt—Q1	R—Kt8!

He carefully avoids 43 . . . Kt—Kt5; 44 R—Q2, R—Kt8; 45 Kt—Kt2, R x Kt? 46 R x R, Kt—Q6ch; 47 K—K2, Kt x R; 48 K—Q2 and the position is a draw.

After Black's last move, however, the QKtP is lost. The longest mode of resistance would have been with 44 K—K1, Kt—R4; 45 K—Q2,

R x P; 46 R x R, Kt x Rch; 47 K—B3 etc.

44 K—K2?	R x P
45 K—K3	R—Kt5
46 Kt—B3	Kt—K2
47 Kt—K2	Kt—B4ch
48 K—B2	P—Kt4
49 P—Kt4	Kt—Q3

Black's eventual objective is to play . . . P—B3 and . . . P—K4, obtaining a decisive passed Pawn; but before doing this, he must reduce White to helplessness by again controlling the seventh rank.

50 Kt—Kt1	Kt—K5ch
51 K—B1	R—Kt8ch
52 K—Kt2	R—Kt7ch

See the previous note. White must now allow his King to be confined to the first rank, for if 53 K—B3? R—B7ch; 54 K—K3, R—KKt7; 55 Kt—K2, R—R7; 56 Kt—Kt1, R—R8 etc.

53 K—B1	R—B7ch
54 K—K1	R—QR7
55 K—B1	K—Kt2

. . . P—B3 etc. would have been a bit quicker; but White is helpless in any event.

56 R—K3	K—Kt3
57 R—Q3	P—B3!
58 R—K3	K—B2
59 R—Q3	K—K2
60 R—K3	K—Q3
61 R—Q3	R—B7ch
62 K—K1	R—KKt7
63 K—B1	R—QR7
64 R—K3	P—K4!
65 R—Q3	P x P
66 R x P	. . . .

If 66 Kt—K2, R—Q7 (or . . . K—B4) wins easily.

66	K—B4
67 R—Q1	P—Q5
68 R—B1ch	K—Q4

White resigns, for if 69 R—Q1, Kt—Kt6ch; 70 K—K1, R—KKt7 winning a piece, as the Knight dare not move because of . . . R—K7 mate. A masterly game!

---

42.   World Championship Match, 1921
(Eleventh Game)
QUEEN'S GAMBIT DECLINED

This game was really the decisive contest of the match. Coming on the heels of the previous game, it convinced Lasker that he could no longer hope to overtake his adversary. One senses very quickly the older man's listless attitude and the challenger's confident and optimistic spirit.

J. R. CAPABLANCA	DR. E. LASKER
White	Black
1 P—Q4	P—Q4
2 Kt—KB3	P—K3
3 P—B4	Kt—KB3
4 B—Kt5	QKt—Q2
5 P—K3	B—K2
6 Kt—B3	O—O
7 R—B1	R—K1

A rather unusual move at this point; but it could have been put to good use later on if followed up properly.

8 Q—B2	P—B3
9 B—Q3	P x P
10 B x P	Kt—Q4
11 B x B	R x B?

A mistake from whose consequences Lasker suffers for the remainder of the game, because of the cramped position he now obtains. Correct was 11 . . . Q x B; 12 O—O, Kt x Kt; 13 Q x Kt, P—K4 or 12 R—Q1, Kt x Kt; 13 Q x Kt, P—QKt3 followed by . . . B—Kt2 with the same general ideas as in Game No. 38.

| 12 O—O | Kt—B1 |
| 13 KR—Q1 | B—Q2 |

Black's game is solid and free from organic defects, but it is unbearably trussed up, with only the barest perspectives of attaining freedom. White's task is to prevent all freeing possibilities (particularly . . . P—K4 and . . . P—QB4); sooner or later Black will have to strike out for additional maneuvering space, and in so doing, he will create a weakness which White will be able to exploit successfully by reason of his superior mobility.

| 14 P—K4 | Kt—QKt3? |

According to the familiar maxim that players with cramped positions should endeavor to lighten their burdens by simplifying, . . . Kt x Kt was indicated. True, Black's position would have remained far from ideal; but at any rate, he would have rid himself of a piece which serves no useful function throughout the game.

| 15 B—B1! | . . . . |

This novel retreat is quite good. The natural B—Kt3 would block the QKtP (see White's next move); B—Q3 would mask the action of White's Rook on the Q file, while B—K2 would interfere with the KR's subsequent pressure on the K file.

| 15 . . . . | R—B1 |

Hoping for . . . P—QB4, which is at once prevented.

| 16 P—QKt4 | B—K1 |
| 17 Q—Kt3 | R (2)—B2 |

Preventing a possible break by P—Q5 and hopefully preparing for an eventual . . . P—QB4.

| 18 P—QR4! | . . . . |

White wants to play P—K5, so as to plant a Knight at Q6 and thus further cramp Black's position. However, he does not want to allow Black's miserably posted Knight to secure the magnificent square Q4; hence he first drives away this piece.

18 . . . .   Kt—Kt3
19 P—R5   Kt—Q2
20 P—K5   . . . .

To play a move of this sort, which, as will be seen, involves a certain amount of compensation for Black, requires courage and keen position judgment. However, almost any decision White takes is favored by his vastly superior mobility.

20 . . . .   P—Kt3
21 Kt—K4   R—Kt1
22 Q—B3   . . . .

Q—R3 at once would have been more accurate, as becomes apparent two moves later; but the essential nature of the struggle remains the same.

22 . . . .   Kt—B5
23 Kt—Q6   Kt—Q4
24 Q—R3   P—B3

This achieves a measure of freedom, as Black is actually threatening to obtain some initiative with . . . B—R4. However, since Capablanca exploits the newly created weakness in convincing fashion, the more patient . . . Q—K2 should have been tried.

25 Kt x B   Q x Kt
26 KP x P   P x BP

Exposes Black's King to attack; but after 26 . . . Kt(2) x P, the weakness of Black's K4 would probably have proved fatal even more rapidly.

27 P—Kt5!   . . . .

Before undertaking action against the hostile King, Capablanca first clears up the situation on the other wing in order to deprive Black of any opportunities for counterplay.

At the same time, the terrain thus opened up on the Queen-side will be of more value to White than to his opponent, because of the former's greater mobility.

At first sight the text seems a mistake, as it gives Black the opportunity for the longed-for freeing move 27 . . . P—QB4. But then comes 28 RP x P, RP x P; 29 B—B4 and Black's position in the center is in danger of imminent collapse.

27 . . . .   R(1)—B1
28 KtP x P   R x P
29 R x R   R x R
30 P x P   P x P
31 R—K1   . . . .

Beginning the final phase. B—Kt5 was a good alternative.

31 . . . .   Q—QB1
32 Kt—Q2!   Kt—B1

Lasker recommends 32 . . . R—B6 here, but after 33 Q—Q6, Kt—B1; 34 Kt—K4, R—B3; 35 Q—R3 we get the same position as in the game.

33 Kt—K4   Q—Q1

Lasker

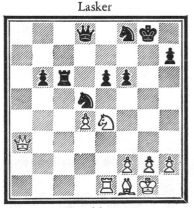

Capablanca

34 P—R4!   . . . .

The strongest continuation of the attack. The RP supports Kt—Kt5 in answer to . . . P—B4, and in some cases the Pawn can advance with good effect.

34 . . . .   R—B2

Capablanca answers 34 . . . P—B4 with 35 B—Kt5, R—B2; 36 Kt—Kt5, R—K2; 37 B—B4 and White has a winning game.

Lasker's suggestion 34 . . . P—B4; 35 Kt—Kt5, P—R3 looks promising, for example 36 Q—R4! (not 36 Kt—B3, R—B6; 37 Q—Kt2, R x Kt!), P—Kt4! 37 B x P, Kt—B6; 38 Q—Kt3, Kt x B; 39 Kt x P! R x Kt; 40 R x R, K—Kt2! with a draw as the likely outcome. However, White has a winning continuation in 35 Q—Kt3ch! K—R1; 36 Q—K5ch, K—Kt1; 37 B—Kt5, R—B2; 38 Kt—Kt5, R—K2; 39 B—B4, Kt—B2; 40 P—R5! P—Kt4; 41 B—Kt3 followed by P—Q5 (Bogolyubov) or Kt x KP!

In view of Black's weaknesses and his exposed position, some such conclusion is inevitable.

35 Q—Kt3   R—KKt2
36 P—Kt3   R—R2
37 B—B4   R—R4

The threat was 38 B x Kt, P x B; 39 Q x Pch etc.

38 Kt—B3   Kt x Kt
39 Q x Kt   K—B2

Black is destined to come to grief now because of the terrible pressure on his game, chiefly against the KP.

40 Q—K3   Q—Q3
41 Q—K4!   R—R5

Some critics have suggested 41 . . . R—R2 as an adequate defense, but White can continue with 42 P—Q5, P—K4; 43 B—B1! followed by B—R3 and a general advance of the King-side Pawns with a winning attack. It is true that the text loses more rapidly.

42 Q—Kt7ch   K—Kt3

If 42 . . . Q—K2; 43 Q—B6

(or even 43 B x Pch, Kt x B; 44 Q x Qch, K x Q; 45 P—Q5), R—R2; 44 P—Q5 wins. If 42 . . . K—Kt1; 43 Q—B8 with a winning position.

43 Q—B8   Q—Kt5

. . . R—R2 would prolong the agony a bit.

44 R—QB1!   Q—K2

Capablanca points out a neat win after 44 . . . Q—R6: 45 B—Q3ch, P—B4 (if 45 . . . Q x B; 46 Q—K8ch or 45 . . . K—R3; 46 R—B7 as in the text); 46 Q—K8ch, K—R3; 47 R—K1, R—R1; 48 R x Pch, Kt x R; 49 Q x Ktch, K—Kt2; 50 Q—K5ch and mate follows.

45 B—Q3ch!   K—R3

If instead 45 . . . P—B4; 46 B x Pch! K—B3; 47 R—B7, Q—Q3; 48 R—B6, Q—Kt5; 49 R—B5! and wins (Bogolyubov).

46 R—B7   R—R8ch
47 K—Kt2   Q—Q3
48 Q x Ktch!   Resigns

An engaging finish to a very fine game.

---

43.   London, 1922

INDIAN DEFENSE

With all its imperfections, this game is one of the most fascinating ever played by Capablanca and therefore richly deserved to be included in this collection.

J. S. MORRISON   J. R. CAPABLANCA

White   Black

1 P—Q4   Kt—KB3
2 Kt—KB3   P—K3
3 P—K3   P—QKt3
4 B—Q3   B—Kt2
5 O—O   . . . .

White's opening play is too timid; for example, QKt—Q2 here or on the next few moves would prevent . . . Kt—K5. For a more aggressive line of play see Game No. 82.

5	B—K2
6 P—QKt3	O—O
7 B—Kt2	Kt—K5
8 P—B4	P—KB4
9 Kt—B3	Q—K1

Capablanca plays for a King-side attack.

10 Q—B2	Kt x Kt
11 B x Kt	Q—R4
12 Q—K2	Kt—R3!?

Hypermodern! Black deliberately loses time in order to encourage the following advance, eventually allowing him to post the Knight favorably on Q4.

13 P—B5	Kt—Kt1
14 P—QKt4	B—KB3
15 QR—B1	Kt—B3
16 P—K4	Kt—K2!

Another subtle move with this Knight, played to provoke a new weakness in White's Pawn position which contributes to his downfall in the ending.

17 P—K5   . . . .

Capablanca

Morrison

17 . . . .   Kt—Q4!

Tartakover has analysed the acceptance of this sacrifice as follows: 18 P x B, Kt—B5.
I 19 Q—K3, Kt x P! 20 Q—Kt5 (obviously 20 K x Kt, Q—Kt5ch loses at once), Q x Q; 21 Kt x Q, Kt—B5; 22 KBP x P (if 22 P—B7 ch, R x P; 23 Kt x R? Kt—R6 mate), R—B3; 23 B—Kt5, R—Kt3 regaining the piece with a winning advantage.
II 19 Q—Q1, Kt x P! 20 Kt—K5! Q—R6! 21 Q—Q2, KKtP x P; 22 P—B3, Kt—R5; 23 Kt—B4, K—B2 with a winning attack.

| 18 B—Q2 | B—K2 |
| 19 Kt—K1 | Q—B2 |

. . . Q x Q was more logical, as it should have proved relatively easy to exploit White's Pawn weaknesses in an endgame. The text leads to a complicated game in which White has more resources than one would suspect at first glance.

20 P—B4	QR—Kt1
21 B—B4	P x P
22 KtP x P!?	P—KR3
23 Kt—B2	P—Kt4
24 R—Kt1	P x P

The game has become extremely interesting again; both players stubbornly pursue their respective objectives.

25 R—Kt3   B—QB3

KR—Kt1 was threatened, winning the QB!

| 26 B x P | Kt x B |
| 27 R x Kt | K—R2? |

A serious mistake, as White could now have won a Pawn and very likely the game, by 28 R x P!
Correct was 27 . . . B—KKt4! with a winning attack.

28 Kt—K3?   B—KKt4!

But now Capablanca is fully prepared for the coming complications!

29 R x P	B x Ktch
30 Q x B	. . . .

Not 30 R x B? Q x R; 31 B—Q3, R—Kt8ch!

30	Q—Kt3!

Forcing White's reply.

31 R—B2	B x P!!

So that if 32 R x B, Q—Kt8ch! and mate in three more moves. This magnificent resource upsets White to such an extent that he misses the best continuation: 32 Q—Kt3, B—K5; 33 Q x Qch, K x Q; 34 R(2)—Kt2 with about an even position.

32 R(3) x R?	B—K5ch
33 Q—Kt3	R x R(Kt1)
34 Q x Qch	K x Q

As a result of White's mistake on move 32, Black's control of the QKt file makes it easy for him to menace White's weak Pawn position.

35 R—B6ch	K—Kt2
36 R—B4	B—B4
37 R—B3	R—Kt8ch

If now 38 R—B1, R—Kt7; 39 R—B2, R—Kt5 etc.

38 K—B2	R—Kt7ch
39 K—Kt3	R—Q7!

Forcing White's Rook to lose contact with the Queen-side.

40 R—B4	P—QR4!
41 P—KR4	. . . .

In order to be able to bring the King to the center. If instead 41 B—Kt3, B—Kt8 with a winning position.

41	P—B3
42 K—B3	P—R5
43 K—K3	R—QB7

Winning the QRP for the QP; Black gets much the better of the bargain.

44 B—R6	R x RP
45 B—B8	R—R6ch
46 K—K2	R—QB6
47 B x P	P—R6
48 P—Q5	. . . .

R—B1 would have prolonged his resistance; after the text, Black has an easy time of it.

48	BP x P
49 P—B6	K—B2
50 R—R4	K—K2
51 R—R8	P—Q5
52 R—K8ch	K—B2
53 R—QR8	B—K5
54 R—R7	R—B7ch
55 K—K1	P—R7
56 K—Q1	P—Q6
57 B—B8ch	K—Kt3

White resigns.   A memorable encounter!

---

44.   London, 1922

RUY LOPEZ

This great fighting game reveals the true stature of a World Champion. Capablanca's victory not only disposed of a formidable rival in the tournament; it also took on genuine historical importance. This magnificent struggle, so taxing in all its phases, was Capablanca's first encounter with an outstanding Hypermodern master.

J. R. CAPABLANCA   E. BOGOLYUBOV

White	Black
1 P—K4	P—K4
2 Kt—KB3	Kt—QB3
3 B—Kt5	P—QR3
4 B—R4	Kt—B3
5 O—O	B—K2
6 R—K1	P—QKt4

| 7 B—Kt3 | P—Q3 |
| 8 P—B3 | O—O |

It is more customary to continue with 8 . . . Kt—QR4; 9 B—B2, P—B4 as for example in Game No. 39; however, Black has a new continuation in mind.

| 9 P—Q4 | . . . . |

As Black is now able to secure a good game, it subsequently became customary to preface the advance of the QP with P—KR3, preventing the annoying . . . B—Kt5.

| 9 . . . . | P x P |

More exact is 9 . . . B—Kt5 and if 10 B—K3, P x P; 11 P x P, Kt—QR4 leading into the text continuation.

| 10 P x P | B—Kt5 |

The inexactitude of Black's opening play could now be demonstrated by 11 Kt—B3! (the early exchange of Pawns has made this effective development possible) as played by Lasker against the same opponent a year later at Maehrisch-Ostrau.

11 B—K3	Kt—QR4
12 B—B2	Kt—B5
13 B—B1	P—B4
14 P—QKt3	Kt—QR4

White's losses of time have been more apparent than real, as Black's QKt has also lost time. But it cannot be denied that Black has obtained a satisfactory position.

15 B—Kt2	Kt—B3
16 P—Q5	Kt—Kt5
17 QKt—Q2	Kt x B

It is indicative of the tense character of the coming struggle that this exchange is advantageous for both (!) players: it rids Black of the useless QKt, while it removes White's KB, which could have little value while hemmed in by White Pawns. Furthermore, Black's Queenside majority of Pawns is compensated for by White's preponderance in the center. Finally, Black has two Bishops, but his best course is to exchange one or both of them!

| 18 Q x Kt | R—K1 |
| 19 Q—Q3 | . . . . |

In order to play Kt—B1, but Capablanca now considers that P—QR4 at once would have been more exact (see Black's 24th move). Black likewise would have continued more effectively by playing . . . Kt—Q2 immediately.

19	P—R3
20 Kt—B1	Kt—Q2
21 P—KR3	B—R4?!

This must not be condemned too harshly, since Black ultimately comes within an ace of winning the game; but the notion of allowing this Bishop to be penned in permanently is highly uneconomical play. Simply 21 . . . B x Kt; 22 Q x B, B—B3 was better.

| 22 Kt(3)—Q2! | B—B3 |

The indicated procedure; but meanwhile he has lost his opportunity to exchange the QB, which will soon be imprisoned.

| 23 B x B | Q x B |
| 24 P—QR4 | P—B5! |

A fighting move, whereby Black secures a strong trump in the form of a passed QRP. In addition, he will have a fine square for his Knight at QB4, as well as the QKt file as the basis for future operations. All told, a promising speculation, and White must do his very best if he is to avoid getting the inferior game.

25 KtP x P	Kt—B4
26 Q—K3	P x RP
27 P—B4	. . . .

Now White's counterplay sets in.

| 27 . . . . | Q—K2 |

| 28 P—Kt4 | B—Kt3 |
| 29 P—B5 | B—R2 |

White's Pawn formation is not a thing of beauty, but he has achieved his object: Black's Bishop is out of play for the balance of the game.

30 Kt—KKt3	Q—K4
31 K—Kt2	QR—Kt1
32 QR—Kt1	P—B3

This move will be needed eventually as part of an attempt to free the Bishop; but the immediate 32 . . . R—Kt7 was more to the point; if then 33 R x R, Q x R; 34 R—QKt1, Q—B7; 35 K—B3, Kt—Kt6 with strong pressure. The inaccurate text allows White to improve his position.

33 Kt—B3	R—Kt7ch
34 R x R	Q x Rch
35 R—K2!	Q—Kt6

Bogolyubov

Capablanca

36 Kt—Q4!   . . . .

A fine positional sacrifice which cannot be accepted. The ending which follows is extremely exciting because of the dangerous QRP.

36 . . . .   Q x Q

On 36 . . . Q x P there would

have followed 37 Kt—K6! (not 37 R—QB2, Q x QP! 38 Kt—K6, R x Kt! with a fine game), R—Kt1; 38 Kt x Kt, P x Kt; 39 R—Q2, R—Kt6; 40 Q—B2 and the passed QP should win quickly (Tartakover). The helplessness of the Bishop is a decisive factor here.

37 R x Q	R—Kt1
38 R—QB3	K—B2
39 K—B3	R—Kt7
40 Kt(3)—K2	B—Kt1
41 Kt—K6!	Kt—Kt6

If 41 . . . Kt x Kt; 42 QP x Ktch with an easy win; or 41 . . . Kt x P; 42 K x Kt, R x Ktch; 42 K—Q4, R—Q7ch; 43 R—Q3 and wins.

42 P—B5!   . . . .

At last White's Pawns come to life; the remaining play is a race between White's QP and Black's QRP.

42	P x P
43 Kt x BP	Kt—Q7ch
44 K—B2	. . . .

If 44 K—K3? P—R6!

44 . . . .   K—K2

Tartakover recommends as Black's last drawing resource 44 . . . Kt—Kt8; 45 R—B4 (45 Kt x P (R4), Kt x R etc.), P—R6; 46 Kt—K6! K—K2! (if 46 . . . P—R7? 47 P—Q6!!); 47 R—B7ch, K—Q3; 48 R—B6ch, K—K2 and Black can hold the position.

| 45 K—K1 | Kt—Kt8 |
| 46 R—Q3 | P—R6 |

After this Capablanca finishes off the game with a well-timed series of forcing moves. Tartakover's 46 . . . K—Q3; 47 Kt x P (R4), R—Kt5; 48 Kt(4)—B3, Kt x Kt; 49 Kt x Kt, B—B2; 50 K—Q2, P—Kt3 still holds out some hope.

| 47 P—Q6ch | K—Q1 |
| 48 Kt—Q4! | R—Kt3 |

Forced by the threat of Kt—B6ch etc.

| 49 Kt(4)—K6ch! | B x Kt |
| 50 P x B | R—Kt1 |

All forced.

| 51 P—K7ch | K—K1 |
| 52 Kt x P! | Resigns |

If 52 . . . P—R7; 53 Kt x R, P—R8(Q); 54 P—Q7ch and mate follows. Or 52 . . . R—Kt2; 53 Kt—B7ch etc. A superb struggle.

---

45. London, 1922

CARO-KANN DEFENSE

This seems to be the first occasion on which Capablanca adopted the defense which later became so great a favorite with him. The game is quite unpretentious, but it shows the stuff of which a World Champion is made.

H. E. ATKINS   J. R. CAPABLANCA

White	Black
1 P—K4	P—QB3
2 P—Q4	P—Q4
3 P—K5	. . . .

Inferior, as will be seen. 3 P x P, P x P; 4 P—QB4 has been the fashionable continuation for some time. Regarding the opening, see also Game No. 63.

3	B—B4
4 B—Q3	B x B
5 Q x B	P—K3
6 Kt—K2	Q—Kt3
7 O—O	Q—R3

Capablanca steers for the ending because his opponent is weak on the white squares and his Bishop is hemmed in by his own Pawns.

| 8 Q—Q1 | P—QB4 |
| 9 P—QB3 | Kt—QB3 |

| 10 Kt—Q2 | P x P |
| 11 P x P | Q—Q6! |

Achieving his object.

12 Kt—QKt3	Q x Q
13 R x Q	KKt—K2
14 B—Q2	P—QR4!
15 QR—B1	P—QKt3!

The two Pawn moves have greatly limited the scope of White's Knights. The following play centers about a struggle for control of the QB file.

| 16 P—QR4 | . . . . |

Unavoidable in the long run; but now White has two weak points (QKt4 and QB4) as well as two weak Pawns (QRP and QP).

16	K—Q2
17 Kt—B3	Kt—R2
18 K—B1	KKt—B3
19 K—K2	R—B1
20 B—K1	. . . .

Note how this Bishop is helpless throughout the game.

20	B—K2
21 Kt—Kt1	P—B4
22 P x P e.p.	. . . .

Exposing the QP to a direct frontal attack, but Atkins must have hoped to be able to get his Bishop into more effective play.

22	B x P
23 B—B3	Kt—Kt5
24 B—Q2	. . . .

A difficult moment for White. Exchanging would rid him of the feeble Bishop, but his pieces would no longer have access to QB3 and his QRP would be exposed to attack.

| 24 . . . . | Kt(2)—B3 |
| 25 B—K3 | Kt—R7! |

An important move which enables Black to control the QB file.

| 26 R—B2 | R—B2 |
| 27 Kt—R3 | KR—QB1! |

Positively decisive. The seemingly strong reply 28 Kt—Kt5? is refuted by . . . Kt x Pch!

Capablanca

Atkins

28 R(2)—Q2	Kt—R2
29 R—Q3	Kt—Kt5
30 R(3)—Q2	R—B3
31 R—QKt1	B—K2!

Planning the elimination of White's Knight at QR3 so as to be able to penetrate at QB7.

32 R—QR1	B—Q3
33 P—R3	R(3)—B2
34 R(1)—Q1	. . . .

If the Rook remains at R1, Black gains his object by 34 . . . Kt(5)—B3; 35 Kt—B2, Kt—K2 etc.

34	Kt—R7!
35 R—QR1	B x Kt
36 R x Kt	B—Kt5
37 R—Q1	R—B5
38 R—QB1	Kt—B3!

Threatening . . . Kt x Pch once more and thus virtually forcing White's reply, which gives Black access to the vital square Q4.

| 39 R x R | P x R |

| 40 Kt—Q2 | B x Kt! |

White's Bishop will be pitiably inferior to the Knight.

41 K x B	K—Q3
42 K—B3	K—Q4
43 R—R1	P—Kt3
44 P—B3	R—QKt1!

Now the opening of the QKt file becomes the road to success.

45 R—R3	P—QKt4
46 P x P	R x P
47 B—B2	Kt—Kt5!

Leaving White no choice, for if 48 B—K3, Kt—Q6; 49 R—R2, R—Kt6ch and wins.

48 P—QKt3	P x P
49 K x P	Kt—B3ch
50 K—B3	R—Kt8
51 R—R4	R—B8ch

If now 52 K—Q3, Kt—Kt5ch; 53 K—K3, R—B6ch; 54 K—Q2, R—B7ch; 55 K—K3, K—B5! wins, for on 56 R x P, Kt—Q4ch is murderous, while on other moves, . . . K—Kt4 decides in short order.

| 52 K—Q2 | R—B5 |
| 53 R—R1 | . . . . |

53 R x R, K x R would of course be quite hopeless in view of the power of the QRP. Black can now win the QP, but he rightly prefers to utilize the superior powers of his Knight.

53	P—R5
54 R—R2	Kt—R2!
55 R—R1	Kt—Kt4
56 R—QKt1	K—B3!
57 K—Q3	R—B6ch
58 K—Q2	R—Kt6
59 R—B1ch	. . . .

59 R x R, P x R is equally hopeless: 60 K—Q3, K—Q4; 61 B—K3, P—Kt7! 62 K—B2, K—B5! 63 K x P, K—Q6 etc.

59	K—Kt2
60 R—B2	P—R6
61 B—Kt3	. . . .

Despair.

61	Kt x P
62 R—B7ch	K—Kt3
63 R—B4	K—Kt4
64 R—B8	Kt—B3
65 R—QR8	R—Kt7ch
66 K—K3	R x P
67 B—B2	Kt—Kt5

White resigns. A very good game.

---

46. London, 1922

QUEEN'S GAMBIT DECLINED

A most instructive game which emphasizes the need for care in playing the moves of even the most routine opening. One slip by Vidmar leaves him with a lost game even before the opening has been completed.

J. R. CAPABLANCA   DR. M. VIDMAR

White	Black
1 P—Q4	P—Q4
2 Kt—KB3	Kt—KB3
3 P—B4	P—K3
4 Kt—B3	B—K2
5 B—Kt5	QKt—Q2
6 P—K3	O—O
7 R—B1	P—B3
8 Q—B2	P x P

Vidmar means to use the system adopted by Capablanca in Game No. 38. But only three moves later, he ruins the whole plan.

9 B x P	Kt—Q4
10 B x B	Q x B
11 O—O	P—QKt3?

A fatal inexactitude. . . . Kt x Kt first, as in the game just cited, was in order.

12 Kt x Kt	BP x Kt

He has no choice but to cede complete control of the QB file to White, for if 12 . . . KP x Kt; 13 B—Q3 wins a Pawn.

13 B—Q3	P—KR3

13 . . . Kt—B3 was somewhat better, although after 14 Q—B7, B—Q2 (if 14 . . . Q x Q; 15 R x Q and White's control of the open file and seventh rank leaves him with a won ending); 15 B—R6! (preventing a Black Rook from coming to QB1) Black is helpless against further strengthening of the pressure by Kt—K5 and the doubling of the Rooks on the QB file.

14 Q—B7!	. . . .

As Black can neither exchange Queens nor develop his Bishop, while the Knight dare not move, he tries a desperate unpinning move whereby he hopes to gain time to rearrange his pieces properly.

14	Q—Kt5

Vidmar

Capablanca

15 P—QR3!	. . . .

A delightful surprise.

15	Q—R5

After a half-hour study of the position, Vidmar realizes that accepting the Pawn sacrifices would soon prove fatal: 15 . . . Q x KtP; 16 R—Kt1! Q x RP (if 16 . . . Q—R7; 17 B—Kt5 followed by R—R1 wins); 17 B—Kt5! Q—K2 (if 17 . . . Kt—B3; 18 R—R1 followed by 19 KR—Kt1 winning t h e Queen!); 18 B—B6! R—Kt1; 19 Kt—K5, Q—Q1; 20 Q x RP, Kt x Kt; 21 P x Kt winning a piece! (Capablanca). If here 19 . . . R—Q1; 20 B x Kt, R—Kt2 (or 20 . . . B x B; 21 Kt—B6); 21 Kt—B6! wins.

16 P—R3!   . . . .

Another remarkable move. Black is virtually in **zugzwang**, for any move of his pieces will result in some material loss. If he confines himself to Pawn moves, he will only postpone the catastrophe for a while without preventing it; thus if 16 . . . P—R3; 17 R—B6, P—QKt4 (else R—Q6 wins); 18 B—B2 winning the Queen.

16 . . . .   Kt—B3
17 Kt—K5   B—Q2

This cannot really be called a mistake, since there are no good moves. If for example 17 . . . B—R3; 18 P—QKt3, Q—R4 (or 18 . . . Q x RP; 19 R—R1 etc.); 19 Kt—B6 winning the Bishop.

18 B—B2   Q—Kt4
19 P—QR4   Q x KtP
20 Kt x B?   . . . .

The only flaw in this excellent game. 20 R—Kt1 wins a piece (20 . . . Q—R7; 21 B—Kt3 or 20 . . . QR—B1; 21 Q x R, Q x R; 22 Q x Rch) and t h u s compels Black's immediate resignation.

20 . . . .   QR—B1
21 Q—Kt7!   . . . .

Winning the exchange and therefore stronger than the plausible

21 Kt x Ktch, P x Kt; 22 Q—Kt3ch, K—R1 etc.

21 . . . .   Kt x Kt
22 B—R7ch   K x B
23 R x R   R x R
24 Q x R   Kt—B3
25 R—B1!   . . . .

Black's Pawn for the exchange becomes meaningless as soon as White's Rook gets into play. The threat is now 26 Q—B2ch, and if 25 . . . Kt—K5; 26 Q—B2 still forces the exchange because of the threatened P—B3.

25 . . . .   Q—Kt5
26 Q—B2ch   K—Kt1
27 Q—B6   Q—R6
28 Q—R8ch   K—R2
29 R—B7!   . . . .

This placement on the seventh is decisive. If now 29 . . . K—Kt3; 30 Q x RP, Q—B1; 31 Q x P and the QRP queens.

29 . . . .   Q x RP
30 R x BP!   Q—Q8ch

The QRP cannot be saved because of the threatened Q—Kt7.

31 K—R2   Q—R4
32 Q x RP   Q—Kt3
33 R—B8   Q—B4
34 R—B7   Q—Kt3
35 R—Kt7   Kt—K5
36 Q—R2   P—K4

There is no point in dragging out such a game.

37 Q x P   P x P
38 R—Kt8   Kt—B3
39 Q x P   Q—B4
40 R x P   Q x P
41 Q—Q3ch   K—Kt1
42 R—Kt8ch   Resigns

47. New York, 1924

DUTCH DEFENSE

Capablanca makes the most of an apparently unpromising middle game and eventually steers into one of his most famous endings.

J. R. CAPABLANCA   S. TARTAKOVER

White   Black

1 P—Q4   P—KB4
2 Kt—KB3   . . . .

Capablanca is content to play the opening in rather an old-fashioned manner, ignoring the modern method of fianchettoing the KB.

2 . . . .   P—K3
3 P—B4   Kt—KB3
4 B—Kt5   B—K2

. . . B—Kt5ch is more promising.

5 Kt—B3   O—O
6 P—K3   P—QKt3
7 B—Q3   B—Kt2
8 O—O   Q K1
9 Q—K2   Kt—K5

Preventing P—K4 and at the same time achieving some useful simplification.

10 B x B   Kt x Kt
11 P x Kt   Q x B

The exchanges appear to have favored Black, who has left his opponent with a doubled QBP which may be a serious weakness for the ending. But Capablanca makes clever use of compensating factors.

12 P—QR4!   B x Kt

Not liking the possibility of 12 . . . Kt—B3; 13 KR—Kt1, Kt—R4; 14 P—B5, P x P? 15 R—Kt5, Black prefers to dispose of the Bishop.

13 Q x B   Kt—B3
14 KR—Kt1   QR—K1
15 Q—R3   R—B3

Waste of time. The immediate . . . P—Kt3 was more to the point.

16 P—B4   Kt—R4
17 Q—B3   P—Q3
18 R—K1!   . . . .

At once accommodating himself to new circumstances. White intends P—K4 with advantageous line-opening. Black's best course was very likely . . . P—B4, but he continues in strangely passive style.

18 . . . .   Q—Q2
19 P—K4   P x P
20 Q x P   P—Kt3
21 P—Kt3!   . . . .

Preparing to advance the KRP and thus weaken Black's position still further. Again Black should counter energetically with . . . P—B4.

21 . . . .   K—B1
22 K—Kt2!   R—B2

Tartakover subsequently pointed out that here or next move he should have played . . . Q—B3. If then Q x Q, Kt x Q; P—B5 (threatening B—Kt5), R—K2 and the reciprocal weaknesses roughly balance each other. As the game goes, Black soon submits to the exchange in a much more unfavorable manner.

23 P—R4!   P—Q4?

Turns out poorly; 23 . . . Kt x P; 24 B x Kt, P—Q4, or 23 . . . Q—B3 offered better chances.

24 P x P   P x P
25 Q x Rch!   . . . .

Rightly heading for the ending, for his Bishop is superior to the Knight, and the King-side Pawns are vulnerable.

25 . . . .   Q x Q
26 R x Qch   K x R
27 P—R5!   . . . .

No matter how Black plays now, he cannot avoid a fatal weakness on the King-side, for example 27 . . . P x P; 28 R—R1, K—B1; 29 R x P and wins.

27 . . . .   R—B3
28 R—R1!   K—B1

If at once 28 . . . R—B3; 29 P x P, P x P; 30 R—R7! with a winning position.

29 P x P   P x P
30 R—R7   . . . .

White now has a number of well-defined advantages: powerful Rook placement on the seventh rank, excellent opportunity of obtaining a passed Pawn, and ability of his King to aid the offensive.

30 . . . .   R—B3
31 P—Kt4!   Kt—B5
32 P—Kt5!   Kt—K6ch

Black has to try to find a defense to the threat of R—R6 followed by P—B5.

33 K—B3   . . . .

Tartakover

Capablanca

Tartakover's original intention was to play 33 . . . Kt—Q8, but he changed his mind after unearthing the following variation: 34 R—R6, K—Kt2 (the Tournament Book refutes 34 . . . K—B2 with 35 P—B5, R x P; 36 P x Pch, K—Kt1; 37 K—K2, Kt—Kt7; 38 B—B5 etc.); 35 P—B5, Kt x P; 36 K—B4! Kt—K5; 37 B x Kt, P x B; 38 P—B6ch! R x P; 39 P x Rch, K x R; 40 K x P, K—R2; 41 K—Q5! K—Kt1; 42 K—B6, P—KKt4; 43 K x P, P—Kt5; 44 P—Q5, P—Kt6; 45 P—Q6, P—Kt7; 46 P—Q7, P—Kt8(Q); 47 P—Q8(Q)ch and wins!

33 . . . .   Kt—B4
34 B x Kt!   P x B
35 K—Kt3!   . . . .

Realizing that the position he will obtain for his King on move 39 is well worth the Pawns sacrificed.

35 . . . .   R x Pch
36 K—R4   R—B6

Fine shows that 36 . . . R—B8 would put up a better, but still not good enough fight: 37 K—R5! (not 37 P—Kt6? R—R8ch; 38 K—Kt5, R x R; 39 P x R, K—Kt2), P—B4; 38 R—Q7! P x P; 39 R x QP, R—Q8; 40 K—Kt6, P—Q6; 41 K—B6, K—K1; 42 P—Kt6, P—Q7; 43 P—Kt7, R—KKt8; 44 R x QP and wins; or 37 . . . R—R8ch; 38 K—Kt6, R x R; 39 K x R, P—B4; 40 P—Kt6 etc.

37 P—Kt6!   R x Pch
38 K—Kt5   R—K5

Black is not happy, despite the two Pawns ahead. If 38 . . . R x P; 39 K—B6, K—K1 (not 39 . . . K—Kt1; 40 R—Q7 and mate follows); 40 R—R8ch, K—Q2; 41 P—Kt7 etc.

39 K—B6   K—Kt1

This is the position Capablanca wanted. Black's game is hopeless.

40 R—Kt7ch!   K—R1
41 R x P   R—K1
42 K x P   R—K5
43 K—B6!   . . . .

Forcing Black's reply and preparing to go after the Queen-side Pawns.

43 . . . .   R—B5ch
44 K—K5   R—Kt5
45 P—Kt7ch   K—Kt1

If 45 . . . R x P; 46 R x R, K x R; 47 K x P and wins. The rest is superfluous.

46 R x P   R—Kt8
47 K x P   R—QB8
48 K—Q6   R—B7
49 P—Q5   R—B8
50 R—QB7   R—QR8
51 K—B6   R x P
52 P—Q6   Resigns

---

48. New York, 1924

KING'S INDIAN DEFENSE

One of Capablanca's greatest positional masterpieces, this game richly deserves to be rescued from obscurity.

J. R. CAPABLANCA   F. D. YATES

White   Black

1 P—Q4   Kt—KB3
2 Kt—KB3   P—KKt3
3 Kt—B3   . . . .

Most unusual, the interpolation of P—B4 being generally preferred.

3 . . . .   P—Q4

Yates is so concerned about the "threat" of P—K4 that he weakens his black squares. . . . P—Q3, as is customary in this variation, was in order.

4 B—B4   B—Kt2
5 P—K3   O—O
6 P—KR3!   . . . .

Providing a retreat for his QB in case of need and at the same time preventing . . . B—Kt5, a move which might enable Black to free himself later with . . . P—K4.

6 . . . .   P—B4

The only alternative freeing method. Plausible as the move is, it is refuted by the Cuban in an incomparably subtle manner.

7 P x P!   . . . .

Seemingly yielding the center and the initiative, but White has seen far ahead.

7 . . . .   Q—R4
8 Kt—Q2!   Q x BP

Not 8 . . . Kt—K5; 9 QKt x Kt, P x Kt; 10 P—QB3 remaining a Pawn ahead.

9 Kt—Kt3   Q—Kt3
10 B—K5!   P—K3

Further weakening the black squares and hemming in the QB—just the objects that Capablanca wished to accomplish with his last move. However, 10 . . . B—K3; 11 B—Q4, Q—B3; 12 Kt—B5 would likewise be unsatisfactory.

11 Kt—Kt5!   Kt—K1

Not 11 . . . Kt—R3; 12 B—Q4. Thus Capablanca has forced the elimination of Black's KB, leaving him with an ineffectual QB and shocking weakness on the black squares.

12 B x B   Kt x B
13 P—KR4!   . . . .

Alekhine comments admiringly in the tournament book on the freshness of Capablanca's treatment of the opening. By threatening an attack, he virtually compels Black to place still another Pawn on a white square (. . . P—B4 or . . . P—KR4), further intensifying the weaknesses already created.

13 . . . .   P—QR3
14 Kt—B3   Kt—B3

15 B—Q3	P—B4
16 Q—Q2	Kt—K4
17 B—K2	Kt—B5

Or 17 . . . B—Q2; 18 Q—Q4! with control of the black squares.

18 B x Kt!	. . . .

He exchanges gladly, securing the open Q file and placing the QP on B5, where it will need protection and cause the creation of new weaknesses.

18	P x B
19 Q—Q4	Q—B2
20 Q—B5!	. . . .

The exchange of Queens simplifies the problem of exploiting Black's difficulties. For the moment, Black can control his QB4; but his QKtP will soon have to advance to QKt4 to guard the QBP, and then White will have this important square in his power once more.

20	Q x Q
21 Kt x Q	P—Kt3
22 Kt(5)—R4	R—Kt1
23 O—O—O	P—QKt4

Inevitable, in view of the threat of R—Q6.

24 Kt—B5	R—Kt3
25 P—R4!	. . . .

This and the next move are played to leave Black with a single weak and advanced Pawn on the Queen-side.

25	Kt—R4
26 P—QKt3!	BP x P
27 BP x P	P x P
28 Kt(3) x P	R—QB3
29 K—Kt2	Kt—B3
30 R—Q2	P—QR4

Relieving his Bishop of one defensive task, but now the QRP becomes a target for White's attack.

31 KR—Q1	Kt—Q4
32 P—Kt3	R—KB2
33 Kt—Q3!	. . . .

Contemplating the exchange of Rooks which takes place in a few moves, and brings this Knight into action against the QRP.

33	R—QKt2
34 Kt—K5	R(3)—B2
35 R—Q4	K—Kt2
36 P—K4!	P x P

In order to keep the Q file closed, Black must permit his KP to become exposed to attack.

37 R x P	R—Kt4
38 R—QB4!	R x R
39 Kt x R	B—Q2

At last!—and still too soon. Capablanca now forces the win of the QRP in a manner which has become a proverbial example of the Knight's agility.

Yates

Capablanca

40 Kt—B3!	R—B4
41 Kt—K4	R—Kt4
42 Kt(K4)—Q6	R—B4
43 Kt—Kt7	R—B2
44 Kt(7) x P	. . . .

The successful outcome of White's profound strategy. However, Black puts up a hard fight now, hoping that he can simplify down to the point where White will remain with only two Knights against the Black King and will therefore be unable to administer mate.

44	....	B—Kt4
45	Kt—Q6	B—Q2
46	Kt(5)—B4	R—R2
47	Kt—K4	....

The winning process is slow but interesting. To begin with, the Knights take command of vital black squares in the center.

| 47 | .... | P—R3 |
| 48 | P—B4 | B—K1 |

Black has been prevented from playing . . . P—Kt4, which was part of his general quest for simplification. White's next step is to create favorable conditions for the advance of his QKtP.

49	Kt—K5	R—R1
50	R—QB1	B—B2
51	R—B6	B—Kt1

The Bishop is still miserably out of play.

52	Kt—B5	R—K1
53	R—R6	R—K2
54	K—R3	B—B2
55	P—QKt4	....

At last. Rendered desperate by the threatened advance of this Pawn, which will win easily against passive play, Black tries a counterattack in the course of which his pieces become so dispersed that his own King is soon enmeshed in a mating net.

55	....	Kt—B2
56	R—B6	Kt—Kt4ch
57	K—Kt2	Kt—Q5
58	R—R6	B—K1
59	P—Kt4!	K—B3
60	Kt—K4ch	K—Kt2
61	Kt—Q6	B—Kt4

| 62 | R—R5 | B—B8 |
| 63 | R—R8! | P—Kt4 |

To stop the mating move P—KKt5, which would make Kt—B6ch possible after Kt—K8ch.

| 64 | BP x P | P x P |
| 65 | P x P | B—Kt7 |

White was again threatening 66 Kt—K8ch with a mating attack.

| 66 | R—K8 | R—QB2 |

Or 66 . . . R x R; 67 Kt x Rch followed by the advance of the KKtP with a quick win.

67	R—Q8	Kt—B3
68	Kt—K8ch	K—B1
69	Kt x R	Kt x R
70	K—B3	B—Kt2
71	K—Q4	B—B1
72	P—Kt6	Kt—Kt2

Or "resigns."

73	Kt—K8!	Kt—Q1
74	P—QKt5	K—Kt1
75	P—Kt7	K—R2
76	P—Kt5	K—Kt1
77	P—KKt6	Resigns

A playful finish. Any move by Black allows a quick mate.

---

49. New York, 1924

QUEEN'S PAWN OPENING

In his **Meet the Masters,** Euwe has described this game perfectly: "A game in the style that earned for Capablanca the description 'chess machine.' We see him obtain a small but definite advantage from the opening, far from sufficient to produce a win of itself but enough to cause his opponent difficulties. The position is just to his taste: slightly to his advantage, simple, straightforward. It is splendid to observe how he holds his advantage and systematically increases it, exploiting each inaccuracy on the part of his opponent. His unsurpassable efficiency produces a game which is a model of modern objectivity."

E. BOGOLYUBOV   J. R. CAPABLANCA

White	Black
1 P—Q4	Kt—KB3
2 Kt—KB3	P—Q4
3 P—K3	P—K3
4 B—Q3	P—B4
5 P—QKt3	. . . .

An old-fashioned line of play which has virtually disappeared from master play because it offers much less promising prospects than the Queen's Gambit in its various forms.

5	Kt—B3
6 O—O	B—Q3
7 B—Kt2	O—O
8 QKt—Q2	. . . .

One of those "obvious" developing moves whose superficiality leads to unexpected difficulties. P—QR3 is preferable.

| 8 . . . . | Q—K2! |

With the double positional threat of 9 . . . P—K4 or 9 . . . P x P; 10 P x P, B—R6—leaving Black with the initiative in either event.

9 Kt—K5	P x P
10 P x P	B—R6
11 B x B	. . . .

The alternative 11 Q—B1, B x B; 12 Q x B would leave his black squares somewhat better protected, but the Queen would be sadly out of play.

| 11 . . . . | Q x B |
| 12 QKt—B3 | . . . . |

In view of his later difficulties on the QB file, 12 Kt x Kt, P x Kt; 13 P—QB4, B—R3; 14 Q—K2 may have been the preferable alternative.

12	B—Q2
13 Kt x Kt	B x Kt
14 Q—Q2	. . . .

White's position is uncomfortable but by no means lost. However, he continues to commit inexactitudes which have a disastrous cumulative effect. Here 14 Q—B1, Q—Kt5; 15 Q—Q2 was in order, to dislodge Black's Queen from its dominating position.

| 14 . . . . | QR—B1 |
| 15 P—B3 | . . . . |

This Pawn is bound to be a troublesome weakness. 15 P—B4, P x P leads either to "hanging Pawns" or to an isolated QP, and while the Pawn was best kept at B2, White would have to have in mind the following maneuver leading to an exchange of Bishops.

| 15 . . . . | P—QR3! |

As Black has an inferior Bishop (hemmed in by its own Pawns) he is naturally eager to exchange Bishops. White might play 16 Q—K2, but then 16 . . . Q—R4 would make . . . B—Kt4 possible after all, unless White is willing to weaken his position catastrophically with 17 P—QKt4?

| 16 Kt—K5 | B—Kt4 |
| 17 P—B3 | . . . . |

17 B x B, P x B would leave White with weak Pawns on two open files.

17	B x B
18 Kt x B	R—B2
19 QR—B1	KR—B1
20 R—QB2	Kt—K1!

Having set up the desired pressure on the QBP, Capablanca proceeds to strengthen it by bringing the Knight to bear on the weak points.

| 21 KR—B1 | Kt—Q3 |
| 22 Kt—K5 | . . . . |

Kt—B5 should have been tried. Evidently White is not fully aware of the danger.

22 . . . .   Q—R4!
23 P—QR4?   . . . .

In order to prevent . . . Kt—Kt4. But 23 Kt—Q3 was better, for if then 23 . . . P—QKt3 (to prevent Kt—B5); 24 P—QR4 can be played, as QKt3 is not available to Black's Queen.

23 . . . .   Q—Kt3!

Wins a Pawn by force, as White has too many weaknesses now to hold everything.

Capablanca

Bogolyubov

24 Kt—Q3   . . . .

Other moves were no better:
I 24 P—QKt4, P—QR4! 25 P—Kt5 (or 25 P x P, Q x P), Kt—B5; 26 Kt x Kt, R x Kt; 27 R—R1, P—K4 winning a Pawn.
II 24 R—Kt1, Kt—B4 and he is helpless against . . . Kt x P.
III 24 R—Kt2, Kt—B4 (threatens . . . Kt x P); 25 R(2)—Kt1 (if instead 25 R(1)—B2, Q—R4! 26 P—QB4, Q x Q; 27 R x Q, P—B3 etc.   Or 25 Kt—Q3, Kt x P! 26 P x Kt, Q x P ch; 27 K—B1, R x R ch; 28 Kt x R, Q x Q; 29 R x Q, R x Kt ch etc.), P—B3; 26 Kt—Kt4 (or 26 Kt—Q3, R x P!), P—K4 etc.

24 . . . .   Q x P
25 Kt—B5   Q—Kt3

At last the Knight is on its best square . . . but it is too late.

26 R—Kt2   Q—R2
27 Q—K1   P—QKt3
28 Kt—Q3   R—B5
29 P—R5   . . . .

Despair. Now the Knight gets to QKt4 after all.

29 . . . .   P x P
30 Kt—B5   Kt—Kt4
31 R—K2   . . . .

Allowing a pretty finish in keeping with this fine game; but there was no hope for him in any event.

31 . . . .   Kt x QP!
32 P x Kt   R(1) x Kt!

White resigns, as 33 P x R, Q x P ch is murderous.

---

50. New York, 1924
(Third Brilliancy Prize)

QUEEN'S GAMBIT DECLINED

Of the many notable games that Capablanca produced, this is one of his most titanic struggles, one of his most gratifying triumphs. It is one of the grandest games on record between contestants of World Championship stature, and is still regarded with awe throughout the chess world.

J. R. CAPABLANCA	DR. E. LASKER
White	Black
1 P—Q4	Kt—KB3
2 P—QB4	P—B3
3 Kt—QB3	P—Q4
4 P x P	P x P

This early exchange of Pawns is part of a system originated and elaborated by Marshall. The basic

ideas are: to avoid complicated
defenses, to preserve a slight but
perceptible initiative, to reduce
Black's possibilities to a minimum.

5 Kt—B3	Kt—B3
6 B—B4	P—K3
7 P—K3	B—K2

This leads to a fuller game than
the spineless 7 . . . B—Q3, which
looks unattractive if only because
the resulting exchange of Bishops
would leave Black with the inferior
Bishop.

| 8 B—Q3 | O—O |
| 9 O—O | Kt—KR4 |

The logical, if somewhat risky
continuation. Lasker rightly realizes that it is important for him
to decrease the menace to his
black squares by removing the QB.

| 10 B—K5! | P—B4 |

Much better than 10 . . . Kt x B?
11 Kt x Kt, Kt—B3; 12 P—B4 (Mar-
shall-Janowski, Match, 1905). Some
annotators have pointed out that
10 . . . P—B3!? would have gained
time, but for over-the-board purposes it is rather difficult to calculate the consequences of the unsound reply 11 Kt—KKt5?!

| 11 R—B1 | Kt—B3 |

Black is now on the point of
bringing this Knight to K5 with
excellent effect.

| 12 B x Kt | P x B! |

Well played: White has permanently lost command of K5, and
Black actually threatens to build
up an attacking formation with
. . . K—R1, . . . Q—K1—R4 and
. . . KR—Kt1. It is true that the
text involves a weakening of Black's
Pawn formation which may make
itself felt later on.

| 13 Kt—KR4 | . . . . |

Capablanca means to forestall a

possible attack by taking the initiative himself on the King-side.

13	K—R1
14 P—B4	KR—Kt1
15 R—B3	B—Q2
16 R—R3	B—K1
17 P—R3!?	. . . .

A move which has its strong
and weak points. Its chief object
seems to be to make QB2 accessible to White's Queen, threatening
P—KKt4 in some cases. On the
other hand, the text weakens
White's Queen-side, as will be seen
later on.

| 17 . . . . | R—Kt2 |
| 18 R—Kt3 | . . . . |

Capablanca's appraisal of the position tells him that the removal
of the Rooks will be to his advantage: he can soon operate on
the newly opened KR file, while
Black will have to lose time bringing his forces to the threatened
sector. Meanwhile, however, Lasker is able to make some progress
on the other wing.

18	R x R
19 P x R	R—B1
20 K—B2	Kt—R4
21 Q—B3	. . . .

This turns out to be a loss of
time which has to be retracted at
once, hence Q—K2 should have
been played.

21	Kt—B5
22 Q—K2	Kt—Q3
23 R—KR1	Kt—K5ch?

Lasker has consolidated very
ably, but this hasty move soon exposes him to a powerful attack.
The Tournament Book points out
that the text should have been postponed until White had played P—
KKt4, after which the latter would
be unable to bring his Queen to
KKt4. Black had several good waiting moves here, as for example . . .
Q—Q2 or . . . R—B2 or . . . B—B2.

24 B x Kt   BP x B

If 24 . . . QP x B; 25 P—KKt4,
B x P (25 . . . P x P; 26 P—B5!);
26 P x P, Q—Kt3; 27 Kt—Kt6ch!
K—Kt1; 28 P x B! R x Kt; 29
R x P!! and wins (Tartakover).

25 Q—Kt4!   P—B4

Black can hardly avoid the following sacrifice, for if 25 . . . R—B3
or 25 . . . B—B2; 26 P—B5 is very
strong.

26 Kt x BP!   P x Kt
27 Q x P   P—KR4
28 P—KKt4   . . . .

As White is bound to get three
Pawns for the sacrificed Knight,
he has good winning chances and
therefore avoids the draw that
would result from 28 Kt x QP, R—
B7ch; 29 K—Kt1, Q—Q3; 30 Q x P,
R—B8ch; 31 K—R2, R x Rch; 32
K x R, B—QB3! 33 Q x B, Q x Kt;
34 Q—K5ch, Q x Q etc. (Tarrasch).
The game has now reached an
extremely exciting stage in which
the tension mounts steadily.

28 . . . .   R—B3

The best defensive chance.

Lasker

Capablanca

29 P—Kt5   . . . .

What a position to have with the
time-control approaching! The best
move was 29 Kt x QP! with the fol-
lowing possibilities:
I 29 . . . R—B7ch; 30 K—Kt3,
P—R5ch; 31 K—R3, Q—Q3; 32
Q—K5ch, Q x Q; 33 QP x Q, B—Q1;
34 R—Q1 followed by P—K6 and
wins (Capablanca).
II 29 . . . B—R5ch; 30 P—Kt3
(not 30 K—Kt1, B—Kt6!), and
now:
(A) 30 . . . B—Kt3; 31 Q—K5ch,
B—B3; 32 Kt x B, Q x Kt; 33 Q x Q
ch, R x Q; 34 P x P, B—B4; 35
R—R4 followed by P—KKt4 and
wins.
(B) 30 . . . R—B7ch; 31 K—Kt1,
R—B8ch; 32 K—Kt2, R—B7ch; 33
K—R3, P x Pch; 34 K x P! B—Q2;
35 R x Bch, Q x Rch; 36 P x Q,
B x Qch; 37 K x B and wins, for ex-
ample 37 . . . R x P; 38 K—K6!
K—Kt2; 39 P—B5, K—B1; 40 P—
R5, R—QR7; 41 P—B6, R x P; 42
P—R6, R—R3ch; 43 K—B5, K—
Kt1; 44 Kt—K7ch etc. (analysis
in the Tournament Book).

29 . . . .   K—Kt1

More exact, says the Tournament
Book, was 29 . . . R—Q3; 30 P—
KKt4, K—Kt1; 31 P x P, Q—Q2!
32 Q x Q, B x Q and Black's Bishops
can hold the Pawns. The text exposes Black to new dangers, although he can still draw.

30 Kt x QP   B—B2
31 Kt x Bch   Q x Kt
32 P—KKt4   P x P?!

The sealed move   Again there
was a fairly simple draw by 32
. . . R—B7ch! 33 K—Kt3 (not 33
K—Kt1? Q—B2! with a mating attack), R—K7; 34 P—Kt6, P—R5
ch! 35 R x P, R x Pch; 36 K—Kt2,
R—K7ch; 37 K—B1, R—K8ch! etc.
But Lasker evidently hopes to retain some winning possibilities.

33 Q—R7ch   K—B1
34 R—R6   B—Kt1

Also possible was 34 . . . R x R;
35 Q x Rch, K—Kt1 with a satisfactory defense.

35 Q—B5ch	K—Kt2

Forced, for if 35 . . . K—K1?
36 R x R, P x R; 37 Q—Kt6ch winning the BP.

36 R x R	P x R
37 K—Kt3	. . . .

Very necessary, for if 37 Q x KtP, P—R4 with an easy draw.

37	Q—K3?

A lapse which loses. Lasker subsequently indicated that the right way was 37 . . . B—B2! 38 Q x KtP (else Black simply plays . . . Q—K3, when the reply K x P?? will be refuted by . . . B—R4ch; this is the finesse that Lasker overlooked), P—B4! 39 P—B5, Q—Q3ch; 40 Q—B4, Q x Qch; 41 K x Q, P x P; 42 K x P, P x P; 43 K x P, B—Kt6 followed by . . . P—R4—5 and draws.

38 K x P	Q x Qch

Black has no choice, for his Queen moves are limited by the two-move mate beginning with Q—B6ch. The following ending is handled very neatly by Capablanca.

39 K x Q	B—Q4
40 P—Kt4	P—R3
41 K—Kt4!	. . . .

More exact than 41 K—K5, K—Kt3; 42 K—Q6 etc. which, however, would also win.

41	B—B5
42 P—B5	B—Kt6
43 K—B4	B—B7
44 K—K5	K—B2
45 P—R4!	K—Kt2

Or 45 . . . B x P; 46 K x P and Black is helpless against the Pawn avalanche.

46 P—Q5	B x P

Similarly, if 46 . . . P x P; 47 K x P, B x P; 48 K x P and the Pawns win easily.

47 P—Q6	P—B4
48 P x P	B—B3
49 K—K6	P—R4
50 P—B6ch	Resigns

A great game, worthy of the occasion.

---

51. New York, 1924

KING'S GAMBIT

Here is one of Capablanca's most delightful games, virtually forgotten now doubtless because his clever attacking play does not conform to the banal description of him as a "chess machine."

S. TARTAKOVER   J. R. CAPABLANCA

White	Black
1 P—K4	P—K4
2 P—KB4	P x P
3 B—K2	. . . .

One of those eccentricities for which Tartakover is famous. It gives Black no trouble.

3	P—Q4
4 P x P	Kt—KB3
5 P—B4	P—B3
6 P—Q4	B—Kt5ch!
7 K—B1	. . . .

A drastic decision, but there was no wholly satisfactory reply to the check, both 7 Kt—B3 and B—Q2 being answered very strongly with . . . Kt—K5!

7	P x P
8 B x P	. . . .

Since it soon becomes evident that the King is too unsafe in an open position, White would have done better to play 8 P—B5, although after 8 . . . P—KKt4 in reply, White's game would retain its unpromising appearance.

8	P x P!

Seemingly losing a piece.

Capablanca

Tartakover

9 B x Kt?   . . . .

Surprising that so experienced a player as Tartakover should be taken in. As a result of the text (which he intends to follow up with Q—R4ch) he is left with a serious weakness on the white squares.

9 . . . .   Kt—Q4!

This sly interpolation was evidently overlooked by Tartakover. If now 10 B—B4, Q—B3, threatening not only the Bishop but . . . Kt—K6ch above all.

10 K—B2   R x B
11 B x P   O—O
12 Kt—KB3   . . . .

As Black's Knight subsequently proves too formidable an attacking piece, B x Kt should have been played here; but Black's two Bishops would be powerful.

12 . . . .   Kt—B3!

White is severely handicapped from now on by his insecure King's position and positional weaknesses.

13 Kt—B3   P—QKt4!

This Pawn offer is even stronger than 13 . . . B x Kt; 14 P x B, Kt—K5ch etc. If now 14 Kt x P (14 B x P?? B x Kt), P—QR3; 15 Kt—B3, B x Kt; 16 P x B, Kt—Kt5ch; 17 K—Kt1, R—Kt7! and there is no satisfactory defense to the threats . . . Kt—K6, . . . R x Pch or . . . Kt—B7. If 18 B—K2, Q—K2! and wins.

14 B—Q3   Kt—Kt5ch
15 K—Kt1   B—Kt2!

The position steadily becomes more threatening. White must not play 16 B x P because of 16 . . . B x KKt; 17 P x B, B x Kt winning a piece (18 P x B, Kt—K6; 19 Q—Q3, Q—Kt4ch; 20 K—B2, R x B; 21 Q x Kt, R—Kt7ch etc.)

16 B—B5   B x KKt
17 P x B   Kt—K6!

Sacrificing a Pawn which is of no consequence compared to the importance of gaining time.

18 B x Pch   K—R1
19 Q—Q3   B x Kt

White's reply is forced (20 Q x B? Q—Kt4ch; 21 K—B2, Kt—Q4 winning a piece).

20 P x B   Kt—Q4!
21 B—K4   Kt—B5

The placement of the Knight on this important square leads to a quickly decisive attack.

22 Q—Q2   Q—R5!
23 K—B1   . . . .

Black was threatening a quickly decisive attack with . . . P—B4 and . . . R—B3—Kt3ch.

23 . . . .   P—B4!
24 B—B6   . . . .

The Bishop is insecure here; but if 24 B—B2, QR—K1 with an easy win.

24 . . . .   R—B3

25 P—Q5   R—Q1!

Leaving White helpless against
the threat of . . . R x B. For if
26 Q—KB2, Q—R6ch wins right
off; or 26 Q—QB2, Q—R6ch; 27
K—K1, R x B; 28 P x R, R—K1ch
(or . . . Q x BP) and White can
resign.

26 R—Q1   R x B!
27 P x R   R x Q
28 R x R   Kt—K3
29 R—Q6   Q—B5ch
30 K—Kt2   Q—K7ch

White resigns. He either runs
into mate (31 K—Kt1, Kt—B5 or
31 K—R3, Q x BPch etc.) or loses
a Rook with 31 K—Kt3, Q—K4ch.

---

52. Moscow, 1925
(Third Brilliancy Prize)

INDIAN DEFENSE

This game exemplifies a kind of
sacrifice which is more subtle and
more profound than the flashy type
of sacrifice which is so much more
popular. There is nothing sensational in such sacrifices, nothing
tangible to be gained quickly; they
require a great deal of self-con-
fidence, of patience and of foresight.

F. J. DUS-CHOTIMIRSKY

            J. R. CAPABLANCA

White   Black

1 Kt—KB3   Kt—KB3
2 P—Q4   P—KKt3
3 P—K3   . . . .

A conservative move which is
not actually bad, but it involves
the likelihood that White will have
a slow and cramped development.

3 . . . .   B—Kt2
4 B—Q3   O—O
5 O—O   P—Q3
6 P—K4   . . . .

White gets around to realizing
that without this move he can
hardly hope to develop his Queen-
side in a satisfactory manner.

6 . . . .   QKt—Q2
7 P—KR3   P—B4
8 P—B3   P—K4

Hoping to induce his opponent
to clarify the situation in the center by 9 P—Q5 (which would enable Black to counter in due course
with . . . P—B4) or else 9 P x P
(which would free Black's game
appreciably).

9 P x KP   . . . .

As already indicated, this only
plays Black's game for him. However, if 9 B—K3, P—Kt3; 10 QKt—
Q2, B—Kt2 followed by . . . R—K1,
White will soon have to be thinking about additional protection for
his KP.

9 . . . .   P x P
10 P—QR4   . . . .

Partly to restrain the Queen-side
advance . . . P—QR3 followed by
. . . P—QKt4, as well as to assure
the future position of his QKt on
QB4.

10 . . . .   Q—B2
11 Kt—R3   P—B5!

An interesting sacrifice, played
to prevent White from achieving
a normal development.

12 Kt x BP   Kt—B4
13 Q—K2   Kt x B
14 Q x Kt   R—Q1
15 Q—K2   B—K3!

So that if 16 QKt x P, Kt—R4;
17 Kt—Q3, B—B5 and the pin will
become intolerable.

16 Kt—R3   P—KR3
17 R—K1   P—R3
18 Q—B2   B—Q2

The Bishop takes a new diagonal,
where it can be more useful.

19 B—K3	B—B3
20 Kt—Q2	P—QKt4

Black gives himself a new open file and reserves the possibility of using the QKtP later on as a battering ram. White cannot very well play 21 P—R5, Kt—Q2 (not 21 . . . Q x P? 22 Kt—B4, Q—B2; 23 B—Kt6); 22 P—QKt4; for that would leave the QBP seriously weak.

21 P x P	P x P
22 P—B3	Kt—R4
23 QR—Q1	B—B1
24 Kt(R3)—Kt1	B—Q2
25 Kt—B1	Kt—B5!

The Knight is very well placed here; and yet White does not dare play B x Kt, for the resultant weakness of his black squares would be serious. Besides, with two unwieldy Knights against two far-ranging Bishops, he would be in a bad way.

26 Kt—Kt3	P—Kt5
27 Kt—K2	P—Kt4
28 Kt—B1	. . . .

Somewhat better would have been 28 Kt x Kt, KtP x Kt; 29 B—B2—although after 29 . . . B—K3 White's position would have remained difficult.

28	KR—B1
29 P—B4	. . . .

Tartakover points out that Black would have the better game after the alternative 29 P—QKt3 (intending P—B4), P x P; 30 Q x P, Q x Q; 31 Kt x Q, R x Kt; 32 B x Kt, KP x B; 33 R x B, B—B4ch; 34 K—R2, B—K6; 35 R(7)—Q1, R—R8.

However, after the text White threatens to obtain an impregnable position with P—QKt3. Striking while the iron is hot, Capablanca makes a courageous decision.

(see diagram next column)

29	P—Kt6!
30 Kt x P	. . . .

Capablanca

Dus-Chotimirsky

It is true that 30 Q x P? would not do because of 30 . . . B—R5; while if 30 Q—B2, B x P! 31 B x Kt, KtP x B; 32 P x B? B—B4. But 30 Q—B3 was probably the safest course.

30	B—R5
31 Kt(1)—Q2?	. . . .

Running into a double pin which soon proves fatal. 31 B x Kt, KtP x B; 32 R—Q3 could have been played, although White's position would still have remained uncomfortable.

31	B—Kt5!
32 P—Kt3	. . . .

Or 32 P—B5, Kt—K3; 33 Q—B4, QR—Kt1; 34 R—R1, QB x Kt winning some material.

32	Kt—K3
33 Q—Q3	R—Q1
34 Q—K2	QR—Kt1!

White cannot save the exchange. His game now collapses in short order.

35 R—KB1	KB x Kt
36 Kt x B	B x R
37 Q x B	R x P
38 Q—B1	R—R7
39 R—B2	R—Q6

40 Kt—B1	R(7)—R6

White could have resigned here.

41 P—B4	R(R6)—B6
42 Q—K1	KP x P
43 P x P	Kt x P
44 B x Kt	P x B
45 Q—K2	P—B6
46 Q—R2	R—B8!
47 R x P	R x R
48 Q—Kt2ch	R—Kt6

White resigns. A most unusual Capablanca game!

---

53. Moscow, 1925
RETI OPENING

Capablanca's use of this opening was very sparing, and it may reasonably conjectured that his adoption of it here was due to Marshall's dislike of the patient position play which is required.

J. R. CAPABLANCA   F. J. MARSHALL

White	Black
1 Kt—KB3	Kt—KB3
2 P—B4	P—K3
3 P—KKt3	P—Q4
4 P—Kt3	P—B4
5 B—KKt2	Kt—B3
6 O—O	B—K2
7 P—Q3	. . . .

If 7 P x P, Kt x P! (better than 7 . . . P x P; 8 P—Q4 and Black finds himself in an inferior variation of the Queen's Gambit Declined); 8 B—Kt2, B—B3 and Black has a good game.

7	O—O
8 B—Kt2	P—Q5

Hemming in White's QB; but Black changes hs mind almost at once.

9 P—K4	P x P e.p.?

A serious strategical error. The diagonal just closed is again open, and in addition the KB file is placed at White's disposal. If Marshall had any hope of demonstrating a weakness in White's center Pawns, he is soon undeceived. Best was 9 . . . P—K4; 10 Kt—K1, Kt—K1; 11 P—B4, P—B3; 12 P—B5 (Tartakover-Janowski, Ghent 1926) with a complicated struggle.

10 P x P	Kt—KKt5

This only loses time. . . . Q—B2 (intending . . . P—K4) was in order.

11 Q—K2	B—B3
12 Kt—B3	Q—R4

Another dubious speculation. He should have continued his development with . . . B—Q2.

13 QR—B1	R—Q1

Another superficial move. Instead of menacing the hostile QP, Black is really weakening his own KBP.

14 P—KR3	KKt—K4?

This virtually loses by force. 14 . . . Kt—R3 had to be tried, although after 15 P—KKt4 White would have a winning advantage.

Marshall

Capablanca

15 Kt—K4! . . . .

There is no good reply. If 15
. . . Kt x Ktch; 16 Q x Kt! wins.

15 . . . . Q x P

Despair.

16 Kt x Bch	P x Kt
17 Kt x Kt	Kt x Kt
18 B—K4!	B—Q2

Too late.

19 R—R1	Q x P
20 KR—Kt1	. . . .

As Capablanca demonstrated directly after the close of the game, he could have concluded with the following magnificent combination: 20 B x Kt, P x B; 21 Q—Kt4ch, K—B1; 22 R x Pch!! K x R; 23 Q—Kt5!! R—KB1; 24 B x RP! B—B3; 25 R—Kt6ch! K—Kt2; 26 B—B5 ch!! K—B2; 27 Q—Kt6ch, K—K2; 28 Q x Pch, K—Q1; 29 Q—Q6ch, K—K1; 30 B—Kt6ch, R—B2; 31 R—KB1 etc.

However, as the text leaves Black without any resource whatever, it has its points.

20	Q—Kt5
21 B x Kt	P x B
22 R x Q	P x R
23 B x P	QR—Kt1
24 R x P	P—Kt6
25 Q—QKt2	B—R5
26 Q x KP	B—B3
27 Q—Kt5ch	K—B1
28 B x B	P—Kt7
29 Q—K7ch	Resigns

---

54. Moscow, 1925
(First Brilliancy Prize)

QUEEN'S GAMBIT

As in Game No. 12, Capablanca winds up with a problem-like finish. He must have taken considerable satisfaction in the fact that it was the weakest unit in his forces which brought about the win!

J. R. CAPABLANCA   L. SUBAREV

White	Black
1 P—Q4	P—Q4
2 P—QB4	P—K3
3 Kt—KB3	P x P
4 P—K4	P—QB4

With 4 . . . Kt—KB3; 5 B—Kt5, B—Kt5ch; 6 Kt—B3, P—B4 Black could transpose into the famous Vienna Variation, which was to produce so many brilliant games in the following decade.

However, after 4 . . . Kt—KB3; 5 P—K5 would be annoying.

5 P—Q5?! . . . .

This leads to an interesting and difficult game. White secures a passed QP, but by way of compensation Black has a strong blockader at Q3 and satisfactory play on the black squares in general. 5 B x P as in the next game is more solid.

5	P x P
6 P x P	Kt—KB3
7 B x P	B—Q3
8 O—O	O—O
9 B—KKt5	. . . .

Only by means of this pin can White hope to give his opponent some trouble in the play that follows.

9	B—Kt5
10 Kt—B3	QKt—Q2
11 Kt—K4	Q—B2

The first of many inexactitudes. It is true that the ripping-up of Black's King-side Pawns need not be fatal, but it does create many difficulties for him. A preferable course was 11 . . . B—K4! and if 12 P—KR3, B x Kt; 13 Q x B, Q—Kt3 with an excellent position.

12 B x Kt   Kt x B

13 Kt x Kt ch	P x Kt
14 P—KR3	B—R4
15 R—K1	KR—K1
16 Q—Kt3	P—QR3
17 P—QR4	B—Kt3

The embarrassments arising from the weak KBP are already beginning to be felt.

18 B—Q3	Q—Q2?

Thoughtless, as Capablanca's reply demonstrates. . . . B—B5 was necessary; Black has played for the two Bishops, but doesn't know how to use them!

19 Kt—Q2!	R—K2

Presumably Black had intended to play to win a Pawn with 19 . . . R x R ch; 20 R x R, B x B; 21 Q x B, Q x QRP; but he notices now that White at once regains the Pawn advantageously with 22 Kt—K4.

20 B x B!	BP x B

This appears to be a colossal strategical blunder, weakening K3 badly. The plausible 20 . . . RP x B would not do, however, because of 21 Kt—K4, K—Kt2; 22 Q—KB3! P—B4; 23 Kt x P! B x Kt; 24 Q—B3 ch, K—Kt1; 25 Q x B, R x R ch; 26 R x R, Q x QRP; 27 Q—K7 with a won ending.
The difference between the two masters is expressed in the fact that Capablanca saw this line before he exchanged Bishops, whereas Subarev saw it after 20 B x B!

21 Kt—K4	K—Kt2
22 Q—QB3	B—K4
23 Q x P	B x P?

Another inexactitude. 23 . . . QR—K1 equalizes, for if 24 QR—Kt1, B x P or 24 Kt—B3? B—R7 ch etc. Black does not realize that only the most economical deployment of his pieces will save him from the consequences of his weakness at K3.

24 Kt—Kt5!	QR—K1

Black has finally doubled Rooks, but his chances have deteriorated considerably now that he has allowed the formidable placement of the Knight at K6.

25 Kt—K6 ch	K—B2
26 QR—Kt1	B—K4
27 Q—B4	R—QB1
28 Q—Kt3	B—Kt1?

Despite his previous sins of omission, Black still had a very good drawing chance in 28 . . . R—B6! 29 Q x P (if 29 Q—R2, P—QKt4), Q x Q; 30 R x Q, R x R; 31 Kt—Q8 ch. Despite the Pawn up, the simplified nature of the position and the strength of Black's Bishop would make the draw fairly certain.

29 P—Kt3	Q—Q3
30 Kt—B4!	QR—K1

White was threatening 31 R x R ch, Q x R? 32 P—Q6 ch.

31 R—K6	Q—Q2
32 R x R ch	. . . .

R—Kt6 also wins, but the text leads to pretty play.

32	K x R

Forced!

33 Q x P!	B x Kt

Overlooking the exquisite combination that follows; but the more prosaic 33 . . . Q x Q; 34 R x Q ch would be quite hopeless for him.

(see diagram next page)

34 R—K1 ch!!	B—K4

There is no better move. If 34 . . . K—Q1; 35 Q—R8 ch; or 34 . . . K—Q3; 35 Q—Kt6 ch, K x P; 36 R—Q1 ch.

35 P—Q6 ch!!	K—K3

Subarev

Capablanca

Not 35 . . . K—Q1; 36 Q—Kt6ch,
K—B1; 37 R—B1ch and mate follows.

36 Q—Kt3ch	K—B4
37 Q—Q3ch	K—Kt4
38 Q—K3ch!	K—B4

If 38 . . . K—R4; 39 P—Kt4ch
wins the Queen.

39 Q—K4ch!   K—K3

Not 39 . . . K—Kt4? 40 Q—
R4ch, K—B4; 41 Q—Kt4 mate.

40 Q—B4ch   K x P

Black has no choice, and thus
the piquant series of checks has
led to the forced win of the Queen.

41 R—Q1ch	K—K2
42 R x Qch	K x R
43 Q x P	R—QKt1
44 Q—R7ch	K—B3
45 Q x P	R—Kt7
46 Q x P	Resigns

---

55.   Moscow, 1925

QUEEN'S GAMBIT

This game was played toward
the end of one of the great tournaments of chess history. Bogolyubov
was in the lead and was naturally
anxious to avoid loss in order to
maintain his advantage in the
score table. Capablanca, on the
other hand, had started badly and
was eager to improve his position.
The result was a struggle which
for tenseness, difficulty and complexity hardly has its equal in
chess literature.

J. R. CAPABLANCA   E. BOGOLYUBOV

White	Black
1 P—Q4	P—Q4
2 P—QB4	P—K3
3 Kt—KB3	P x P
4 P—K4	P—QB4
5 B x P	. . . .

Stronger than P—Q5, as played
in an analogous position in the previous game. Black's position will
soon turn out to be difficult, as he
has trouble with his development
and he has little freedom for his
pieces.

5	P x P
6 Kt x P	Kt—KB3
7 Kt—QB3	B—B4

Black already has reason to be
dissatisfied with his position. If
7 . . . B—K2; 8 P—K5, Kt—Q4;
9 Q—Kt4 (or 9 B x Kt) with a
strong game for White.
The possibility of 7 . . . P—K4
was dismissed by Bogolyubov because of the variation 8 KKt—Kt5,
Q x Qch; 9 K x Q, Kt—R3; 10 B—
K3! Kt—KKt5; 11 B x RP! R x B;
12 Kt x R, Kt x Pch; 13 K—K2,
Kt x R; 14 Kt x B, B—B4; 15 R x
Kt, O—O; 16 B x Kt, P x B; 17
Kt—R4 and White remains a piece
ahead.
Note that if 15 . . . K—Q2; 16
B x Kt, P x B; 17 Kt—R4, R x Kt;
18 R—Q1ch! K—K3 (if the Bishop
interposes, Kt—Kt6ch wins); 19
R—QB1, K—Q3; 20 P—QKt4 wins

8 B—K3   QKt—Q2

Deciding to provoke the following sacrifice, because on other

moves (such as . . . O—O) White can continue advantageously with P—K5.

9 B x P!   . . . .

"Feeling morally obligated to win, Capablanca played this move without a moment's hesitation" (Bogolyubov). For another example of this sacrifice, see also Game No. 75.

9 . . . .   P x B
10 Kt x P   Q—R4

This move has been questioned in some quarters, 10 . . . Q—Kt3; 11 Kt x B, Kt x Kt; 12 O—O (threatening Kt—R4), Q—B3 being suggested as preferable. Capablanca refutes this defense as follows: 13 R—B1! QKt x P; 14 Kt x Kt, Q x Kt; 15 R—K1, K—B2; 16 R—B7ch, K—Kt3; 17 B—Q4, Q—B5; 18 R(1)—K7, R—Q1; 19 R x Pch, K—R3; 20 R x Pch!! Kt x R; 21 R x Kt ch! K x R; 22 Q—R5ch, K—Kt1; 23 Q—Kt6ch, K—B1; 24 B—B5ch and wins. Pretty play!

11 O—O!   . . . .

The following deterioration in White's Pawn position is far less important than the opening of the KB file.

11 . . . .   B x B
12 P x B   K—B2

Forced in view of the threats of Kt x Pch or Q—Q6 or Kt—Q5.

13 Q—Kt3   K—Kt3
14 R—B5!   . . . .

A powerful move which should have led to a quick forced win.

14 . . . .   Q—Kt3

The plausible 14 . . . Kt—K4 is refuted surprisingly by 15 Kt—Q5!

15 Kt—B4ch   K—R3

Bogolyubov

Capablanca

16 P—Kt4?   . . . .

A bad mistake which might have lost the game. Correct was the following line subsequently pointed out by Capablanca:

I 16 Q—B7! (threatening 17 Q—R5ch!! and mate next move), P—Kt3; 17 P—KKt4, Q x Pch; 18 K—Kt2! P x R (or 18 . . . Kt x KtP; 19 R—R5ch, P x R; 20 Q x P(5)ch, K—Kt2; 21 Q x Ktch and wins); 19 P—Kt5ch, K x P; 20 Q—Kt7ch, K x Kt; 21 R—B1ch, K—K4; 22 Q—K7ch, K—Q5; 23 R—Q1ch, K—B5; 24 Q—K6ch, K—B4; 25 P—Kt4ch, K x P; 26 Q—Kt3ch and mate follows.

II 16 Q—B7! P—Kt4; 17 R x P! Q x Pch; 18 K—R1, KR—Kt1; 19 R x R and wins.

III 16 Q—B7! Q x Pch; 17 K—R1, P—KKt3; 18 R x Kt, Kt x R; 19 Q x Kt, R—K1; 20 QKt—Q5! Q—B7; 21 P—KR4! and wins.

16 . . . .   P—Kt4

This move is so necessary that it cannot be missed. Nor can White play 17 Q—B7 because of . . . R—B1. He must therefore exchange Queens, and rely on the exposed position of Black's King and his superior development to make up for the piece minus.

17 Q x Q   P x Q

18 R—Q1	KR—Kt1?

Black in turn misses his chance. The right way was 18 . . . P x Kt! 19 P—Kt5ch, K—Kt2; 20 P x Ktch, Kt x P; 21 R x P (or 21 R—Kt5ch, K—B2; 22 P x P, P—R3), R—R4! and in either event the outcome is highly dubious, though in any case Black would have much better prospects than in the actual game.

19 Kt(4)—Q5!	Kt x KtP

Better than 19 . . . R—Kt3; 20 Kt—K7, Kt—B4; 21 R—Q8! with strong pressure.

20 Kt—K7	R—Kt2
21 R—Q6ch	K—R4
22 R—B3!	Kt(5)—B3

After his opponent's slip on move 18, Capablanca has again worked up a formidable position, and has at least a draw . . . if he wants it.

23 R—R3ch	K—Kt5
24 R—Kt3ch	K—R4
25 Kt—B5	R—Kt3
26 Kt—K7?	. . . .

With both players in terrible time pressure, Capablanca repeats moves in order to gain some much-needed time. Later, he unearthed the following exquisite win, reminiscent of the choicest composed problems: 26 R—R3ch! K—Kt5; 27 K—Kt2!! Kt x P (or 27 . . . Kt—B4; 28 Kt—R6ch, R x Kt; 29 R x R, Kt(4) x P; 30 Kt x Kt, Kt x Kt; 31 R—Q5! and Black is helpless against P—R3 mate!); 28 R—Q5! Kt x Kt; 29 R—R4ch!! P x R; 30 Kt—R6ch, R x Kt; 31 P—R3 mate!!

26	P—Kt5?

Again missing his chance. 26 . . . Kt—B4! 27 Kt x R, Kt(3) x P! 28 R—Q8! K x Kt; 29 R—Kt2, Kt—K3; 30 R x B! R x R; 31 Kt x Kt would have led to equality. But of course such moves cannot be expected from players suffering from acute time pressure.

27 Kt x R	K x Kt?

. . . P x Kt would have prolonged his resistance.

28 R x Pch	K—B2
29 R—B4	K—Kt2
30 P—K5	Kt—K1

The time pressure is over, but so is the game.

31 R—K6	Resigns

For if 31 . . . Kt—B2; 32 R—K7ch wins a piece. A great fighting game, for all its mistakes ("errare humanum est").

---

56.   Lake Hopatcong, 1926

QUEEN'S GAMBIT DECLINED

This game is one of the finest examples of Capablanca's simple and direct style at its best. The reader will find it instructive to see how White smothers every attempt at counterattack and brings his own attack to a successful conclusion.

J. R. CAPABLANCA	E. LASKER
White	Black
1 Kt—KB3	Kt—KB3
2 P—B4	P—B3
3 P—Q4	P—Q4
4 Kt—B3	P—K3
5 B—Kt5	QKt—Q2
6 P—K3	Q—R4

By means of several transpositions, the opening has finally turned into the Cambridge Springs Variation.

7 P x P	. . . .

Although this move was popular during the New York 1924 Tournament, it has been generally replaced by the older 7 Kt—Q2, as Black has good counterplay now with 7 . . . Kt x P.

7	KP x P
8 B—Q3	Kt—K5
9 O—O!?	. . . .

A Pawn sacrifice recommended in the New York 1924 Tournament Book.

| 9 . . . . | QKt—B3 |

If 9 . . . Kt x Kt; 10 P x Kt, Q x BP; 11 P—K4! with strong attacking possibilities (for example 11 . . . P—B3; 12 P x P! P x B; 13 R—K1ch).

Black's best course is probably 9 . . . Kt x B; 10 Kt x Kt, Kt—B3.

| 10 QB x Kt | Kt x Kt |

Evidently Black does not like the alternative 10 . . . Kt x B; 11 Kt—K5, B—Q3; 12 P—B4 and White is strongly entrenched in the center.

| 11 P x Kt | P x B |
| 12 Q—B2 | B—Q3 |

Black appears to have obtained a fine game, with his two Bishops and open KKt file; but Capablanca neutralizes these factors very easily.

| 13 B—B5! | . . . . |

But not 13 B x P? B—KKt5; 14 Kt—Q2, P—KB4!

The text eliminates Black's Bishop-pair and highlights the weakness of his KBPs (13 . . . B x B; 14 Q x B with distinct advantage to White). Lasker therefore plays a move which leads to the undoubling of his KBP, but new Pawn weaknesses turn up.

| 13 . . . . | B—K3 |
| 14 QR—Kt1 | . . . . |

The subsequent play will indicate that this open file is of more value than is the other Kt file.

14	Q—B2
15 B x B!	P x B
16 P—K4	O—O—O

Very enterprising, but it is more risky than aggressive. In view of the further possibility of KR—K1 etc., the Black King could no longer remain in the center; and while 16 . . . O—O was feasible, Black would thereby renounce all attacking possibilities and still remain with a positional disadvantage.

| 17 P—B4 | B—B5 |

Evidently in order to prevent KR—B1. If instead 17 . . . P x KP; 18 Q x P, Q—B2; 19 R—Kt3 followed by doubling Rooks on the QKt or K file and Black has too many weak points to defend; or 17 . . . P x BP; 18 Q x P, Q—B2; 19 KR—B1 and again White has the initiative while Black is thrown back on an irksome defensive policy.

| 18 R—Kt3 | P x BP |

Black is of course loath to open lines for his opponent; but if 18 . . . Q—B2; 19 KR—Kt1, R—Q2; 20 KP x P, KP x P; 21 Q—KB5 and wins.

19 Q x P	Q—B2
20 KR—Kt1	R—Q2
21 P—K5!	. . . .

The winning move. If now 21 . . . P—KB4 White has the same Queen "sacrifice," or if 21 . . . R—B2; 22 P—Q5! B x P; 23 Kt x B, P x Kt; 24 P—Q6, R—Q2; 25 Q x P ch, K—Kt1; 26 Q—K4 with much the better game.

(see diagram next page)

| 21 . . . . | P x P |
| 22 P x P | KR—Q1 |

This has been criticized, but it does not seem to have been an oversight if one studies the alternative 22 . . . R—B2; 23 P—Kt3, R—Kt1; 24 K—B1, B—R3; 25 Kt—Q4, R—K1; 26 Kt x BP! P—R3 (if 26 . . . R x Kt; 27 Q x Rch or 26 . . . Q—Q2; 27 Q—KR4 and wins);

Lasker

Capablanca

27 R x P! R x R; 28 Q x P (threatening Q—R8ch), Q—B2; 29 Q—R8ch, K—Q2 (or 29 . . . Q—Kt1; 30 Q x Qch and wins); 30 R—Q1 ch, K x Kt; 31 Q x Rch, K—B4; 32 Q x P and wins.

    23 Q x Pch!   K—Kt1

If 23 . . . R—B2; 24 R x P! wins. The rest is easy.

    24 P—Kt3   R—Q8ch
    25 K—Kt2   R x R
    26 R x R   R—Q4

Vainly hoping to win the KP. White must of course refrain from 27 P x B? Q—Kt3ch.

    27 Q—B3   Q—B4?

Losing by force. 27 . . . B—R3 would hold out longer.

    28 Q—Kt4!   P—Kt4

Or 28 . . . P—Kt3; 29 Kt—R4 winning the Bishop.

    29 Kt—R4   P—QR4
    30 Q x Pch!   Resigns

He will be at least the exchange down.

----

57. Lake Hopatcong, 1926

DUTCH DEFENSE (in effect)

Even the unskillful chess player is familiar with the trap and the "swindle." More refined by far than these tactical weapons is the type of psychological chess which Capablanca produces in this game: he inveigles White into shifting his pieces to the King-side, and then exploits their absence by a decisive advance on the other wing.

A. KUPCHIK   J. R. CAPABLANCA

White	Black
1 P—Q4	Kt—KB3
2 Kt—KB3	P—K3
3 P—K3	P—QKt3
4 B—Q3	B—Kt2
5 O—O	Kt—K5
6 QKt—Q2	P—KB4

Cf. the opening of Game No. 43. As in that game, White's opening play is timid, but good enough for equality.

    7 P—B3   . . . .

P—B4 would be more natural, but the plan White has in mind (driving out the advanced Knight and playing P—K4) is quite good.

7	B—K2
8 Q—B2	P—Q4
9 Kt—K5	O—O
10 P—B3	. . . .

This is the move on which White has relied.

10	Kt x Kt
11 B x Kt	Kt—Q2
12 Kt x Kt	Q x Kt
13 QR—K1	. . . .

13 P—K4! here or next move was logical and correct.

13	P—B4!
14 Q—Q1	R—B3
15 Q—K2	QR—KB1

16 B—Kt5?   . . . .

Waste of time. P—KB4 at once was better.

16 . . . .   Q—B2

As White must now stop for P—KB4 anyway (else . . . P—K4), his KB will be locked out and will be driven back with gain of time.

17 P—KB4   P—B5
18 K—R1   B—Q3
19 R—B3   P—KR4!

A very fine move. It seems to be played to guard against an eventual P—KKt4 (although Black would have little to fear from that advance); its effect—and intention —is, however, is to fascinate White and focus all his attention, so that he forgets about the real danger zone: the Queen-side.

20 QR—KB1   . . . .

If White had recognized the danger, he would have retreated his KB to B2 and placed his Rooks at QR1 and QKt1 and perhaps would have returned in time to make the first "break" with P—QKt3. However, it was not easy to see through Black's crafty plan.

20 . . . .   R—R3
21 B—K1   P—Kt3

This has the double value of making the King-side absolutely solid and at the same creating the false impression that the black squares are weak.

22 B—KR4   K—B2
23 Q—K1   . . . .

All according to plan. But now the time has come for Black to show his cards.

(see diagram next column)

23 . . . .   P—R3!
24 B—R4   P—QKt4
25 B—Q1   B—B3
26 R—R3?   . . . .

Capablanca

Kupchik

Even now White does not realize the danger. Black intends to push up his Queen-side Ps, with the result that he will eventually obtain an open file against the backward QKtP, or that he will obtain a passed QBP, or that he will secure pressure against the isolated QRP and QBP—all these possibilities arising, of course, after he has played . . . P—QR4 and . . . P—Kt5.

In order to combat this plan, it is essential for White to bring his forces to the beleaguered Queen-side. Instead, he actually makes matters worse with this and his next three moves.

26 . . . .   P—R4
27 B—Kt5?   KR—R1
28 Q—R4?   P—Kt5
29 Q—K1   . . . .

Beginning the retreat; but the damage has been done.

29 . . . .   R—QKt1
30 R(3)—B3   P—R5
31 R(3)—B2   . . . .

Or 31 P x P, R x P; 32 either R—B2, R(1)—QKt1 winning the QKtP —a variation which shows the serious effects of White's incorrect plan.

31 . . . .   P—R6!

This rolls up the Queen-side completely and forces a passed QBP for Black and a weak QRP for White.

32 P—QKt3? . . . .

A final weak move which loses a Pawn and leads to a quick collapse.

```
32 . . . .        BP x P
33 B x KtP        B—Kt4
34 R—Kt1          Q x P
35 Q x Q          P x Q
36 R—B2           KR—QB1
37 B—KR4          . . . .
```

Much too late; but if 37 R(1)—QB1, B—Kt5 followed by . . . B—Q6 with an easy win.

```
37 . . . .        B—Q6
38 R(2)—B1        R x B!
39 P x R          P—R7
```

White resigns, as he cannot avoid a decisive loss of material:
I 40 B—K1? B—Kt8 and wins.
II 40 R—R1, B—Kt8; 41 R x B (else . . . P—B7 and . . . B—R6. If instead 41 B—K1, B—R6 followed by . . . B—Kt7 or . . . P—B7), P x R(Q); 42 R x Q, P—B7; 43 R—QB1, B—R6 and wins. A neat finish to a most instructive game.

---

58. Lake Hopatcong, 1926

CARO-KANN DEFENSE

One of the queerest psychological quirks to be observed in tournament chess is the tendency of even experienced chess masters to head for complicated lines in time pressure. It is true, of course, that sometimes a player commits himself to grave consequences because he lacks the time to calculate them.

G. MAROCZY   J. R. CAPABLANCA

White   Black

```
1 P—K4            P—QB3
```

```
2 P—Q4            P—Q4
3 P x P           P x P
4 B—Q3            . . . .
```

The old continuation, which has now given way almost completely to the more fashionable 4 P—QB4 —a move that sets both players many problems.

```
4 . . . .         Kt—QB3
5 P—QB3           Kt—B3
6 B—KB4           . . . .
```

After 6 P—KR3 (to prevent . . . B—Kt5), Black can play either 6 . . . P—K4; 7 P x P, Kt x P freeing his game at the expense of being left with an isolated QP—or else 6 . . . P—KKt3 followed by . . . B—Kt2 and . . . B—B4.

```
6 . . . .         B—Kt5
7 Q—Kt3           . . . .
```

7 Kt—K2 is recommended by some opening authorities, but Black should obtain a perfectly satisfactory game with 7 . . . P—K3; 8 Q—Kt3, Q—Q2; 9 Kt—Kt3, Kt—KR4! or 7 . . . B—R4! 8 Q—Kt3, Q—Q2; 9 Kt—Kt3, B—Kt3 etc.

```
7 . . . .         Kt—QR4
8 Q—R4ch          B—Q2
9 Q—B2            Q—Kt3
10 Kt—B3          P—K3
11 O—O            B—Kt4
```

Wisely removing White's KB, which had obviously brighter prospects than Black's QB. At the same time, such attacking possibilities as White may have hoped for on the King-side are considerably minimized.

```
12 QKt—Q2         B x B
13 Q x B          R—B1
```

Of course not 13 . . . Q x KtP? 14 KR—Kt1, Q—R6; 15 Q—Kt5ch and serious disadvantage is unavoidable for Black.

```
14 QR—Kt1         B—K2
```

15 P—KR3   . . . .

KR—K1 or Kt—K5 looks more
energetic here. The text has the
drawback of preempting the square
KR3—for example, in the event of
KR—K1—K3 White cannot play
the otherwise useful attacking
move R—R3.

15 . . . .   O—O
16 KR—K1   Kt—B5
17 Kt x Kt   R x Kt

Although the Rook will be driven
off at once, Black's judgment is
probably sound in rejecting 17 . . .
P x Kt; for although he would gain
time thereby and secure Q4 for his
pieces, his Queen-side counterplay
would proceed more slowly and
White's attacking chances on the
other wing would be greater.

18 Kt—K5   QR—B1
19 B—Kt5   . . . .

White does not relish being left
with his Bishop in a subsequent
ending, as this piece would be
hemmed in by White's Pawns on
black squares.

19 . . . .   Q—Q1
20 B x Kt   P x B!

After 20 . . . B x B the position
would be quite level, with a paucity
of possibilities for both players.
The text leads to a more lively
kind of game, at no great risk.

21 Kt—Kt4   K—R1
22 P—KB4   P—B4

P—B5 must not be allowed. The
second occupation of K5 by the
Knight will be of short duration.

23 Kt—K5   B—Q3
24 Q—B3   B x Kt
25 R x B   R—KKt1

Black has some initiative now
because of the open KKt file.

26 R—K2   Q—R5
27 K—R2   R—Kt3

28 P—KKt3   Q—B3
29 R—Kt1   K—Kt2
30 Q—Q3   . . . .

See the introduction. In the
Tournament Book, Howell wisely
comments, "White, if anything, at
a disadvantage on the King-side,
now evolves a plan to break
through on the Queen-side. However, as he can hardly hope to win
such a game, it would be better for
him to simply keep his pieces ready
to shift to whichever side Black
attacks and hold the draw in hand.
With only the heavy pieces left,
Black probably could not break
through."

30 . . . .   P—QR3
31 R—QB1   P—KR4
32 P—KR4   K—R3

Evidently poised for the play
which follows.

33 P—B4   . . . .

While this is not a mistake viewed objectively, it is nevertheless
ill-judged because White is short
of time. Aside from that, 33 P—
Kt3 would prepare this advance
in a more promising form without
allowing the combination which
follows.

33 . . . .   P x P
34 R x BP   . . . .

Capablanca

Maroczy

34 . . . .   R x P!?
35 Q x R?   . . . .

This loses, as do also the fol-
lowing:
I 35 K x R, R—Kt1ch; 36 K—
R2, Q x Pch; 37 Q—R3, Q x Pch;
38 K—R1, R—Kt6 and wins.
II 35 K x R, R—Kt1ch; 36 K—
B2, Q x RPch; 37 K—K3, R—Kt6
ch; 38 K—Q2, R x Qch; 39 K x R,
Q x P and wins.
III 35 K x R, R—Kt1ch; 36 K—
B3, Q x RP and wins.
The above variations are given
by Howell, who shows a draw with
35 K x R, R—Kt1ch; 36 K—R3!
Maroczy adds to this: 36 . . . R—
Kt5; 37 K—R2! Q x Pch; 38 Q—
R3, Q—B3; 39 Q—KB3 and Black
must take a draw.
However, with only one correct
choice in five tries, it is no wonder
that White goes astray, having so
little time available.

35 . . . .   R x R

As White is a Pawn down and
the QP is weak, the rest is quite
easy. Black's King will head for
Q4.

36 R—Q2   Q—Kt3!
37 Q—Kt5ch   . . . .

It is relatively better to exchange
on this square than to allow . . .
Q—Kt5, after which the exchange
will be even more favorable for
Black.

37 . . . .   Q x Q
38 RP x Qch   K—Kt3
39 K—Kt3   R—B3!

Preventing the only counterchance P—Q5, which would now
be answered by . . . R—Q3.

40 K—B3   R—Q3
41 K—Kt3   P—B3
42 P x P   K x P

If now 43 K—R4, R—Q1! threatening . . . R—KKt1—Kt5ch.

43 K—B3   P—R5

44 R—R2   R x P
45 R x P   P—Kt4
46 R—R6ch   K—K2
47 R—R7ch   K—Q3
48 R—R7   R—R5
49 P—R3   K—Q4

White resigns — seemingly prematurely, but he is helpless. If
his Rook remains on the QR file,
Black's King goes to QKt6. If
White's Rook is planted on the K
file, then . . . P—R4 followed by
. . . P—Kt5 forces the issue.
The respective amounts of time
consumed by the players are interesting: Maroczy, three hours;
Capablanca, an hour and a half.

---

59. Lake Hopatcong, 1926
(First Brilliancy Prize)

QUEEN'S PAWN OPENING

Capablanca pursues the same
policy here as in Game No. 52: he
gives up a Pawn for positional
pressure, obtaining a powerful bind
which eventually brings about the
collapse of the hostile position.

E. LASKER   J. R. CAPABLANCA

White   Black

1 P—Q4   Kt—KB3
2 Kt—KB3   P—K3
3 P—KKt3   P—B4
4 P—B4   P x P

An unusual line of play. After
4 . . . P—Q4 we would have a
position which was to become very
popular about a decade later.

5 Kt x P   P—Q4
6 B—Kt2   P—K4!

Seizing the first opportunity to
free his game, despite the likelihood that it will involve the sacrifice of a Pawn.

7 Kt—KB3   P—K5

If 7 . . . Kt—B3? 8 P x P, Kt x P;
9 Kt x P etc.

8 KKt—Q2 . . . .

If 8 Kt—K5, B—Q3; 9 Q—R4ch,
QKt—Q2 or 8 Kt—Q4, P x P; 9
Q—R4ch, B—Q2; 10 Q x BP, Kt—
B3 and Black has an excellent
game in either event.

8 . . . . P x P
9 Q—R4ch B—Q2
10 Q x BP P—K6!

Although this move had to be
foreseen when Black played 6 . . .
P—K4, it nevertheless has a surprising effect. White derives little
benefit from the extra Pawn, as
he remains with a doubled and
isolated KP which is virtually
worthless and at the same time
hampers his development.

Capablanca

Lasker

11 P x P . . . .

And not 11 B x P, P x Ktch; 12
Kt x P, B—K3; 13 Q—R4ch, QKt—
Q2; 14 B x R, Q x B and Black
wins.

11 . . . . B—B3
12 O—O B x B
13 K x B B—K2
14 Kt—QB3 . . . .

It would be interesting to know
whether Capablanca intended to
answer 14 Q—Kt5ch with . . . Q—
Q2, playing for the ending, or with
14 . . . QKt—Q2, offering another
Pawn.

14 . . . . O—O
15 Kt—B3 QKt—Q2
16 P—K4 . . . .

In order to be able to bring
out the Bishop; but the KP thereby becomes more vulnerable.

16 . . . . R—B1

Black continues to develop favorably.

17 Q—Kt5 P—QR3!

Demonstrating to White that he
was wrong if he expected to gain
time with his last move. If now
18 Q x KtP, Kt—B4; 19 Q—Kt4
(not 19 Q—R7?? R—R1), QKt x P;
20 Q—Kt3, Kt x Kt; 21 P x Kt, Kt—
K5 with lasting pressure on the BP.
This variation is characteristic:
fighting to hold the extra Pawn
occasions White all sorts of inconvenience; yet if he loses the
Pawn, he is likely to be left with
an inferior game anyway.

18 Q—KB5 R—B4
19 Q—B4 R—B5
20 B—K3 B—B4

Risky-looking at first, because it
seems as if the QR may get into
trouble. However, the move is
perfectly feasible, and has the merit of making way for new pressure
by Black on the K file.

21 Kt—Q2 . . . .

Howell's suggestion of simplifying by returning the Pawn is likewise not quite satisfactory: 21
B x B, Kt x B; 22 QR—Q1, Q—K2;
23 Kt—K5, R—Kt5; 24 Kt—Q3,
Kt x Kt; 25 P x Kt, R x Pch; 26
R—B2 and now 26 . . . Q—Kt5!

21 . . . . R—Kt5
22 P—Kt3 Q—K2

23 P—QR3	B x B
24 Q x B	R—Kt3
25 QR—Q1	R—K3
26 P—QKt4	. . . .

To prevent . . . Kt—B4. But White's game has become too difficult for successful resistance.

26	R—B1
27 Q—Q4?	. . . .

R—B5 might have been tried here; certainly the text is useless. However, White is already in time pressure, making his troubles altogether intolerable!

27	R—Q3!

Regains the Pawn, for if 28 Q—K3, Kt—Kt5; 29 Q—B3, QKt—K4 and wins.

28 Kt—Q5	Kt x Kt
29 P x Kt	Q x Pch
30 K—Kt1	Kt—B3
31 Kt—Kt3	. . . .

QR—K1 would have prolonged his resistance. After the text, Black wins prettily.

31	R x P
32 Q—B2	Q x R!
33 R x Q	R x Rch
34 K—Kt2	Kt—Kt5

If now 35 Q—K2? R—B7!

35 Q—Kt6	P—R4!
36 Kt—B5	R—K1

White resigns. The finish might have been 37 K—B3, R—K6ch; 38 K—B4, R—Q5ch; 39 K—Kt5, R—K4ch; 40 K—R4, Kt—B7ch etc. An object lesson in the art of constantly creating difficulties for one's opponent.

---

60. New York, 1927

QUEEN'S GAMBIT DECLINED

One of Capablanca's most enjoyable games. There is artistry of a high order in the clarity and logic of his play, and in the perfectly natural way in which his pretty combinative attack arises out of his positional manoeuvring.

A. NIMZOVICH   J. R. CAPABLANCA

White	Black
1 P—QB4	Kt—KB3
2 Kt—KB3	P—K3
3 P—Q4	P—Q4
4 P—K3	. . . .

Both this and the next move are unnecessarily conservative, ceding equality to Black at once.

4	B—K2
5 QKt—Q2	O—O
6 B—Q3	P—B4

Giving Black his fair share of the center by discouraging the intended P—K4.

7 QP x P	Kt—R3!

A good reply, played to avoid the waste of time resulting from . . . B x P. However, 8 Kt—Kt3 (instead of White's colorless reply) would have maintained equality.

8 O—O	Kt x P
9 B—K2	P—QKt3
10 P x P?	. . . .

A further error of judgment, more serious than the previous inexactitudes. Black now acquires a slight but imperceptible pressure which is steadily augmented. 10 P—QKt3 followed by B—Kt2 was the proper course.

10	Kt x P

Now it is too late for 11 P—QKt3 (11 . . . B—B3; 12 Kt—Q4, Kt—B6).

11 Kt—Kt3   . . . .

White embarks on a policy of simplification, but Black manages to retain his advantage.

11 . . . .   B—Kt2
12 Kt x Kt   B x Kt
13 Q—R4   . . . .

Continuing the policy of simplification, but 13 B—Q2 would have been preferable.

13 . . . .   Q—B3!

Capablanca could have prevented the following exchange by . . . P—QR3; but as a matter of fact, he welcomes the removal of White's KB, because of the resulting weakness of White's white squares and because the main problem is to hamper the development of White's QB.

14 B—R6   B x B
15 Q x B   Kt—Kt5

The Knight is headed for Q6, exploiting the freshly-created weakness of the white squares.

16 Q—K2   KR—Q1
17 P—QR3   . . . .

17 Kt—K1, in order to play 18 P—QR3 without allowing . . . Kt—Q6, seems more natural. However, Kmoch shows that this would likewise be inadequate: 17 Kt—K1, QR—B1; 18 P—QR3, Kt—B3; 19 Kt—Q3, B—K2; 20 B—Q2, Q—B4! 21 Kt—B1, B—B3; 22 R—R2, Q—Q4; 23 R—Q1, Kt—R4 and White has a lost game.

17 . . . .   Kt—Q6
18 Kt—K1   Kt x Kt
19 R x Kt   QR—B1
20 R—Kt1   . . . .

It is time to take stock of the situation. Black's development is superior in every respect, and yet it appears that White can achieve approximate equality with P—QKt4 and B—Kt2. How does Capablanca meet the challenge?!

20 . . . .   Q—K4!

This subtle centralizing move, combining threats on both wings, assures Black's advantage a lasting character.

21 P—KKt3   . . . .

Now White has all his Pawns on black squares, with the prospect that even after his Bishop is "developed," it will be just as useless as it has been hitherto. Yet the weakening advance of the KKtP could hardly have been averted:

I 21 B—Q2, B—Q3; 22 P—KKt3 (or 22 P—B4, Q—K5 with clear advantage to Black), R—B7; 23 Q—Q3, R x P! 24 B—B3, R x R; 25 B x Q, R x Rch; 26 K—Kt2, B—K2 and Black should win.

II 21 P—QKt4, B—Q3; 22 P—KKt3, Q—K5; 23 R—Kt2, P—QR4! (a characteristic move in this and later variations: White's Pawns on black squares are targets for Black's Bishop); with a very superior game for Black (Kmoch).

21 . . . .   Q—Q4!

Black is now in a position to menace the vulnerable white squares on the Queen-side.

22 P—QKt4   B—B1
23 B—Kt2   Q—R7!

White is now powerless against the decisive advance . . . P—QR4! which if played, will win a Pawn.

24 R—R1   . . . .

Alekhine criticizes this move, and gives a long variation to prove that 24 QR—Q1, R x R; 25 R x R, P—QR4; 26 Q—R6! R—B7; 27 R—Q8 gives Black a draw. However, 25 . . . P—QR4 is premature here, whereas the simple 25 . . . Q—Kt6 continues to maintain the pressure.

In the event of 24 QR—B1 there would have followed 24 . . . R x R! 25 R x R, P—QR4 with decisive advantage.

24 . . . .   Q—Kt6
25 B—Q4   . . . .

In order to prevent . . . P—QR4,
he must allow the inroad of Black's
Rooks.

25 . . . .   R—B7
26 Q—R6?   . . . .

It is true that 26 Q—B3 is impossible because of R x B. Yet the
removal of the Queen is suicidal,
and should have been replaced by
Q—B1 or Q—Q1; although Black
would have retained a marked advantage.

Capablanca

Nimzovich

26 . . . .   P—K4!

Making way for the doubling of
the Rooks, with some pretty play
in prospect.

27 B x KP   R(1)—Q7
28 Q—Kt7   . . . .

White is at a loss for a good
move:
I 28 R—KB1, Q x KP! 29 B—
B4, R x P! and mate follows.
II 28 Q—B1, Q—Q4; 29 B—Q4,
Q—KR4! (a subtle move; if 29
. . . Q—B6; 30 QR—B1, R x P; 31
R x R with some chances); 30 P—
KR4 (else . . . R x P wins easily),
Q—B6 and now 31 QR—B1 is im-
possible because of 31 . . . R x P

forcing mate (Capablanca).
III 28 QR—B1, R x P; 29 R x R,
Q x R and wins.

28 . . . .   R x P
29 P—Kt4   Q—K3
30 B—Kt3   R x P!

Breaks White's resistance. If
now 31 B x R, Q x KtPch; 32 K—
R1, Q—R6! followed by mate.
White has nothing left to play for.

31 Q—B3   R(R7)—Kt7ch
32 Q x R   R x Qch
33 K x R   Q x KtP
34 QR—Q1   P—KR4
35 R—Q4   Q—Kt4
36 K—R2   P—R4
37 R—K2   P x P
38 P x P   B—K2
39 R—K4   B—B3
40 R—KB2   Q—Q4
41 R—K8ch   K—R2
White resigns. A fine game.

---

61. New York, 1927
QUEEN'S INDIAN DEFENSE

Capablanca's clear, simple and
correct play makes mincemeat of
Alekhine's nervous and badly timed
"attack." This is one of the most
crushing defeats ever administered
to Alekhine.

A. ALEKHINE   J. R. CAPABLANCA

White	Black
1 P—Q4	Kt—KB3
2 P—QB4	P—K3
3 Kt—KB3	P—QKt3
4 P—KKt3	B—Kt2
5 B—Kt2	P—B4?!

A move whose merits have been
hotly disputed; the question is
whether, a f t e r White's reply,
Black has a cramped game or
whether White's center is weak.
In actual practice, White has had

much the better of the argument.

| 6 P—Q5 | P x P |
| 7 Kt—R4 | P—Kt3 |

In the Nottingham Tournament Alexander introduced a novel line of play against Vidmar: 7 . . . Q—B2; 8 P x P, P—Q3; 9 O—O, QKt—Q2; 10 Kt—QB3, P—QR3; 11 P—K4, P—Kt3; 12 P—B4, O—O—O! 13 B—K3, B—Kt2 and Black is well prepared to absorb the shock of an eventual P—K5.

8 Kt—QB3	B—Kt2
9 O—O	O—O
10 B—B4	. . . .

A questionable move, for at best it is a loss of time. Two superior continuations are 10 B—Kt5! (manifestly superior to the text, because of the pin and the resulting indirect menace against Q5) and 10 P x P, P—Q3; 11 P—K4, QKt—Q2; 12 P—B4, R—K1; 13 R—K1 (as in a famous game Vajda-Monticelli, Budapest 1926) and the formidable push P—K5 will soon be feasible.

10	P—Q3
11 P x P	Kt—R4
12 B—Q2	Kt—Q2
13 P—B4	. . . .

Evidently fearing that 13 P—K4 would allow 13 . . . Kt—K4; 14 P—B4, Kt—Q6.

| 13 . . . . | P—QR3! |

Well-timed, for if White stops for the logical move P—K4, then . . . P—QKt4 gains considerable ground for Black on the Queenside.

| 14 B—B3? | . . . . |

This does not leave White's KKt with very promising prospects. 14 P—R4, P—B5; 15 K—R1! was better.

| 14 . . . . | KKt—B3 |
| 15 P—R4 | P—B5! |

Good; this creates a fine square for the QKt at QB4, and also makes possible . . . P—QKt4, as White could not capture twice on QKt5 because of the ultimate . . . Q—Kt3ch.

| 16 B—K3? | . . . . |

Whereas Capablanca makes the most of his opportunities, Alekhine flits from one project to another. 16 P—K4 was still the logical course, and had to be played at all cost. As White plays, he is soon left with a lost game.

| 16 . . . . | Q—B2 |
| 17 P—KKt4 | . . . . |

This is all of a piece with the previous play. It gives no attack and only creates new weaknesses which are later ruthlessly exploited.

17	Kt—B4
18 P—Kt5	KKt—Q2
19 P—B5	KR—K1!

A useful gain of time against the threatened P—B6. Black now takes the initiative, with results that are soon apparent. White's aggressive setup is only make-believe, while Black's iron grip on the center squares will soon tell heavily in his favor.

Capablanca

Alekhine

20 B—B4	B—K4!
21 B—Kt4	. . . .

Alekhine suggests Kt—Kt2 as somewhat better; White's position has become altogether too disjointed.

21	Kt—Kt6
22 P x P	RP x P

Not 22 . . . Kt x R? 23 P x BPch.

23 R—Kt1	B x Kt

And now White's QP must go; he is punished for his neglect of the center.

24 P x B	Q—B4ch
25 P—K3	Kt—K4
26 B—B3	Kt—Q6!

For he can answer 27 R x Kt with . . . Kt x B.

27 K—R1	B x P
28 R x Kt	Kt x B
29 QR—Kt1	. . . .

Or 29 B x B, Kt x B; 30 R—QKt1, Kt x KP.

29	R x P!
30 Kt—Kt2	R x B!
31 R x R	Kt x Kt
32 K x Kt	R—K1
33 K—B1	. . . .

Alekhine could have resigned here without a qualm, but he says he was too pressed for time to find the right moment!

33	B x R
34 Q x B	Q x P
35 R—K1	R x Rch
36 K x R	Q—Kt8ch
37 K—Q2	Q x Pch
38 K—B1	Q—K4
39 K—Kt2	K—Kt2
40 Q—B2	P—QKt4
41 Q—Kt6	P x P
42 Q x RP	Q—K7ch

White resigns. Alekhine: "I am ashamed of this game, but freely admit that my opponent took excellent advantage of my mistakes."

---

62. New York, 1927
(First Brilliancy Prize)

QUEEN'S GAMBIT DECLINED

This might well be considered the classic Capablanca game. It shows his proverbial clean-cut and logical simplicity in its most attractive form.

J. R. CAPABLANCA   R. SPIELMANN

White	Black
1 P—Q4	P—Q4
2 Kt—KB3	P—K3
3 P—B4	QKt—Q2
4 Kt—B3	KKt—B3
5 B—Kt5	B—Kt5

It is now White's task to demonstrate that this early attempt at counterattack is premature. In the first-round game between the same players there followed 6 P x P, P x P; 7 Q—Kt3? P—B4! 8 P—QR3, B x Ktch; 9 Q x B, P—B5! 10 Q—K3ch! Q—K2; 11 Q x Qch, K x Q and Capablanca had to fight hard to maintain himself against the hostile Queen-side majority.

6 P x P	P x P
7 Q—R4	. . . .

An improvement, but still not the best course, which seems to consist in 7 P—K3, P—B4; 8 B—Q3, Q—R4; 9 Q—B2, P—B5; 10 B—B5 and White has strong trumps in the later possibilities of P—K4 or Kt—K5.

7	B x Ktch?

Very plausible, but inferior to 7 . . . P—B4! Spielmann thought that this could be answered successfully by 8 P x P, B x Ktch; 9 P x B, O—O; 10 P—B6—realizing

only after the game that 10 . . .
Q—B2! would have given him an
excellent game.

| 8 P x B | O—O |
| 9 P—K3 | P—B4? |

After the more discreet . . .
P—B3 Black would still have the
inferior game because of his weakness on the Black squares and the
power of the hostile Bishops. After
the text these difficulties are even
more intensified.

| 10 B—Q3 | P—B5 |
| 11 B—B2 | Q—K2 |

Viewed superficially, Black's position looks quite promising because of the Queen-side Pawns.
However, the threatened smash-up
of Black's position by P—K4 looms
ever more threateningly.

| 12 O—O | P—QR3 |
| 13 KR—K1 | . . . . |

Already menacing the deadly advance P—K4.

| 13 . . . . | Q—K3 |

Unpinning to prevent P—K4. But
this is a palliative whose effect
wears off at once.

| 14 Kt—Q2! | . . . . |

Renewing the threat of P—K4.

| 14 . . . . | P—QKt4 |

Virtually forced, as the QBP has
become too shaky.

| 15 Q—R5! | . . . . |

Black's position has become more
uncomfortable than ever. He is
threatened with catastrophe by P—
QR4 and the standing threat P—
K4; aside from which the pressure
on the black squares (chiefly expressed by the possibility of Q—B7
in some positions) is distinctly
uncomfortable.

| 15 . . . . | Kt—K5 |

Preventing P—K4, but leading
to a different kind of refutation.
However, if 15 . . . B—Kt2; 16 P—
B3! is crushing, as P—K4 would
then follow with heightened effect.

| 16 Kt x Kt | P x Kt |

P—K4 has been ruled out, but
now Black's downfall comes on the
Queen-side.

| 17 P—QR4! | Q—Q4 |

Spielmann hopes to save the situation by gaining a move with his
attack on the Bishop for protecting
the Queen-side Pawns.

This wan hope meets with a
brusque refutation, but passive defense with 17 . . . R—Kt1 would
have been futile: 18 KR—Kt1, Q—
Q4; 19 B—B4, R—Kt3; 20 P x P,
R x P; 21 R x R, P x R; 22 B—R4
etc.

Spielmann

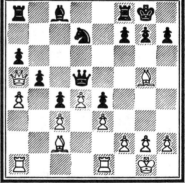

Capablanca

| 18 P x P! | . . . . |

Beginning a combination which
is enchanting not so much because
of its brilliancy, but **because it
refutes Black's faulty strategy in
so convincing a manner.**

| 18 . . . . | Q x B |
| 19 B x P | R—Kt1 |

19 . . . R—R2 looks like the
logical move, but then comes 20

P—Kt6! Q x Q; 21 P x R! B—Kt2
(or 21 . . . Q x R; 22 R x Q, Kt—
Kt3; 23 P—R8(Q), Kt x Q; 24
B x Kt etc.); 22 R x Q, B x B; 23
R x P, R—R1; 24 R—K2, B—Kt2;
25 R—R5, K—B1; 26 R—Kt2, B—
B1; 27 R—Kt4, K—K2; 28 R x P
winning easily.

20 P x P!   . . . .

Amusing: with a piece down
White can offer the exchange of
Queens and Black dare not accept.
The QRP must cost Black at least
a piece.

20 . . . .   R Kt4
21 Q—B7   . . . .

And this deadly penetration
clinches matters.

21 . . . .   Kt—Kt3
22 P—R7   B—R6

P—R8(Q) is now good enough,
but Capablanca plays for higher
game.

23 KR—Kt1!   R x Rch

Or 23 . . . R—B1; 24 Q x Kt,
R x Q; 25 R x R and the double
threat of P—R8(Q) or R—Kt8 is
conclusive.

24 R x R   P—B4
25 B—B3   P—B5
26 P x P   Resigns

Perfect play by Capablanca all
the way.

---

63. New York, 1927
(Prize for the best-played game)
CARO-KANN DEFENSE

A very fine game, despite its
lack of fireworks or other showy
features. The final **zugzwang** phase,
which lends the game a particularly instructive character must (almost!) have been enjoyed by
Nimzovich himself.

A. NIMZOVICH	J. R. CAPABLANCA
White	Black
1 P—K4	P—QB3
2 P—Q4	P—Q4
3 P—K5	B—B4
4 B—Q3	B x B
5 Q x B	P—K3

Black has an easy game. Despite
the inevitable weakness of White's
white squares and the ineffectual
state of his Bishop, Nimzovich had
a fondness for this line of play.
Black will have promising possibilities in operations on the QB
file, as well as fine placements for
his Knights at QB5 and KB4.

6 Kt—QB3	Q—Kt3
7 KKt—K2	P—QB4
8 P x P	B x P
9 O—O	. . . .

9 Q—Kt3, Kt—K2; 10 Q x P,
KR—Kt1 would be distinctly unfavorable for White.

9	Kt—K2
10 Kt—R4	Q—B3
11 Kt x B	Q x Kt
12 B—K3	Q—B2
13 P—KB4	Kt—B4

As Black's position is quite satisfactory, it is time for White to
be mapping a permanent plan of
action. This Nimzovich proceeds
to do, but it takes the form of
establishing an "overprotected"
and seemingly impregnable strong
point on Q4. This turns out to be
inadequate, and therefore it would
have been better to play for the
opening of the QB file, as recommended in the Tournament Book:
14 QR—B1, Kt—B3; 15 B—B2, P—
KR4; 16 P—B4, P x P; 17 Q x P,
O—O; 18 KR—Q1 followed by Kt—
B3—K4 etc. with equality.

14 P—B3	Kt—B3
15 QR—Q1?	. . . .

It was still possible to switch to
the right plan.

15 . . . .   P—KKt3!

Most players would automatically continue with . . . P—KR4, in order to fortify the position of the Knight on KB4. But Capablanca deliberately provokes the following thrust, foreseeing the weakening effect it will have on White's game.

16 P—KKt4?   . . . .

A serious positional blunder, as Capablanca demonstrates in short order. Much better would have been 16 B—B2, P—KR4; 17 R—Q2 followed by R—B1 in the hope of advancing the QBP.

16 . . . .   Kt x B
17 Q x Kt   P—KR4
18 P—Kt5   . . . .

Completely negating the purpose of his sixteenth move, and yet what is he to do? After the natural 18 P—KR3 there follows 18 . . . P x P; 19 P x P, O—O—O and the threats of . . . R—R5 and . . . P—KKt4 are still decisive.

From this point on, White has a positionally lost game, and the most he can expect is to find some way of prolonging his resistance.

18 . . . .   O—O
19 Kt—Q4   Q—Kt3
20 R—B2   KR—B1
21 P—QR3   R—B2
22 R—Q3   Kt—R4

As Capablanca soon realizes, . . . Kt—K2 is more exact.

23 R—K2   R—K1

Black changes his mind, observing that the intended 23 . . . Kt—B5; 24 Q—B2, Kt x RP (25 P x Kt? Q—Kt8ch!) can be answered by 25 P—B5! with unpleasant complications.

24 K—Kt2   Kt—B3!

The right idea. White's Knight must be removed, so that Black can play . . . R—B5 and menace White's weak KBP. This explanation makes the text seem quite obvious; yet most players would have adopted the mechanical move . . . Kt—B5.

25 R(2)—Q2   . . . .

Nimzovich is still busily "overprotecting." 25 Kt x Kt, Q x Kt would eventually lead to the same kind of position, but White could have put up a better fight.

25 . . . .   R(1)—QB1
26 R—K2   Kt—K2!
27 R(2)—Q2   R—B5!

At last. The next step is to remove White's Knight.

28 Q—R3   . . . .

White could stop the attack on the fifth rank with P—Kt3, but in that event his Queen-side as well would be fatally weak.

28 . . . .   K—Kt2!

The point of this will be seen two moves later.

29 R—KB2   P—R4
30 R—K2   Kt—B4!
31 Kt x Ktch   . . . .

Slightly better was 31 R(2)—Q2, Kt x Kt; 32 R x Kt, R x R; 33 P x R, R—B8ch; 34 K—B2, Q—Kt4 with a winning position.

31 . . . .   KtP x Kt!

For if 32 Q x RP, R—KR1! 33 Q—B3, R—R5 and the KBP falls. The position is now ripe for the exploitation of White's weak Pawn structure.

32 Q—B3   K—Kt3
33 R(2)—Q2   R—K5!

Magnificent centralization, and meanwhile he makes room for the other Rook.

34 R—Q4   R—B5
35 Q—B2   . . . .

Here or next move it would have been somewhat better to play R x R (B4), but in the long run White could not escape the effects of being left exclusively on the defensive.

35 . . . .   Q—Kt4!
36 K—Kt3   R(B5) x R!

Forcing White's reply, for if 37 R x R? R—K7. The rest is a beautiful study in how to reduce one's opponent to helplessness.

37 P x R   Q—B5

Seizing the only open file.

38 K—Kt2   P—Kt4!

This Pawn will be advanced to Kt6, if necessary, in order to eliminate possible moves at White's disposal.

39 K—Kt1   P—Kt5
40 P x P   P x P
41 K—Kt2   Q—B8!

(see diagram next column)

Neither the White Queen nor Rook can now move. If 41 P—R4, P—Kt6 wins. Hence the King must move, allowing a new intrusion.

42 K—Kt3   Q—KR8!

If now 43 R—K2, R x R; 44 Q x R, Q—Kt8ch wins the QP. If 43 Q—B3, P—R5ch wins. If 43 P—R4, R—K8 wins. If 43 Q—Kt2, Q x Qch wins a Pawn. A delicious position!

43 R—Q3   R—K8

Capablanca

Nimzovich

44 R—KB3   R—Q8
45 P—Kt3   . . . .

On 45 K—R3, R—Q7 is decisive, while if 45 R—Kt3, Q—K5! 46 R x P, R—Q6ch; 47 K—R4, R—KB6 wins.

45 . . . .   R—QB8!

Leaving White helpless, for example 46 P—R3, R—Kt8ch; 47 K—R4, R—Kt5 mate; or 46 Q—Q2, P—R5ch! and wins; or 46 K—R3 (or K—R4), R—B7! and wins; finally, if 46 Q—K2, Q—Kt8ch with a rapid collapse of White's game in order.

46 R—K3   R—B8

White resigns, as he must lose the Queen. (If 47 Q—K2, Q—Kt8 ch; 48 K—R3, R—K8!) A classic ending.

Part V
Ex-Champion
1927-1942

During this final period of Capablanca's career, he continued his avoidance of 1 P—K4. We find it here in an exhibition game (Game no. 93, a brilliant Four Knights' Game against Steiner) ; also in Game no. 112 against Czerniak, a cut-and-thrust affair all the way. Game no. 88, with Colle, begins as a Reti Opening, but soon transposes into a Dragon Variation in which Capablanca's crystalline position play extracts every bit of advantage from the opening and middle game.

In Games no. 65 and 67, Capablanca refutes Alekhine's Cambridge Springs Defense in interesting style. The ending in the latter encounter is particularly worthy of study. Game no. 69 shows how difficut it is for Black to make headway in the Orthodox Defense when the center Pawns are exchanged at an early stage. In Game no. 74, Steiner undertakes to play Capablanca's own version of the Orthodox Defense; but the Cuban produces one of his most perfect games—an enchanting example of his style at its very best. In Game no. 77 we have a welcome bit of variety in this opening, in that Capablanca plays the less hackneyed B—B4 instead of B—Kt5. Becker tries too hard for a counterattack, and is crushed in double-quick time. Game no. 78 is a classic example of how to defeat an opponent who is content to shift his pieces back and forth, saying in so many words "Come and get me." In Games no. 81 and 83, against Gilg and Maroczy, Capablanca's success is due in the first case to superior handling of the middle game, and in the second to keen exploitation of his opponent's faulty treatment of the opening. Game no. 92 is one of the most important milestones in the evolution of the Slav Defense, and the later play is extremely interesting. In Game no. 98, Levenfish's Meran Defense undergoes a smashing refutation in short order. A defeat just as drastic but of a different kind is meted out to Znosko-Borovsky after his adoption of the Tarrasch Defense (Game no. 108) with its inevitable positional weaknesses. The Queen's Gambit with Havasi (Game no. 75) echoes Capablanca's famous encounter with Bogolyubov at Moscow 1925; but it is interesting in its own right as well. It is instructive to study the lines of play adopted by Capablanca against the Nimzoindian Defense during this period. In the earliest example (Game no. 71, against Nimzovich himself) Capablanca botches the opening, but handles the balance of the game with wonderful resourcefulness. The next game (no. 76) is very neatly handled by the Cuban, who wins a piece early in the middle game by means of artistic play. Equally convincing is his demolition of the defense in Game no. 80 against Mattison. In Game no. 89, Colle is just on the point of getting a powerful attack; but Capablanca comes first with a clever sacrifice of the exchange. Game no. 96, in which poor Ragozin is tied up in knots, is another of the great Capablanca classics; it was awarded a special prize. Game no. 110 is an important theoretical landmark in this opening, and incidentally represents a crushing defeat of Euwe. Nor does Mikenas fare any better in Game no. 111, which is rounded off with a neat combination.

There is only one example of the Queen's Indian (Game no. 94), in which Thomas has a bad game from the beginning. The comical way in which his Queen is subsequently trapped is diverting! Capablanca's first and only victory against Rubinstein takes place in Game no. 72, and shows the Cuban playing flawlessly in a very difficult struggle. Game no. 87 transposes into a King's Indian Defense, in which Yates is outplayed in short order. In Game no. 107, Romih's weakening of the black squares soon turns out to have catastrophic effect. Ever the innovator, Tartakover introduces a tricky variation of the Budapest Defense (Game no. 68), which leads to such complications that both players go wrong! But in due course Capablanca winds up with a nicely handled ending with Bishops of opposite color.

In Game no. 99 Capablanca plays the English Opening in unconventional fashion and then proceeds to deploy his Bishops to good effect. The three examples of Reti's Opening have diverse characters: in Game no. 90 Santasiere adopts the London System and is trounced in short order; Lilienthal (Game no. 102) adopts the same system, plays too timidly and finally succumbs in a well-played ending by Capablanca; Game no. 105 is one of the earliest specimens of the Catalan System, and after starting out with an initial disadvantage, Capablanca steers into a favorable ending, which he eventually wins after some exciting play.

With the black pieces, Capablanca's choice of openings is equally interesting. Defending the Ruy Lopez against Thomas (Game no. 104), he obtains a won game with astounding rapidity. In Game no. 103 (a Vienna Game with Kan), it is interesting to see how skilfully he evades the draw and always manages to maintain some initiative. The Sicilian serves him well against Lasker (Game no. 101)—the last decisive encounter between these two great masters. A French Defense adopted against Fine (Game no. 109) brings the Cuban to the verge of ruin; but he makes a marvellous recovery in what is one of the most attractive middle games of his whole career.

Capablanca's use of the Orthodox Defense was somewhat curtailed after the Championship Match of 1927. An outstanding example is the celebrated game from this match which is so fine a specimen of Capablanca's defensive skill. In Game no. 95 Alatortsev plays without energy, and is bowled over very quickly by a neat Rook sacrifice. Game no. 97 is still another fine example of Capablanca's resourcefulness in difficult situations; the ending is full of interest right to the very last move. In Game no. 100, a vigorous counterattack wins neatly and quickly. There is one example of the Slav, in which Capablanca easily refutes Ragozin's enterprising but unsound Pawn sacrifice (Game no. 106).

In Games 79 and 84 against Johner and Winter, Capablanca adopts the Nimzoindian Defense to good effect, maneuvering cleverly against hostile Pawn weaknesses. But it was with the Queen's Indian Defense that he achieved some of his finest victories during this period. For example, there is the splendid win against Bogolyubov (Game no. 70), which can probably be explained adequately only in psychological terms; Game no. 73, in which Marshall's premature attack is repulsed with decisive effect; Game no. 82, an even finer game, along much the same lines; Game no. 85, in which Canal's combinations prove inferior to those of Capablanca; Game no. 86, in which Monticelli is forced into a lost postion without making any overt mistake; and Game no. 91, in which Marshall is made to pay the penalty for inferior opening play. An instructive set of games!

64. World Championship
Match, 1927

(Third Game)

INDIAN DEFENSE

Capablanca shows to great advantage here, while his opponent, as he later admitted, lets his nerves get the better of him. The second half of the game is a remarkable example of a powerful and concentrated attack carried on by only a few pieces.

J. R. Capablanca A. Alekhine

White	Black
1 P—Q4	Kt—KB3
2 Kt—KB3	P—QKt3
3 P—KKt3	B—Kt2
4 B—Kt2	P—B4
5 O—O	P x P
6 Kt x P	B x B
7 K x B	P—Q4

A dubious move. The opening variation adopted by White is perfectly harmless, and Black need only play 7 . . . P—KKt3, followed in due course by . . . Q—B1—Kt2 ch to obtain a perfectly even and perhaps superior position. The text is playable, but it may involve a premature opening up of the game which can be very troublesome for Black.

8 P—QB4!	P—K3

Better was 8 . . . P x P; 9 Q—R4ch, Q—Q2; 10 Kt—Kt5, Q—B3ch.

9 Q—R4ch	Q—Q2
10 Kt—Kt5!	Kt—B3
11 P x P!	P x P

The opening of new lines is un-pleasant for Black, in view of his backward development. If 11 . . . Kt x P; 12 P—K4 followed by R—Q1 with a decidedly inferior game for Black.

12 B—B4	R—B1
13 R—B1!	B—B4?

White was threatening 14 Kt—B7ch, R x Kt; 15 B x R, Q x B; 16 R x Kt etc.

While Black's situation has admittedly become critical, he could still have saved himself with Rabinovich's suggestion 13 . . . Kt—K5! If 14 Kt—B7ch, R x Kt; 15 B x R, Kt—B4; 16 Q—KB4, Kt—K3; 17 Q—QR4, Kt—B4 with a draw by repetition of moves.

14 P—QKt4!	B x KtP

And here Dr. Lasker's recommendation 14 . . . Kt x P; 15 Kt—Q6ch, K—Q1; 16 Q x Qch, K x Q; 17 Kt x R, R x Kt would offer better drawing prospects.

15 R x Kt!	. . . .

Stronger than the win of the exchange with Kt—B7ch.

15	R x R
16 Q x B	Kt—K5
17 Kt—Q2	Kt x Kt
18 Q x Kt	O—O
19 R—Q1	. . . .

The following play is most instructive. Capablanca soon demonstrates in a highly convincing manner the superiority of the two minor pieces against the Rook. His immediate object is to remove the weak QP.

19	R—B4
20 Kt—Q4	R—K1

| 21 Kt—Kt3 | QR—B1 |
| 22 P—K3 | Q—R5 |

Deciding that the QP cannot last much longer in any event, Black decides to exchange it for the QRP. This looks like a good bargain, as Black secures two connected passed Pawns on the Queen-side; but so powerful a r e Capablanca's threats on the other wing, that these passed Pawns never advance a single square.

| 23 Q x P! | R—B7 |

If 23 . . . Q x P; 24 R—QR1 and 25 R x P.

| 24 R—Q2! | R x RP |

. . . Q x P would lead to much the same kind of play.

| 25 R x R | Q x R |
| 26 Q—B6! | . . . . |

Beginning the final a t t a c k. Black's reply is forced, for if 26 . . . R—Q1; 27 B—B7, R—QB1; 28 Q—Q7, Q—R3; 29 B—Q8, P—R3; 30 Kt—Q4 followed by Kt—B5 with a winning attack.

| 26 . . . . | R—KB1 |
| 27 Kt—Q4 | . . . . |

Alekhine

Capablanca

White threatens B—K5 followed by B x P with a mating attack.

Black appears to have no adequate defense, for example 27 . . . R—Q1 (angling for . . . Q—Q4ch. If instead 27 . . . P—B3; 28 Kt—K6 and the Rook is lost wherever it moves! Or 27 . . . Q—R3; 28 Kt—B5, P—Kt3; 29 Q—B6! or 28 . . . K—R1; 29 Kt x P! and wins); 28 P—K4, P—KR3; 29 B—K5! threatening B x P.

| 27 . . . . | K—R1 |
| 28 B—K5 | P—B3 |

B x Pch was threatened. If 28 . . . R—KKt1; 29 P—R4! forcing fatal weaknesses in Black's position.

| 29 Kt—K6 | R—KKt1 |
| 30 B—Q4 | P—KR3 |

The threat was 31 Kt x P, R x Kt; 32 Q x BP, Q—Kt1; 33 P—R4 followed by the further advance of the RP to R6.

| 31 P—R4! | . . . . |

Kt x P can be played at once, but the text is even more forcing.

| 31 . . . . | Q—Kt8 |
| 32 Kt x P! | Q—Kt3 |

If instead 32 . . . R x Kt; 33 Q x BP, Q—K5ch; 34 K—Kt1, Q—Kt2; 35 Q x Pch, K—Kt1; 36 Q x R ch, Q x Q; 37 B x Q, K x B; 38 K—B1! and wins.

33 P—R5!	Q—B2
34 Kt—B5	K—R2
35 Q—K4	R—K1
36 Q—B4	Q—B1

Black is receiving a terrible battering; he cannot hold out much longer.

| 37 Kt—Q6 | R—K2 |

Or 37 . . . R—Q1; 38 B x BP! etc.

| 38 B x BP | Q—R1ch |
| 39 P—K4 | R—KKt2 |

40 B x R	K x B
41 Kt—B5ch	K—B2
42 Q—B7ch	Resigns

An admirable game by Capablanca, who exploited every possibility throughout the game.

---

65. World Championship Match, 1927

(Seventh Game)

QUEEN'S GAMBIT DECLINED

Again Alekhine proceeds too nervously in the opening. The manner in which Capablanca snatches the attack from him is most interesting.

J. R. CAPABLANCA   A. ALEKHINE

White	Black
1 P—Q4	P—Q4
2 P—QB4	P—K3
3 Kt—KB3	Kt—Q2
4 Kt—B3	KKt—B3
5 B—Kt5	P—B3
6 P—K3	Q—R4
7 Kt—Q2	B—Kt5
8 Q—B2	O—O
9 B—R4	....

Thus far Capablanca has been content to proceed along the orthodox lines of the Cambridge Springs Defense; the object of the somewhat novel text is to be able to play B—Q3 without having to worry about ... P x P.

| 9 .... | P—B4 |

Black considered the alternative 9 . . . P—K4 for an hour, finally discarding the move because of the variation 10 QP x P, Kt—K5; 11 KKt x Kt, P x Kt; 12 P—K6! Kt—K4; 13 P x Pch, R x P; 14 O—O—O! and while Black is likely to regain his Pawn, he will be left with an inferior ending, despite the coming weakness of the Queenside Pawns.

| 10 Kt—Kt3 | Q—R5 |

Intending a speculative Pawn sacrifice, for after the peaceful 10 . . . Q—B2 White will obtain a two-Bishop game and leave Black with an isolated QP by simply exchanging Pawns.

| 11 B x Kt | Kt x B |

This is virtually forced, since 11 ... P x Kt; 12 BP x P, KP x P would leave Black with a shattered Pawn position.

| 12 QP x P | Kt—K5? |

Relatively better would have been 12 . . . Q—B3 or 12 . . . B x Ktch; 13 Q x B, Kt—K5. It must be admitted, however, that at first glance the Knight move looks promising.

| 13 P x P | B x Ktch |

Or 13 . . . Kt x QBP; 14 R—B1! P x P; 15 Kt x Kt, Q x Q; 16 R x Q, B x Kt; 17 Kt x P remaining a Pawn ahead.

| 14 P x B | Kt x P (B4) |
| 15 R—Q1! | .... |

More effective than 15 P x P, B x P which would only gain time for Black and give him some attacking chances.

| 15 . . .. | P x P |
| 16 R x P | Kt x Kt |

Uniting his opponent's Pawns, but if instead 16 . . . P—QKt3; 17 B—K2, B—Kt2; 18 R—Q4 with considerable advantage to White.

| 17 P x Kt | Q—B3 |
| 18 R—Q4 | R—K1 |

Played to prevent P—B3; while if 19 Q—Q2 (to prepare P—B3), B—K3; 20 P—QB4, P—QR4! intending . . . P—R5 with counterchances. But Capablanca continues to play in the same admirable style:

| 19 B—Q3! | Q x KtP |

20 B x Pch	K—B1
21 B—K4	Q—R6
22 Q—Q2	B—K3
23 P—QB4	P—R4

A g a i n intending counterplay; White must find new attacking methods.

| 24 R—Kt1! | Q x P |

. . . Q—R3 was more discreet; but the temptation to equalize in material was probably too great for Black.

| 25 R—R1 | Q—B2 |
| 26 Q—Kt2! | . . . . |

Threatening 27 Q—R3ch, K—Kt1; 28 B—R7ch, K—R1; 29 R(4)—R4 and wins.

| 26 . . . . | Q—B4 |
| 27 B—Q5! | R—R3? |

White threatened 28 B x B, P x B; 29 R—B4ch, K—Kt1; 30 Q—B2 and wins. The best defense was 27 . . . QR—Q1! 28 B x B! R x R; 29 R—R8ch, K—K2; 30 R x Rch, K x R; 31 D x Pch, K x B, 32 P x R, Q—Kt5ch; 33 K—Q1! P—R5; 34 K—B2 and White should win the ending.

After the inferior text, White wins with a crisply executed attack.

Alekhine

Capablanca

| 28 R—K4 | R—Q3 |

If 28 . . . K—Kt1; 29 R—Kt1 with a winning position.

| 29 R—R7! | K—K2 |

There is no good move: if 29 . . . P—KKt3; 30 Q—B6 forces mate; if 29 . . . P—B3; 30 R—R8 ch wins a piece; if 29 . . . Q—Kt5ch; 30 K—K2, R x B; 31 Q x P ch, K—K2; 32 Q x Pch followed by Q—B7 mate.

| 30 Q x P | K—Q1 |
| 31 B x B | P x B |

If 31 . . . QR x B; 32 Q x P or 31 . . . KR x B; 32 Q—B8ch etc.

| 32 Q x P | Q—Kt5ch |

Forced.

33 Q x Q	P x Q
34 P—B5	R—B3
35 R x KtP	R x P
36 R—R7!	Resigns

There is nothing to be done about White's threat to exchange all the Rooks by 37 R—Kt8ch, R—B1; 38 R x Rch, K x R; 39 R—R8ch etc. If 36 . . . R—QB1? 37 R—Q4 mate!!

---

66.   World Championship Match, 1927

(Twenty-second Game)

QUEEN'S GAMBIT DECLINED

One of the most celebrated games of the match. Capablanca's superhuman patience and defensive genius in this inordinately difficult game earned him the enthusiastic praise of all the critics.

A. ALEKHINE	J. R. CAPABLANCA
White	Black
1 P—Q4	Kt—KB3
2 P—QB4	P—K3
3 Kt—QB3	P—Q4

4 B—Kt5	QKt—Q2
5 P—K3	B—K2
6 Kt—B3	O—O
7 R—B1	P—B3

As is well-known, Capablanca relied exclusively on this defense throughout the match.

8 B—Q3	P x P
9 B x P	Kt—Q4
10 B x B	Q x B
11 Kt—K4	KKt—B3
12 Kt—Kt3	Q—Kt5ch

As the sequel indicates, the exchange of Queens leads to a dreary game for Black in which he is permanently on the defensive. A far preferable equalizing method, discovered subsequently, is 12 . . . P—K4; 13 O—O, P x P; 14 Kt—B5, Q—Q1; 15 KKt x P, Kt—K4; 16 B—Kt3, B x Kt; 17 Kt x B, P—KKt3! (Euwe-Flohr, Nottingham, 1936) and Black has nothing to fear.

13 Q—Q2	Q x Qch
14 K x Q	R—Q1
15 KR—Q1	P—QKt3

It is desirable for Black to free himself by means of . . . P—K4 or . . . P—QB4, but unfortunately this is not easily accomplished! Thus if 15 . . . P—K4; 16 K—K2, P x P; 17 R x P, R—B1; 18 Kt—B5 with powerful pressure (for example 18 . . . Kt—Kt3; 19 Kt—K7ch, K—R1; 20 B x P). Thus, while a freeing move is desirable, it cannot be made safely until Black has obtained more development. A maddening difficulty!

16 P—K4	B—Kt2
17 P—K5	Kt—K1

Not inviting, but he wants to prevent Kt—K4—Q6.

18 K—K3	K—B1

If 18 . . . P—QB4; 19 P—Q5 is in White's favor.

19 Kt—Kt5	P—KR3

20 Kt(5)—K4	K—K2
21 P—B4	P—KB4

It was necessary to prevent P—B5, and either the text or . . . P—Kt3 weakens Black's Pawn structure.

22 Kt—B3	Kt—B2
23 Kt(Kt3)—K2	P—KKt4

If 23 . . . Kt—Q4; 24 B x Kt! BP x B (or 24 . . . KP x B; 25 P—KKt4); 25 Kt—Kt5 with advantage. The text is played with a view to some counterchances, but this hope is stifled by White's reply.

24 P—KR4!	P—Kt5

This soon leads to trouble; better was 24 . . . P x P; 25 R—KR1, R—KKt1!

25 Kt—Kt3	P—QR4
26 B—Kt3!	QR—B1
27 P—R3	R—B1
28 R—Q2	B—R1

It is still too soon for . . . P—B4, which would still be answered advantageously with P—Q5.

29 R(2)—QB2!	P—B4

Now or never.

30 P x P	Kt x BP

In view of the difficulties to which this move leads, . . . P x P has been suggested. But it is anything but inviting.

31 Kt—R4!	Kt(2)—R3

(see diagram next page)

32 B x P!	. . . .

An interesting sacrifice which leads to lively and difficult play.

32	K x B
33 Kt x KtP	QR—Kt1

According to Alekhine, the only line to hold the game was 33 . . .

Capablanca

Alekhine

QR—Q1; 34 R x Kt, Kt x R; 35 R x Kt, QR—Kt1; 36 Kt—R4, KR—B1; 37 R x R, R x R or 34 Kt x B, R—Q6ch; 35 K—B2, KR x Kt; 36 P—Kt4? P x P; 37 P x P, Kt x P; 38 R x Kt, R—R7ch; 39 Kt—K2, R(6)—Q7 etc.

34 Kt x B   R—Kt6ch

If 34 . . . R x Kt; 35 Kt—K2! Kt—Kt6 (else Kt—Q4ch); 36 R—B6ch followed by R—Q1 with a winning position.

35 R—B3   R x Rch
36 P x R!   . . . .

This move looks paradoxical, because it gives up the QB file; but 36 R x R? would be answered by 36 . . . R x Kt; 37 P—Kt4, P x P; 38 P x P, Kt x P; 39 R x Kt, R—R6ch and wins!

36 . . . .   R x Kt
37 R—Q1!   R—KB1

There is nothing better, for if 37 . . . Kt—Kt2; 38 R—QKt1! with decisive advantage.

38 R—Q6ch   K—K2
39 R x P   Kt—B2
40 R—R7ch   K—Q1
41 P—B4!   . . . .

An important move which cuts

down Black's mobility by preventing either . . . Kt—Q4ch or . . . Kt—Kt4.

41 . . . .   Kt(2)—K3

But not 41 . . . Kt—R5; 42 R—R5, Kt—Kt7; 43 R x P, Kt x Pch; 44 K—Q3! R x R; 45 Kt x R, Kt x P; 46 P—R5, Kt—K3; 47 P—Kt3 and White's Pawns are very strong (Tartakover).

42 R—R7?   . . . .

The winning continuation (according to Alekhine) was 42 Kt—K2 (permanently ruling out the possibility of . . . Kt x P), K—B1; 43 Kt—B3, R—Q1; 44 Kt—Q5 and wins. The text allows Capablanca to slip out.

42 . . . .   Kt—B2!

Not 42 . . . Kt x P? 43 R—R8ch. The Knight's move, as will be seen, is an important link in Black's defensive plan.

43 R x P   Kt(4)—K3
44 P—R5   . . . .

Or 44 Kt—K2, K—Q2; 45 Kt—Q4, Kt x Kt; 46 K x Kt, R—QKt1! 47 R—R7, K—B3; 48 P—K6, K—Kt3; 49 R—R4, Kt x Pch; 50 K—K5, R—K1; 51 K x P, P—Kt6! and Black has adequate defensive resources (Alekhine).

44 . . . .   K—Q2!

But not 44 . . . Kt x P; 45 K x Kt, Kt—K3ch; 46 K—K3, P—B5ch; 47 K—K4! P x Kt; 48 R—R8ch and wins (Tartakover).

45 P—R6   Kt x P!

Now this move is playable, although it requires close calculation.

46 K x Kt   Kt—K3ch
47 K—K3   P—B5ch
48 K—B2   P x Ktch
49 K x P   R—KR1!

Black need not fear 50 R—R7ch,

Kt—B2; 51 P—K6ch, K—B3; 52 P—K7, K—Kt3!

50 R—Q5ch	K—K2!
51 P—B5	R x P
52 P—B6	Kt—B1
53 R—B5	K—Q1
54 K x P	R—Kt3ch

White's four Pawns are all disconnected and therefore harmless.

| 55 K—B3 | K—B2 |
| 56 P—Kt4 | Kt—K3 |

56 . . . R x P? 57 R x Rch, K x R; 58 K—K4 would be much more troublesome for Black, and might involve losing possibilities.

57 R—Q5	Kt—B1
58 R—B5	Kt—K3
59 R—Q5	Kt—B1
60 R—R5	R x BP

The game could have been given up as a draw here. The remaining moves were: 61 K—K4, R—B8; 62 R—R7ch, K—B3; 63 R—R6ch, K—Q2; 64 R—R7ch, K—K3; 65 R—R6ch, K—K2; 66 P—R4, Kt—Q2; 67 R—R6, R—K8ch; 68 K—Q4, Kt x P; 69 P—R5, Kt x P; 70 R—R7ch, K—Q3; 71 P—R6, R—QR8; 72 P—R7, Kt—B3; 73 R—QKt7, Kt—Q2; 74 R—Kt2, R x P; 75 R—Q2, Kt—B4; 76 K—B4ch, K—B3; 77 R—KR2, R—R5ch; 78 K—B3, R—KKt5; 79 K—Q2, R—Kt6; 80 R—R5, K—Kt4; 81 K—K2, K—B5; 82 R—R4ch, K—B6; 83 K—B2, R—Q6; 84 R—KB4, K—Q7; 85 K—Kt2, R—Q4; 86 K—B3, K—Q6; drawn. A titanic struggle!

---

67. World Championship, 1927
(Twenty-ninth Game)

QUEEN'S GAMBIT DECLINED

Another hard-fought battle from this epochal struggle. Capablanca's opponent puts up a good fight, but weakens toward the close.

J. R. CAPABLANCA   A. ALEKHINE

White	Black
1 P—Q4	P—Q4
2 P—QB4	P—K3
3 Kt—QB3	Kt—KB3
4 B—Kt5	QKt—Q2
5 P—K3	P—B3
6 Kt—B3	Q—R4

The Cambridge Springs Defense, rehabilitated by Alekhine during this match. The object of Black's 8th move is to secure two Bishops at the expense of what he hopes will be only a temporarily cramped position.

7 Kt—Q2	B—Kt5
8 Q—B2	P x P
9 B x Kt	Kt x B
10 Kt x P	Q—B2
11 P—QR3	B—K2
12 P—KKt3!	. . . .

As Black's policy involves the eventual freeing of his position by . . . P—B4, the Bishop will be well placed at Kt2.

12	O—O
13 B—Kt2	B—Q2
14 P—QKt4	P—QKt3?

The indicated reply to Capablanca's last move, obviously played to prevent or to postpone . . . P—B4. And yet it will soon be apparent that Black should have considered m o r e conservatively with . . . QR—B1, . . . KR—Q1 and . . . B—K1.

| 15 O—O | P—QR4 |

(see diagram next page)

The thrust of the QRP seems to assure Black a clear advantage, for if 16 P—Kt5 (the most plausible. 16 KR—Kt1 loses a Pawn; 16 QR—Kt1 gives up the QR file; 16 P x P, P—QKt4! 17 Kt—Kt6, R x P leaves White with a fatally weak QRP), P x P! 17 B x R, Q x

Alekhine

Capablanca

Kt; 18 B—B3, P—Kt5 and wins; or even more simply 16 . . . QR—B1! and White is lost!
But Capablanca has a convincing reply!

| 16 Kt—K5! | P x P |
| 17 P x P | R x R |

Or 17 . . . B x P; 18 Kt—Kt5 and White regains his Pawn advantageously.

| 18 R x R | R—B1 |

Again if 18 . . . B x P; 19 Kt—Kt5 wins back the Pawn with advantage.

| 19 Kt x B | Q x Kt |

This leads to a difficult game, but if 19 . . . Kt x Kt; 20 Q—Kt3 and Black's game is far from easy.

| 20 Kt—R4! | Q—Q1 |
| 21 Q—Kt3 | Kt—Q4 |

The Pawn weaknesses which are a heritage of Black's impetuous 15th move continue to be noticeable. 21 . . . P—QKt4; 22 Kt—B5 is not an attractive alternative.

| 22 P—Kt5! | P x P |

Black has no choice but to submit to the loss of the QKtP, for 22 . . . P—QB4; 23 P x P, P x P would leave White with an easy win because of the passed QKtP.

| 23 Q x P | R—R1 |

Or 23 R—Kt1; 24 B x Kt, Q x B; 25 Q x Q, P x Q; 26 R—Kt1, P—QKt4; 27 Kt—B3, P—Kt5; 28 Kt x P etc.

| 24 R—QB1 | . . . . |

Not 24 R—Kt1, R x Kt!

24	R—R4
25 Q—B6	B—R6
26 R—Kt1	B—B1

Again threatening . . . R x Kt; but it is too late.

| 27 B x Kt | R x B |
| 28 Kt x P | R—Q3 |

Capablanca has finally won the Pawn, but due to the fact that there are no Queen-side Pawns left, Black has good drawing chances. Hence the following jockeying for position, in which both players endeavor to improve the position of their pieces.

29 Q—Kt7	P—R4
30 Kt—B4	R—Q2
31 Q—K4	R—B2
32 Kt—K5	Q—B1
33 K—Kt2	B—Q3
34 R—QR1	R—Kt2
35 Kt—Q3	P—Kt3
36 R—R6	B—B1
37 R—B6	R—B2

Black offers the exchange because White's Rook is too well posted on the sixth rank.

38 R x R	Q x R
39 Kt—K5	B—Kt2
40 Q—R8ch	K—R2
41 Kt—B3	B—B3
42 Q—R6	K—Kt2
43 Q—Q3	Q—Kt2
44 P—K4	. . . .

Preparing his only winning chance: a passed QP.

44	Q—B3
45 P—R3	Q—B2
46 P—Q5	P x P
47 P x P	Q—B6!

Black's judgment in offering the exchange of Queens is excellent.

48 Q x Q	B x Q
49 K—B1	K—B3
50 K—K2	B—Kt5!

The Bishop is headed for QB4, from where it can prevent the further advance of the QP and at the same time keep an eye on White's KBP, preventing White's King from taking an active part in the game.

51 Kt—Q4	B—B4
52 Kt—B6	K—B4
53 K—B3	K—B3
54 P—Kt4	P x Pch
55 P x P	K—Kt4?

Overlooking a subtle resource. Either . . . B—Q3 or . . . B—Kt3 would have drawn. The text is premature: in his anxiety to simplify further with . . . P—B4, Black overlooks the full effect of White's reply.

| 56 Kt—K5! | . . . . |

For if 56 . . . P—B4 (56 . . . K—B3? is impossible, and if 56 . . . P—B3; 57 Kt—B7ch, K—R5; 58 P—Q6 and Black must give up the Bishop for the Pawn); 57 P—Q6! P x Pch; 58 K—Kt2! B—Kt3; 59 P—Q7, K—B4; 60 Kt—B6! and wins. Note that 58 K—K2? or K—K4? would only draw because of 58 . . . B x QP; 59 Kt—B7ch, K—R5; 60 Kt x B, P—Kt6 etc.

| 56 . . . . | B—Q5? |

. . . B—R6 would still have given very good drawing chances because of the weakness of White's QP.

| 57 Kt x Pch | K—B3 |
| 58 Kt—Q8 | B—Kt3 |

He cannot play 58 . . . K—K4 because of 59 Kt—B6ch. See the previous note.

| 59 Kt—B6 | B—B4 |

Even now the ending is anything but easy. Thus if 60 K—Kt3, B—Q3ch; 61 P—B4, P—Kt4; or 60 K—K2, K—Kt4; 61 P—B3, K—B5. But Capablanca finds the right way!

| 60 K—B4! | B x P |

For if 60 . . . P—Kt4ch; 61 K—B3 followed by K—K2 and P—B3; then, since Black's King is shut out from invasion, White simply brings his King to the Queen-side. Very neat!

| 61 P—Kt5ch | K—B2 |
| 62 Kt—K5ch | K—K2 |

Or 62 . . . K—Kt2; 63 P—Q6 etc.

63 Kt x Pch	K—Q3
64 K—K4	B—Kt6
65 Kt—B4	K—K2
66 K—K5	B—K8
67 P—Q6ch	K—Q2
68 P—Kt6	B—Kt5
69 K—Q5	K—K1
70 P—Q7ch	Resigns

A terrific struggle which has produced some highly instructive play.

---

68. Bad Kissingen, 1928

BUDAPEST DEFENSE

After excusable mistakes by both players in a novel and complicated opening variation, Capablanca produces a characteristically instructive and exactly played ending.

J. R. CAPABLANCA   S. TARTAKOVER

White	Black
1 P—Q4	Kt—KB3
2 P—QB4	P—K4

| 3 P x P | Kt—Kt5 |
| 4 P—K4 | P—Q3?! |

The selection of this tricky opening, especially with a difficult and unfamiliar line of play, is excellent psychology on Black's part. But, whatever the merit of this line of play may be theoretically, the stronger player triumphs over the board.

| 5 P x P | B x P |

This move is less easy to answer than it might seem at first sight: thus if 6 P—KR3, Q—R5; 7 Q—B2, Kt x P; 8 Kt—R3 (8 Q x Kt?? B—Kt6), Q x Pch etc.; or 6 Kt—KB3, B—Kt5ch; 7 B—Q2, B—QB4 etc.

| 6 B—K2! | P—KB4 |

This move of Dr. Balogh's leads to extremely complicated play.

| 7 P x P | Q—K2?! |

White can now win a piece with 8 P—B5, B x BP; 9 Q—R4ch, Kt—B3; 10 Q x Kt, but Black obtains a counter-attack which can be quite dangerous in view of White's retarded development. Capablanca therefore prefers to indulge his bent for simplicity—doubtless the wisest course with limited time at one's disposal.

8 Kt—KB3	B x BP
9 B—Kt5	Kt—KB3
10 Kt—B3	Kt—B3
11 Kt—Q5	Q—B2
12 O—O	O—O—O

Tartakover subsequently concluded that . . . O—O would have been better. The text looks formidable enough, as all of Black's pieces are fully in play and White's position on the King-side and on the Q file is somewhat precarious.

| 13 Kt—Q4 | QKt x Kt |
| 14 Q x Kt | P—B3 |

Now White's Knight dare not play to B3 or K3 (. . . B x Pch),

while after 15 Kt—B4, KR—K1 (threatening to win a piece); 16 B—B3, B—Kt1; 17 Q—B3, P—KR3; 18 B x Kt, P x B; 19 B—R5, Q—B2; 20 B x R, Q x Kt; 21 P—KKt3, Q—Kt4; 22 B—B7, R—B1 Black wins. This variation is not absolutely forced, but it is a good indication of the strength of Black's position.

| 15 B x Kt | P x B |

Tartakover

Capablanca

The crucial position. As will be seen, Capablanca's next m o v e (played in his favorite simplifying style) is not adequate to meet the situation. In the Tournament Book, Tartakover pooh-poohs the sacrifice 16 Q x RP! P x Kt; 17 P x P etc., but this was the correct line of play, as it would have left Black's King badly exposed:

I 17 . . . Q x P; 18 B—B3.
(A) 18 . . . Q—Kt4; 19 QR—B1ch, B—B2 (if 19 . . . K—Q2; 20 B x P, K—K3; 21 KR—K1ch regaining the piece); 20 R—B5, Q—Q6; 21 KR—B1 and wins.
(B) 18 . . . B—K5; 19 QR—B1ch, B—B2 (19 . . . K—Q2; 20 Q—R4ch); 20 Q—R8ch, K—Q2; 21 Q—R4ch and wins.
II 17 . . . K—Q2; 18 KR—K1! B—K4 (18 . . . Q x P; 19 Q—R4ch! K—B1; 20 B—B3 and wins); 19 B—Kt5ch, K—K2; 20 Q—R3ch! R—Q3; 21 P—B4 winning.

Other moves (such as 17 . . .
B—B2 or . . . KR—K1) would
not diminish the force of White's
attack.

16 Q x BP?	Q x Q?

A sad necessity, says Tartakover
—but it isn't!! As Balogh has
shown, Black could have obtained
the advantage here with 16 . . .
Q—Kt3!!
  I 17 Q x Q, P x Q! 18 Kt—B3,
B x Pch; 19 K—R1, R—Q7 with
advantage.
  II 17 Kt—K7ch? B x Kt; 18
Q x B, KR—K1 and wins.
  III 17 P—B5! B x P; 18 Q x Q,
P x Q; 19 Kt—B3, R—Q7; 20 B—
B3, B—Q3! with a fine game.

17 Kt x Q	B—K4
18 B—Kt4!	B x Kt
19 B x Bch	K—B2

After this move Black will have
the "choice" of ceding the seventh
rank or losing the KRP. Hence
Tartakover gives 19 . . . K—Kt1;
20 QR—Q1, R x R; 21 R x R, B x P;
22 R—Q7, P—KR3 as preferable
—although Black is thereby reduced to complete passivity and
could consequently hardly stave
off defeat in the long run.

20 QR—Q1!	B x P

20 . . . P—KR3; 21 P—QKt3 is
equally unattractive.

21 R x R	R x R

Or 21 . . . K x R; 22 R—Q1ch and
23 R—Q7 (ch).

22 B x P	R—Q5

. . . R—Q7 was better; but Tartakover evidently did not appreci-
ate the full force of White's reply.

23 P—Kt3!	. . . .

Far better than 23 B—Kt8, R—
Kt5; 24 B—B7, R—B5; 25 B—K6,
R—K5 etc., after which White must
relinquish the QBP if he wishes to
play for a win. The text wins
some valuable tempi.

23	R x P
24 P—KR4	P—Kt4

. . . R—Q5 followed by the ad-
vance of the BP would likewise be
unavailing, e.g. 24 . . . R—Q5; 25
K—Kt2, P—B4; 26 P—B4, P—B5;
27 P—B5, P—B6; 28 P—B6, R—
Q7ch; 29 K—R3, P—B7; 30 B x P,
R x B; 31 P—B7, B—Kt2; 32 P—
B8(Q), B x Q; 33 R x B and wins.

25 K—Kt2	P—R4
26 P—R5!	B—Kt2
27 P—B4	B—R3

Temporarily preventing P—Kt4.

28 R—K1!	R—R5
29 B—Kt8	R—Q5
30 R—K7ch!	R—Q2
31 R x Rch	K x R
32 K—B3	P—B4

32 . . . K—K2; 33 P—Kt4, K—
B3; 34 K—K4! is no better (Tar-
takover); for example 34 . . . P—
R5; 35 P—Kt5ch, B x P; 36 P x B
ch, K x P; 37 K—Q4, P—Kt5; 38
K—B5! P—Kt6; 39 B x P! etc.

33 P—Kt4	P—B5
34 P—Kt5	B—B1
35 P—R6	P—R5
36 P—B5!	K—B3
37 P—R7	. . . .

Or 37 P—B6 etc.

37	B—Kt2
38 P—B6	P—B6
39 K—K2	B—R1
40 P—B7	Resigns

Black's reliance on the Bishops
of opposite color has proved futile.
A slick ending.

---

69. Bad Kissingen, 1928

QUEEN'S GAMBIT DECLINED

The theme of this simple but most
instructive game is the remorse-
less exploitation of a positional ad-

vantage (in this case, White's pressure on the black squares, and his successful attempt to prevent the development of Black's QB). Black's helplessness carries a moral: avoid opening variations which are distasteful to you, no matter how highly they may be recommended.

J. R. CAPABLANCA	J. MIESES
White	Black
1 P—Q4	Kt—KB3
2 P—QB4	P—K3
3 Kt—QB3	P—Q4

3 . . . B—Kt5 is much favored nowadays because of its aggressive character; but Mieses, being a player of the old school, naturally prefers the more orthodox text. However, his lively style is poorly suited to the somewhat unimaginative type of game enjoined upon Black in this variation.

4 B—Kt5	B—K2
5 P—K3	QKt—Q2
6 Kt—B3	O—O
7 R—B1	P—QR3
8 P x P!	. . . .

Capablanca had already realized that this reply gives White the most promising game against Black's 7th move after playing the characterless 8 P—QR3 in the title match against Alekhine; the latter replied 8 . . . P x P; 9 B x P, P—QKt4 followed by . . . P—B4 with a fine game.

8	P x P
9 Q—Kt3	P—B3
10 B—Q3	Kt—R4

This involves a loss of time which is hard to understand; . . . Kt—K5 should have been played directly, and if then 11 B—KB4, Kt x Kt; 12 P x Kt, Kt—B3 and Black is better off than after the text.

11 B x B	Q x B
12 O—O	Kt (4)—B3

13 Kt—QR4!   . . . .

Initiating what proves to be extremely troublesome pressure on Black's Queen-side. Mieses is now confronted with this dilemna: in order to get out his Bishop, he must move his QKt—but this would permit Kt—B5 or Kt—Kt6 with powerful pressure on the black squares.

13	Kt—K5
14 B x Kt!	. . . .

A surprising reply, but a very good one.

14 . . . .   Q x B

One would have expected 14 . . . P x B; but after 15 Kt—Q2, Kt—B3; 16 Kt—B5 Black's Queen-side would be in a woeful state.

15 Q—Kt4!   . . . .

More pressure on the black squares.

15 . . . .   Q—Kt3

A difficult decision, he wants to prevent Q—Q6—B7 which would cripple his position. 15 . . . Q—K3 looks better than the text, but White simply doubles Rooks on the QB file, quietly waiting for a Knight move, which will be answered resoundingly with Kt—B5.

16 Q—K7!   . . . .

Further utilization of the black squares to impede Black's development, for . . . R—K1 is prevented. How is Black to proceed? The natural move . . . Kt—B3 would be met by Kt—K5, leaving Black with no reasonably quick method of shaking off the pressure. He therefore decides to play for the exchange of Queens.

16	P—B3
17 R—B3	Q—K1
18 Q—Q6!	. . . .

Capablanca is willing to exchange Queens . . . for a price. First he gains a useful tempo.

18	R—B2
19 KR—B1!	Q—B1
20 Q x Qch	K x Q

See the previous note: Black would like to play 20 . . . Kt x Q (hoping for the eventual liberation of his Queen-side pieces); but then 21 Kt—Kt6, R—Kt1; 22 Kt x P! wins a Pawn.

The ending is much in White's favor, as he has more mobility and the initiative—plus the undiminished pressure on the black squares. Black not only has trouble in getting out his Bishop, but this piece is doomed to inactivity in any event, as it will be restricted in scope by the Black Pawns on white squares.

| 21 Kt—K1! | . . . . |

More pressure on the black squares!

| 21 . . . . | K—K1 |

The choice of moves is not luxurious: if 21 . . . P—QKt4? 22 R x P, B—Kt2; 23 R—B7 etc.

| 22 Kt—Q3 | R—Kt1 |

In order to play . . . Kt—B1 (see the note to his 20th move). The alternative was 22 . . . K—Q1; 23 P—B3, K—B2; 24 R—Kt3, P—QR4 (not 24 . . . Kt—B1? 25 Kt—Kt6, R—Kt1; 26 Kt x Pch) followed by . . . R—Kt1, . . . Kt—B1 and . . . B—K3; but Black's game would still be inferior.

23 P—B3	R—K2
24 K—B2	Kt—B1
25 R—Kt3	Kt—Q2

Such indecisiveness can avail very little in this type of position. He should have played 25 . . . B—B4; 26 Kt(3)—B5, P—QR4.

| 26 P—Kt4 | P—QKt4? |

Realizing after White's last move that Capablanca is prepared for a leisurely advance on both wings, Mieses loses patience and makes a violent attempt to free himself. As is usual in such cases, he only hastens the end!

Mieses

Capablanca

| 27 Kt(4)—B5 | Kt—Kt3 |

If instead 27 . . . Kt x Kt; 28 R x Kt, B—Kt2; 29 Kt—Kt4 with a winning positional advantage; or 27 . . . P—QR4 (to prevent White's next move); 28 R—R3, P—R5; 29 P—Kt3, P x P; 30 Kt x P, B—Kt2; 31 Kt—Kt4, R—B1; 32 R—R7, Kt—Kt3; 33 Kt—R5 with decisive pressure.

| 28 Kt—Kt4! | . . . . |

After this powerful stroke, Black's Queen-side collapses in ruins.

28	B—Kt2
29 Kt x B	QR x Kt
30 R x P	P—QR4
31 R x Kt!	P x Kt
32 R x R	R x R
33 R x P	Resigns

---

70. Bad Kissingen, 1928

QUEEN'S INDIAN DEFENSE

As in Game No. 55, Capablanca

has the pleasure of defeating the first prize-winner. Just how this is accomplished must in the last analysis remain a psychological secret. Both players start out from a perfectly level position, and Bogolyubov begins to commit errors none of which seem fatal; yet he is imperceptibly slipping, and the eventual catastrophe is all the more crushing because it has made its appearance so unobtrusively.

E. Bogolyubov J. R. Capablanca

White	Black
1 P—Q4	Kt—KB3
2 P—QB4	P—K3
3 Kt—KB3	P—QKt3

An opening which was frequently seen in Capablanca's games beginning about this time; his favorite Orthodox Defense had been analysed overmuch.

4 Kt—B3	B—Kt2
5 B—Kt5	B—K2
6 P—K3	. . . .

Q—B2 would be more aggressive, carrying on the fight for the center. But, as will be seen, Bogolyubov is playing for a draw.

6	Kt—K5
7 B x B	Q x B
8 Kt x Kt	B x Kt
9 Kt—Q2	. . . .

Good enough, but B—K2 is still simpler.

9	B—Kt2
10 B—K2	Q—Kt4

10 . . . B x P; 11 KR—Kt1 followed by R x P would obviously favor White.

11 B—B3	B x B
12 Q x B	Kt—B3
13 Q—Kt3	. . . .

Still concentrating on the draw!

| 13 . . . . | Q x Q |

14 RP x Q	K—K2
15 P—KKt4	P—R3
16 P—R3?	. . . .

Instead of continuing in the same cautious vein, Bogolyubov now switches to misplaced displays of energy. The text has the drawback of creating a potential weakness on the Queen-side. Simply K—K2 was in order.

16	P—R3!
17 K—K2	KR—QKt1!

Revealing his intentions of attacking on this wing; thus if 18 P—Kt4? P—Kt4; 19 P—B5, P—QR4 with a strong initiative.

| 18 Kt—K4 | . . . . |

As the Knight is soon driven back with loss of time, it would have been preferable to play KR—QKt1 followed by K—Q3—B2.

18	P—QKt4
19 P—B5	P—Q4!

Black has already gained considerable ground and now he virtually forces the opening of the QB file, for if 20 Kt—Q2, P—K4! or 20 Kt—B3, P—Kt5! in either case with disadvantage to White.

20 P x P e.p. ch	P x P
21 P—B4?	. . . .

Bogolyubov seems to have lost his head completely. It was necessary to dispute the control of the QB file with KR—QB1.

21	R—QB1
22 P—B5?	. . . .

Another feeble move, which assures Black a won ending, in case of considerable exchanges, by bringing his King to KKt4. Thus from now on, White dare not go too far in trying to ease the pressure by exchanges!

22	Kt—R4
23 K—Q3	Kt—B5

This practically forces the immobilization of White's QR, for after 24 P—QKt3, Kt—R4 the QKtP still requires protection, while if 24 R—QR2, R—B3; 25 P—QKt3, Kt—R4; 26 R—QB2, R(1)—QB1; 27 R x R, R x R; 28 R—QKt1, Kt—Kt2; 29 K—Q2, P—Q4; 30 Kt—B3, K—B3! and Black goes after the KKtP.

24 QR—QKt1   P—Q4!

Beginning a series of energetic strokes which soon reduce White to helplessness. The reply 25 Kt—B5 looks good at first sight, but . . . P—K4 is a strong reply.

25 Kt—B3   R—B3
26 P x P   P x P
27 P—Kt5   . . . .

Preventing . . . K—B3—Kt4—an admission of previous bad play.

27 . . . .   P x P
28 R—R5   K—B3
29 R—R3   R(1)—QB1

Capablanca

Bogolyubov

By way of showing his appreciation of the gift of the QB file, Capablanca now turns it to decisive account. The immediate threat is . . . Kt x P ch.

30 Kt—K2   P—R4!

The process of encirclement is gathering momentum.

31 R—B3 ch   K—Kt3
32 P—KKt4   Kt—Q3!

And now the mating possibilities of this position begin to make their appearance.

33 Kt—B3   P—Kt5
34 P x P   P x P
35 Kt—Q1   . . . .

An amusing alternative line would be 35 Kt—R2, Kt—K5! 36 Kt x P, R—B5; 37 Kt—R2, R—B7; 38 R—Q1, R x P; 39 Kt—B1, R x Kt!! (Spielmann).

35 . . . .   R—B7
36 R—B2   P—Kt6!

Nailing down the coffin.

37 R—R1   Kt—K5
38 R—K2   R(1)—B3
39 R—Kt1   P—K4!

If now 40 P x P, Kt—B4 ch or . . . R(3)—B5 wins. The text prepares a pretty finish.

40 R—R1   R(3)—B5!
41 R—R5   Kt—B4 ch!

White resigns, as . . . P—K5 mate cannot be prevented. A very remarkable game.

---

71.   Bad Kissingen, 1928

INDIAN DEFENSE

Capablanca was lucky to extract a half-point from this game, but one can hardly begrudge him this fortunate result. A thrilling struggle all the way.

J. R. CAPABLANCA   A. NIMZOVICH

White   Black

1 P—Q4   Kt—KB3
2 P—QB4   P—K3
3 Kt—QB3   B—Kt5

4 Q—B2   P—Q4

The best reply to this popular move is either 5 P x P (Flohr) or 5 P—K3 (Rubinstein). The move selected by Capablanca is unsatisfactory, as it loses a Pawn without compensation.

5 B—Kt5   P x P!
6 Kt—B3   P—Kt4
7 P—QR4   P—B3
8 B x Kt?!   . . . .

The idea is to obtain some attacking chances by breaking up Black's King-side, since if 8 . . . Q x B; 9 P x P, P x P; 10 Q—K4 etc. However, subsequent analysis has shown that even this variation is playable, for Black has the resource 10 . . . Q—Kt3!! 11 Q x R, Q—B7 with a terrific attack: I 12 Q x Kt, O—O; 13 Kt—Q2, Q x P; 14 QR—Kt1, Q x Kt and wins, or 14 Q x P, B x Kt; 15 R—Q1, B x P; 16 Q—B7, P—B6 winning. II 12 Q x P, Q x P; 13 R—Q1, B x Ktch; 14 Kt—Q2, B x Ktch; 15 R x B, Q—Kt8ch; 16 R—Q1, Q—Kt5ch; 17 R—Q2, P—B6! 18 Q x Kt, O—O! 19 Q B7 (19 P—K3, P—B7! or 19 K—Q1? Q—Kt8 mate), Q—Kt8ch; 20 R—Q1, P—B7!

8 . . . .   P x B
9 P—KKt3   . . . .

With a view to exerting pressure on the diagonal, which has been weakened by Black's 6th move.

9 . . . .   P—QR3
10 B—Kt2   R—R2

An original but clumsy maneuver, intended to take the Rook out of the range of White's Bishop. The simpler course would be 10 . . . B—Kt2; 11 O—O, Kt—Q2; 12 Kt—R4, QR—Kt1.

11 O—O   R—Q2
12 Q—B1   . . . .

In order to menace Black's King-side after he castles: but P—K4

might have had more lasting effect.

12 . . . .   O—O
13 Q—R6   B x Kt

This weakens the black squares, but seems to be a disagreeable necessity; the plausible 13 . . . K—R1 would have been refuted by 14 Kt—K4, B—K2; 15 Kt(3)—Kt5! P x Kt; 16 Kt—B6! B x Kt; 17 B—K4 and mate follows!

14 P x B   K—R1
15 Kt—Q2   P—KB4
16 KR—Kt1   . . . .

Rather slow; P—K4 would have given better chances.

16 . . . .   P—K4!

Best; if 16 . . . B—Kt2; 17 P x P, RP x P (or 17 . . . BP x P; 18 B x B, R x B; 19 Kt x P with advantage); 18 R—R7 with a good game— while 16 . . . R—Kt2 would lead to an interesting draw by 17 Kt x P! P x Kt; 18 R x R, B x R; 19 R—Kt1, B—R1; 20 R x Kt! Q x R; 21 Q—B6ch (Tartakover).

17 Kt—B3   . . . .

Capablanca changes his mind. Nimzovich stated afterwards that he expected 17 Kt x P, KP x P; 18 Kt—K5, R—Q3; 19 Q—B1, QP x P; 20 Q x P, Q—B3 with a complicated game.

17 . . . .   R—Q3!

An important intermediary move. If at once 17 . . . P—K5; 18 Kt—Kt5, P—B3; 19 Kt—K6.

18 Q—K3   P—K5
19 Kt—Q2   Kt—Q2

As Black is now on the way toward consolidating his position with . . . Kt—B3—Q4, Capablanca adopts a wild course which is far from characteristic of his style.

20 P—Kt4?!   Kt—B3
21 P x P   . . . .

Nimzovich

Capablanca

Having obtained a won game against Capablanca for the first time in his life, Nimzovich should have continued with 21 . . . Kt—Q4! 22 Q—R3 (if 22 Q x P? Kt x P or 22 Q—Kt3, R—Kt1 etc.), Kt—B5; 23 Q—K3, Q—Kt4; 24 Q x P, B x P etc.

21 . . . .   B x P?

Perhaps reckoning only on 22 Kt x P, R—K3; 23 P—B3, R—Kt1; 24 K—R1, Kt x Kt; 25 P x Kt, R x B; 26 K x R, B x Pch followed by . . . B x R.

22 Q—B4   Q—Q2

At last Black has completed his development and threatens . . . Kt—Q4 very strongly.

23 B x P   . . . .

Preparing to sacrifice the exchange; if 23 Kt x KP, B x Kt; 24 B x B, R—Kt1ch; 25 B—Kt2 (on K moves, . . . R—Kt5 wins), Kt—Q4; 26 Q—K5ch, P—B3 wins.

23 . . . .   Kt x B
24 Kt x Kt   R—Kt3ch
25 Kt—Kt3   . . .

Forced; if 25 K—B1 (or 25 K—R1, Q—Q4; 26 P—B3, R—K1 and wins), R—K1; 26 P—B3, B x Kt; 27 P x B, Q—R6ch wins quickly.

25 . . . .   B x R
26 R x B   P—KB4

Preventing P—K4 (Black threatens . . . R—Kt5 followed by . . . P—B5).

27 P—B3   Q—KKt2

A weak move, possibly in time pressure. More direct was 27 . . . Q—Q3; 28 Q x Q, R x Q; 29 P—K4, P x P; 30 P x P, R—B6.

28 K—B2   Q—B3
29 P x P   BP x P

If 29 . . . RP x P; 30 P—Q5!

30 R—Q1   K—Kt1?

Again . . . Q—Q3 was in order. Now the game begins to be extremely difficult for Black.

31 P—Q5!   Q x P?

But now . . . Q—Q3 was absolutely essential. There might have followed 32 Q x Q, R x Q; 33 P—K4, P x P; 34 Kt x P, R—R3! 35 P—Q6, K—B2 and Black wins (Tartakover).

32 P—Q6   Q—B3
33 P—Q7   P—B6
34 Kt x P!   P—B7!

An exciting position! The text is better than 34 . . . R—Kt4; 35 R—Q5! (not 35 Kt—R6ch, Q x Kt; 36 P—Q8(Q), R—Kt7ch; 37 K x R, Q x Q with advantage), R x Kt; 36 R x R, Q—Kt3ch; 37 K—Kt2, R x R; 38 Q x R (Tartakover) and White wins!

35 R—Q6!   Q—Q1

35 . . . Q x R is no better: 36 Kt x Q, R x Q; 37 P—Q8(Q)ch, R—B1; 38 Q—B7, R x Kt! 39 Q x P—or 35 . . . P—B8(Q); 36 Q x Q, Q x Kt; 37 P—Q8(Q), R x Q; 38 R x Rch with a likely draw.

36 Q—K5!!   R x Kt

Mate in two was threatened. If 36 . . . R—Kt7ch; 37 K x R, Q—

Kt4ch; 38 K—B2, P—B8(Q); 39
Q—Q5ch! with perpetual check.

37 R x Rch	P x R
38 Q—K8ch	R—B1!
39 Q x Pch	Drawn

A tense finish.

---

72.   Berlin, 1928

QUEEN'S PAWN OPENING

This was Capablanca's first and
only win against Rubinstein. The
play is quite intricate and difficult,
and the manner in which the Cuban
exploits his advantage is most instructive.

J. R. CAPABLANCA   A. RUBINSTEIN

White	Black
1 P—Q4	P—Q4
2 Kt—KB3	P—QB4

A move which often leads—as
here—to an isolated QP, compensated for in great measure by
Black's excellent development.

| 3 P x P | P—K3 |

He could prevent White's next
move with 3 . . . Kt—KB3, after
which White, if so inclined, could
continue along the lines of the
Queen's Gambit Accepted with a
move in hand.

| 4 P—K4 | B x P |

4 . . . P x P; 5 Q x Qch, K x Q;
6 Kt—Kt5 is in White's favor. The
text leads to a position which
might also be reached from the
French or Sicilian Defense.

5 P x P	P x P
6 B—Kt5ch	Kt—B3
7 O—O	KKt—K2
8 QKt—Q2	. . . .

One of White's Knights is headed
for Q4.

| 8 . . . . | O—O |

| 9 Kt—Kt3 | B—Kt3 |
| 10 R—K1 | . . . . |

Simpler and more efficacious was
10 P—KR3, in order to continue
with P—B3, QKt—Q4 and B—K3
followed by pressure on the isolated QP.

| 10 . . . . | B—Kt5 |

Threatening 11 . . . B x Pch; 12
K x B, Q—Kt3ch etc.

| 11 B—Q3 | Kt—Kt3 |

White was threatening to return
the compliment with 12 B x Pch,
K x B; 13 Kt—Kt5ch etc.

12 P—KR3	B x Kt
13 Q x B	QKt—K4
14 Q—B5	Kt x B
15 Q x Kt	P—Q5?

. . . Q—B3! would have freed
Black's game and given him at
least equality. The move actually
adopted leads to a totally different
kind of game. Black cuts down
the mobility of his own Bishop
without really strengthening the
QP. On the other hand, the QBP
is now backward. The play which
follows is exceedingly difficult; but
whereas Capablanca's play from
this point on is admirable, Rubinstein does not make the most of
his opportunities.

| 16 B—Q2 | Q—B3 |
| 17 R—K4 | QR—Q1 |

Here for example 17 . . . Kt—
K4; 18 Q—K2, Kt—B3 looks good;
the QP would then be adequately
defended, and both B—R5 and
R—K7 would be impossible. In
any event, . . . KR—Q1 was superior to the text (which at once
leads to difficulties), in order to
reserve the possibility of . . . QR—
B1 with counter-pressure on the
QBP.

| 18 QR—K1 | Q—B3 |

In order to oppose Rooks on the

K file (White was threatening B—Kt4).

19 P—Kt3   . . . .

The text is a preparation for B—R5, which if played at once, would be refuted by 19 . . . P—B4! 20 R—K6, Kt—B5.

Rubinstein

Capablanca

19 . . . .   KR—K1

In order to exchange Rooks. Znosko-Borovsky convincingly demonstrates that the attempt to secure a loophole for Black's King would be inadequate:

I 19 . . . P—KR3; 20 B—Kt4, KR—K1; 21 R x Rch, R x R; 22 R x Rch, Q x R; 23 Kt x P, Kt—K4; 24 Q—Kt5, Kt—B6ch; 25 K—Kt2 and wins.

II 19 . . . P—B3; 20 P—KB4, P—B4; 21 R—K6, Q—Q4 (not 21 . . . R—Q3; 22 R x R, Q x R; 23 Q—B4ch winning the exchange); 22 P—KR4!

(a) 22 . . . R—B1; 23 P—R5, Kt—R1; 24 B—Kt4, KR—Q1; 25 R(1)—K5, Q—B5; 26 R—K8ch, R x R; 27 R x Rch, K—B2; 28 Q x P ch! K x R; 29 Q—B8ch, K—Q2; 30 Q—Q6ch and mate next move.

(b) 22 . . . R—B2; 23 P—R5, Kt—B1; 24 R(6)—K5, Q—Q2; 25 B—Kt4,Q—R5; 26 P—R3, P—Kt3; 27 R—K7 and wins.

20 B—R5!   . . . .

Not 20 R x Rch, R x R; 21 R x R ch, Q x R; 22 Kt x P? Kt—K4; 23 Q—Kt5, Q x Q; 24 Kt x Q, Kt—B6ch etc.

20 . . . .   R x R
21 Q x R   Kt—B1

A futile attempt to get the Knight into play. Capablanca recommends as best 21 . . . Q x Q; 22 R x Q, B x B; 23 Kt x B, P—B4; but in that event Black would soon lose a Pawn after 24 R—K2.

However, Black had little choice in view of the threatened 22 B x B, Q x B; 23 R—Q1.

22 Q x Q   P x Q
23 R—K7   R—Q4

Now Black finds that the contemplated 23 . . . Kt—K3 (White threatens 24 R x RP) would not do because of 24 B x B, P x B; 25 R—Kt7, P—QKt4; 26 R—Kt6, R—QB1; 27 Kt—R5, Kt—Q1; 28 K—B1, K—B1; 29 K—K2, K—K2; 30 K—Q3, K—Q3; 31 K x P etc.

Another equally instructive line is 23 . . . P—Q6; 24 P x P, R x P (threatening . . . R x Pch in addition to . . . R x Kt); 25 B x B, P x B; 26 R—Kt7, P—Q8ch; 27 K—Kt2, R—Kt8 (or 27 . . . P—QKt4; 28 Kt—R5, R—Kt8; 29 Kt x P, R x P; 30 Kt—K7ch, K—R1; 31 R—Kt8 and wins—always the Knight of the Rueful Countenance!); 28 R x P, R x P; 29 P—QR4, P—QB4 (the only counterchance); 30 P—R5, P—B5; 31 Kt—Q4, P—B6 (if 31 . . . R x R; 32 P x R, Kt—Q2; 33 P—Kt7, K—B1; 34 K—B1, Kt—Kt1; 35 K—K2, K—K2; 36 K—Q2, K—Q3; 37 K—B3, K—B2; 38 K x P, K x P; 39 Kt—B5, P—Kt3; 40 Kt—Q6ch and wins; or 37 . . . K—Q4; 38 Kt—B5, P—Kt3; 39 Kt—R6, P—B4; 40 Kt—Kt8 and wins); 32 R—QB6, R—R7; 33 P—R6, P—Kt3; 34 Kt—Kt5, P—B7; 35 P—R7! and wins.

24 B x B   P x B
25 R—Kt7   Kt—Q2

One of the Pawns must fall; thus

if 25 . . . P—QKt4; 26 R—B7,
R—Q3; 27 Kt—R5.

| 26 R—B7 | R—Q3 |

Or 26 . . . P—QB4; 27 R—B8ch,
Kt—B1 (again the absence of a
loophole makes itself felt!); 28
R—B6 and wins.

| 27 R—B8ch | Kt—B1 |
| 28 Kt—Q2 | P—QB4 |

If 28 . . . P—QKt4; 29 Kt—Kt3
followed by Kt—R5.

29 Kt—B4	R—K3
30 R—Kt8	R—K8ch
31 K—Kt2	P—KKt4

. . . P—KKt3 would make possible a longer resistance.

32 P—QR4	R—QR8
33 Kt x P	K—Kt2
34 R—B8	Kt—K3
35 Kt—Q7	R x P
36 Kt x P	R—Kt5

If 36 . . . R—B5? 37 Kt x Ktch;
or if 36 . . . Kt x Kt; 37 R x Kt,
R—Kt5; 38 P—Kt3 and Black's
game is hopeless.

37 Kt—Q3	R—Kt4
38 K—B3	P—R3
39 P—QKt4	P—R4
40 P—Kt4	P x Pch
41 P x P	P—B3
42 R—B4	K—B2
43 Kt—B5	Kt—Q1
44 Kt—Kt3	. . . .

Black overstepped the time limit,
although he could equally well
have resigned. An ending worthy
of careful study.

---

73. Berlin, 1928

INDIAN DEFENSE

Because White's attack is not
grounded in the realities of the
position, he suffers a stinging set-
back.

F. J. MARSHALL J. R. CAPABLANCA

White	Black
1 P—Q4	Kt—KB3
2 Kt—KB3	P—K3
3 P—B4	B—Kt5ch
4 B—Q2	Q—K2
5 Kt—B3	. . . .

The more customary P—KKt3
gives White better chances of obtaining the initiative.

5	P—QKt3
6 P—K3	B x Kt
7 B x B	Kt—K5
8 R—B1	. . . .

This appears rather clumsy, as
the Rook will later on be out of
play at QB3. However, the classic
game with this variation resulted
in an even more promising position for Black after 8 Q—B2, B—
Kt2; 9 B—K2, P—Q3; 10 O—O,
O—O; 11 QR—Q1, Kt—Q2; 12 B—
K1, P—KB4 (Vidmar-Nimzovich,
New York 1927).

8	B—Kt2
9 B—Q3	O—O
10 O—O	P—Q3

. . . P—KB4 or . . . Kt x B would
be more accurate, for after the
text White could continue 11
B x Kt! B x B; 12 Kt—Q2, B—Kt2;
13 P—K4 as played by Marshall
against Kashdan the following
year.

| 11 Kt—Q2 | Kt x B |
| 12 R x Kt | P—QB4 |

Black has a shade the better of
it because of his opponent's misplaced Rook. However, White
could doubtless have maintained
equality by some such move as
Kt—B3 or B—K4.

| 13 P x P | QP x P |

Because of the superior placement of his Rooks, Black will be able to command the Q file. But it is by no means certain that this factor would have been absolutely decisive; whereas the line of play White now adopts, leads to irremediable ruin in a few moves.

14 Q—R5?   P—KR3
15 P—B4?   Kt—Q2
16 P—K4   P—K4!

A simple but very powerful reply: if now 17 P x P, Kt x P and Black has pressure on the KP (which cannot hold out very long) supplemented by play in the Q file, supported by the admirably posted Knight at K4. Or if 17 P—B5, Kt—B3 likewise with advantage to Black.

17 Kt—B3   QR—K1!

Capablanca

Marshall

The KP must fall: if 18 P—B5, Kt—B3; 19 Q—R4, Kt x P! etc. Hence White makes a last despairing attempt—which is easily repulsed.

18 Kt—R4   P x P!
19 R x P   Q—Kt4!

Clearly forcing a retreat.

20 Q—B3   Kt—K4

If now 21 Q—K3 Black wins

easily with 21 . . . P—B4! 22 B—B2 (22 Kt x P, R x Kt! or 22 P x P? Kt x B), P x P; 23 R x Rch, R x R; 24 B x P, Q x Qch; 25 R x Q, Kt x P etc.

21 Q—B2   Kt x B
22 R x Kt   R x P

Black's position is still so superior that the remainder offers a minimum of technical difficulties.

23 R x R   B x R
24 R—K3   P—B4
25 P—KR3   R—Q1
26 P—R3   R—Q5
27 K—R2   Q—B3
28 Q—B4   P—KKt4
29 R—Kt3   K—B1
30 Q—Kt8ch   R—Q1
31 Q—K5   . . . .

White's ingenuity is wasted on a barren cause.

31 . . . .   Q x Q
32 Kt—Kt6ch   K—B2
33 Kt x Qch   K—B3

White resigns; the finish might have been 34 Kt—B3, P—B5; 35 R—Kt4, P—KR4; 36 Kt x P (36 R x P, B x Kt), B—B4.
Such games are the graveyard of the romantic attacking style.

---

74. Budapest, 1928

QUEEN'S GAMBIT DECLINED

One of the great Capablanca games. A slight inaccuracy in the opening leaves Black exposed to relentless pressure for the remainder of the game. The exploitation of the open QB file is most instructive.

J. R. CAPABLANCA   H. STEINER
White   Black

1 P—Q4   Kt—KB3
2 P—QB4   P—K3

3	Kt—QB3	P—Q4
4	B—Kt5	QKt—Q2
5	P—K3	B—K2
6	Kt—B3	O—O
7	R—B1	P—B3
8	B—Q3	P x P
9	B x P	Kt—Q4

Using one of Capablanca's favorite weapons against him! However, Black soon misses an important finesse.

10	B x B	Q x B
11	O—O	. . . .

Capablanca's indifference toward exchanges was proverbial. For the more complicated Kt—K4 see Game No. 66.

11	. . . .	Kt x Kt
12	R x Kt	P—QKt3

Intending . . . B—Kt2 and . . . P—QB4. Reasonable as this intention is, the move is soon stamped as a bad mistake. Best is 12 . . . P—K4, which avoids the creation of any weakness.

13	Q—B2!	P—QB4

White was threatening to win a Pawn with B—Q3. If 13 . . . B—Kt2; 14 B—Q3, P—Kt3 (or 14 . . . Kt—B3; 15 Kt—K5 with the same result); 15 B—K4 winning the weak QBP.

The text is therefore forced, but it has the unfortunate sequel of leading to the opening of lines which will be controlled by White because of his superior development.

14	P x P!	Kt x P
15	P—QKt4!	Kt—R3

The Knight is of course wretchedly placed here, but Black has little choice; for the more orthodox retreat to Q2 would give White a won game after 16 B—Q3!:
I 16 . . . Q x P? 17 B x Pch, K—R1; 18 R—B4! Q—K2; 19 R—KR4, P—Kt3; 20 B x Pch, K—Kt2 (if 20 . . . K—Kt1; 21 B—R7ch, K—Kt2; 22 Q—K4, QR—Kt1; 23

Q—Kt4ch etc.); 21 B x P! and wins.
II 16 . . . P—Kt3; 17 R—B7! with innumerable threats, such as Q—B6, B—Kt5, B—K4, Kt—K5 or R—Q1. Some loss of material would be unavoidable.

16	P—QR3	B—Kt2
17	B—Q3!	. . . .

Just in time to stop . . . QR—B1.

17	. . . .	P—Kt3
18	R—B1!	QR—Q1

He cannot dispute the QB file, for if 18 . . . QR—B1; 19 R x R, R x R; 20 Q x Rch! B x R; 21 R x B ch, K—Kt2; 22 B x Kt wins.

19	Kt—K5	. . . .

Improving his position by establishing the Knight on a magnificent post. Meanwhile White gains time by threatening to win the exchange by B x Kt and Kt—B6.

19	. . . .	Q—Q3
20	P—B4	. . . .

Steiner

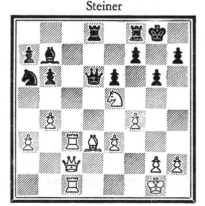

Capablanca

From the further course of the game, it is clear that Black's last chance to free himself was 20 . . . P—B3. His reasons for not playing it are most interesting: 20 . . . P—B3; 21 Kt x P! P x Kt; 22 B x

Kt, B x B; 23 Q x Pch, K—R1; 24 P—Kt5!! (not 24 P—K4?? Q—Q5ch and **Black** forces mate!), B x P (if 24 . . . B—Kt2? 25 P—K4! Q—Q5ch; 26 K—B1! and wins); 25 Q—R5ch followed by Q x B with an easy win.

20	Kt—Kt1
21 R—B7	B—R1
22 R x RP	Kt—B3

Hoping for some complications, but Capablanca selects the simplest and most conclusive course.

23 R x B!	Kt x Kt
24 R x R	R x R
25 B—K2!	Q—Q7

He had no choice, for if 25 . . . Kt—Q2 (25 . . . Kt—Q6; 26 R—Q1); 26 R—Q1, Q—K2 (or 26 . . . Q—Kt1; 27 Q—Q2! maintaining the pin); 27 Q—B7, K—B1; 28 B—Kt5 exchanging all the pieces and winning the King and Pawn ending.

| 26 Q x Q! | . . . . |

Simplicity is still the keynote; 26 P x Kt, Q x Pch; 27 K—R1, R—Q7; 28 Q—B8ch, K—Kt2; 29 B—B3 would win a piece, but would prolong the game.

26	R x Q
27 R—B8ch!	K—Kt2
28 K—B1!	Kt—Q2

Or 28 . . . Kt—Q6; 29 R—Q8.

| 29 R—Q8 | . . . . |

Forcing the win of the exchange. This was the point of 23 R x B! and it was the logical outcome of White's relentless utilization of the QB file.

| 29 . . . . | K—B3 |
| 30 B—Kt5 | R—Q4 |

Of course if . . . K—K2, White exchanges all the pieces winning easily.

| 31 P—QR4! | . . . . |

Much simpler than 31 B x Kt, K—K2; 32 R—QKt8, R x B; 33 R x P, R—R2 etc.

| 31 . . . . | R x B |

There is nothing better; but White has an easy win, for all that is needed is penetration by his King.

| 32 P x R | K—K2 |
| 33 R—QB8! | . . . . |

But now 33 R x Ktch? would only draw, because of the doubled QKtP.

| 33 . . . . | P—K4 |

This hastens the end, as now White's King will come in at Q5.

34 R—B6!	P—K5
35 K—K2	P—B4
36 K—Q2	K—B2
37 K—B3	Resigns

Black is helpless. A gem of a game.

---

75.   Budapest, 1928
QUEEN'S GAMBIT

Although this game echoes Capablanca's celebrated encounter with Bogolyubov at Moscow (Game No. 55), it has attractive qualities of its own.

J. R. CAPABLANCA	K. HAVASI
White	Black
1 P—Q4	P—Q4
2 P—QB4	P—K3
3 Kt—KB3	P x P
4 P—K4	P—QB4

About this time White's last move was thought to give him a definitely superior game; however, the later fashionable "Vienna Variation" (4 . . . B—Kt5ch; 5 Kt—B3, Kt—B3; 6 B—Kt5, P—B4) has caused the theorists to suspend judgment.

5 B x P	P x P
6 Kt x P	Kt—KB3
7 Kt—QB3	P—QR3

In the Bogolyubov game the continuation was 7 . . . B—B4; 8 B—K3, QKt—Q2; 9 B x P! etc.

8 O—O	B—B4

Black's game has already become critical, but 8 . . . P—K4; 9 Kt—B3, Q x Qch; 10 R x Q, B—KKt5 appears preferable.

9 B—K3	QKt—Q2?

Allowing the sacrifice in an even stronger form, since White has already castled. But it is difficult to suggest a wholly satisfactory move.

10 B x KP!	. . . .

More of a sound investment than a sacrifice: White will have three Pawns and a lasting attack to boot for the piece.

10	P x B
11 Kt x P	Q—R4

The only move, now that White is castled. 11 . . . Q—Kt3 would be refuted by 12 Kt x B, Kt x Kt; 13 Kt—QR4.

12 Kt x Pch	K—B2
13 Kt—B5	Kt—K4
14 Q—Kt3ch	K—Kt3

14 . . . B—K3; 15 Q x Pch, KKt—Q2! would set White a more difficult problem.

15 QR—B1	. . . .

(see diagram next column)

15	B—B1

White was intending 16 B x B, Q x B; 17 Kt—K2! winning the Queen because of the threatened mate with 18 Kt—B4ch etc. 15 . . . B x B; 16 P x B would lead to a devastating attack against Black's lonesome King.

Havasi

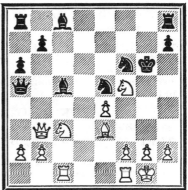

Capablanca

16 Kt—K2!	P—R4

Creating a much-needed flight square; 16 . . . Kt x P? would be refuted by 17 R x B!

17 KR—Q1	. . . .

The immediate 17 B—Kt6, Q—Kt4; 18 Kt—B4ch, K—R2; 19 R—B7ch, B—Q2; 20 Q—K6 would be less conclusive because of the reply 20 . . . B—Kt2.

17	KR—Kt1
18 Kt—B4ch	K—R2
19 B—Kt6	Q—Kt4
20 R—B7ch	K—R1

Other moves are no better:
I 20 . . . B—Q2; 21 Kt—Q5! Kt x Kt; 22 R x Kt, Q x Q; 23 P x Q and wins.
II 20 . . . B—Kt2; 21 Q x Rch! K x Q; 22 R x Bch, K—B1; 23 R—Q8ch, Kt—K1; 24 R x B! Q x B forced; 25 R x R and wins.

21 Q x Q!	. . . .

This seemingly "dull" move is really the point of departure for a charming combination.

21	P x Q
22 R—Q8!	R x P
23 R(8) x QB	Kt—B5

This is the position Black had aimed for; he threatens mate and attacks the Bishop. But there is a simple defense.

24 P—R3!   Kt x B
25 R x B!   . . . .

The point: . . . R x R would now lead to mate in two.

25 . . . .   Kt (Kt3)—Q2
26 R—B7!   R x P
27 Kt—Q5   Resigns

He must lose at least a piece. A very pleasing game.

---

76. Budapest, 1928

INDIAN DEFENSE

In some quarters Capablanca was often accused of a lack of originality. It is difficult to reconcile such a charge with the ingenuity of his play in games like the present one. Incidentally, some of his moves here bespeak a sly sense of humor!

J. R. CAPABLANCA   Z. VON BALLA

White   Black

1 P—Q4   Kt—KB3
2 P—QB4   P—K3
3 Kt—QB3   B—Kt5
4 Q—B2   P—B4

See Game No. 71 for the better move 4 . . . P—Q4.

5 P x P   B x P
6 P—QR3   Kt—B3
7 P—QKt4!   . . . .

An improvement on 7 Kt—B3, Kt—Q5! 8 Kt x Kt, B x Kt; 9 P—K3, B x Ktch; 10 Q x B, O—O; 11 P—QKt4, P—Q4! as played in a game between Capablanca and Marshall several rounds earlier. After the text Black does not have the resource of exchanging at Q5.

7 . . . .   B—K2
8 Kt—B3   Q—B2?

Not only a loss of time, but it soon involves Black in serious tactical difficulties. Correct was 8 . . . P—Q4; 9 P—K3 with a slight advantage to White.

9 P—Kt3   P—QKt3

Perhaps he should have played . . . P—QR3 to guard against Kt—QKt5. Balla evidently does not realize that White's last move not only provides for the fianchetto, but also prepares a troublesome attack on the Queen.

10 B—KKt2   B—Kt2
11 B—B4!   P—Q3

If 11 . . . Q—Q1; 12 R—Q1 with strong pressure. And on 11 . . . P—K4 White has an excellent reply in 12 B—Kt5! (not 12 Kt x P? Kt x Kt; 13 B x Kt, P—Q3! and Black wins a piece!

12 Kt—QKt5   Q—Kt1
13 P—B5!   P—K4
14 P x QP!   B x P

Or 14 . . . P x B; 15 Kt—B7ch, K—Q1; 16 P x Bch! K x Kt; 17 Kt—K5 winning. The text seems to give Black a relatively playable game, since he is now ready to castle.

Von Balla

Capablanca

15 R—Q1!   . . . .

The winning move! (15 Kt x Bch, Q x Kt; 16 Kt x P would not do because of 16 . . . Kt x P!).

If now 15 . . . P x B; 16 Kt x Bch, K—B1; 17 Kt x B, Q x Kt; 18 Kt—R4, R—B1; 19 R—B1 and wins; or 15 . . . B—K2; 16 Kt x KP, Kt x P (16 . . . Kt x Kt; 17 B x Kt with advantage); 17 P x Kt, B x B (if 17 . . . B x Pch; 18 K—B1 etc.); 18 Kt—B7ch, K—B1; 19 Q—B4! and wins (Kmoch).

An extraordinary position!

| 15 . . . . | O—O |

The "safe" move, but now White wins a piece!

16 Kt x B	P x B
17 Kt—R4!	Kt—Q1
18 Kt x B	Kt x Kt
19 Q—B6!	. . . .

Tartakover would call this "stealing a Knight in broad daylight."

19	P x P
20 RP x P	Q—K4
21 Q x QKt	Q—B6ch
22 K—B1	QR—Q1

"Hoping" for 23 R x R?? Q—B8ch and mate next move.

| 23 R—K1 | Q x RP |

Capablanca could now retain the QKtP with P—Kt5; but he rightly prefers to go right after Black's King, since the two passed Pawns are no equivalent for the piece.

24 Kt—B5	R—Q2
25 Q—B3	Q x P
26 R—R4	Q—Kt7
27 Q—B4	KR—Q1
28 B—B6!	R—Q7
29 Q—Kt5	P—Kt3

Now we see the point of White's 28th move (if here 29 . . . Kt—K1? 30 B x Kt, R x B; 31 Kt x P!).

| 30 Kt—K3! | Q—B6 |

The only move to take the sting out of Kt—B4.

| 31 R—QB4! | Q—Kt7 |
| 32 R—B4! | Kt—R4 |

Forced; the way in which Capablanca has gained time is extremely interesting.

| 33 Kt—B4 | P—B3 |

Again the only move, for if 33 . . . Q—B6; 34 Kt x R and the other Black Rook is en prise. But now Black's game must fall apart.

34 Q—Kt4	Q—R7
35 Q—K6ch	K—R1
36 R—K4	R—Q8
37 R x R	R x Rch
38 K—Kt2	Resigns

---

77. Carlsbad, 1929

QUEEN'S GAMBIT DECLINED

It is a tragedy to obtain a position which promises more than it can perform. This is what happens to Black in the following game; his judgment turns out to be quite fallacious, whereas Capablanca's appraisal of the position is proven correct with dazzling rapidity.

J. R. CAPABLANCA	A. BECKER
White	Black
1 P—Q4	P—Q4
2 P—QB4	P—K3
3 Kt—KB3	Kt—Q2
4 Kt—B3	. . . .

For other ways of answering Black's last move, see also Game No. 62.

| 4 . . . . | Kt—B3 |
| 5 B—B4 | . . . . |

Not the best, to be sure, but a welcome departure from the routine 5 B—Kt5.

| 5 . . . . | P x P |
| 6 P—K3 | Kt—Q4 |

An attractive idea, since White cannot very well try to preserve the QB (7 B—Kt3, B—Kt5; 8 R—B1, Kt(2)—Kt3 with a good game for Black). However, Black loses valuable time with this maneuver; hence it would have been preferable to play 6 . . . Kt—Kt3; 7 KB x P, Kt x B; 8 Q—R4ch, P—B3; 9 Q x B, Kt—Q4 (Alekhine-Spielmann, Carlsbad, 1923; Black soon obtained the initiative and eventually won).

7 KB x P	Kt x B
8 P x Kt	B—Q3
9 P—KKt3	. . . .

The exchange on move 7 seems to have conferred considerable advantages on Black: White has an isolated QP, doubled KBP and a potential weakness on the long diagonal. In return, however, White can operate on the QB and K files, and has a generally more aggressive position.

9	Kt—B3
10 O—O	O—O
11 Q—K2	P—QKt3
12 KR—Q1	. . . .

It was subsequently discovered that Kt—K5 is even stronger.

12	B—Kt2
13 QR—B1	P—QR3
14 B—Q3	B—Kt5?

Simply . . . Q—K2 was better; but Black is led astray by the hope of exploiting what he considers White's weakness on the long diagonal.

15 Kt—K4	Q—Q4?

More of the same. Black hopes for 16 R x P (if 16 Kt x Ktch, P x Kt with strong pressure), QR—B1! 17 R x R, R x R.

16 Kt(3)—Kt5!   . . . .

An unexpectedly strong move because the Knights seem to be so insecure. Nevertheless, the fact remains that White is threatening 17 Kt x Ktch, P x Kt; 18 B—K4, or 17 R x P etc.

16 . . . .   Kt—K1

It was no longer possible to guard against all theats, for example 16 . . . K—R1; 17 R x P! threatening R x B! with decisive effect.

Becker

Capablanca

17 Kt x RP!   P—KB4

Of course if 17 . . . K x Kt? 18 Kt—B6ch wins the Queen.

The text can be answered in a variety of ways, for example 18 Kt x R, K x Kt (or 18 . . . P x Kt; 19 B—B4, Q—Q3; 20 Kt x P); 19 P—B3! Q x Pch; 20 K—Kt2, P x Kt; 21 B x KP etc. However, Capablanca's choice is still more forcing.

18 Kt(7)—Kt5!   Resigns

If 18 . . . P x Kt; 19 B—B4 and Black must resign. Or 18 . . . Q—Q2; 19 Q—R5, Kt—B3 (if 19 . . . P—Kt3; 20 Q x Pch, K—R1; 21 B—B4! etc.); 20 Kt x Ktch, P x Kt; 21 Q—Kt6ch, K—R1; 22 Kt x P with the deadly threats of R x P and B x BP.

78. Carlsbad, 1929

QUEEN'S GAMBIT DECLINED

An instructive positional battle, which shows h o w weaknesses which are lightheartedly created in the opening can remain to plague a player for the remainder of the game.

J. R. CAPABLANCA   DR. K. TREYBAL

White	Black
1 P—Q4	P—Q4
2 P—QB4	P—QB3
3 Kt—KB3	P—K3
4 B—Kt5	. . . .

An interesting novelty which is best answered by the normal move . . . Kt—B3. The attempt to win a Pawn by 4 . . . P—B3? 5 B—Q2, P x P would turn out badly after 6 P—K3, P—QKt4; 7 P—QR4, Q—Kt3; 8 P x P, P x P; 9 P—QKt3, P x P; 10 Q x P, B—Q2; 11 Kt—B3, P—Kt5; 12 Kt—QR4 etc. (Kmoch).

4	B—K2
5 B x B	Q x B
6 QKt—Q2!	P—KB4?

A serious strategical error. The Stonewall formation is completely out of place here, for the black squares are irretrievably weakened and Black's Bishop's lack of scope becomes catastrophic.

7 P—K3	Kt—Q2
8 B—Q3	Kt—R3
9 O—O	O—O
10 Q—B2	P—KKt3

Much as in Game No. 14. But here the refutation is purely positional.

11 QR—Kt1!	Kt—B3
12 Kt—K5	Kt—B2
13 P—B4	B—Q2

. . . Kt x Kt might have been tried. In any event, the position is not attractive.

14 QKt—B3	KR—Q1
15 P—QKt4	B—K1
16 KR—B1	P—QR3
17 Q—B2	Kt x Kt
18 Kt x Kt	Kt—Q2
19 Kt—B3!	. . . .

As White's pieces have a more promising future, he avoids further exchanges.

| 19 . . . . | KR—B1 |

Allowing himself to be trussed up completely. . . . P x P was a bit better.

| 20 P—B5! | . . . . |

White's objective is now to break through with P—Kt5. This requires quite a bit of preparation, but it will be absolutely decisive when it finally comes.

20	Kt—B3
21 P—QR4	Kt—Kt5
22 Q—K1	Kt—R3
23 P—R3!	Kt—B2

The object of the Knight moves was to prepare for . . . P—KKt4. But White comes first.

24 P—Kt4!	B—Q2
25 R—B2	K—R1
26 R—KKt2	R—KKt1
27 P—KKt5	Q—Q1

Being exposed to attack on both wings now, Black has nothing left to do but wait for the ax to fall.

28 P—R4	K—Kt2
29 P—R5	R—R1
30 R—KR2	Q—B2
31 Q—B3	Q—Q1

. . . P—R4 would bring no relief, as it would be answered by P—Kt5.

32 K—B2	Q—B2
33 QR—KR1	QR—KKt1
34 Q—R1	R—Kt1
35 Q—R3	QR—Kt1

This move permits White to undertake decisive action on the Queen-side. There was in any event at least one more winning method, consisting of R—R3, R(1)—R2 followed by Q—B1—KR1. Black would be helpless against the pressure on the KR file.

Treybal

Capablanca

| 36 | P—Kt5! | RP x P |

Of course if 36 . . . BP x P? 37 P—R6ch, K—B1; 38 P—B6ch and the unfortunate Bishop is lost.

| 37 | P—R6ch! | . . . . |

Deliberately blocking the King-side because all his forces are to be switched to the Queen-side.

37	. . . .	K—B1
38	P x P	K—K2
39	P—Kt6	Q—Kt1

Now comes a classic winning procedure, based on occupation of the QR file, the establishment of an outpost at QR7, and finally irresistible pressure on the QKtP.

40	R—R1	R—QB1
41	Q—Kt4	KR—Q1
42	R—R7	K—B1
43	R—KR1	B—K1

This wretched Bishop has been useless throughout.

44	R(1)—R1	K—Kt1
45	R(1)—R4	K—B1
46	Q—R3	K—Kt1
47	K—Kt3	B—Q2
48	K—R4	. . . .

White marks time hereabouts until the 52nd move.

48	. . . .	K—R1
49	Q—R1	K—Kt1
50	K—Kt3	K—B1
51	K—Kt2	B—K1
52	Kt—Q2!	. . . .

The Knight heads for QR5 with decisive effect.

| 52 | . . . . | B—Q2 |
| 53 | Kt—Kt3 | R—K1 |

No better is 53 . . . B—K1; 54 Kt—R5, R—Q2; 55 Kt x KtP! R x Kt; 56 R—R8. Beautiful exploitation of Black's fantastically cramped position!

54	Kt—R5	Kt—Q1
55	B—R6!	P x B
56	R x B	R—K2

On other moves Kt—Kt3 wins easily.

| 57 | R x Ktch! | R x R |
| 58 | Kt x P | Resigns |

A perfect example of the "encirclement" of a cramped position. It is not too much to say that Black's sixth move cost him the game.

79. Carlsbad, 1929

INDIAN DEFENSE

An unpretentious but most instructive game. The way in which Capablanca exploits a positional weakness and solves the resulting technical difficulties makes chess seem a simple game indeed.

P. JOHNER   J. R. CAPABLANCA

White   Black

1 P—Q4   Kt—KB3
2 P—QB4   P—K3
3 Kt—QB3   B—Kt5
4 P—K3   O—O
5 B—Q3   P—B4
6 Kt—K2   Kt—B3
7 P—QR3?   . . . .

White has handled the opening in
so easy-going a manner that after
7 Q—B2 (probably best), Black
would have effortless equality with
. . . P—Q4.

7 . . . .   B x Ktch
8 P x B   P—QKt3
9 O—O   B—R3

The classic method of exploiting
the weakness of White's Pawn on
QB4. White's best course would
have been to counter with Kt—Kt3
and Q—K2. The method he adopts
to protect the QBP is soon shown
to be inadequate.

10 P—K4   Kt—K1

An interesting preventive move.
Black does not like to have his
plans disrupted by a possible P—
K5, and in some positions it would
be useful to be able to answer
P—B4 with . . . P—B4.

11 B—K3   P—Q3
12 Q—R4   Kt—R4

The fate of the menaced QBP is
as good as decided. Thus if 13
Kt—B1 (intending Kt—Kt3), P x P!
14 P x P, R—B1! etc. Or 13 P—
Q5, Kt—B2; 14 Kt—B1, Q—K1;
and again the Pawn falls.

13 KR—Q1   Q—B2
14 QR—B1   Q—B3!
15 Q x Q   Kt x Q

The exchange of Queens has left
the QBP without adequate defense,
for example 16 P—Q5, Kt—K4; 17
P x P, P x P; 18 Kt—B4, Kt—QB2;

19 B—B1, QR—Q1 and the Pawn
falls. Johner therefore tries an
interesting diversion which, however, is cleverly refuted.

Capablanca

Johner

16 P—K5?!   BP x P
17 BP x P   P x P
18 P—Q5!   P x P
19 P x P   B x B
20 R x B   . . . .

Black is apparently in difficulties,
for his forces are divided and the
QP looks formidable.

20 . . . .   P—K5!
21 KR—Q1   Kt—K4
22 R—Q4   P—B4
23 B—B4   Kt—Q6
24 R—B6   R—Q1

If now 25 P—Q6, R—Q2 followed
by . . . R—B3 and the QP will
be lost in short order. As Black
has now consolidated his position,
White has nothing better than the
following simplifying attempt.

25 P—B3   Kt—B3
26 P x P   P x P
27 B—Kt5   Kt—B4
28 Kt—B3   QR—K1

White must exchange, as the
pressure against his QP (. . . R—
K4 etc.) coupled with such threats

as . . . P—K6 followed by . . .
KKt—K5, leave him little choice.

29 B x Kt	R x B
30 R x R	P x R
31 K—B2	P—B4
32 Kt—Kt5	K—Kt2!

For if 33 Kt x P, R—QR1; 34
Kt—Kt5, R—R4; 35 Kt—Q6 (35
R—Kt1?? Kt—Q6ch), K—B3 with
an easy win.

33 P—Kt3	K—B3
34 K—K3	P—QR3
35 Kt—Q6	R—Q1
36 Kt—B4	Kt—Kt6

Good. After the immediate . . .
P—Kt4 White's Knight could go
to QR5, preventing a subsequent
centralization with . . . K—K4.

37 R—Q1	P—Kt4
38 Kt—Kt6	K—K4

Now the game is as good as
over, . . . R—Q3 being threatened.

39 P—Q6	R x P
40 Kt—Q7ch	K—K3
41 Kt—B8ch	K—K2
42 R x R	K x R
43 P—Kt4	. . . .

Despair; if 43 Kt x P, K—K4; 44
Kt—B8, Kt—R4 winning easily.

43	P x P
44 K x P	Kt—Q7ch
45 K—Q3	Kt—B6
46 Kt x P	Kt x P
47 Kt—B6	K—K4!
48 Kt—R5	P—R4

White resigns. An admirable
game.

---

80.   Carlsbad, 1929
INDIAN DEFENSE

This game is a convincing indication of the difference between
a master and a grandmaster. Capablanca's subtle and incisive play
makes his opponent look like a
tyro. Particularly enjoyable is the
beautiful timing of White's moves.

J. R. CAPABLANCA	H. MATTISON
White	Black
1 P—Q4	Kt—KB3
2 P—QB4	P—K3
3 Kt—QB3	B—Kt5
4 Q—B2	P—B4

Regarding the preferable alternative . . . P—Q4, see Game No. 71.
The drawback of the text is that
it is likely to lead to trouble on
the Q file.

5 P x P	Kt—B3

To this the strongest reply may
be 6 P—QR3 as in Game No. 76.

6 Kt—B3	B x P
7 B—B4	P—Q4

The alternative course . . . B—
K2 followed by . . . P—Q3 would
lead to a very cramped game which
is not to everyone's taste; it would
also facilitate White's plan (clearly
revealed by his last move) of bearing down on Q6.

8 P—K3	Q—R4?

. . . Q—K2 is better. The plan
initiated with this move turns out
poorly.

9 B—K2	B—Kt5

The resulting doubling of the
QBP does White no harm, as his
far superior development allows
him to dissolve the BP advantageously.

10 O—O	B x Kt

The logical corollary of the previous move; but the Bishop will
be sorely missed later.

11 P x B	O—O
12 QR—Kt1!	. . . .

A fine move, which hampers the development of the hostile Bishop, and leaves Black's Queen in rather a precarious position.

12 . . . .   Q—R6

Somewhat better was an attempt at consolidation by 12 . . . P x P; 13 B x P, Q—QB4 followed by . . . Q—K2 and . . . R—Q1. As the game goes, Black's game is disorganized while White's pieces work together harmoniously.

13 KR—Q1!   P—QKt3

After this Capablanca demolishes the hostile position with a few convincing strokes; but unfortunately . . . P x P is now impossible because of the reply B—Q6.

14 P x P   Kt x P

Leads to an energetic refutation; but 14 . . . P x P would not do because of 15 P—B4!

15 Kt—Kt5!   P—B4

There is no satisfactory alternative; if 15 . . . Kt—B3; 16 B—Q6 wins; while if 15 . . . P—Kt3; 16 B—B3 as in the text.

16 B—B3!   . . . .

Mattison

Capablanca

White's Bishops are complete masters of the situation, as the following analysis demonstrates:

I   16 . . . Kt(3)—K2; 17 P—B4.
II 16 . . . Kt(4)—K2; 17 B—Q6.
III 16 . . . Kt x B; 17 B x Kt.
IV 16 . . . R—Q1; 17 P—B4, Kt(4)—Kt5; 18 R x Kt, R x Rch; 19 Q x R.
V   16 . . . P—KR3; 17 R x Kt! P x Kt; 18 B—Q6, Q—R3; 19 B x R, P x R; 20 B x Pch, K x B; 21 B x Kt, R—Kt1; 22 Q—Q2! K—K2; 23 R—Q1 and wins.

16 . . . .   Q—B4

Parries the chief threat of R x Kt; but now White wins with a very fine move.

17 P—B4!!   . . . .

O divine simplicity! White threatens to win a piece with R—Kt5. If (a) 17 . . . Kt—B3 or . . . R—Q1; 18 R—Kt5 wins; or (b) 17 . . . Kt x B; 18 R—Kt5! Q—K2; 19 B x Kt, Q x Kt; 20 P x Kt wins.

17 . . . .   Kt(4)—Kt5
18 Q—Kt3   P—K4

Else B—Q6 is crushing.

19 P—QR3!!   Kt—R3

What else? (If 19 . . . P x B; 20 P x Kt wins a piece.)

20 B x Kt   Resigns

For if 20 . . . Q x B; 21 P—B5ch, K—R1; 22 Kt—B7ch leads to mate. One of Capablanca's best games in this great tournament.

---

81. Carlsbad, 1929

QUEEN'S GAMBIT DECLINED

Capablanca operates throughout the game with simple but cogent moves. The impression of easy achievement is deceptive.

J. R. CAPABLANCA   K. GILG

White	Black
1 P—Q4	P—Q4
2 P—QB4	P—K3
3 Kt—KB3	Kt—KB3
4 B—Kt5	B—K2
5 P—K3	QKt—Q2
6 QKt—Q2	. . . .

Probably played to get off the beaten track, this move is weaker than in Game No. 37; Black has not played . . . P—QB3 and can therefore play the equalizing . . . P—B4 without loss of a tempo. In playing the text, therefore, Capablanca relies on his superior abilities rather than on any inherent merit of the move.

6	P—KR3
7 B—R4	O—O
8 R—B1	P—B4!
9 BP x P	Kt x P
10 B—Kt3!	P—QKt3
11 B—Q3	P x P
12 P x P	. . .

This isolated Pawn may later become weak, but White has little choice; after 12 Kt x P, Kt—B4 Black has too easy a game.

12	B—Kt2

Tartakover suggests the interesting continuation 12 . . . Kt—QKt5; 13 B—K4, B—R3! But 13 B—QB4 is better.

13 O—O	QKt—B3
14 R—K1	. . . .

The customary procedure in such situations. Occupation of K5 and attacking possibilities are to compensate for any possible difficulties with the QP.

14	R—B1
15 R x R	Q x R
16 Kt—K5	Q—Q1
17 P—QR3	P—R3
18 Kt—Kt3	B—Q3

19 Q—K2	P—QR4

Naturally not 19 . . . P—QKt4 because then White has a fine post for the QKt at B5.

20 Kt—Q2	Q—K2
21 B—Kt1	. . . .

By setting up a potential mating threat along the diagonal, White hopes to keep several of his opponent's pieces tied up.

21	R—B1
22 Q—Q3	B—Kt1
23 P—B4	Q—B1

Not liking to have his Queen on the K file with P—B5 in the offing. The more natural 23 . . . Q—Q1 would not be satisfactory because of 24 B—R4, hence Gilg has recourse to the clumsy-looking but feasible text-move.

24 Kt—Q7	Q—K1
25 Kt x B	. . . .

At any rate, Capablanca has extracted some benefit from the last few moves in the form of the two Bishops.

25	R x Kt
26 P—B5!	R—Q1

The Rook must get out of the QB's range, and it is well placed here, with a view to future action against the QP.

27 Kt—B3	B—B1
28 P x P	B x P
29 Kt—K5	Q—B1
30 Kt—Kt6!	. . . .

Not a "brilliancy"; White's object is to remove the defenses of Black's KR2.

30	Q—K1
31 Kt—B4!	Kt x Kt
32 B x Kt	Q—Q2

At last it seems as if Black has counterplay on the QP; but White's threats come first.

33 B—K5   K—B1
34 P—R3   . . . .

. . . Kt—Kt5 must not be allowed.

Gilg

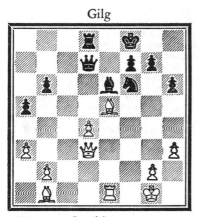

Capablanca

34 . . . .   Kt—K1

No better was 34 . . . Kt—Kt1 (recommended in the Tournament Book) for then White plays 35 Q—KKt3! (not 35 Q—R7? P—B3), P—B3; 36 B—B7! and wins, for if the Rook moves, 37 B x P wins; or if 36 . . . Q x Pch; 37 K—R2 winning the exchange.

35 Q—R7!   P—B3
36 Q—R8ch   K—K2

If 36 . . . B—Kt1; 37 B—R2 wins; or if 36 . . . K—B2; 37 R—KB1! with a winning attack.

37 B—Kt3   Q—Q4

Somewhat better was 37 . . . K—B2 (not 37 . . . Q x Pch; 38 B—B2 winning a piece because of the threat of B—KB5 or B—R2); 38 Q—R7, P—B4; 39 R x B! Q x R; 40 B x P, although Gilg admitted after the game that the advantage would still be with White.

38 B—Kt6   Resigns

There is no good defense to the threat of 39 B x Kt and 40 Q x Pch. If 39 . . . Q—KKt4; 39 Q—Kt8! is the strongest.

---

82. Carlsbad, 1929

INDIAN DEFENSE

After the game was over, Colle remarked naively, "I didn't make a single mistake, but my opponent's moves were still better." There are many ways to win a game of chess, but that is one of the best.

E. Colle   J. R. Capablanca

White   Black

1 P—Q4   Kt—KB3
2 Kt—KB3   P—QKt3
3 P—K3   . . . .

Intending to set up the dreaded Colle System, with which the brilliant Belgian master scored so many beautiful wins. It is fascinating to see how effortlessly Capablanca extracts the venom from this famous formation.

3 . . . .   B—Kt2
4 QKt—Q2   P—K3
5 B—Q3   P—B4
6 O—O   Kt—QB3
7 P—B3   B—K2

Interestingly enough, Black makes no attempt to prevent a possible P—K4, foreseeing the likelihood that his Q4 may be advantageously occupied by his pieces later on.

8 P—K4   P x P
9 Kt x P   . . . .

9 P x P looks imposing, but it allows the troublesome rejoinder 9 . . . Kt—QKt5; 10 B—Kt1, B—R3.

9 . . . .   O—O
10 Q—K2   . . . .

As will soon be apparent, White should have exchanged Knights first.

| 10 . . . . | Kt—K4 |
| 11 B—B2 | Q—B1! |

Gaining mastery of a vital diagonal.

| 12 P—B4 | B—R3 |
| 13 Q—Q1 | Kt—B3 |

Of course not 13 . . . B x R? 14 P x Kt obtaining two pieces for the Rook.

| 14 R—B3 | P—Kt3! |

By closing the important attacking diagonal, Black provides against such possibilities as P—K5 followed by B x Pch and R—R3ch. White is anxious to attack, but his development is too much in arrears at the present moment; thus if 15 Kt x Kt, Q x Kt; 16 P—B5? B—B4 ch; 17 K—R1, Kt—Kt5 and the attack has changed hands.

| 15 Kt(2)—Kt3 | Kt x Kt |
| 16 Kt x Kt | B—Kt2 |

Returning to his first love. The idea is either to keep the KP under observation or else to induce its advance, which will open the diagonal for Black's QB.

| 17 Q—K2 | B—B4! |

Preventing the development of White's QB at this point; the best reply was K—R1, but being anxious to attack, Colle overlooks this precaution and soon finds himself in a difficult situation.

| 18 R—R3 | Q—B3! |

Practically forcing White's reply, for if 19 R—K3, Q—B2; 20 R—B3, P—K4! with considerable advantage.

| 19 P—K5 | Kt—Q4 |
| 20 Q—B2 | . . . . |

In order to play Q—R4. Note that 20 B—K4? is refuted by 20 . . . Kt x QBP!

| 20 . . . . | B x Kt! |

Forcing White's reply, for if 21 Q x B? Kt x KBP.

| 21 P x B | QR—B1! |

He does not fear 22 Q—R4, P—KR4; 23 B—Q1 (threatening B x P), Kt x P! Note that White's KB has only one retreat, thus if 22 B—Kt3, Q x Bch! 23 R x Q, R x Rch with a piece to the good.

| 22 B—Q1 | P—B3! |

Partly for defensive purposes (see his next move); but there is also a threat: 23 B—Q2, Kt x P! 24 B x Kt, P x P; 25 B—B3 (if 25 P x P, R x B!), P—K5! 26 B—K2, P—K6! 27 R x KP, R x B and wins!

| 23 Q—R4 | R—KB2 |
| 24 B—B3 | Q—B5! |

Capablanca

Colle

All of Black's pieces are now placed to advantage and he must win a Pawn (if 25 Q—B2? Q x B). Nor does White's ingenious reply stave off the evil hour.

| 25 B—K3?! | Kt x B |
| 26 B x B | Kt—B4! |

If now 27 Q—B2, Q—QB8ch with an easy endgame win.

| 27 Q—K1 | R—B2 |
| 28 B—K4 | Q x Pch |

29 K—R1   P x P

White's position now disintegrates rapidly.

30 B x Kt	KP x B!
31 P x P	R—K2
32 R—K3	Q x KtP
33 P—K6	P x P
34 R x P	K—B2!

White resigns, for after 35 R x R ch forced, R x R further play would be pointless. A very fine game.

---

83. Carlsbad, 1929

QUEEN'S GAMBIT DECLINED

In this game Capablanca executes a strategem dear to Nimzovich's heart—the establishment of an outpost in a controlled open file—in a manner that must have made the Baltic master swell with pride.

J. R. CAPABLANCA   G. MAROCZY

White	Black
1 P—Q4	Kt—KB3
2 P—QB4	P—K3
3 Kt—KB3	P—Q4
4 B—Kt5	B—K2
5 P—K3	O—O
6 Kt—B3	QKt—Q2
7 R—B1	P—B3
8 Q—B2	P—KR3
9 B—R4	P—R3
10 P x P	Kt x P

Maroczy was a master of the old school, and as such never quite assimilated the spirit of this opening; in consequence his games with it often contain slight inaccuracies. 10 . . . KP x P was better, since White has no need of exchanging Bishops, with his QB on R4.

11 B—Kt3!   Q—R4

This is waste of time, as the sequel indicates. . . . Kt x Kt fol-

lowed by . . . P—QB4 was in order.

| 12 Kt—Q2! | Kt x Kt |
| 13 P x Kt | P—QB4 |

As Capablanca at once demonstrates in clever fashion, this should have been preceded by . . . P—QKt4.

| 14 Kt—B4 | Q—Q1 |
| 15 R—Q1! | . . . . |

Capablanca means to make use of the Q file, even at the expense of leaving himself with a weak QBP; he foresees that the exploitation of the Q file will outweigh the weakness of the QBP.

15 . . . .   P x P

Or 15 . . . P—QKt4; 16 P x P! B x P (or 16 . . . P x Kt; 17 P—B6); 17 Kt—K5 with considerable advantage.

| 16 R x P! | B—B4 |
| 17 R—Q2 | . . . . |

Thoughtfully reserving Q1 for the other Rook.

| 17 . . . . | Q—K2 |
| 18 B—K2 | P—QKt3 |

Seemingly timid, but the more forceful 18 . . . P—QKt4 would be answered by Kt—R5! with embarrassing effect. White has already established a strong bind.

19 Kt—Q6   Kt—B3

. . . P—K4 would cut off the Knight, but then Kt—B5 would be a formidable reply. This consideration applies to the later play as well.

20 O—O   R—R2

This clumsy move can hardly be avoided, for if 20 . . . R—Q1 (not 20 . . . B—Kt2? 21 Kt x B, Q x Kt; 22 B—B3); 21 KR—Q1 (threatening Kt—B5!), B—Q2; 22 B—B3, R—R2; 23 Kt—Kt7 with strong pressure.

| 21 B—B3 | B—Q2 |
| 22 KR—Q1 | P—K4 |

If Black had hoped to obtain a measure of freedom with this move, he soon discovers his mistake.

| 23 B—R4! | P—KKt4? |

Black's position had already become too shaky for such weakening advances. However, if 23 . . . Q—K3; 24 B x Kt, Q x B; 25 Kt—K4, Q—K2; 26 Kt x B, P x Kt; 27 R—Q6 with a winning position.

| 24 B—Kt3 | K—Kt2 |
| 25 B—K2! | P—Kt4 |

In order to release the QR for more fruitful action; but it never comes to that.

Maroczy

Capablanca

| 26 P—KR4! | R—B2 |

This loses quickly, but as the Tournament Book points out, Black had no good continuation: 26 . . . Q—K3; 27 P x P, P x P; 28 Kt—K4, Kt x Kt; 29 Q x Kt, P—B3; 30 B—Q3 and wins (this is one of the useful aspects of 25 B—K2!). Or 26 . . . B x Kt; 27 R x B, R—QB1; 28 P x P, P x P; 29 P—KB4! and Black cannot last very long.

| 27 P x P | P x P |
| 28 Kt—B5ch | . . . . |

Naturally.

| 28 . . . . | B x Kt |
| 29 Q x B | Resigns |

A bit premature, but the outcome is a foregone conclusion:
I 29 . . . K—R3; 30 B x P, R—B3; 31 R—Q7! and wins.
II 29 . . . R—K1; 30 Q x Pch, K—R1; 31 Q—R6ch, Kt—R2; 32 B—Q3 (again the effect of 25 B—K2!), P—B3; 33 B x Kt etc.
A very pleasing game.

---

84.   Ramsgate, 1929

INDIAN DEFENSE

A subtle, difficult game, in which Capablanca makes quite a few far from obvious moves.

W. WINTER   J. R. CAPABLANCA

White	Black
1 P—Q4	Kt—KB3
2 P—QB4	P—K3
3 Kt—QB3	B—Kt5
4 Kt—B3	P—QKt3
5 P—K3	B—Kt2
6 B—Q3	Kt—K5
7 Q—B2	P—KB4

Capablanca seems to be playing for the control of K5—yet at the very next move he has a change of heart.

| 8 O—O | Kt x Kt |

In accordance with the spirit of the previous play, one would now expect 8 . . . B x Kt; 9 P x B, O—O and if 10 Kt—Q2, Q—R5; 11 P—Kt3, Kt—Kt4! (12 P—K4, P x P!).
Instead Capablanca drops the hypermodern motif and actually exchanges the long-range Bishop.

9 P x Kt	B x Kt!?
10 KtP x B	Q—Kt4ch
11 K—R1	B—Q3
12 P—B4	Q—R3

13 R—KKt1   Kt—B3

Capablanca's intention, w h e n
making the previous exchanges,
must have been to create weaknesses in his opponent's Pawn position, with the idea of exploiting
them later on. White should therefore be seeking ways of posting
his pieces to the best advantage:
as for example, B—K2—B3! followed by Q—R4. Fortunately for
Capablanca, his opponent follows
a will-o'-the-wisp in the form of
trying to utilize the KKt file for
attack.

14 Q—K2   Q—B3
15 Q—B3   O—O
16 B—Q2   P—Kt3
17 R—Kt2   R—B2
18 QR—KKt1   . . . .

Black's last two moves should
have been sufficient indication that
a King-side attack is doomed to
failure. But Winter stubbornly
continues with his faulty plan.

18 . . . .   QR—KB1
19 Q—R5   R—Kt2

Putting an end to the transparent threat of R x P ch. If now
20 Q—R6, Kt—Q1; 21 P—KR4??
Kt—B2 and the Queen is lost!

20 Q—R3   Kt—K2!
21 B—K1   Q—B2
22 P—B3   Kt—B1
23 B—R4   B—K2

Capablanca has timed his last
few moves with a view to preventing B—Kt5—R6.

24 B x B   Q x B
25 Q—Kt3   P—Q4!
26 P—K4   . . . .

Black was on the point of improving his position still more with
. . . Kt—Q3; but this nervous move
makes matters worse for White
by exposing his KBP to attack.
The opening of the Bishop's diagonal is no compensation.

26 . . . .   BP x P
27 KBP x P   P x KP
28 B x P   Q—Q3
29 R—KB2   . . . .

The logical course is now 29 . . .
R(2)—B2 to strengthen the pressure on the KBP. But this would
be a serious blunder!

Capablanca

Winter

29 . . . .   Kt—K2!

Not 29 . . . R(2)—D2? 30 B x P!
P x B; 31 Q x P ch, K—R1; 32 R—
B3, R—R2 (if 32 . . . Q—B3; 33
P—Q5); 33 Q x R ch, K x Q; 34 R—
R3 mate!

30 R—K1   R(2)—B2
31 R(1)—KB1   Kt—B4

Forcing the following exchange,
in view of the threat of . . . Kt—
Kt2—R4.

32 B x Kt   R x B
33 K—Kt1   Q—B3
34 Q—Q3   K—R1!

Threatening . . . P—KKt4 and
thus forcing the following weakening reply. White is very much on
the defensive and Capablanca is
in his element.

35 P—KR4   R—R4
36 R—R2   R(4)—KB4

| 37 | R(2)—KB2 | Q—Q3 |
| 38 | Q—K3 | Q—Q1 |

White must consent to the following exchange, for on some such move as 39 Q—Kt3 there follows . . . Q—B3 and eventually . . . P—B4! with new pressure.

39	Q x P	Q x RP
40	Q—K3	R—KR4
41	R—KKt2	Q—R8ch
42	K—B2	Q—R6!

This leaves White without a satisfactory reply, for if 43 Q x Q, R x Q and White's Pawns are due for a massacre. Or 43 Q—B3, R x P! 44 Q x R, R—KB4; 45 Q x R, Q x Q ch; 46 K—Kt1, Q—Q6 and wins.

| 43 | Q—Kt3 | Q—K3! |

Winning a Pawn, with more in sight.

44	K—Kt1	Q x P
45	R—K1	Q—B2
46	R—KB2	R(4)—KB4
47	R—K4	. . . .

Or 47 R(1)—KB1, P—KKt4 and wins.

| 47 | . . . . | P—KKt4 |

White resigns, as his position collapses. The final phase has been most instructive.

---

85.   Budapest, 1929

INDIAN DEFENSE

The Peruvian master Esteban Canal is famous for his aggressive play and the critical portion of this game proves no exception. However, Capablanca meets the crucial test with his customary coolness and comes out victorious.

E. CANAL	J. R. CAPABLANCA
White	Black
1 P—Q4	Kt—KB3

2	P—QB4	P—K3
3	Kt—KB3	P—QKt3
4	P—KKt3	B—Kt2
5	B—Kt2	B—Kt5ch
6	B—Q2	B x Bch
7	QKt x B	. . . .

Q x B is more promising, so as to reserve the more useful square QB3 for the QKt. The text permits Black an easy development.

7	. . . .	O—O
8	O—O	P—B4
9	P x P	. . . .

This gives Black the QKt file, while the pressure on his QP will prove quite bearable. However, P—K3 is intolerably passive, while Kt—Kt3 leaves the QKt stranded on a bad square.

9	. . . .	P x P
10	Q—B2	Kt—B3
11	KR—Q1	Q—Kt3
12	P—QR3	. . . .

This and his next move indicate that he is angling for P—QKt4—an ambition impossible to satisfy if Black plays correctly.

| 12 | . . . . | QR—Kt1 |
| 13 | QR—Kt1 | KR—B1 |

Indirectly aimed against an eventual P—QKt4; but the more direct . . . P—QR4 would have been more to the point.

| 14 | P—K4 | P—K4 |

Both players now strive for the occupation of the opponent's Q5, but Black gets there first (see the note to White's seventh move).

| 15 | Q—Q3 | . . . . |

Hoping to prevent . . . Kt—Q5 because the KP would thereby lose its protection. But the unexpected reply solves this problem neatly.

| 15 | . . . . | P—Q3! |
| 16 | Kt—B1 | Kt—Q5 |

Virtually forcing White's reply, which prevents his occupation of Q5. But Canal finds an ingenious continuation.

| 17 | Kt x Kt | KP x Kt |
| 18 | P—QKt4! | Q—B3!? |

This move has been criticized, and . . . Q—B2 recommended in its stead. But Capablanca shows a masterly understanding of the position in playing the text, for if 18 . . . Q—B2; 19 P x P, P x P; 20 P—B4 followed by P—K5 with a strong game. The text is played to prevent the KP from advancing and involves a far-sighted combination.

| 19 | P x P | P x P |

Capablanca

Canal

| 20 | R x B | . . . . |

Ingenious! The KP advances after all!

20	. . . .	Q x R
21	P—K5	Q—Kt6!
22	P x Kt	Q x Q
23	R x Q	R—Kt8!

The point of Capablanca's combination is now apparent. He is playing to win the QRP, followed by the advance of his passed QRP. The success of this plan is based on the relative helplessness of White's minor pieces. It is this immobility which outweighs their formal superiority to the Black Rook.

24	B—Q5	KR—Kt1
25	K—Kt2	R(1)—Kt6
26	R x R	R x R
27	Kt—Q2	. . . .

P—QR4 would be too slow. White must try to rush all his pieces to the threatened sector as soon as possible.

27	. . . .	R x P
28	Kt—K4	P—QR4
29	Kt x P	P x P

Not 29 . . . P—R5? 30 B—B6.

| 30 | K—B1? | . . . . |

Giving the RP the opportunity of advancing; necessary was 30 B—B6! K—B1; 31 K—B1, K—K2 and the outcome is doubtful.

| 30 | . . . . | P—R5 |

For if 31 B—B6, R—R8ch and the RP continues to march.

31	K—K2	R—R8
32	Kt—Q3	P—R6
33	P—B5	P—R7

Winning a piece; the win is certain but somewhat slow, due to the unfavorable position of Black's King-side Pawns.

34	K—B3	R—Q8
35	B x P	R x Ktch
36	K—K4	R—Q7
37	B—B4	K—B1!

The King is to stop the QBP if need be; of course not 37 . . . R x P? 38 P—B6 etc.

38	P—B3	R x P
39	K x P	K—K2
40	B—Q3	P—R4
41	K—K3	R—KKt7

42	K—B4	R—Kt8
43	B—K4	R—QB8
44	P—B6	R—B6!
45	P—B7	. . . .

Incomprehensible at first sight, but if 45 K—B5, R—B4ch; 46 K—B4, K—K3 (threatens . . . P—B4); 47 P—Kt4, P—R5 and the RP wins easily for Black.

45	. . . .	R x P
46	B—Q5	R—B4
47	B—R2	R—QKt4
48	K—K3	R—R4
49	B—B4	R—QB4
50	B—R6	. . . .

Or 50 B—R2, P—B4 winning in much the same manner.

50	. . . .	K—K3
51	K—B4	R—B6
52	B—B1	P—B4!

White is steadily forced back now.

53	B—R6	K—B3
54	B—Kt7	R—B5ch
55	K—K3	K—Kt4
56	K—B2	P—B5
57	K—Kt2	P—B4

White resigns. There are any number of winning methods, such as 58 B—Q5, R—B7ch; 59 K—R3, P x P; 60 K x P, P—R5ch; 61 K—R3, K—B5.

---

86.   Barcelona, 1929

INDIAN DEFENSE

This is one of those "simple" games in which the Cuban triumphs by means of clear, "obvious" and imperturbable moves. As one plays over the game, it seems as if White were condemned from the very start to lose it!

M. MONTICELLI J. R. CAPABLANCA

White	Black
1 P—Q4	Kt—KB3
2 Kt—KB3	. . . .

More accurate is 2 P—QB4, P—K3; 3 Kt—KB3, P—QKt3; 4 P—KKt3, B—Kt2; 5 B—Kt2 and if 5 . . . P—B4; 6 P—Q5!

2	. . . .	P—QKt3
3	P—KKt3	B—Kt2
4	B—Kt2	P—B4

Now White cannot push by with P—Q5. Regarding this line of play, see also Game No. 64.

5	P x P	P x P
6	P—B4	P—Kt3
7	P—Kt3	B—Kt2
8	B—Kt2	O—O
9	O—O	P—Q3

Despite the superficial symmetry of the position, Black has a slight edge because of his more compact Pawn position, and the eventual possibility of weakening his opponent's game with . . . P—QR4—5. Of course this is only a hope at present.

10	Kt—B3	Kt—K5!
11	Q—B1	Kt x Kt
12	B x Kt	B x B
13	Q x B	P—QR4!

As a result of the removal of White's Knight, . . . P—R5 has now become a real menace.

| 14 | KR—Q1 | Kt—Q2 |
| 15 | Q—K3 | K—Kt2 |

Guarding against the threat of Q—R6 followed by Kt—Kt5.

| 16 | P—KR3 | Kt—B3 |
| 17 | P—KKt4 | . . . . |

Vainly hoping to obtain some attack on the King-side to compensate for Black's threat on the other wing. It should of course be noted that P—QR4 here or on the next two moves would leave a terribly weak QKtP on an open file.

17	P—R3
18 Kt—K1	Q—B2
19 Kt—Q3	. . . .

Tartakower suggests 19 B x B, Q x B; 20 Q—KB3 as offering better chances. This may be correct, but in any event Black would retain the initiative.

19	B x B
20 K x B	P—R5

Thus Black has achieved the first part of his strategical plans. The next step is to increase the pressure.

21 Kt—B4	KR—QKt1!
22 P—B3	P x P
23 P x P	R x R
24 R x R	P—K4!

Surprising at first sight, for it seems to weaken the QP; but since the Knight cannot return to Q3, the actual effect is a strengthening of Black's Pawn formation and an accompanying weakening of White's Pawn position.

25 Kt—Q5	Kt x Kt
26 P x Kt	. . . .

Capablanca

Monticelli

Black appears to win a Pawn with 26 . . . Q—Kt2; but there follows 27 Q—Q3, Q x KtP; 28 Q x Q, R x Q; 29 R—R6 regaining the Pawn.

26 . . .	R—Kt5!

Threatening . . . Q—Kt2 as well as . . . R—Q5. White cannot hold out much longer.

27 Q—Q3	Q—Kt2!

Avoiding the last trap: 27 . . . R—Q5; 28 Q—R6, R x P; 29 Q—R8, R—Q7; 30 R—R7, Q—Kt3; 31 R—Kt7, R x Pch; 32 K—Kt3, R—QR7; 33 R x Q, R x Q; 34 R x P and White can hold the ending (Tartakover).

28 Q—R6	Q x P
29 Q—B8	Q—Kt2!

Black must consolidate his position before capturing more booty. Thus if 29 . . . R x P? 30 R—R8 etc.

30 Q—Q8	Q—Kt1
31 Q—Q7	R—Kt2

Much better than 31 . . . R x KtP; 32 R—R7 etc.

32 Q—B6	R x P
33 R—R6	R—Kt7

White resigns, as he must remain two Pawns down without any compensation.

---

87.   Barcelona, 1929

KING'S INDIAN DEFENSE
(in effect)

Yates a d m i r e d Capablanca's handling of this game so much that he included it as his only loss in the collection of his own best games!   An unusual example of sportsmanship.

J. R. CAPABLANCA   F. D. YATES

White	Black
1 Kt—KB3	Kt—KB3
2 P—B4	P—KKt3
3 P—QKt3	B—Kt2
4 B—Kt2	O—O
5 P—Kt3	P—Q3
6 B—Kt2	Kt—B3
7 O—O	P—K4
8 P—Q4	. . . .

By some rather unusual transpositions, we have reached a position in the King's Indian Defense, of which Yates was so fond.

| 8 . . . . | Kt—Q2 |

A difficult situation for Black. If 8 . . . P x P; 9 Kt x P, B—Q2; 10 Kt—Q2 White's pressure along the diagonal from KKt2 is painful. If on the other hand 8 . . . P—K5; 9 KKt—Q2, R—K1; 10 P—K3 and the exposed state of Black's KP promises to be embarrassing.

| 9 P x P! | . . . . |

Much stronger, of course, than 9 P—Q5, Kt—K2 and Black stands well. The text can hardly be answered by 9 . . . P x P; 10 Kt—B3, Kt—B3; 11 Kt—Q5 with a distinct positional superiority for White.

9	Kt(2) x P
10 Kt—B3	R—K1
11 Kt x Kt!	Kt x Kt

Again if 11 . . . P x Kt; 12 Q x Q followed by Kt—Q5 with marked advantage.

| 12 Q—Q2 | P—QR4 |

. . . R—Kt1 at once was a bit better. The text is played with a view to 13 . . . P—R5; 14 Kt x P, Kt x P!; but Capablanca's reply kills this possibility.

| 13 QR—B1 | R—Kt1 |
| 14 P—KR3 | B—Q2 |

| 15 Kt—Q5! | . . . . |

This is the key to White's strategy. Sooner or later the black-squared Bishops will have to be exchanged, giving White opportunities to exploit the weakness of the black squares. In addition, the ultimate removal of this Knight will give White a very strong center as well as pressure on the newly-opened QB file. All very advantageous perspectives for White.

| 15 . . . . | P—Kt3 |

. . . P—QB3 would weaken the QP critically, while if 15 . . . B—QB3; 16 Q x P, R—R1; 17 Q x P, R x P; 18 Q x Q, R x Q; 19 B x Kt, B x B; 20 P—K3 (Tartakover) and Black has nothing to show for the lost Pawn.

16 P—B4	Kt—B3
17 B x B	K x B
18 Q—Kt2ch	P—B3

Forced. Capablanca proceeds at once to the exploitation of the new weakness.

| 19 P—KKt4 | Kt—Kt5 |

It is clear that the murderous Knight must be removed at once.

| 20 P—Kt5 | Kt x Kt |
| 21 P x Kt | QR—B1 |

White was threatening to win a Pawn with 22 Q x Pch.

| 22 P—K4! | . . . . |

(see diagram next page)

Black must now realize that there is no good defense to the threat of P x Pch followed by P—K5. Tartakover indicates the following possibilities:
I 22 . . . K—B2; 23 P x P, Q x P; 24 P—K5!
II 22 . . . R—B1; 23 P x Pch, Q x P; 24 P—K5! P x P; 26 P x P etc.
III 22 . . . B—Kt4; 23 R—KB2, R—B1; 24 P x Pch, Q x P; 25 P—

Yates

Capablanca

K5, P x P; 26 P x P, Q x Rch; 27 Q x Q, R x Q; 28 K x R and Black has avoided a middle-game catastrophe.

Although this last variation yields only a favorable ending, there is no reason why White should open up the position so quickly. For example, he could simply maintain the pressure with 24 P—KR4.

22	P—B3?
23 P x P	R x BP
24 P x Pch	K—B2

Naturally this Pawn cannot be captured (24 . . . Q x P? 25 Q x Q ch, K x Q; 26 P—K5ch); but after White's reply, which maintains the advanced Pawn, the situation is manifestly hopeless for Black.

25 P—K5	R x R
26 R x R	P x P
27 P x P	Q—Kt1
28 Q—Q4	B—B4

Desperation; if 28 . . . B—K3; 29 R—B6, P—QKt4; 30 Q—B5 wins easily.

| 29 B—Q5ch | K—B1 |

Or 29 . . . B—K3; 30 B x Bch, K x B (if 30 . . . R x B; 31 Q—Q7 ch); 31 R—B6ch, K—B4 (if 31 . . . K—B2; 32 Q—Q7ch); 32 P—B7! and wins.

| 30 Q—KB4! | R x P |

Or 30 . . . R—Q1; 31 Q—R6ch, K—K1; 32 Q—Kt7 etc.

| 31 Q—R6ch | K—K1 |
| 32 P—B7ch! | Resigns |

A nice finish. If 32 . . . K—K2; 33 R—B7ch, B—Q2; 34 P—B8(Q) ch, Q x Q; 35 R x Bch etc.

---

88. Barcelona, 1929

SICILIAN DEFENSE (in effect)

A much admired game in which Capablanca makes faultless use of a positional advantage obtained in the opening.

J. R. CAPABLANCA	E. COLLE
White	Black
1 P—QB4	Kt—KB3
2 Kt—KB3	P—B4
3 Kt—B3	Kt—B3

A careless move which leaves Black with a lasting positional inferiority. Better is 3 . . . P—Q4; 4 P x P, Kt x P etc.

| 4 P—Q4 | P x P |
| 5 Kt x P | Kt x Kt |

Somewhat better was 5 . . . P—KKt3; 6 P—K4, P—Q3, although this Dragon Variation formation always favors White. Likewise unsatisfactory would be 5 . . . P—Q4; 6 P x P, Kt x P; 7 KKt x Kt, P x Kt and Black has a serious weakness for the ending.

6 Q x Kt	P—KKt3
7 P—K4	P—Q3
8 B—K3	B—Kt2
9 P—B3	Q—R4

This turns out to be waste of time, but it is already apparent that the nature of the Pawn formation (White's permanent control of Q5!) gives White a clear advantage in any event.

10 Q—Q2	P—QR3
11 B—K2	B—K3
12 QR—B1!	....

An important preliminary to the natural move P—QKt3, which if played at once would be answered by 12 ... Kt—Kt5! (not 12 ... Kt x P; 13 Kt x Kt, Q x Qch; 14 K x Q, B x R; 15 R x B); 13 B—Q4, B x B; 14 Q x B, Q—K4! and Black has greatly improved his position.

12	QR—B1
13 P—QKt3	Kt—Q2

Giving his KB more scope, but this does not improve the situation appreciably. The fact is that Black is dying a lingering death.

14 O—O	O—O
15 Kt—Q5!	Q—Q1

Since ... Q x Q? would lose a Pawn, Black must return to Q1 with further loss of time.

16 Q—Kt4	B x Kt

Giving White two Bishops and control of the QB file, but there was little choice: 16 ... R—Kt1? 17 B—R7.

17 BP x B	R x R

He cannot dispute control of the QB file; after 17 ... P—QKt4 White could play 18 R x R, Q x R; 19 R—B1, Q—Kt2; 20 P—QR4! or simply 18 Q—R3 with decisive pressure on the Queen-side.

18 R x R	Q—Kt1
19 Q—B4	....

In order to maintain control of the QB file. Tartakover suggests that Black's best chance here is 19 ... Kt—B4; 20 B x Kt, R—B1; 21 Q—Kt4, P x B; 22 R x P, R x R; 23 Q x R, B—K4; 24 P—Kt3, Q—B2 and the Bishops of opposite color offer Black considerable drawing chances.

19	B—Kt7

20 R—B2	B—B3
21 P—B4!	....

White now plays for the further advance of the KP, which must be decisive.

21	R—Q1
22 Q—B7!	....

Colle

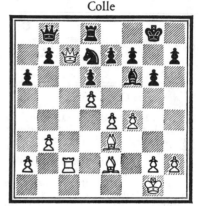

Capablanca

22	Q—R1

A wretched place for the Queen, but Tartakover shows that the seemingly preferable 22 ... Kt—B4 would also be unsatisfactory: 23 Q x Q, R x Q; 24 P—K5, B—Kt2; 25 B x Kt, R—QB1; 26 P—QKt4, P—Kt3; 27 B x RP, R—B2; 28 B—Q3 (the simplest; 28 R—Q2 also wins), QP x B; 29 P x P, P x P (or 29 ... R x P; 30 R x R, P x R; 31 P—QR4 and the RP can't be stopped!); 30 B—Kt5 winning easily.

23 B—Kt4!	Kt—B4

Desperation; if 23 ... Kt—B1; 24 P—K5, P x P; 25 P x P, B—Kt2; 26 B—B8! with a murderous position.

24 P—K5!	B—Kt2
25 Q x KP	P—KR4

Trying to free himself, he gets

into even greater trouble. However, after 25 . . . B—B1 White
simply continues 26 Q—B7 leaving
Black in a hopeless state.

26	P—K6!	P x B
27	P x Pch	K—R2
28	Q—R4ch	B—R3
29	P—B5	P—KKt4

Or 29 . . . K—Kt2; 30 Q x Bch,
K x P; 31 Q x Pch, K—K2; 32 Q—
Kt7ch, K—K1; 33 P—B6, R—Q2;
34 Q—Kt8 mate.

| 30 | B x P | K—Kt2 |
| 31 | Q x Bch | Resigns |

Black has been drastically punished for his unsatisfactory handling of the opening and the resulting poor position of his pieces.

---

89. Hastings Christmas Tournament, 1930-1931

INDIAN DEFENSE

It is curious that in his games
with the great Belgian master of
the attack, Capablanca generally
obtained the initiative early in the
game and thereafter dictated its
further progress.

J. R. CAPABLANCA   E. COLLE

White   Black

1	P—Q4	Kt—KB3
2	P—QB4	P—K3
3	Kt—QB3	B—Kt5
4	Q—B2	P—Q4
5	P x P	Q x P

. . . P x P is safer, but it leads
to rather a dull game in which
White's prospects are more promising.

| 6 | Kt—B3 | O—O |
| 7 | B—Q2 | B x Kt |

| 8 | P x B | . . . . |

For the more natural-looking 8
B x B, see Game No. 110.

8	. . . .	QKt—Q2
9	P—K3	P—B4
10	P—B4	Q—Q3

The issue is clearly joined:
White has the freer game, and two
Bishops; Black on the other hand,
has prospects of exploiting the
somewhat shaky Pawn position of
his opponent.

| 11 | R—Q1 | . . . . |

Clearly foreshadowing his intention of operating on the Q file.

| 11 | . . . . | P—QKt3 |
| 12 | B—B3 | P—KR3 |

. . . B—Kt2 at once was in order.
It is not clear what Black had in
mind in playing the text.

13	B—K2	B—Kt2
14	O—O	Q—B2
15	P x P	P x P

15 . . . Q x P looks attractive,
in order to keep the QB file open
for pressure on the QBP; but then
Q—Kt2! (primarily threatening B—
Kt4) is quite strong.

| 16 | Q—Kt2! | QR—Kt1 |
| 17 | Q—R1! | . . . . |

Capablanca maintains his hold
on the long diagonal, even at the
seeming cost of putting the Queen
out of play. What he has in mind
soon becomes apparent.

| 17 | . . . . | Kt—Kt5?! |

Threatening . . . B x Kt with
ruinous consequences for White.
As Capablanca naturally does not
care for the position which arises
out of 18 P—Kt3, P—K4; 19 P—
KR3, P—K5 etc., he must find
some better way of meeting the
mating threat.

Colle

Capablanca

| 18 R x Kt! | Q x R |
| 19 B x P | Q—B2 |

After this there is no fight left in Black's game, as he goes steadily downhill. But if 19 . . . KR—K1; 20 Kt—K5! Kt x Kt; 21 Q x Kt, P—B4; 22 B x P and White has both positional and material compensation for the sacrificed exchange.

| 20 B x R | R x B |
| 21 P—Kt3 | . . . . |

This move has proved unavoidable, but after the foregoing exchanges, White has little to fear in the way of attack.

| 21 . . . . | P—B3 |
| 22 Kt—R4 | Kt—K4 |

Still dreaming of exploiting the long diagonal. Capablanca defends himself deftly.

| 23 P—B4! | Q—B3!? |
| 24 K—B2! | Q—K5 |

Hoping to fish in troubled waters after 25 P x Kt, P x Pch. But as usual, Capablanca takes the simplest way:

| 25 Q—Kt1! | Q x Q |

After this forced exchange of Queens, Black's attack vanishes, and all that remains for White is the technical task of making use of his extra Pawn.

26 R x Q	B—K5
27 R—Kt3	Kt—Q2
28 R—R3	R—R1
29 R—R5	. . . .

The ideal place for the Rook, as it attacks two weaknesses simultaneously.

| 29 . . . . | K—B2 |
| 30 Kt—B3 | . . . . |

The Knight comes into strong play in short order.

30	K—K2
31 Kt—Q2	B—B3
32 B—B3!	B x B
33 K x B	K—Q3

Striving to get to QKt3.

34 Kt—K4ch	K—B3
35 R—R6ch	Kt—Kt3
36 Kt x KBP	K—Kt2
37 R—R5	R—QB1
38 Kt—K4	Kt x P
39 R—Kt5ch!	Resigns

For if 39 . . . K—R3; 40 R x P with an easy win. Note that if 39 Kt x Pch? K—Kt3; 40 Kt—Kt3, Kt—Q7ch. Or 39 R x BP? Kt—Q7ch! etc.

---

90. New York, 1931

RETI OPENING

It is instructive to see how Capablanca opens up vital lines in a seemingly blocked position, by means of a temporary sacrifice. The preferable position of his pieces gives him a superiority in the sequel which soon proves decisive.

J. R. Capablanca   A. Santasiere

White	Black
1 Kt—KB3	Kt—KB3
2 P—QKt3	P—Q4
3 B—Kt2	B—B4
4 P—Kt3	P—K3
5 B—Kt2	QKt—Q2
6 O—O	B—Q3
7 P—Q3	P—KR3
8 QKt—Q2	Q—K2
9 R—K1	P—K4

White was threatening to win a piece with P—K4—K5. The system of development used here by Black was first adopted by Capablanca himself in his game with Reti in the London 1922 Tournament, and has since then been known as the London System. The position now arrived at, became famous as a result of the memorable encounter between Reti and Dr. Lasker in the New York 1924 Tournament. In that game Reti strove to secure the advantage by relying exclusively on his fianchettoed Bishops. In the present game, White relies on an advance in the center (P—K4). The whole system was first worked out for White by Kevitz.

10 P—B4	P—B3

Note that the seemingly attractive move . . . P—K5? is refuted by 11 Kt—Q4! winning a Pawn.

11 P x P!	P x P
12 P—K4!	P x P

Virtually compulsory, as he must not permit the opening of the K file.

13 P x P	B—K3
14 Kt—R4!	P—KKt3

If 14 . . . O—O; 15 Kt—B5, B x Kt; 16 P x B opening the diagonal of White's KB and giving him a distinct positional advantage.

15 Kt—B1!	O—O
16 Kt—K3	KR—B1?

Relatively better would have been . . . B—QKt5 followed by . . . Kt—Kt3, although even then White's game would have been preferable. The superficial text is refuted in drastic fashion.

Santasiere

Capablanca

17 Kt(4)—B5!	P x Kt
18 P x P	P—K5

Closing the diagonal of White's KB, but opening the diagonal of the other Bishop with disastrous effect. 18 . . . R—B2; 19 P x B, Q x P; 20 Kt—Q5! Kt x Kt; 21 B x Kt was the lesser evil.

19 P x B	Q x P
20 B—KR3!	. . . .

He parts with this Bishop gladly, as its usefulness is over.

20	Q x B
21 Q x B	R—B3
22 Q—B4	R—K1

So that if 23 Kt—B5? Kt—Q4 etc.

23 QR—B1!	Kt—R4
24 Q—B5	Q x Q
25 Kt x B	R(1)—K3

The exchange of Queens enables White to concentrate on his opponent's weaknesses in the most effective manner. There is hardly

anything better than the text, for
if 25 . . . R(1)—QB1? 26 Kt—
K7ch.

| 26 R x R | P x R |

A new weakness, but an unavoidable one.

| 27 R—Q1 | Kt—K4 |

Losing a Pawn, but 27 . . . Kt—
Kt3; 28 R—Q8ch, K—R2; 29 R—
R8ch, K—Kt3; 30 P—KKt4! is
even worse.

28 Kt x Pch	K—Kt2
29 Kt—Kt4	P—B3
30 B x Kt	P x B
31 R—K1	K—Kt3

Black might just as well resign;
the position is hopeless.

32 R x P	K—B4
33 P—B3	Kt—Kt2
34 Kt—K3ch	K—B3
35 R—QR4	R—Q3

Or 35 . . . R—K2; 36 R—R6
winning another Pawn just the
same (36 . . . R—QB2? 37 Kt—
Q5ch).

| 36 R x P | R—Q7 |
| 37 Kt—Kt4ch | Resigns |

Just in time. If 37 . . . K—Kt3;
38 Kt x Pch followed by Kt x P.
The instructive exploitation of
Black's weaknesses has resulted in
a remarkably quick finish.

---

91. New York, 1931

QUEEN'S INDIAN DEFENSE

This game teaches a valuable
lesson about the importance of
developing one's pieces on squares
where they will be able to play a
useful part in the subsequent unfolding of the game. White disregards the necessity for the
effective placement of his pieces
and suffers accordingly.

F. J. MARSHALL   J. R. CAPABLANCA

White	Black
1 Kt—KB3	Kt—KB3
2 P—Q4	P—K3
3 P—B4	P—QKt3
4 P—KKt3	B—Kt2
5 B—Kt2	B—Kt5ch
6 B—Q2	B x Bch
7 QKt x B	. . . .

As already pointed out in Game
No. 85, White does better to retake with the Queen, so that he
can bring his QKt to the far preferable square QB3. In combination
with Q—B2 and P—K4, he would
then have an excellent game.

| 7 . . . . | O—O |

Had White played 7 Q x B, he
could now continue with 8 Kt—B3
and if 8 . . . P—B4; 9 P—Q5. But
as matters stand, the advance of
the QP is now impossible.

8 O—O	P—B4!
9 P x P	P x P
10 R—B1	. . . .

Rather pointless. White's proper course is to double Rooks on the
Q file, at the same time posting his
QKt more effectively by means of
Kt—Kt1—B3. As White plays, he
soon drifts into a bad game.

10	Q—B2
11 Kt—Kt3?	P—Q3
12 Q—Q2	Kt—B3
13 KR—Q1	KR—Q1
14 Kt—R4	P—QR4!

While Marshall has not played
so well as Canal in Game No. 85,
Capablanca has improved on his
play in that game. The maneuver
P—QR3 followed by P—QKt4 is
virtually ruled out, and Black prepares comfortably to exercise
pressure on the QKt file.

| 15 P—QR4? | . . . . |

A natural reaction to Black's last move, but it merely exposes the QRP to later attack. Far superior was the posting of the QKt on a better square by means of Kt—R1—B2—R3 intending Kt—Kt5.

15 . . . .   QR—Kt1
16 R—B3   B—R1
17 P—R3   . . . .

Or 17 R—Q3, Kt—K4; 18 R—QB3 (if 18 R x P? R x R; 19 Q x R, Q x Q; 20 R x Q, Kt—K1! and wins), B x B followed by . . . R—Kt5. White is already reduced to helplessness.

17 . . . .   Kt—QKt5
18 B x B   R x B
19 Q—B4   Q—B3!

20 R—R1 is now virtually impossible because of 20 . . . P—Q4! followed by . . . P—Q5 with a winning advantage.

20 R—B3   R—Q2!

Partly in order to defend the KBP against a possible P—Kt4—5 but also to make the win of a Pawn possible two moves later.

21 P—Kt4   Q x P
22 R x P   . . . .

Capablanca

Marshall

22 . . . .   Kt(5)—Q4!

Wins a Pawn. If Black's KR were still on Q1, White could save himself—temporarily, at any rate —with R x Rch.

23 Q—K5   R x R
24 Q x R   Kt—K5
25 Q—K5   Q x P

Black has an easy win now. Capablanca winds up neatly and quickly.

26 R—Q3   P—R5!
27 P—B3   Kt(5)—B3
28 Kt—Q2   Q—B8ch
29 K—B2   P—R3
30 P—B4   P—B5
31 R—Q4   P—B6!

Not 31 . . . Q x P?? 30 R x Kt.

32 P x P   P—R6
33 P—Kt5   P—R7
34 Kt—Kt3   Q x P
35 P x Kt   Q x Kt
36 R—Q1   Q x R

White resigns. A simple but pleasing game.

---

92. Match, 1931
(Ninth Game)

QUEEN'S GAMBIT DECLINED

This game contains one of those strange "double errors" which sometimes attack even the greatest masters. Somewhat favored by l u c k , Capablanca subsequently winds up the game with a number of trenchant and elegant moves.

J. R. CAPABLANCA   DR. M. EUWE

White   Black

1 P—Q4   P—Q4
2 Kt—KB3   Kt—KB3
3 P—B4   P—B3

4 Kt—B3	P x P
5 P—QR4	B—B4

For more than a decade the merits of this line of play have been hotly disputed, and even now the last word has not been said.

6 Kt—K5	QKt—Q2
7 Kt x QBP(4)	Q—B2
8 P—KKt3	P—K4
9 P x P	Kt x P
10 B—B4	KKt—Q2
11 B—Kt2	B—K3

The alternative 11 . . . P—B3 seems to have been disposed of at once for all in the first game of the return match between Alekhine and Euwe (1937): 12 O—O, R—Q1; 13 Q—B1, B—K3; 14 Kt—K4! B—QKt5; 15 P—R5! with a decided positional advantage for White.

12 Kt x Kt	Kt x Kt
13 O—O	Q—R4

In his first World Championship Match in 1935, Euwe varied with 13 . . . B—K2; 14 Q—B2, R—Q1; 15 KR—Q1, O—O; 16 Kt—Kt5!; Black lost very quickly. As will be seen, the text also leads to a precarious position.

14 Kt—K4	R—Q1
15 Q—B2	B—K2

Relatively better was 15 . . . B—QKt5 and if 16 Kt—Kt5, B—QB1; 17 Q—K4, B—Q3; 18 KR—Q1, P—B3. Black's position would then be uncomfortable but playable.

16 P—QKt4	. . . .

A characteristic sacrifice in this variation. Black has little choice, for if 16 . . . Q—B2; 17 Kt—B5 with a position much in White's favor.

16	B x P
17 Q—Kt2	P—B3
18 KR—Kt1?	. . . .

This move has a serious tactical flaw—something quite unusual in Capablanca's games. The point is that **White is not even threatening to take the Bishop because of the reply . . . R—Q8ch.**
The correct move was 18 QR—Kt1, B—K2; 19 B x Kt followed by the capture of the QKtP, with a very superior game for White.

18	O—O?

Not the best, 18 . . . Kt—B5 being the proper reply.
However, it was not easy to see that White would obtain the advantage after the text; and in addition, 18 . . . Kt—B5 may have seemed unfavorable because of the possible reply 19 Kt x Pch? — although this would at once be refuted by 19 . . . K—B2.

19 B x Kt	P x B
20 Kt—Kt5!	B—B6

20 . . . B—B2 would have been a bit better, but then 21 B—K4 would have left White with a vastly superior game.

21 Q—B2	B—B4

Euwe

Capablanca

22 B—K4!	P—KKt3

There was no wholly satisfactory move. Thus if 22 . . . B x R; 23

BxB, P—KKt3 (if 23 . . . P—
KR3?? 24 B—K6ch etc.); 24 BxP
etc. Or 22 . . . P—KR3; 23 BxB,
PxKt; 24 R—R3! B—Q5; 25 P—
Kt4! R—B3; 26 R—R3, R—R3; 27
RxR, PxR; 28 B—K6ch, K—R1
(or 28 . . . K—Kt2; 29 RxPch);
29 Q—Kt6 and wins.

23 Q—R2ch   K—Kt2
24 RxPch   R—Q2
25 QR—Kt1   . . . .

White has regained his Pawn
and in addition has enough pressure to assure himself an easy win.

25 . . . .   Q—R3
26 Q—Kt3!   RxR

The plausible alternative 26 . . .
B—Q5 leads to the loss of a piece
by means of 27 RxRch, BxR; 28
Q—Kt7, QxQ; 29 RxQ, since 29
. . . R—Q1? would now be refuted
by 30 Kt—K6ch. The kaleidoscopic
collapse of Black's position in only
a handful of moves is quite remarkable.

27 QxRch   QxQ
28 RxQch   K—Kt1

If 28 . . . K—R3; 29 P—KR4 is
immediately decisive.

29 BxP   R—Q1
30 RxQRP   R—Q3
31 B—K4   B—Q2
32 P—R4   B—Q5
33 R—R8ch   K—Kt2
34 P—K3   B—B6
35 B—B3   Resigns

Black has nothing left to play
for.

---

93. Los Angeles, 1933
(Exhibition Game)

FOUR KNIGHTS' GAME

This game, played with "living
pieces," turns out to be vastly en-

tertaining and must have delighted
the spectators.

J. R. Capablanca   H. Steiner
White   Black

1 P—K4   P—K4
2 Kt—KB3   Kt—QB3
3 Kt—B3   Kt—B3
4 B—Kt5   B—Kt5
5 O—O   O—O

In adopting this game, Capablanca has harked back to a favorite line of play of his younger
years. In consequence the game
takes on a certain nostalgic quality.

6 P—Q3   P—Q3
7 B—Kt5   BxKt
8 PxB   Kt—K2

It is pretty well established nowadays that 8 . . . Q—K2 is preferable to the text, which is likely to
cause trouble for Black because of
the resulting broken-up King-side.

9 Kt—R4   P—B3

9 . . . Kt—Kt3 is simply answered
by 10 KtxKt and 11 P—KB4 with
excellent prospects for White.

10 B—QB4   B—K3

The position is a difficult one.
The attempt to simplify by 10 . . .
P—Q4; 11 B—Kt3! PxP; 12 PxP,
QxQ; 13 QRxQ, Kt—Kt3; 14 Ktx
Kt, PxKt turns out in White's
favor after 15 BxKt, PxB; 16 P—
KB4!

11 BxKt   PxB

Not 11 . . . BxB? 12 Q—Kt4
and wins.

12 BxB   PxB
13 Q—Kt4ch   K—B2
14 P—KB4!   . . . .

Naturally. White has an easy
initiative, and his opponent finds
himself in a most uncomfortable
position.

14	KR—Kt1

. . . Kt—Kt3 was relatively better, although his game would have remained inferior.

15 Q—R5ch	K—Kt2
16 P x P	QP x P

Steiner

Capablanca

17 R x P!!	. . . .

A stormy break-through which leaves Black defenseless.

17	K x R
18 R—B1ch	Kt—B4
19 Kt x Kt!	. . . .

Played in the grand manner, and much more forcing than P x Kt.

19	P x Kt
20 R x Pch	K—K2
21 Q—B7ch	K—Q3
22 R—B6ch	K—B4

It is clear that after 22 . . . Q x R; 23 Q x Qch etc. White's Pawn preponderance would win easily.

23 Q x KtP!	Q—Kt3

Seemingly guarding against the two-fold mating threat.

24 R x Pch	Q x R
25 Q—Kt4 mate	

A charming game.

---

94. Margate, 1935
INDIAN DEFENSE

It is a source of never-ceasing wonder to see how quickly a bad game can be obtained in a variation which has virtually been analysed to death. One or two little inexactitudes, and the remainder of the game is "only a matter of technique."

J. R. CAPABLANCA   G. A. THOMAS

White	Black
1 P—Q4	Kt—KB3
2 P—QB4	P—K3
3 Kt—KB3	B—Kt5ch
4 B—Q2	Q—K2
5 P—KKt3	P—QKt3
6 B—Kt2	B—Kt2
7 O—O	B x B

As is well-known, the exchange cannot be postponed any longer (7 . . . O—O? 8 B—B4! or B—Kt5! and Black's KB is badly out of play).

8 QKt x B	. . . .

Surprising, as Capablanca had had ample opportunity to realize the value of Q x B from some of his earlier games (see Games No. 85 and 91).

8	P—Q3

Routine play. Correct was 8 . . . P—B4! forcing a clarification in the center, as in the games just quoted. The plausible text soon leaves Black with a distinctly inferior game.

9 Q—R4ch!	P—B3

Not the best reply to White's surprising check. If 9 . . . Kt—B3?
10 P—Q5 wins a piece, and if 10
. . . Q—Q2 or 10 . . . B—B3; 11
Q—B2 and Black must lose further
time to develop properly. However,
9 . . . QKt—Q2 (the most natural
reply); 10 KR—K1, P—B4; 11 P—
K4 is not quite satisfactory for
Black.

| 10 P—K4 | O—O |
| 11 P—K5 | Kt—K1 |

Even at so early a stage, Black's
game has already taken on an
appearance of hopelessness. If 11
. . . P x P; 12 P x P followed by
Kt—K4 and White has gained the
use of the Q file for bearing down
on the weak point Q6.

| 12 KR—K1 | P—QB4 |

Necessary if Black is to free himself somewhat; but, as is to be expected, it is White who benefits
from the resulting open lines.

| 13 KP x P | Kt x P |

This results in a weak QBP, but
after 13 . . . Q x P; 14 P—Q5!
Black would be left with an isolated
KP, which if anything would be
even weaker.

14 P x P	P x P
15 Q—R5!	Kt—Q2
16 P—Kt3	KR—Q1
17 QR—Q1	QR—B1
18 Kt—B1	. . . .

Beginning a long tour with this
Knight with the object of bringing
it to bear on Black's weak Queenside. White's position is of the
kind which plays itself. All his
pieces are posted to good advantage, while Black must always
worry about his weak Pawns.

| 18 . . . . | P—QR3 |

It is true that the Pawn was not
menaced at the moment, as Q x
RP?? would lose the Queen; but
sooner or later the Pawn would
require direct protection.

| 19 Kt—K3 | Kt—Kt1 |

Obviously played with a heavy
heart; but the alternative 19 . . .
Q—B1 is equally uninviting, the
simplest reply being the doubling
of White's Rooks on the Q file.

| 20 Kt—Q5! | Q—B1 |

Or 20 . . . B x Kt; 21 P x B and
Black's KP will be fatally weak
(B—R3 etc.).

| 21 Kt—Kt6 | R—B2 |
| 22 Kt—QR4 | . . . . |

The Knight is now posted to good
effect after its remarkable tour.

| 22 . . . . | R(1)—B1 |
| 23 Kt—K5! | . . . . |

Bringing this Knight as well into the attack on the QBP, and also
causing a general weakening of
Black's game by the exchange of
Bishops.

23	B x B
24 K x B	Kt—B4
25 Kt—Q3	Q—Q3?!

He gives up a Pawn in what
proves to be a vain effort to obtain
some counterattack. Against other
moves White would continue to
strengthen his position.

| 26 Kt(3) x P | Q—B3ch |

With this and the next few
moves, Black tries to obtain some
counterchances. But Capablanca
repulses the attack with ease.

| 27 K—Kt1 | P—R4 |
| 28 Kt—Q3 | P—R5 |

Just as it begins to look as if
Black might accomplish something,
White takes command.

29 Kt—K5	Q—Kt2
30 Q—Kt6	P x P
31 RP x P	Q—R1

Naturally the exchange of Queens
would be quite hopeless.

32 R—Q8ch!	R x R

Or 32 . . . K—R2; 33 R x R, R x R; 34 Kt x P and Black can resign.

33 Q x R	R—KB1
34 Kt—QKt6	Resigns

Thomas

Capablanca

An extraordinary finish.

---

95.   Moscow, 1935

QUEEN'S GAMBIT DECLINED

Many of Capablanca's wins remind one of the "painless" extraction of a tooth. The game meanders along placidly, the opponent suspects nothing, and . . . suddenly he realizes that his resignation is in order.

V. ALATORTSEV   J. R. CAPABLANCA

White	Black
1 P—Q4	Kt—KB3
2 P—QB4	P—K3
3 Kt—QB3	P—Q4
4 B—Kt5	B—K2
5 P—K3	O—O
6 P x P	Kt x P

With this simplifying move, Capa-

blanca avoids the somewhat troublesome line 6 . . . P x P; 7 Q—B2, P—B3; 8 B—Q3 followed by KKt—K2, which was used against him to such good effect in the 1927 World Championship Match.

7 B x B	Q x B
8 Kt—B3	. . . .

By making this rather lackadaisical move, White indicates that he is not interested in trying to secure an opening advantage. More energetic alternatives are Q—Kt3, Q—B2 and R—B1.

8	Kt x Kt

This additional exchange will make it possible for Black to obtain the initiative later on with . . . P—QB4.

9 P x Kt	P—QKt3
10 B—K2	. . . .

Even at this early stage, White realizes that he must content himself with modest moves. Thus, 10 B—Q3, B—Kt2; 11 P—K4 looks more forceful; but after . . . O—O, . . . P—QB4, . . . Kt—B3 and . . . KR—Q1 White would find that his aggressive-looking center would be more of a liability than an asset.

10	B—Kt2
11 O—O	P—QB4
12 Kt—K5	Kt—B3
13 Kt x Kt	. . . .

Or 13 Kt—Q3, P x P; 14 BP x P, Kt—R4 and Black stands well.

13	B x Kt
14 B—B3	QR—B1
15 P—QR4	. . . .

Hoping to continue in due course with P—R5; but this possibility never materializes.

15	P x P
16 BP x P	P—Kt3

The creation of such a flight-square is always advisable when an ending with only the heavy pieces is in the offing.

17 B x B   R x B

An attempt to dispute control of the QB file is now impossible: 18 R—B1, KR—B1; 19 R x R, R x R; 20 Q—Kt3 (if 20 Q—Q2, Q—R6), Q—B2 with appreciable advantage for Black despite the previous simplifications.

18 Q—Q3   . . . .

Preparing for P—R5, which if played at once, could be answered by ... P—QKt4.

18 . . . .   Q—Kt2
19 KR—Kt1   . . . .

See the previous note. Nevertheless, QR—Kt1 would have been better.

19 . . . .   KR—B1
20 P—R3   . . . .

For if 20 P—R5, P—QKt4! 21 R x P? R—B8ch and White must resign. This explains why it would have been better to play 19 QR—Kt1.

20 . . . .   P—QR3!

Now P—R5 can always be answered by ... P—QKt4.

21 Q—R3?   . . . .

Failing to see the possibilities in the following occupation of the second rank. Q—K2 was better; if then ... R—B7; Q—B3 etc.

21 . . . .   R—B7!
22 Q—Q6?   . . . .

He does not see Black's terrible reply. However, Alatortsev later admitted that after the following replies, Black would still maintain a clear advantage:
I 22 R—R2, R(1)—B6; 23 R—Kt3, R—B8ch; 24 K—R2, Q—B2ch; 25 P—B4 (if 25 P—Kt3, Q—B3!),

R x R; 26 Q x R, R—B6 etc.
II 22 R—Kt2, R—B8ch; 23 R x R, R x Rch; 24 K—R2, Q—B2ch etc.
Also if 22 Q—Kt3, R(1)—B3 followed by ... Q—B2 and Black's positional advantage should suffice to win.

Capablanca

Alatortsev

22 . . . .   R x P !

A terrible surprise for White. The game is as good as over.

23 Q—Kt3   . . . .

If instead 23 K x R, R—B7ch; 24 K—Kt3 (if 24 K—K1, Q x P; 25 Q—Kt8ch, K—Kt2; 26 Q—K5ch, P—B3 and White is helpless), R x Pch (... Q x Pch also wins); 25 K—B4 (if 25 K—R4, Q—K5ch; 26 Q—B4, P—Kt4ch; 27 K—R5, Q—Kt3 mate), R—B7ch; 26 K—Kt5, Q—Kt7ch; 27 K—R4, P—Kt4 ch; 28 K—R5, Q x Pch; 29 K x P, R—B4 mate.

23 . . . .   R—K7

White resigns, for after 24 R—QB1, R x Rch; 25 R x R, Q—K5 he lacks the slightest chance of saving the game.

96. Moscow, 1935
(Special Prize)
INDIAN DEFENSE

This is one of the famous Capablanca games in which the opponent is systematically throttled until he has no moves left. Despite the absence of sensational details, such games have a quiet artistry which is deeply impressive.

J. R. CAPABLANCA	V. RAGOZIN
White	Black
1 P—Q4	Kt—KB3
2 P—QB4	P—K3
3 Kt—QB3	B—Kt5
4 P—QR3	. . . .

An unusual kind of move for Capablanca, who loved clarity above all. The text gives White two Bishops and attacking chances at the cost of a weak Queen-side.

| 4 . . . . | B x Ktch |
| 5 P x B | P—Q3 |

. . . P—B4 is more elastic, leaving Black a later choice of . . . P—Q3 or . . . P—Q4.

6 Q—B2	O—O
7 P—K4	P—K4
8 B—Q3	P—B4
9 Kt—K2	Kt—B3
10 P—Q5	Kt—K2?

A highly illogical move which condemns Black to permanent passivity. Correct was . . . Kt—QR4 to be followed by . . . P—QKt3 and . . . B—R3; the text, on the other hand, leaves Black without counterplay.

| 11 P—B3 | Kt—Q2 |

Another ill-judged move. The right way was 11 . . . Kt—K1! and if then 12 P—Kt4 (to prevent the freeing move . . . P—B4), Kt—Kt3 and Black's position is much better than in the actual

game. Likewise if 12 Kt—Kt3, White will have to content himself with a less threatening position on the King-side.

| 12 P—KR4! | . . . . |

Alertly taking advantage of his opponent's lapse. If now 12 . . . Kt—KKt3; 13 P—R5 and Black has only lost time.

| 12 . . . . | Kt—QKt3 |
| 13 P—Kt4 | P—B3? |

Losing his head completely. The text creates a target which makes it possible for White to open the KKt file; which means that Black's King will be dangerously insecure. A much better plan was later indicated by Ragozin: 13 . . . B—Q2; 14 Kt—Kt3 (if 14 P—R4, Q—K1; 15 P—QR5, Kt(3)—B1 followed by . . . P—QKt3), Kt—R5 followed by . . . P—QR3 and . . . P—QKt4.

| 14 Kt—Kt3 | K—B2 |

Foreseeing the eventual attack, Black begins to remove the King from the danger zone.

| 15 P—Kt5! | Kt—Kt1 |

There is little choice: if 15 . . . P x P; 16 P x P, K—Kt1 (with the idea of making the KR useful on the KB file); 17 Q—KR2 and wins.

| 16 P—B4! | . . . . |

Ordinarily this is out of place because it usually gives one's opponent an opportunity of posting a Knight on K4. But here, after 16 . . . KP x P; 17 B x P the weakness of Black's QP would become painfully noticeable.

| 16 . . . . | K—K1 |
| 17 P—B5! | . . . . |

The encirclement process is now shaping up. However, it requires considerable skill, as will be seen, to batter down Black's Steinitzian position.

17 . . .	Q—K2
18 Q—KKt2	K—Q1
19 Kt—R5	K—B2
20 P x P	P x P

In view of the heavy concentration of White's forces on the Kingside, Black has been wise to remove his King. But his troubles are only beginning!

| 21 Kt—Kt7 | B—Q2 |
| 22 P—R5 | . . . . |

It is worth noting that Capablanca does not play the Knight to K6 at once, but defers the move until it will have the most effect.

| 22 . . . . | QR—B1 |

Unfortunately, . . . P—R3 would leave the KRP in too weak a state. White is therefore able to reinforce the terrible Knight.

23 P—R6	K—Kt1
24 KR—Kt1	R—KB2
25 R—Kt1	. . . .

Black has in effect castled all over again, but his King is still insecure, as the text indicates.

25	Q—B1
26 B—K2!	K—R1
27 B—R5	R—K2

Ragozin points out that an attempt to propitiate the enemy with 27 . . . Kt x BP would not do because of 28 B x R, Q x B; 29 Q—K2, Kt—Kt3; 30 Q—R5, Q—K2; 31 Kt—K6 and White's penetration at K6 will be decisive.

28 Q—QR2	Q—Q1
29 B—Q2	Kt—R5
30 Q—Kt3	Kt—Kt3

At first sight . . . R—Kt1 (intending P—Kt4) looks better. But Ragozin refutes the move as follows: 31 Kt—K6! Q—Kt3 (there is nothing better, for White was not only attacking the Queen but also threatening R x Kt! Note also that

if 31 . . . B x Kt; 32 QP x B, Kt—Kt3; 33 B—B7 wins. Or if 31 . . . Q—R4; 32 R x Kt wins); 32 Q x Q, P x Q; 33 Kt—B7ch, K—R2; 34 Kt—Kt5ch, B x Kt; 35 R x B and Black has no defense against the threatened B—Q1. Or here 34 . . . K—R3; 35 Kt x P followed by B—B7 and wins. Amazing variations!

Ragozin

Capablanca

| 31 P—R4! | R—Kt1 |

The wretched state of Black's game is now beginning to tell against him. He cannot answer the surprising advance of the QRP with 31 . . . B x P because of 32 Q—R2, B—Q2 (R x Kt was threatened; if 32 . . . Q—Q2; 33 R x Kt, P x R; 34 B—Q1); 33 Kt—K6, B x Kt; 34 QP x B and again Black has no resource against the coming B—B7.

| 32 P—R5 | Kt—B1 |

Again Black has no choice: 32 . . . Kt—R5; 33 Kt—K6, B x Kt (if 33 . . . Q x P; 34 R x Kt); QP x B and the double threat of Q x Kt or B—B7 is decisive.

33 Q—R2	Q—B1
34 B—K3	P—Kt3
35 P—R6!	Q—Q1

The encirclement is now complete; if 35 . . . P—Kt4; 36 P x P,

B x KtP; 37 Kt—K6 and wins.

36	K—Q2	Q—B1
37	R—QKt2	Q—Q1
38	Q—Kt1!	P—Kt4

Black has been glumly waiting for the ax to fall, but now he finds he must make more room for his pieces, in view of White's contemplated 39 Q—KB1 followed by 40 Kt—K6, B x Kt; 41 BP x B and 42 B—B7.

39	P x P	Kt—Kt3
40	Q—R2	P—B5

To prevent White from solidifying his Pawn position with P—B4.

41	Q—R3	Q—B2
42	K—B1	R—KB1
43	R(2)—Kt2!	Q—Kt1

Black is of course helpless against the coming Kt—K6.

44	Q—Kt4	R—Q1
45	R—Kt3	R—KB1
46	Kt—K6!	. . . .

There are few players in the world who could have resisted for so long a time the natural desire to make this powerful move.

46	. . . .	B x Kt
47	QP x B	R—QB2
48	Q x QP	Kt—K2

Equally disastrous would be 48 . . . R—Q1; 49 Q x R(8), Q x Q; 50 R x Kt etc.

49	R—Q1	Resigns

Masterly position play of the highest order. Black has been left without any play.

---

97. Moscow, 1935

QUEEN'S GAMBIT DECLINED

Although Capablanca was on the defensive throughout, this is one of his best games. The skill he displays in warding off defeat is of a high order, resulting in one of his most instructive games.

S. FLOHR	J. R. CAPABLANCA
White	Black
1 P—Q4	P—Q4
2 P—QB4	P—K3
3 Kt—QB3	Kt—KB3
4 Kt—B3	QKt—Q2
5 B—Kt5	B—K2
6 P—K3	O—O
7 Q—B2	P—B4

A variation popularized by Capablanca in the 1927 World Championship Match. It has little to recommend it, as it leaves White with an easy initiative all the way.

8 BP x P	Kt x P
9 B x B	Q x B

After 9 . . . Kt x B there might follow 10 R—Q1 or 10 P x P, Kt x P; 11 R—Q1 with an uncomfortable game for Black in either event.

10 Kt x Kt	P x Kt
11 B—Q3	P x P

He does not bother to defend the RP, for if 12 B x Pch? K—R1 and White has no time for Kt x P because of the threatened . . . P—KKt3.

12 Kt x P	Q—Kt5ch
13 Q—Q2	Kt—B4
14 B—Kt5	Q x Qch
15 K x Q	P—QR3
16 B—Q3	B—K3

From now on, it is an uphill fight for Black all the way. His isolated QP is bound to give trouble, and White's command of Q4 is very useful.

17 QR—QB1	KR—B1
18 R—B2	Kt x B

Else White doubles on the QB

file and plays P—QKt4. The Tournament Book points out that if 18 ... Kt—Q2; 19 KR—QB1, Kt—Kt3; 20 B—B5 with marked advantage to White.

19 K x Kt	R x R
20 K x R	K—B1
21 K—Q2	R—B1
22 KR—QB1	R x R
23 K x R	....

Flohr now has a position dear to his heart, and the defense requires constant vigilance and foresight. There are not many players in the world who could hold this position against Flohr.

23	K—K2
24 K—Q2	K—Q3
25 K—B3	P—QKt3
26 P—B4	B—Q2
27 Kt—B3	P—B3!
28 K—Q4!	P—QR4!
29 Kt—Q2	B—B1
30 Kt—Kt1	B—K3
31 Kt—B3	K—B3
32 P—QR3	P—R3

As will soon become apparent, Black is in great danger.

33 P—KKt3	P—R4!
34 P—QKt4!	....

Threatening 35 P—Kt5ch, K—Q3; 36 P—B5! B—B2; 37 Kt—K2 followed by Kt—B4. Black would then be reduced to King-moves, and all that would be necessary to win would be to play Kt—K6 at a moment when the Black King is at QB3.

34	P x P
35 P x P	K—Q3
36 P—Kt5!	P—Kt3

Again P—B5 was threatened.

37 Kt—R4	K—B2
38 Kt—B3	K—Q3

39 P—B5!   ....

Initiating a new and very dangerous phase. The sacrificed Pawn is soon recovered, with the result that Black is left with a permanently weakened Pawn position.

39	P x P
40 Kt—K2	B—Q2
41 Kt—B4	B—K1!

Not 41 ... B x P; 42 Kt x RP! and White must win either the KBP or the QP, aside from which his passed RP will be a formidable menace.

42 Kt x QP	B x P
43 Kt x KtP!	....

Again the proper capture, for if 43 Kt x BP, B—K7 followed by ... P—Kt4 etc. and Black should have no difficulty in drawing.

43	B—B3
44 Kt—B4ch	K—K3
45 Kt—Kt2	B—Kt4
46 Kt—Q1	B—K7
47 Kt—B2	B—B8

White's Knight cannot be permitted to reach the deadly square KB4.

48 Kt—Q3!   ....

As he cannot make any further headway with the Knight against the Bishop, Flohr tries the King and Pawn ending. In view of the numerous losing possibilities which beset Black, the following phase is most promising for White. The basic motif of the following play is White's attempt to land his King on KB4; if he ever succeeds in doing so, he will win automatically. But the ending abounds in delicious finesses.

48	B x Kt
49 K x B	....

Capablanca

Flohr

49 . . . .   K—K4!

The natural-looking move 49 . . .
K—Q4? loses after the reply 50
K—Q2!!
I 50 . . . P—R5; 51 P x P, P—
B5; 52 P x P, K—K5; 53 P—R5,
K—B4; 54 K—K3 etc.
II 50 . . . K—K5; 51 K—K2, K—
Q4 (if 51 . . . P—R5; 52 P x P,
P—B5; 53 P—R5! K—B4; 54 P x P
as in the previous variation); 52
K—B3, K—K4; 53 P—R3 (waiting
for Black to exhaust his moves),
K—Q4; 54 K—B4 K—K3; 55 P—
R4. Now Black's moves are ex-
hausted and White wins.
III 50 . . . K—K4; 51 K—K1!!
K—Q4 (if 51 . . . K—K5; 52 K—
K2 wins); 52 K—B2! K—K5; 53
K—K2 and wins as in Variation II.
(Rabinovich in the Tournament
Book.)

50 K—K2   . . . .

If 50 K—Q2, P—R5!! (not 50 . . .
K—K5? 51 K—K2 and White wins
as already shown); 51 P x P, P—
B5! 52 P—R5, P x Pch and draws.
Note that the move . . . P—R5
saves Black in this line of play.

50 . . . .   K—K5!

This is the only move to hold
the game!

51 P—R3   . . . .

Or 51 K—B2, P—R5! (again the
drawing move); 52 P x P (if 52
K—K2, P x P; 53 P x P, K—K4; 54
K—B3, K—Q4; 55 K—B4, K—K3
and now we have the same position as in Variation II above, with
the important exception that because of . . . P—R5 **White has no
tempo moves**, so that the game is
a draw!), P—B5! 53 P—R5 (or 53
P x P, K x P and draws), P x Pch;
draw.

51 . . . .   K—Q4!

Again Capablanca finds the only
move to draw:
I 51 . . . K—K4? 52 K—B3, K—
Q4; 53 K—B4, K—K3; 54 P—R4
(White still has this tempo move
available) and wins.
II 51 . . . P—R5? 52 P x P,
P—B5; 53 P—R5 and wins.

52 K—B3   . . . .

A last hope: 52 . . . K—K3?? 53
K—B4 wins. Or if 52 . . . K—Q3??
53 K—B4, K—K3; 54 P—R4 wins.

52 . . . .   K—K4!

Drawn. If 53 P—R4, K—Q4; 54
K—B4, K—K3 and White can make
no progress, having consumed all
his tempo moves. A magnificent
example of resourceful play in an
unusually difficult position.

---

98. Moscow, 1935

QUEEN'S GAMBIT DECLINED

Capablanca outplays his opponent
all the way and winds up with a
murderous attack. The forceful
timing of the final moves is notable.

J. R. CAPABLANCA   G. LEVENFISH

White	Black
1 P—Q4	P—Q4
2 P—QB4	P—QB3
3 Kt—KB3	Kt—B3

4 P—K3	P—K3
5 Kt—B3	QKt—Q2
6 B—Q3	P x P
7 B x BP	P—QKt4

The Meran Defense, which has been badly battered in recent years.

8 B—Q3	P—QR3
9 P—K4	....

Considerable analysis, supported by a number of important games, has demonstrated conclusively that this forceful continuation is best.

9	P—B4
10 P—K5	P x P
11 Kt x KtP	Kt x P
12 Kt x Kt	P x Kt
13 Q—B3!	....

This is the basic improvement which gives White the better game.

13	R—R4

Likewise after 13 . . . B—Kt5ch; 14 K—K2, QR—Kt1; 15 Q—Kt3! (if 15 Kt—B6, B—Kt2), Q—Q3; 16 Kt—B3! White has the better game.

14 O—O	P—Kt5
15 B—KB4	B—K2

The position calls for extreme caution on Black's part: If 15 . . . B—Q3? 16 Q—B6ch, K—K2; 17 Kt x P! wins.

16 KR—B1!	O—O
17 Q—R3!	....

This wins. It not only threatens Kt—B6, but it is chiefly directed against Black's KR2, which turns out to be inadequately defended.

17	R—B4

There was no defense. Some critics have recommended 17 . . . B—Kt2, overlooking that 18 Kt—Kt4 wins because of the double menace 18 Kt x Ktch and 18 B—B7.

18 R x R	B x R

Levenfish

Capablanca

19 B—KKt5	P—KR3

What to do?! If 19 . . . R—K1; 20 Kt—B6 followed by B x Kt and wins. If 19 . . . P—Kt3; 20 Kt—B6, Q—Q2; 21 B x Kt, Q x Kt; 22 Q—R6 and wins.

20 Kt—Kt4!	B—K2

If 20 . . . P x B? 21 Kt x Ktch forces mate. Or if 20 . . . P—K4; 21 Kt x Pch, P x Kt; 22 Q x P winning in a move or two.

21 B x Kt	P x B

Or 21 . . . B x B; 22 Kt x Pch, P x Kt; 23 Q x RP, R—K1; 24 B—R7ch and mate follows.

22 Kt x Pch	K—Kt2
23 Q—Kt4ch!	K—R1
24 Q—R5	K—Kt2
25 Kt x P!	R—R1

Capablanca's last move has completed the demolition of Black's position. If 25 . . . R x Kt; 26 Q—R7ch, K—B1; 27 Q—R8 mate.

26 Q—Kt6ch	Resigns

An energetic last-round win.

99. Margate, 1936

ENGLISH OPENING

Black's wholly incorrect appraisal of the position reached in the early middle game gets him into lasting difficulties. Capablanca's inexorable demolition of his opponent's game is highly instructive.

J. R. Capablanca

P. S. Milner-Barry

White	Black
1 P—QB4	P—K4
2 Kt—QB3	Kt—QB3
3 P—KKt3	P—KKt3
4 B—Kt2	B—Kt2
5 P—Q3	KKt—K2
6 P—KR4	. . . .

A most unusual move. Black's reply (making . . . P—KKt4 possible in answer to P—R5) seems to dispose of any possibilities of a King-side attack.

6	P—KR3
7 B—Q2	P—Q3
8 R—Kt1	. . . .

With this and the next move, he shifts his attention to the Queenside. A bewildering policy for Black, who cannot foresee where the lightning will ultimately strike.

8	O—O
9 P—QKt4	Kt—Q5

As the game goes, the wanderings of this Knight turn out to be of no value. The logical course for Black is to play . . . P—KB4, seeking counterplay in the center.

10 P—K3	Kt—K3
11 KKt—K2	P—QB3
12 Q—Kt3	B—Q2

Beginning a whole series of pointless moves. He should have played either . . . P—KB4 or else . . . Kt—B2 followed by P—Q4.

13 O—O	Q—B2
14 KR—B1	KR—B1

The Rook remains here for almost the balance of the game, accomplishing nothing whatever. The correct plan for Black has already been indicated.

15 P—R4	QR—Kt1
16 Q—R3	B—B1?

. . . P—KB4 was still possible.

17 Kt—K4!	P—KB4

Black should have swallowed his pride and played . . . B—Kt2, even at the cost of admitting that his last move was a mistake.

18 Kt—B6ch	K—B2
19 Kt x B	Q x Kt
20 B—QB3	. . . .

Having two Bishops now, White's course is clearly indicated: he must work consistently to open up the position, after which the Bishops will have a field day.

20	B—Kt2
21 Q—Kt2!	Q—B2
22 P—Q4!	Kt—B1

There is little choice. If 22 . . . P—K5; 23 P—B3, P x P; 24 B x P followed in due course by P—K4.

23 P x P	B x P

Forced, for if 23 . . . P x P; 24 P—B4 exposes Black to terrific pressure.

24 Kt—Q4	Kt—Q2
25 P—K4!	B x Kt

Black is helpless. If 25 . . . P—B5; 26 B—R3 is very strong.

26 B x B	Kt—K4
27 Q—Q2	P x P
28 B x KP	Kt—B4

Milner-Barry

Capablanca

It has already become painfully apparent that Black's game will soon fall apart.

29 B—QR1!   . . . .

He could have won a Pawn with 29 QB x Kt, P x B; 30 B x Kt, P x B; 31 Q x P. But the text method cuts short Black's resistance by a considerable margin.

29 . . . .   R—Kt1
30 P—KR5!   . . . .

At last White's sixth move proves to be of service!

30 . . . .   QR—QB1
31 P—B5!   . . . .

Now a murderous stroke from the other side. Black's position now collapses very rapidly.

31 . . . .   P—Q4

It is clear that 31 . . . QP x P; 32 R x P is equally bad for Black.

32 B x Pch   P x B
33 Q x Pch   K—B3
34 P—B4   Q—B3
35 B x Ktch   K—K2
36 B—Q6ch!   Resigns

Capablanca's last move made fur-

ther resistance impossible. If 36 . . . K—B3; 37 Q—K5ch, K—B2; 38 P x Pch, K x P; 39 Q—K6ch etc. Or 36 . . . Kt x B; 37 P x Ktch, Q x P; 38 R—K1ch, K—Q2; 39 Q—B7ch, K—B3; 40 R—K6.

This game was an easy one to win; yet it is a game from which the average player can learn a great deal.

---

100. Margate, 1936

QUEEN'S GAMBIT DECLINED

While Capablanca consistently exploits all his chances, White remains in an undecided state throughout the game, and suffers accordingly.

G. A. Thomas   J. R. Capablanca

White	Black
1 P—Q4	Kt—KB3
2 P—QB4	P—K3
3 Kt QB3	P—Q4
4 B—Kt5	B—K2
5 P—K3	O—O
6 Kt—B3	QKt—Q2
7 R—B1	P—B3
8 B—Q3	P—KR3

Thus far the game has proceeded on conventional lines. But now Capablanca branches out with a line of play which is novel in his games.

9 B—R4	P x P
10 B x P	P—QKt4
11 B—Q3	P—R3
12 O—O	. . . .

Thomas proceeds too placidly. 12 P—R4! would confront Black with all sorts of difficulties in the attempt to iron out the unlovely Pawn formation on the Queen-side.

| 12 . . . . | P—B4 |
| 13 P—R4 | P—B5!? |

The usual move is . . . P—Kt5, but Capablanca is playing for the Queen-side majority of Pawns, even at the risk of creating weaknesses with the far-advanced QBP.

14 B—K2?   . . . .

The more energetic B—Kt1 naturally deserved preference.

14 . . . .   Kt—Q4!
15 B x B   Q x B
16 Q—Q2   . . . .

The alternative 16 P x P, Kt x Kt; 17 R x Kt, P x P; 18 P—QKt3, R—R6! 19 Q—B2, Q—Kt5! is difficult to appraise.

16 . . . .   B—Kt2
17 P x P   Kt x Kt
18 Q x Kt   P x P

If now 19 P—QKt3, R—R6! would still be awkward for White.

19 R—R1   KR—B1
20 KR—B1   Kt—Kt3

Black is systematically strengthening the QBP, a policy which must naturally give him the advantage.

21 Kt—K1   P—B4!

It is important to restrain White from eventually playing P—K4.

22 B—B3   B—Q4
23 Q—B2   Q—Q3

Capablanca evidently c a n n o t make up his mind to play . . . P—Kt5, and therefore waits to see if White will worsen his position. This hope is at once gratified.

24 Q—Q2   Q—B1
25 Kt—B2?   . . . .

Vainly hoping to stop . . . P—Kt5; but he seriously weakens his position.

25 . . . .   B x B

Naturally.

26 P x B   Kt—Q4

Black is now ready to play . . . P—Kt5; hence White's desperate reply.

27 P—K4   P x P
28 P x P   . . . .

Capablanca

Thomas

28 . . . .   Q—B5!

Thomas either overlooked this move, or failed to foresee its consequences. The position is now clearly lost; if 29 Q x Q, Kt x Q; 30 K—B1, Kt—Q6; 31 R x R, R x R; 32 R—Kt1, R—R7 and wins.

29 Q—K2   Q—Kt4ch!
30 K—R1   Kt—B5
31 Q—B3   Kt—Q6
32 R—KKt1   . . . .

Or 32 KR—QKt1, Q—Q7 etc.

32 . . . .   R x R
33 Kt x R   Q—Q7

White resigns. This was a triumph of planning over planlessness.

---

101.   Moscow, 1936

SICILIAN DEFENSE

Purdy describes one of the immortal encounters between these two famous rivals in the following words: "In playing over this game, imagine the thousands of faces intently studying the duplicate board above the heads of the two great rivals, and the question in everyone's mind—would the old wizard once again lower his conqueror's colors, as he had twelve months before, in the same place? It was not to be."

DR. E. LASKER   J. R. CAPABLANCA

White   Black

1 P—K4   P—QB4

A defense which Capablanca took up late in life and played rarely. By adopting it, he announces at once that he means to play for a win.

2	Kt—KB3	Kt—QB3
3	P—Q4	P x P
4	Kt x P	Kt—B3
5	Kt—QB3	P—Q3
6	B—K2	. . . .

It would have been interesting to see Capablanca reacting to Richter's Attack (6 B—KKt5). But Lasker, with his well-known contempt for fashionable variations, lets the opportunity slip.

6	. . . .	B—Q2
7	B—K3	P—K3
8	Q—Q2	P—QR3
9	P—B4	. . . .

Here and later on, we have examples of Lasker's indifference toward the idea of playing the very best moves in the opening. 9 P—QR4 would have had a far more cramping effect on Black's position.

9	. . . .	Q—B2
10	Kt—Kt3	P—QKt4

Profiting by his opponent's previous inexactitude.

11	B—B3	QR—Kt1
12	Kt—K2	B—K2

13	O—O	O—O
14	Kt—Kt3	P—QR4!

Beginning an interesting and novel kind of counterplay, all the more in order since White has omitted, by his last move, the normal procedure which consists in his advancing the King-side Pawns (14 P—KKt4!).

15	Kt—Q4	P—R5
16	QR—K1	KR—B1
17	R—B2	Kt—K1
18	Kt x Kt	. . . .

In order to play P—B5 without allowing the retort . . . Kt—K4, and also with the idea of evading the well-known Queen-side attack . . . Kt—R4—B5.

18	. . . .	B x Kt
19	P—B5?	. . . .

As the faulty effects of this move soon become painfully apparent, White would have done better to continue "swimming."

19	. . . .	P—K4!

" 'What about the backward Pawn?' shrieks the pious student, brought up on sound positional principles. The answer is that there ain't goin' to be no backward Pawn." (Purdy)

20	Kt—R5	Q—Kt2
21	B—Kt5	P—B3
22	B—K3	Kt—B2

. . . B x P? would of course lose the exchange. Black is systematically preparing for the important strategic push . . . P—Q4, which will greatly increase the scope of his pieces.

23	Q—Q1	R—Q1
24	R—Q2	K—R1!

An important preliminary to . . . P—Q4, as will be seen.

25	P—QR3	QR—B1
26	B—B2	P—Q4

27	P x P	Kt x P
28	B x Kt	R x B
29	Q—Kt4	B—B4!

Had Black played . . . P—Q4 while his King was still at Kt1, he would have had to play the modest . . . B—Q1 at this point.

Note the pretty trap involved in Lasker's last move: 29 . . . P—Kt3? 30 P x P! R x R; 31 P—Kt7ch, K—Kt1; 32 Q—K6 mate!

30	R(1)—Q1	B x Bch
31	K x B	QR—Q1
32	R x R	. . . .

Or 32 Q—Kt4, P—R3 with about the same kind of position as in the text.

32	. . . .	R x R
33	R x R	B x R
34	Q—Kt4	Q—R2ch
35	K—K2	B—B5ch
36	K—B3	Q—R1ch
37	K—B2	Q—Q1

Lasker has managed to minimize most of his positional inferiority, and Black has been able to retain only a slight advantage due to the superior mobility of his Bishop.

38 Q—B3?   . . . .

A blunder which allows Capablanca to penetrate into White's game with fatal effect. The right move was 38 K—K1! after which White seems to be safe, as the Black queen cannot engage in too much gallivanting because of the latent threat Q—B8ch.

| 38 | . . . . | Q—Q8! |
| 39 | Kt—Kt3 | P—R3! |

Suddenly White finds himself in **Zugzwang**! For example 40 P—R3, K—R2; 41 P—R4, K—R1; 42 P—R5, K—R2 etc.

40	P—Kt3	P x P
41	P x P	B x P
42	Kt—B1	. . . .

42 Kt—K2, B—B5 would lose even more rapidly for White.

| 42 | . . . . | Q—Kt8! |
| 43 | P—Kt4 | B—B5 |

Not 43 . . . Q—R7ch; 44 K—Kt3, Q x P? 45 Kt—Q2.

44 Kt—K3   . . . .

Or 44 Kt—Kt3 (to prevent Black's next move), Q—R7ch; 45 K—Kt1, B—Q4 and wins.

44 . . . .   Q—KR8

This leads to a massacre of White's Pawns, for if 45 K—Kt3, B—K7 is deadly. But the win is still troublesome.

45	Kt x B	Q x Pch
46	K—K1	Q—Kt8ch
47	K—Q2	Q—B7ch
48	K—B1	Q—B8ch
49	K—Q2	P x Kt
50	P—R4	Q—B5ch

Capablanca

Lasker

51 K—B2   . . . .

Against 51 K—K1 Capablanca intended . . . Q—K5ch; 52 K—Q2, Q x KtP; 53 P—R5, Q—Kt7ch; 54 K—K3, Q—QR7. The QRP is destined to give Black some anxious moments!

51	Q x P
52 P—R5	Q x Pch
53 K—B1	Q—B7

Played after half an hour's reflection. Capabalnca saw that he could win with 53 . . . P—K5; 54 P—R6, Q—B4; 55 Q—Kt2, P—B6; 56 Q—Kt8ch, K—R2; 57 P—R7, Q—K6ch; 58 K—Kt1, Q—Q6ch; 59 K—R2, P—B7; 60 P—R8(Q), Q—B5ch. However, fearing that there might be some miscalculation, he determined to play the ending in the very simplest way.

54 Q—QR3	. . . .

If 54 Q—Q2, Q—B4! wins; while on 54 Q x BP Capablanca had prepared the following winning line: 54 . . . Q—K8ch; 55 K—B2, Q x P; 56 Q—D8ch, K—R2; 57 Q—B5ch, K—Kt1; 58 Q—K6ch, K—B1; 59 Q—Q6ch, K—K1; 60 Q—K6ch, K—Q1; 61 Q—Kt8ch, K—K2; 62 Q x P ch, K—K3; 63 Q—Kt8ch, K—Q3; 64 Q—B8ch, K—Q4; 65 Q x BP, Q—R5ch etc.

54	K—R2

White resigns, as 55 P—R6 is simply answered by 55 . . . P—B6! 56 Q x BP, Q—B8ch. A curious ending.

---

102. Moscow, 1936

RETI OPENING

This is a lesson in the fine art of making something out of nothing. At first the game gives little promise of developing into anything noteworthy; but Capablanca works up a powerful pressure which soon leads to some extremely interesting play.

J. R. CAPABLANCA A. LILIENTHAL

White	Black
1 Kt—KB3	P—Q4
2 P—B4	P—QB3
3 P—QKt3	B—B4
4 B—Kt2	P—K3
5 P—Kt3	Kt—B3
6 B—Kt2	QKt—Q2
7 O—O	P—KR3

Black has adopted the well-known London System. Instead of continuing with the line of play (characterized by the advance of White's KP) which he used in Game No. 90, Capablanca harks back to the development adopted by Reti in his famous encouter with Dr. Lasker at New York in 1924.

8 P—Q3	B—K2

It is very difficult to decide whether this or . . . B—Q3 is preferable.

9 QKt—Q2	O—O
10 R—B1	P—QR4
11 P—QR3	. . . .

A natural reaction to Black's last move: he wants to answer an eventual . . . P—R5 with P—QKt4.

11	R—K1
12 R—B2	B—R2
13 Q—R1	B—B1

Lackadaisical. Here and later Black should be thinking about playing . . . P—K4, with . . . B—Q3 as a preparatory move.

14 R—K1	Q—Kt3
15 B—R3	B—QB4
16 R—KB1	B—B1
17 R(2)—B1	QR—Q1
18 KR—K1	B—QB4

Doubtless in order to provoke P—Q4, which would shut in White's QB and be correspondingly favorable for Black's QB.

19 R—B1	B—B1
20 B—Kt2	B—Q3

At last he has the idea of playing . . . P—K4. Capablanca prevents the move with the following continuation, which requires accurate appraisal of its consequences.

21 Kt—K5	B x Kt
22 B x B	Kt x B
23 Q x B	Kt—Q2

If instead 23 . . . P—Q5 Capablanca intended 24 P—B5, Q—Kt4; 25 Kt—B4, R—K2; 26 Kt—Q6, Q x KtP; 27 R—Kt1, Q x RP; 28 Kt x KtP, R—QB1; 29 R—R1, Q—Kt5; 30 Kt x P with clear advantage to White.

| 24 Q—Kt2 | Kt—B3 |

Still playing a waiting game. 24 . . . P—QB4 has been suggested, for if 25 P x P, P x P; 26 B x P, R x P etc.

| 25 P—QKt4! | RP x P |
| 26 Q x P! | . . . . |

The proffered exchange of Queens is not woodshifting. Black's QKtP is in real danger no matter how he plays; for example 26 . . . Q—B2; 27 R—Kt1, R—K2; 28 R—Kt3 followed by KR—Kt1 with strong pressure.

26	Q x Q
27 P x Q	R—R1
28 R—R1	Kt—Q2

White intends to establish an outpost on QR5. If Black's position is not lost, it is certainly critical.

| 29 Kt—Kt3 | K—B1 |
| 30 R—R5! | P x P? |

This loses because of the opening of the long diagonal, permitting the "Reti Bishop" to make his presence felt. Correct was . . . K—K2—Q3—B2, when the outcome would be doubtful.

31 P x P	Kt—Kt3
32 R x R!	R x R
33 Kt—R5!	R—R2
34 R—Q1	K—K1

There was no defense. The threat was 35 B x P! P x B; 36 R—Q8ch, K—K2; 37 Kt x Pch. If 34 . . .

K—K2; 35 B x P. If 34 . . . P—B3; 35 R—Q8ch followed by R—QKt8 (Capablanca).

Lilienthal

Capablanca

| 35 Kt x KtP! | . . . . |

A far-sighted positional sacrifice. The resulting passed Pawns leave Black helpless, and the poor position of his Bishop does not help matters.

35	R x Kt
36 B x Pch	R—Q2
37 P—B5	K—K2

Alternatives are (a) 37 . . . B—K5; 38 R x R! Kt x R; 39 B x B or 38 . . . B x B; 39 R—B7 and wins; (b) 37 . . . Kt—Q4; 38 P—B3, P—B4; 39 P—Kt5, K—K2; 40 B x R, K x B; 41 R—R1 with an easy win.

38 B x R	Kt x B
39 P—B6	Kt—Kt3
40 P—B7	B—B4
41 R—Q8	P—K4
42 R—QKt8	Kt—B1

Or 42 . . . Kt—Q4; 43 P—B8(Q), B x Q; 44 R x B, Kt x P; 45 R—B7ch, K—K3; 46 P—K4 and wins.

43 P—Kt5	K—Q3
44 P—Kt6	Kt—K2
45 R—KB8	. . . .

45 P—B8(Q), B x Q; 46 P—Kt7 also wins.

45 . . . .   B—B1
46 R x P   Kt—Q4

Or 46 . . . P—Kt3; 47 R—B6ch, K—Q2; 48 P—R4 and White has matters his own way.

47 R x P   Kt x KtP
48 R—R7   Kt—Q4
49 R x Pch   K x P
50 P—K4   Kt—K2
51 P—B3   K—Q2
52 P—R4   K—K1
53 R—B6   Kt—Kt1

. . . B—Q2 would save the KP, but the advance of White's Pawns would win easily enough.

54 R—B6   Resigns

For R—B5 will win the KP.

———

103. Moscow, 1936

VIENNA GAME

The early exchange of Queens leads White to believe that a draw is his for the asking. That this is not necessarily true is amply demonstrated in the further course of the game. If one of the players is in a fighting mood, the early exchange of Queens need be no hindrance to interesting play.

I. Kan   J. R. Capablanca

White   Black

1 P—K4   P—K4
2 Kt—QB3   B—B4
3 Kt—B3   P—Q3
4 Kt—QR4   . . . .

At once steering for the two Bishops; but Black, as will be seen, has his compensations. 4 P—Q4 may be more promising.

4 . . . .   B—Kt3
5 Kt x B   RP x Kt
6 P—Q4   P x P
7 Q x P   Q—B3

Practically forced, as 7 . . . Kt—KB3; 8 B—Kt5 is anything but attractive for Black.

8 B—Kt5   Q x Q
9 Kt x Q   B—Q2

White has some lead in development, and his Bishops may become powerful. The way in which Capablanca demonstrates that these advantages are only temporary, is quite interesting.

10 B—QB4   Kt—K2
11 O—O   Kt—Kt3

Just in time to prevent the aggressive advance 12 P—B4, which would now be refuted by . . . P—R3 (13 P—B5, Kt—K4).

12 P—QR3   O—O
13 QR—Q1   Kt—B3!

This move, so harmless in appearance, is well thought out. In the first place, . . . R—R5 is threatened.

14 Kt x Kt   . . . .

Superficial, as the exchange deprives White of control of the square Q5.

14 . . . .   P x Kt
15 B—Q2   . . . .

Better B—B1 (this by the way was the proper continuation a move earlier) so as to be able to play P—QKt3 in answer to a possible . . . R—R5.

15 . . . .   R—R5
16 B—Q3   Kt—K4
17 B—B3   P—B3
18 P—B3   R—K1
19 R—B2   B—B1
20 B—B1   B—R3!

Forcing that exchange of the Bishops. This will be in Black's favor, because he may be able to gain ground on the white squares.

| 21 B x B | R x B |
| 22 B x Kt | BP x B |

The position now arrived doesn't seem to offer much of a winning chance. The fact remains that Black has more maneuvering space for his pieces and that he has some chances for breaking through on the King-side by means of . . . P—KKt4—5.

23 R—Q3	P—QKt4
24 R(2)—Q2	P—B4
25 K—B2	R—R5
26 K—K2	K—B2
27 R—Q1	K—K3
28 K—Q2	R—QKt1
29 R—B3	P—Kt4

After a preliminary period of consolidation and jockeying for position, Capablanca is at last ready for his great winning attempt on the King-side.

30 P—R3	P—R4
31 R—KR1	R—Q5ch
32 K—K2	R—Kt1

Something had to be done about White's contemplated P—R4, which would have left him with pressure on Black's RP (after . . . P x P) or with a passed Pawn (after . . . P—Kt5).

| 33 R—Q3 | R—R5 |
| 34 R(1)—Q1 | P—KKt5 |

This is feasible, now that White's Rook is gone from the KR file; yet, had the Rook remained there, Black could have tried a different kind of advance with . . . P—B3 and . . . P—Q4.

| 35 RP x P | P x P |
| 36 K—K3 | . . . . |

White is putting up a good defense. Euwe points out that if

36 R—KR1, P x P ch; 37 P x P (or 37 K x P, R—B1ch; 38 K—K3, R—KB5 and wins), R—Kt7ch and White's game is untenable.

| 36 . . . . | R—KR1! |

Black's initiative is beginning to shape up very strongly; the text is more promising than 36 . . . P x P; 37 P x P, R—Kt7; 38 R(3)—Q2 and White's defensive set-up is quite adequate.

| 37 R—Kt3 | . . . . |

Relatively best. Capablanca was hoping for 37 P x P, R—KKt1; 38 K—B3, R—B1ch; 39 K—K3, R—KB5 and wins.

| 37 . . . . | R—R7 |
| 38 R—Q2 | R—Q5! |

A splendid post for the Rook, which can hardly be removed; for if 39 R x R, BP x Rch; and Black's formidable Pawn mass in the center is a powerful contributory factor in making victory possible for him.

| 39 R—K2 | P—B3 |
| 40 R—B3 | P—Kt6!? |

Threatening to reduce White to helplessness with . . . R—R8—KB8. However, White still has one more drawing chance.

Capablanca

Kan

41 R—Q3? ....

Missing his chance. The right way, as later demonstrated by Capablanca, was 41 P—B4! R—KR5; 42 P x P, R(Q5) x Pch; 43 K—B3, R(R5)—B5ch; 44 K x P, R—Kt5ch; 45 K—B3, R x R; 46 K x R(K2), R x Pch; 47 K—B3, R—R7; 48 K—Kt3! with a draw.

41 ....   R—R8!

Now Black has a clear win, and Capablanca winds up in instructive fashion.

42 P—KB4   R—KB8!
43 P—B5ch   ....

43 P x P, K x P is no better, as . . . R—KB5 will be decisive.

43 ....   K—B3
44 P—B3   R x Rch
45 K x R   P—Q4!

With the double threat of . . . P x Pch or . . . P—B5ch.

46 P—Kt3   P—B5ch
47 P x P   KtP x Pch
48 K—K3   ....

Hoping for 47 . . . R—B8; 48 R—R2 and the RP pushes ahead. The idea is faulty, but 47 K—B2, P—Q5 or 47 K—Q2, R—QR8 is no better.

48 ....   R—QR8!
49 K—B3   R x P

If now 50 R—K3, R—Kt6; 51 K x P, P—Q5 wins.

50 K x P   R x Pch
51 K—R4   R—B8!

Not 51 . . . P—Q5 because of 52 P—Kt4 and 53 P—Kt5ch.

52 P—Kt4   R—R8ch

The point of the previous move.

53 K—Kt3   P—Q5
54 R—QR2   P—Q6

55 K—Kt2   R—K8
56 K—B2   R x P
57 K—B3

Kan resigned without awaiting his opponent's reply, for after 57 . . . R—B5ch; 58 K—Kt3, K—Kt4 White's remaining Pawns must fall. An uncommonly instructive ending.

---

104. Nottingham, 1936

RUY LOPEZ

White spoils his chances quite early in the game with a poor opening move. Nevertheless, Capablanca's crisp exploitation of his advantage lends the game lasting interest.

G. A. Thomas   J. R. Capablanca

White	Black
1 P—K4	P—K4
2 Kt—KB3	Kt—QB3
3 B—Kt5	P—QR3
4 B—R4	P—Q3
5 B x Ktch	P x B
6 P—Q4	P—B3

This has been a fashionable defense for some time, although it is not certain that one fares well with it if White adopts the best attacking formation.

7 B—K3!   Kt—K2

There is no point in aiming for the more desirable formation of . . . P—Kt3 in conjunction with . . . Kt—R3—B2; for after 7 . . . P—Kt3 White would answer 8 Q—Q2!

8 Kt—B3   Kt—Kt3
9 Q—Q2   B—K3
10 P—QKt3?   ....

A stodgy reply which allows Black to carry out the transparent object of his last move. With 10 O—O—O! White could have prevented the intended . . . P—Q4 and assured himself of a fine development. It is a pity that the game departs from the usual course at this early stage, as it would have been interesting to see how Capablanca would have overcome the resulting difficulties.

10 . . . .   P—Q4!

Taking the initiative.

11 O—O?   . . . .

11 KP x P was not appetizing but relatively better than the text, which soon leads to the loss of a Pawn.

11 . . . .   QP x P!
12 QKt x P   B—Q4
13 Kt—Kt3   . . . .

The smash-up of the King-side is unavoidable, 13 Q—Q3 being out of the question because of . . . P—KB4 followed by . . . P—K5.

13 . . . .   B x Kt
14 P x B   Kt—R5

Capablanca

Thomas

15 Q—Q3   . . . .

Resigning himself to the inevitable, for if 15 Q—Q1, P x P; 16 B x P, Q x B; 17 Q x Q, Kt x Pch; or 15 Q—K2, Q—Q4; 16 Kt—K4, P—KB4; 17 Kt—Q2, B—Kt5; 18 P—QB4, Q—B2 and wins: the

threat is . . . Q—Kt3ch or . . . P—B5.

15 . . . .   Kt x Pch
16 K—R1   Kt x QP
17 Q—K4   Q—Q4!

Black decides to return one of the Pawns, as he realizes that trying to retain both Pawns would only create technical difficulties.

18 Q x Q   P x Q
19 B x Kt   P x B
20 QR—Q1   B—B4

Better than 20 . . . P—QB4, when White has advantageous replies in P—Kt4 or P—QB3.

21 Kt—B5   . . . .

If instead 21 P—QB3, K—B2; 22 P x P, B—Kt3 etc.

21 . . . .   K—B2
22 Kt x QP   KR—K1
23 P—QB3   R—K4
24 R—Q3   QR—K1
25 P—QR4?   . . . .

Thoughtlessly creating a new weakness which hastens the end. 25 K—Kt2 was better.

25 . . . .   B x Kt
26 R x B   . . . .

Or 26 P x B, R—K8; 27 K—Kt2, R x R; 28 K x R, K—K2; 29 R—QB3, K—Q3; 30 R—B5, R—QKt1 with an easy win.

26 . . . .   P—QB4
27 R—Q2   R—QKt1
28 R—QKt1   P—QR4!

All very clear and energetic.

29 K—Kt2 ·   K—K3
30 R—B2   K—Q3
31 P—B3   P—Kt4
32 K—Kt3   P—R4
33 P—R4   P x Pch
34 K x P   R—K6
35 K—Kt3   . . . .

Or 35 K x P, R—Kt1 and the White King is in a mating net!

35 . . . .   P—B5!

This wins a second Pawn in an amusing manner.

36 P—Kt4   P x P
37 P x P   R—Kt6!
Resigns

---

105. Nottingham, 1936

RETI OPENING (in effect)
Catalan System

One of the most crucial games in this great tournament. The inexactitude of some of the early play bears witness to the great strain under which both players labored. But the inexorable precision of Capablanca's endgame play outweighs these drawbacks. Reshevsky puts up his usual fierce resistance, but this time it is of no avail.

J. R. CAPABLANCA   S. RESHEVSKY

White	Black
1 P—Q4	P—Q4
2 Kt—KB3	Kt—KB3
3 P—B4	P x P
4 Q—R4ch	QKt—Q2
5 Q x BP	. . . .

Or 5 P—KKt3, P—QR3; 6 Kt—B3, QR—Kt1; 7 Q x BP, P—QKt4 with much the same kind of position.

| 5 . . . . | P—K3 |
| 6 P—KKt3 | . . . . |

This is the move that gives the game its Catalan character. 6 Kt—B3 (intending P—K4), would lead to a totally different kind of game, more aggressive and more risky.

| 6 . . . . | P—QR3 |
| 7 B—Kt2 | P—QKt4 |

8 Q—B6   . . . .

If Capablanca thought that this would prevent . . . P—B4, he is soon undeceived. Q—B2 was better.

| 8 . . . . | R—R2 |
| 9 B—B4 | B—Kt2! |

Simple and good. Capture of the QBP would of course lose a piece.

10 Q—B1	P—B4
11 P x P	B x P
12 O—O	O—O

As a result of White's time-wasting moves with the Queen and the lack of a good square for this piece, Black has a fine game. He has only one difficulty, which can be solved without much trouble: developing the QR.

13 QKt—Q2	Q—K2
14 Kt—Kt3	B—Kt3
15 B—K3	R—B1

The phase which now follows is very trying for White and requires all of Capablanca's patience.

16 Q—Q2	Kt—K5
17 Q—Q3	Kt(5)—B4
18 Kt x Kt	Kt x Kt
19 Q—Q1	B—R1

Much too elaborate. Simply . . . B—Q4 or . . . B—K5 followed by the doubling of Black's Rooks on the Q file would have given him a fine game.

20 R—B1	QR—B2
21 P—Kt3	Kt—Q2
22 R x R	R x R
23 B x B	Kt x B
24 Q—Q4	. . . .

It is now apparent that Reshevsky has not made the most of his chances, and White's position is now quite satisfactory.

| 24 . . . . | Kt—Q4 |
| 25 R—Q1 | P—B3 |

| 26 Kt—K1 | B—Kt2 |
| 27 B x Kt | P x B? |

An astounding positional blunder whereby Black voluntarily creates a serious positional weakness and relegates his Bishop to a purely defensive role. . . . B x B was the natural and correct move, resulting in an even game.

28 P—K3	Q—K5
29 P—KR4	P—QR4
30 P—B3	Q x Q?

This leads to a very inferior ending. . . . Q—K4 was better.

| 31 R x Q | R—B8? |

Reshevsky is unrecognizable here. Bringing up the King to the center, in order to guard the QP, offered the best chances.

32 K—B2	R—R8
33 R—Q2	P—R5
34 Kt—Q3	R—QKt8?

. . . P x P would have offered better chances of resistance. The text allows Capablanca to force the exchange of Rooks, leading to an ending in which the Bishop, hemmed in by its own Pawns, is decidedly inferior to the Knight.

35 R—Kt2!	R x Rch
36 Kt x R	B—B3
37 Kt—Q3	P—Kt4!?

Reshevsky realizes that passive play is hopeless once White gets his King to Q4. He therefore tries a sortie on the King-side which forces Capablanca to play with the utmost accuracy.

38 RP x P	BP x P
39 Kt—Kt4	P x P
40 P x P	B—Kt2
41 P—Kt4!	. . . .

Naturally, Black is not permitted to secure an outside passed KRP.

| 41 . . . . | K—Kt2 |

| 42 K—K2 | K—Kt3 |
| 43 K—Q3 | P—R4 |

Not 43 . . . P—Q5? 44 P—K4.

| 44 P x Pch | K x P |
| 45 K—Q4 | K—R5 |

The probabilities have been fulfilled in the loss of the QP; but Reshevsky has the consolation of a close finish.

| 46 Kt x P | K—Kt6 |
| 47 P—B4! | P—KKt5 |

Other attempts are equally hopeless:

I 47 . . . B x Kt; 48 K x B, P x P; 49 P x P, K x P; 50 K—B5 and wins.
II 27 . . . B x Kt; 48 K x B, P—KKt5; 49 P—B5, K—R7; 50 P—B6, P—Kt6; 51 P—B7, P—Kt7; 52 P—B8(Q), P—Kt8(Q); 53 Q—R8ch followed by Q—Kt8ch and wins.

| 48 P—B5 | B—B1 |
| 49 K—K5 | B—Q2 |

Or 49 . . . K—R7; 50 P—B6, P—Kt6; 51 Kt—B4 and wins.

| 50 P—K4 | B—K1 |
| 51 K—Q4 | . . . . |

Before trying to win the Bishop, White must settle accounts with the KKtP.

51	K—B6
52 P—K5	P—Kt6
53 Kt—K3	. . . .

(see diagram next page)

| 53 . . . . | K—B5 |

Against . . . B—Q2 (or 53 . . . P—Kt7; 54 Kt x P, K x Kt; 55 P—K6 and wins), Capablanca had calculated the following win: 54 P—K6, B—B1; 55 P—K7, B—Q2; 56 P—B6, B—K1; 57 Kt—B5, P—Kt7; 58 Kt—R4ch, K—B5; 59 Kt x Pch, K—B4; 60 Kt—K3ch, K x P; 61 Kt—Q5ch, K—B2; 62 Kt—B7, K x P; 63 Kt x B, K x Kt; 64 K—B5 and wins.

Reshevsky

Capablanca

54 P—K6   P—Kt7

Black is helpless. If 54 . . .
P—Kt5; 55 P—B6 etc. or 54 . . .
K—Kt4; 55 K—K5 etc.

55 Kt x Pch   K x P
56 K—Q5   K—Kt5
57 Kt—K3ch   K—B5
58 K—Q4!   Resigns

There is nothing to be done
against the maneuver Kt—Q5ch—
B7. One of Capablanca's classic
endings.

---

106. Semmering-Baden, 1937
QUEEN'S GAMBIT DECLINED

It is interesting to see how Capablanca refutes his opponent's speculative Pawn sacrifice and then
proceeds to take the initiative.

V. RAGOZIN   J. R. CAPABLANCA

White	Black
1 P—Q4	P—Q4
2 P—QB4	P—QB3
3 Kt—KB3	Kt—B3
4 Kt—B3	P x P

5 P—QR4   B—B4
6 P—K3   . . . .

Capablanca's preference in this
position was apparently for 6 Kt—
K5, as in Game No. 92.

6 . . . .   P—K3
7 B x P   B—QKt5

Played with a view to restrain an
eventual P—K4.

8 O—O   O—O
9 Q—Kt3   . . . .

Q—K2 is the move. The text
seems to give Black some trouble,
but its effects can be neutralized
easily enough.

9 . . . .   Q—K2
10 Kt—K5   . . . .

And here 10 B—Q2 (threatening
Γ—K4) looks more promising.

10 . . . .   P—B4!

This had to be calculated very
exactly, as will be seen.

11 Kt—R2?!   B—R4
12 Q—Kt5   . . . .

White's last two moves appear
to be quite powerful, and it is
difficult to see how Capablanca is
to avoid loss of a Pawn. However,
he handles the following play so
cleverly that White soon has to
retreat his Queen with loss of time
and his QKt remains out of play
for the rest of the game.

12 . . . .   P—QKt3
13 P—B3   P x P!

(see diagram next page)

How is Black to answer 14 P—
QKt4, which seems to win his QB?
The continuation would be 14 . . .
P—QR3! 15 Kt—B6, Kt x Kt; 16
Q x Kt, KR—B1 and White's Queen
is lost!

14 P—K4?   . . . .

Capablanca

Ragozin

A superficial Pawn sacrifice whose effect is transitory. But he realizes that after 14 P x P Black would have an excellent game.

14 ....   B—Kt3
15 B—Kt5   ....

Of course, if 15 P—QKt4, P—QR3 etc.

15 ....   P—QR3
16 Q—Kt3   Q—B4

Obtaining the Bishop-pair and seizing the initiative. It will be amusing to see how Capablanca always succeeds in taking the sting out of a possible P—QKt4.

17 B x Kt   P x B
18 Kt—Q3   Q—Q3
19 Q—Q1   R—B1!

Gaining time to stop P—QKt4.

20 P—QKt3   Kt—Q2
21 Q—K2   Kt—B4

Threatening . . . Kt x RP and thus practically forcing White's reply.

22 Kt x Kt   Q x Kt
23 B—Q3   P—B4!

Opening new lines. If now 24

P x P, P x P! (not 24 . . . B x P; 25 B x B, Q x B; 26 P—QKt4 or 25 . . . P—Q6ch; 27 Q—B2, Q x B; 28 P—QKt4. It is true that in these variations Black could save his KB by playing . . . P x B instead of . . . Q x B but this procedure is clearer in the main variation); 25 P—B4 (else . . . P—B5), R—K1; 26 Q—Q1, R—K6 with irresistible pressure.

24 QR—Kt1   P x P
25 P x P   B—B6

Now the position of this Bishop is definitely assured, and Black can continue the process of penetration.

26 P—QKt4   Q—K4
27 Kt—B1   P—QR4!

Gaining the square QB4 for his pieces, regardless of what White does; although 28 P—Kt5 was relatively best.

28 P x P   B x RP
29 R—Kt5   R—B4
30 Q—B3   R x R
31 P x R   B—Q7

The Bishops are getting dangerous . . .

32 Kt—K2   B—K6ch
33 K—R1   R—R6!

Leaving White no choice, as the unfortunate Bishop cannot budge.

34 R—Q1   P—R4!

But not 34 . . . R x B; 35 R x R, B x P; 36 Q—Kt4ch. If, after the text, 35 Kt—Kt3, P—R5; 36 Kt—K2, B—R4; 37 Q—B1, P—R6! with an easy win.

35 P—R3   R x B!

Winding up neatly.

36 R x R   B x P
37 R x B   P x R
38 Q—B1   Q x P
39 Q—B4   B x Pch

40 K—R2   Q x Kt

White resigns. An admirable game by Capa all the way.

---

107.   Paris, 1938

INDIAN DEFENSE (in effect)

This is the kind of game in which thoughtless handling of the opening can lead to an amazingly rapid debacle.

J. R. CAPABLANCA   M. ROMIH

White	Black
1 P—Q4	P—Q4
2 P—QB4	P—QB3
3 Kt—KB3	Kt—B3
4 P—K3	P—KKt3
5 Kt—B3	B—Kt2

By means of a familiar transposition, we have reached a well-known line in the Gruenfeld Variation.

| 6 Q—Kt3 | O—O |
| 7 Kt—K5 | .... |

A novelty, the usual course being B—Q2 followed by R—B1. But the text has its points, especially if Black plays inaccurately.

7 ....   P—K3?

Too passive. Correct was 7 . . . QKt—Q2; 8 P—B4, Kt x Kt; 9 BP x Kt, Kt—K5.

8 P—KB4	QKt—Q2
9 B—K2	Kt x Kt
10 BP x Kt	Kt—Kt5?

Reckoning only on 11 B x Kt, Q—R5ch. It was no longer possible to play . . . Kt—K5 because of 11 Kt x Kt, P x Kt; 12 Q—B2 and the KP falls. 10 . . . Kt—Q2 was apparently best.

11 O—O   Q—R5

Romih

Capablanca

12 B x Kt!   . . . .

This has been criticized as an example of Capablanca's over-developed desire for simplicity, but it happens to be stronger than the colorless P—KR3. The point of the unexpected exchange is to take advantage of the Black Queen's poor position.

| 12 .... | Q x B |
| 13 R—B4! | Q—Kt4 |

. . . Q—R4 is equally unattractive.

14 P—K4!	P x BP
15 Q x BP	Q—K2
16 R—Kt4!	. . . .

It is clear that Capablanca will have a field day on the black squares.

16	P—B3
17 P x P	Q x P
18 B—K3	B—Q2
19 P—KR3	K—R1

Hoping for . . . P—K4, which is of course at once prevented.

20 P—K5	Q—Q1
21 Kt—K4	P—Kt3
22 B—Kt5	Q—B2
23 B—K7	KR—K1

| 24 B—Q6 | Q—Q1 |

In view of his opponent's overwhelming position, Black cannot hope to hold out very long.

| 25 R—KB1 | P—B4 |
| 26 Kt—Kt5! | Q—B1 |

After 26 . . . K—Kt1 there would be many ways of winning, for example 27 Q—B2, P—KR3; 28 Q x KtP, P x Kt; 29 R x P, R—K2; 30 R—R5 etc.

| 27 R—R4 | P—KR3 |
| 28 Q—Q3 | Resigns |

Simplicity itself!

---

108. Paris, 1938

QUEEN'S GAMBIT DECLINED

This is one of those "simple" Capablanca games that make chess seem so deceptively easy. His opponent displayed singularly bad judgment in selecting an opening variation which gave the great Cuban the opportunity to hammer away at an obvious weakness.

J. R. CAPABLANCA
              E. ZNOSKO-BOROVSKY

White	Black
1 P—Q4	P—Q4
2 P—QB4	P—K3
3 Kt—QB3	P—QB4
4 BP x P	KP x P
5 Kt—B3	Kt—QB3
6 P—KKt3	Kt—B3
7 B—Kt2	B—K2
8 O—O	O—O
9 P x P!	. . . .

Regarding the opening, see also Game No. 7. Capablanca's play is a distinct improvement on White's handling of the opening in the earlier game.

9 . . . .   B x P

| 10 Kt—QR4! | B—K2 |
| 11 B—K3 | Kt—K5 |

It has already become apparent that it will be White's policy to combine pressure on the QP with observation of the important square QB5. Black's position is very difficult.

| 12 Kt—Q4 | Kt—K4? |

Plausibly aiming for QB5; but the whole idea is refuted easily enough. . . . Kt x Kt followed by . . . B—K3 and . . . Q—R4 is somewhat better.

| 13 R—B1 | Q—R4 |

This aggressive-looking m o v e soon leads to inextricable difficulties; however, if 13 . . . Kt—B5? 14 R x Kt! wins.

| 14 B—B4! | Kt—Kt3 |

As is well-known, a Knight is badly placed here in positions when the hostile KKtP is already on KKt3. But the alternatives are uninviting: after 14 . . . P—B3; 15 Q—Kt3 White has a manifestly superior position, while if 14 . . . B—Q3? 15 QB x Kt, B x B; 16 B x Kt wins some material.

| 15 B—B7 | Q—R3 |

From now on Black's Queen will be in serious danger, but 15 . . . P—Kt3? is out of the question (16 Kt—B6), while 15 . . . Q—Q7; 16 Q x Q, Kt x Q; 17 KR—Q1 leads to a lost ending for Black.

16 P—QR3!	B—Q2
17 Kt—B3	Kt x Kt
18 R x Kt	B—K3

With the weakness of his QP uncovered, Black's position has taken a distinct turn for the worse. If 18 . . . B—QB3; 19 Kt x B, P x Kt; 20 Q—B2 winning a Pawn.

| 19 P—QKt4 | P—Kt3 |

White was actually threatening to win the Queen with P—Kt5!

20 P—K4! . . . .

White could have won the QP here with P—B4, but he deliberately decides to renounce the win of the Pawn in favor of opening up new lines for his pieces—certainly the more artistic procedure.

20 . . . . P x P
21 B x KP QR—K1

Black's choice of moves is steadily narrowing: if 21 . . . QR—B1; 22 Kt x B, P x Kt; 23 Q—Q7 wins a Pawn.

22 Kt x B P x Kt
23 B—B6 B—B3

Forced (if 23 . . . R—B1; 24 B—Q7). But White's Bishops are irresistible.

24 P—Kt5 Q—B1

Just as hopeless is 24 . . . Q—R4; 25 R—Q3, R—B1; 26 B—Q6, B—K2 (else B—Kt4); 27 Q—Kt3 etc. The non-participation of Black's Queen must lead to a catastrophe.

25 R—B2 R—K2
26 B—Q6 R—Q1
27 P—B4! . . . .

Primarily threatening P—B5 (when . . . P x P will be impossible); still more important, the KR is going to Q2.

27 . . . . K—R1
28 KR—B2! R—KB2

Else 29 R(KB2)—Q2 wins the exchange!

29 R(KB2)—Q2 . . . .

Threatening B—K8. White has built up a crushing concentration of force; small wonder that Black's game collapses in short order.

Znosko-Borovsky

Capablanca

29 . . . . R—Kt1
30 Q—R5 Q—Q1

There was no saving move.

31 B—K4 Resigns

A model game.

---

109. Avro Tournament, 1938

FRENCH DEFENSE

This is one of the finest examples in all chess literature of a remarkable recovery from a lost position. The way in which the older player manages to snatch the half-point from his gifted opponent is nothing short of miraculous!

R. FINE J. R. CAPABLANCA

White Black

1 P—K4 P—K3
2 P—Q4 P—Q4
3 Kt—QB3 B—Kt5
4 P—K5 . . . .

The most aggressive course. Fine had already scored a sensational victory with this move against Botvinnik in the first round, and was destined to achieve an even more crushing triumph against Flohr a few rounds later with the same move.

4	P—QB4
5 B—Q2	P x P

This leads to trouble. The simpler course is 5 . . . Kt—K2 and if 6 Kt—Kt5, B x Bch; 7 Q x B, O—O, when Black will secure a satisfactory development.

6 Kt—Kt5	B x Bch
7 Q x B	Kt—QB3
8 Kt—KB3	P—B3?!

As 8 . . . KKt—K2; 9 Kt—Q6ch, K—B1; 10 Q—B4, Kt—B4; 11 Kt x Kt, P x Kt; 12 Kt x P yields a positionally lost game, Capablanca rightly decides on aggressive defense.

9 Q—B4!	Kt—R3

Of course not 9 . . . P x P? 10 Kt x KP with a winning position.

10 Kt—Q6ch!	. . . .

Not 10 P x P, O—O! and Black escapes.

10	K—B1
11 B—Kt5!	. . . .

Very strong; it is clear that the disappearance of Black's vital QKt will enhance his difficulties.

11	Kt—B2

. . . K—Kt1 was safer, but Capablanca wants to clear the situation in the center at once. If 11 . . . Kt x P; 12 Kt x Kt, P—KKt4; 13 Q—Kt3, P x Kt (13 . . . Q x Kt?? 14 Kt—Kt6ch); 14 Q x KP with marked advantage.

12 Kt x Kt	K x Kt
13 B x Kt	P x B
14 P x P	P x P

Material disadvantage was unavoidable in any event, and the text is certainly preferable to 14 . . . Q x P; 15 Q—B7ch etc.

15 Kt—K5ch	K—Kt2
16 Q—Kt3ch	K—B1
17 Kt x P	Q—Q2

If 17 . . . Q—Kt3? 18 Q—Q6ch with a quick win in the offing.

18 Kt x QP	P—K4
19 Kt—Kt3	Q—B4

Black has a lost game, but Capablanca fights back with desperate ingenuity.

20 Q—Q3	P—Q5
21 O—O	. . . .

As 21 Q x Q, B x Q; 22 K—Q2, QR—B1 would result in technical difficulties, Fine prefers to play to win in the middle game. His judgment is correct, but he goes astray later on.

21	KR—Kt1
22 P—KB4!	. . . .

Seemingly crushing . . . and it should have been, with proper play.

22	B—Kt2!

At last he gets counterplay. Naturally the Queen cannot be captured.

23 R—B2	B—K5
24 Q—Q2	K—B2
25 R—K1	R—Kt5

Capablanca

Fine

26 Kt—B5?   . . . .

An understandable mistake in this crucial position (Fine had six minutes left for thirteen moves, Capablanca only one minute left!). The proper course was 27 P x P! as pointed out by Belavenetz: 27 . . . R x Pch; 28 R x R, B x R; 29 P— K6ch! and wins; or 27 . . . Q x P; 28 Q x P, Q x Qch; 29 Kt x Q, B x KtP; 30 R x B, R x Kt; 31 R(2)— K2 and White wins the ending.
After the faulty text, the advantage passes to Black.

26	B x KtP!
27 R x B	QR—KKt1
28 R(1)—K2	P x P!

This is the key to Capablanca's counterplay. A magnificent move in such time pressure.

29 Kt—Kt7	Q—Q4!
30 R x R	R x Rch
31 R—Kt2	R x Rch
32 Q x R	P—B6
33 Q—R3	. . . .

Now it looks as if White will maintain his piece, as . . . Q x Kt? would cost the Queen.

33 . . . .   Q—Kt4ch!

Forcing White's reply, for if 34 K—B1? Q—B8ch; 35 K—B2, Q— K6ch; 36 K—B1, Q—K7ch; 37 K— Kt1, P—B7ch forcing mate. 34 K—B2? Q—K6ch leads to the same variation.

34 Q—Kt3	Q—B8ch
35 K—B2	Q—K6ch
36 K—B1	Q—K7ch
37 K—Kt1	Q—Q8ch
38 K—B2	Q x Pch
39 K x P	Q—B3ch
40 K—K2	Q x Kt

The time pressure is over, but both players have been moving so rapidly that they don't realize it!

41 P—Kt3   Q—K5ch

42 K—Q2	Q—K4
43 Q—R3	Q—Kt4ch
44 K—Q3	. . . .

At this point a draw was agreed on, as White must regain the extra Pawn. An imperfect game, but a magnificent struggle!

---

110. Avro Tournament, 1938

INDIAN DEFENSE

Capablanca consistently outplays his famous opponent here and scores a well-earned win.

J. R. CAPABLANCA   DR. M. EUWE

White	Black
1 P—Q4	Kt—KB3
2 P—QB4	P—K3
3 Kt—QB3	B—Kt5
4 Q—B2	P—Q4
5 P x P	Q x P

. . . P x P leads to a colorless kind of game for Black in which his KB would be posted to more advantage at K2 than at Kt5.

6 Kt—B3	P—B4
7 B—Q2	B x Kt
8 B x B	. . . .

Simpler than 8 P x B (Game No. 89), the text leaves White with a slight advantage. As the two Bishops may easily become formidable, Black must play with care.

8 . . . .   P x P

Two rounds later, the game Capablanca-Fine continued 8 . . . Kt—B3; 9 R—Q1! O—O; 10 P— K3, P—QKt3; 11 P—QR3, B—Kt2; 12 P x P! Q x P; 13 P—QKt4 and Black was able to keep his head above water only as a result of exceptionally resourceful play.

9 Kt x P   . . . .

Later analysis unearthed a very strong alternative in 9 R—Q1! Q x P; 10 B—Kt4! or 9 . . . P—K4; 10 P—K3 with advantage to White.

9	P—K4
10 Kt—B5	B x Kt
11 Q x B	Kt—B3

A difficult position to appraise. Black's more aggressive position in the center probably makes up for his opponent's two Bishops.

12 P—K3	O—O
13 B—K2	Q—K5

Not 13 . . . Q x KtP; 14 B—B3, Q—Kt3; 15 Q x Q, RP x Q; 16 B x Kt, P x B; 17 B x P and the ending is clearly in White's favor.

14 Q—B3	Q—B7?

In his anxiety to keep the dreaded Bishops at bay, Black miscalculates. . . . KR—K1 is better, but the text has a superficial attraction because it apparently stops 15 O—O in view of the reply . . . P—K5.

Euwe

Capablanca

15 O—O!	QR—Q1

Realizing that 15 . . . P—K5; 16 Q—Kt3, Q x KB; 17 B x Kt would leave Black with a lost game. But the text leads to new difficulties; . . . P—QR3 was relatively best.

16 B—Kt5!	R—Q4

The KP had to be protected; however, White has a strategically won game, as he now demonstrates.

17 QR—B1	Q—K5
18 Q—K2	R—Q3

Or 18 . . . R—B1; 19 P—B3, Q—Kt3; 20 P—K4, R—B4; 21 P—QKt4, Kt—Q5; 22 Q—Q3, R x QB; 23 R x R, Kt—K7ch; 24 Q x Kt, R x R; 25 Q—Kt2 winning the KP (Kmoch).

19 P—B3	Q—B4
20 B x Kt	R x B

Capablanca is exploiting his advantage in admirable style. The text allows the loss of a Pawn, but if 20 . . . P x B; 21 B—Kt4 wins.

21 Q—Kt5	KR—B1
22 Q x KtP	Q—Q6
23 P—K4!	Kt—R4

Hoping to take advantage of the White Queen's absence for a desperate attack. If 23 . . . Q—K6ch; 24 K—R1, Kt—R4 (threatens . . . Kt—Kt6ch); 25 Q x Rch! R x Q; 26 B—Q2, R x R; 27 R x R and wins.

24 P—KKt3!	. . . .

Simple and strong. If 24 K—R1?? Kt—Kt6ch; 25 P x Kt, R—R3 ch; 26 K—Kt1, Q—K6ch wins. If 24 Q x P, Kt—B5 with good counterchances.

24	Q—K6ch
25 K—Kt2	Q—Kt4
26 K—B2!	P—B4

Giving up a piece to continue the attack. This is inadequate, but he has no good line.

27 P x P	Q x P
28 P—KKt4	Q—B5
29 P x Kt	Q x RPch
30 K—K3	Q—B5ch
31 K—K2	Q—B5ch
32 K—K1	Q—Q6

White now consolidates his position without much effort.

33	Q—Kt3ch	K—R1
34	R—QB2!	R—B3
35	R—Q2	Q—B4
36	Q—B2	Q—B5
37	Q—K4	Q—Kt6ch
38	R(1)—B2	Q—Kt8ch
39	K—K2	R(3)—B1
40	P—R6!	Resigns

---

111. Buenos Aires Team Tournament, 1939

INDIAN DEFENSE

In commenting on this game, one could not do better than quote Golombek's summary: "A beautiful game by Capablanca, whose apparent simplicity hides a good deal of art."

J. R. CAPABLANCA	V. MIKENAS
(Cuba)	*(Lithuania)*
White	Black

1	P—Q4	Kt—KB3
2	P—QB4	P—K3
3	Kt—QB3	B—Kt5
4	Q—B2	Kt—B3

For . . . P—Q4 here, see Game No. 89.

5	Kt—B3	P—Q4

The basic idea of Black's last move is to continue with . . . P—Q3 and—in due course— . . . P—K4. The text, on the other hand, leads to a Pawn formation in which Black's QB is likely to have a severely limited field of action.

6	P—QR3	B x Ktch
7	Q x B	P—QR4

Not absolutely essential, for if 7 . . . B—Q2; 8 P—QKt4, P—QR4; 9 P—Kt5, Kt—R2; 10 P—QR4, P—

B3 (a line worked out by Ragozin) and Black has a good game. However, White would answer 7 . . . B—Q2 advantageously with 8 B—Kt5.

8	P—QKt3	. . . .

Not so much with the idea of fianchettoing the QB, as to prevent his Queen-side from being fixed with . . . P—R5.

8	. . . .	O—O
9	B—Kt5	P—R3
10	B x Kt!	. . . .

Better than the plausible 10 B—R4, which could be met by 10 . . . P—KKt4; 11 B—Kt3, Kt—K5; 12 Q—B2, P—R4! and Black stands well.

10	. . . .	Q x B

Black is now left with the inferior Bishop, which will give him trouble for the remainder of the game.

11	P—K3	B—Q2
12	B—Q3	KR—B1

Portentously preparing for some Queen-side play which never materializes.

13	O—O	P—R5
14	P—QKt4	P x P
15	B x P	Kt—R2
16	Kt—K5	B—K1

. . . B—Kt4 was somewhat better, although it would have left White with a clear positional advantage.

17	P—B4	P—QKt3

. . . Kt—Kt4—Q3 had to be tried. After the text, Capablanca decides the game by a neat combination.

18	Q—Q3	R—Q1
19	P—B5!	. . . .

Decisive line-opening. Black's reply is sheer despair.

19	. . . .	P—QKt4

Apparently winning a piece, for if 20 B—R2? Q x Kt.

Mikenas

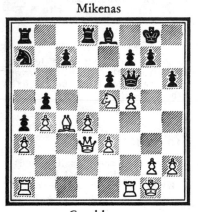

Capablanca

20 P x P!	P x B
21 R x Q	P x Q
22 P x Pch	B x P
23 R x B	Kt—Kt4

Or 23 . . . Kt—B3; 24 R x P, Kt x Kt; 25 P x Kt, P—Q7; 26 R—Q1 winning easily.

24 R—B2	R—Q4
25 Kt x P	R—K1
26 R—B3	Resigns

---

112.   Buenos Aires Team Tournament, 1939

CARO-KANN DEFENSE

This is a very original game, handled with delightful freshness and verve by both players. The second phase, in which Capablanca demonstrates the middle game superiority of a minor piece against three Pawns, is also most rewarding.

J. R. CAPABLANCA   M. CZERNIAK
    (Cuba)   (Palestine)

White   Black

1 P—K4   P—QB3

2 P—Q4	P—Q4
3 P x P	P x P
4 P—QB4	. . . .

As Capablanca is playing against one of his favorite defenses, he prefers to adopt the novel Panov Attack, which he has never been called upon to meet with the Black pieces.

4 . . . .   Kt—QB3

. . . Kt—KB3 is safer. However, Czerniak is a very aggressive player, and prefers to try for pressure on White's QP, which is likely to become isolated.

5 Kt—KB3   B—Kt5

Continuing with his plan, although . . . Kt—B3 would be safer.

| 6 P x P | Q x P |
| 7 B—K2 | . . . . |

Capablanca is not intimidated by his opponent's plans, and proceeds with simple and clear developing moves.

| 7 . . . . | P—K3 |
| 8 O—O | . . . . |

He defers Kt—B3 so that Black will not be able to pin the Knight.

| 8 . . . . | Kt—B3 |
| 9 Kt—B3 | Q—QR4 |

. . . Q—Q1 was safer, but Czerniak is not interested in safe moves.

| 10 P—KR3 | B—R4 |
| 11 P—R3 | R—Q1 |

. . . B—K2 followed by . . . O—O was the normal course; but Black wishes to concentrate on the only weak point in White's position.

12 P—KKt4!   . . . .

This wild looking move is something one would never expect from Capablanca; but it protects the QP and initiates an interesting combination.

| 12 . . . . | B—Kt3 |
| 13 P—Kt4! | B x P |

Black could avoid the sacrifice with . . . Q—B2, but his position would remain unpleasant in any event.

| 14 P x B | Q x R |
| 15 Q—Kt3 | . . . . |

The point: White threatens B—Kt2 winning the Queen.

Czerniak

Capablanca

| 15 . . . . | R x P! |

This cannot be answered by 16 B—Kt2? R x P! 17 Q x R, Q x Rch! nor by 16 Kt x R, Kt x Kt; 17 Q—B4, Q x Kt! All very ingenious, but White has something better in reply.

| 16 B—R3 | B—B7 |

The only move!

| 17 Q x B | Q x B |
| 18 Kt—QKt5! | . . . . |

And again not 18 Kt x R? Kt x Kt; 19 Q—Q2 (19 Q—R4ch, Q x Q; 20 Kt x Q, Kt x Bch), Q x Kt etc.

18	Q x P
19 KKt x R	Kt x Kt
20 Kt x Kt	. . . .

Not 20 Q—B8ch? K—K2; 21 Q x R, Kt x Bch followed by . . . Q x Kt.

| 20 . . . . | O—O |

Of course not 20 . . . Q x Kt? 21 R—Q1 and wins (21 . . . Q—K4; 22 Q—B8ch, K—K2; 23 Q x R, Q x B; 24 Q—Q8 mate). The position now arrived at is extremely interesting. Black has three Pawns, two of them passed, for the piece. Yet the Pawns are unable to play an important part at this stage, so that White has a fairly easy win in prospect.

| 21 R—Q1 | Kt—Q4 |

. . . R—Q1 would be answered very strongly by Q—B7!

| 22 B—B3 | Kt—B5 |
| 23 K—R2 | P—K4 |

Leading to an unfortunate weakening of his KB4 and Q4, but what is he to do? If 23 . . . Q—Q3; 24 Kt—K2, Q—K4; 25 Kt x Kt, Q x Kt ch; 26 K—Kt2, P—QKt3; 27 R—Q7 (Kmoch) winning easily. On other moves White would have played Kt—K2 in any event, with the eventual conclusive threats of R—Q7 or R—QKt1.

| 24 Kt—B5 | P—KKt3 |

One weakness leads to another; but the White Knight was too strongly posted.

| 25 Kt—K3 | Kt—K3 |
| 26 Kt—Q5! | . . . . |

The Field points out that this is more forcing than 26 R—QKt1, Q—B5ch; 27 K—Kt2, Q x Bch; 28 K x Q, Kt—Q5ch; 29 K—Kt3, Kt x Q; 30 Kt x Kt, R—B1 followed by . . . P—Kt3. If in this 29 K—K4, Kt x Q; 30 Kt x Kt, P—Kt3; 31 K x P, R—K1ch followed by . . . R—K7.

26	Q—R6
27 R—Q3	Q—R8
28 R—Q1	Q—R6

29 R—Q3	Q—R8
30 Q—Q2!	. . . .

Having gained time on the clock, Capablanca threatens to exploit the King-side weaknesses with 31 Q—R6, P—B3; 32 Kt—K7ch and wins.

30	K—Kt2
31 Q—K2!	. . . .

Remorselessly forcing another weakness because of the threatened R—Q1.

31	P—B3
32 Q—K3!	P—R3

R—R3 was threatened.

33 R—Q1!	Q—Kt7

34 Kt—B3	. . . .

This makes the win clear. The primary threat is R—QKt1, and if 34 . . . P—QKt4; 35 R—Q7ch, R—B2; 36 R x Rch, K x R; 37 B—Q5! and wins.

34	Kt—Q5

Or 34 . . . R—B2; 35 B—Q5 etc.

35 R—QKt1	Q—B7

As Black would lose very quickly after the normal reply 35 . . . Q—R6, the fact that the text loses the Queen does not much matter.

36 B—K4	Resigns

An outstanding game even among the many fine ones produced by Capablanca.

Index of Openings

All numbers refer to games. Bold type indicates games in which Capablanca had the white pieces.

A CATALOG OF SELECTED
DOVER BOOKS
IN ALL FIELDS OF INTEREST

A CATALOG OF SELECTED DOVER
BOOKS IN ALL FIELDS OF INTEREST

CONCERNING THE SPIRITUAL IN ART, Wassily Kandinsky. Pioneering work by father of abstract art. Thoughts on color theory, nature of art. Analysis of earlier masters. 12 illustrations. 80pp. of text. 5⅜ x 8½. 23411-8 Pa. $3.95

ANIMALS: 1,419 Copyright-Free Illustrations of Mammals, Birds, Fish, Insects, etc., Jim Harter (ed.). Clear wood engravings present, in extremely lifelike poses, over 1,000 species of animals. One of the most extensive pictorial sourcebooks of its kind. Captions. Index. 284pp. 9 x 12. 23766-4 Pa. $12.95

CELTIC ART: The Methods of Construction, George Bain. Simple geometric techniques for making Celtic interlacements, spirals, Kells-type initials, animals, humans, etc. Over 500 illustrations. 160pp. 9 x 12. (USO) 22923-8 Pa. $9.95

AN ATLAS OF ANATOMY FOR ARTISTS, Fritz Schider. Most thorough reference work on art anatomy in the world. Hundreds of illustrations, including selections from works by Vesalius, Leonardo, Goya, Ingres, Michelangelo, others. 593 illustrations. 192pp. 7⅛ x 10¼. 20241-0 Pa. $9.95

CELTIC HAND STROKE-BY-STROKE (Irish Half-Uncial from "The Book of Kells"): An Arthur Baker Calligraphy Manual, Arthur Baker. Complete guide to creating each letter of the alphabet in distinctive Celtic manner. Covers hand position, strokes, pens, inks, paper, more. Illustrated. 48pp. 8¼ x 11. 24336-2 Pa. $3.95

EASY ORIGAMI, John Montroll. Charming collection of 32 projects (hat, cup, pelican, piano, swan, many more) specially designed for the novice origami hobbyist. Clearly illustrated easy-to-follow instructions insure that even beginning papercrafters will achieve successful results. 48pp. 8¼ x 11. 27298-2 Pa. $3.50

THE COMPLETE BOOK OF BIRDHOUSE CONSTRUCTION FOR WOODWORKERS, Scott D. Campbell. Detailed instructions, illustrations, tables. Also data on bird habitat and instinct patterns. Bibliography. 3 tables. 63 illustrations in 15 figures. 48pp. 5¼ x 8½. 24407-5 Pa. $2.50

BLOOMINGDALE'S ILLUSTRATED 1886 CATALOG: Fashions, Dry Goods and Housewares, Bloomingdale Brothers. Famed merchants' extremely rare catalog depicting about 1,700 products: clothing, housewares, firearms, dry goods, jewelry, more. Invaluable for dating, identifying vintage items. Also, copyright-free graphics for artists, designers. Co-published with Henry Ford Museum & Greenfield Village. 160pp. 8¼ x 11. 25780-0 Pa. $10.95

HISTORIC COSTUME IN PICTURES, Braun & Schneider. Over 1,450 costumed figures in clearly detailed engravings—from dawn of civilization to end of 19th century. Captions. Many folk costumes. 256pp. 8⅜ x 11¾. 23150-X Pa. $12.95

STICKLEY CRAFTSMAN FURNITURE CATALOGS, Gustav Stickley and L. & J. G. Stickley. Beautiful, functional furniture in two authentic catalogs from 1910. 594 illustrations, including 277 photos, show settles, rockers, armchairs, reclining chairs, bookcases, desks, tables. 183pp. 6½ x 9¼. 23838-5 Pa. $9.95

AMERICAN LOCOMOTIVES IN HISTORIC PHOTOGRAPHS: 1858 to 1949, Ron Ziel (ed.). A rare collection of 126 meticulously detailed official photographs, called "builder portraits," of American locomotives that majestically chronicle the rise of steam locomotive power in America. Introduction. Detailed captions. xi + 129pp. 9 x 12. 27393-8 Pa. $12.95

AMERICA'S LIGHTHOUSES: An Illustrated History, Francis Ross Holland, Jr. Delightfully written, profusely illustrated fact-filled survey of over 200 American lighthouses since 1716. History, anecdotes, technological advances, more. 240pp. 8 x 10¾. 25576-X Pa. $12.95

TOWARDS A NEW ARCHITECTURE, Le Corbusier. Pioneering manifesto by founder of "International School." Technical and aesthetic theories, views of industry, economics, relation of form to function, "mass-production split" and much more. Profusely illustrated. 320pp. 6⅛ x 9¼. (USO) 25023-7 Pa. $9.95

HOW THE OTHER HALF LIVES, Jacob Riis. Famous journalistic record, exposing poverty and degradation of New York slums around 1900, by major social reformer. 100 striking and influential photographs. 233pp. 10 x 7⅞. 22012-5 Pa. $10.95

FRUIT KEY AND TWIG KEY TO TREES AND SHRUBS, William M. Harlow. One of the handiest and most widely used identification aids. Fruit key covers 120 deciduous and evergreen species; twig key 160 deciduous species. Easily used. Over 300 photographs. 126pp. 5⅜ x 8½. 20511-8 Pa. $3.95

COMMON BIRD SONGS, Dr. Donald J. Borror. Songs of 60 most common U.S. birds: robins, sparrows, cardinals, bluejays, finches, more—arranged in order of increasing complexity. Up to 9 variations of songs of each species.
Cassette and manual 99911-4 $8.95

ORCHIDS AS HOUSE PLANTS, Rebecca Tyson Northen. Grow cattleyas and many other kinds of orchids—in a window, in a case, or under artificial light. 63 illustrations. 148pp. 5⅜ x 8½. 23261-1 Pa. $4.95

MONSTER MAZES, Dave Phillips. Masterful mazes at four levels of difficulty. Avoid deadly perils and evil creatures to find magical treasures. Solutions for all 32 exciting illustrated puzzles. 48pp. 8¼ x 11. 26005-4 Pa. $2.95

MOZART'S DON GIOVANNI (DOVER OPERA LIBRETTO SERIES), Wolfgang Amadeus Mozart. Introduced and translated by Ellen H. Bleiler. Standard Italian libretto, with complete English translation. Convenient and thoroughly portable—an ideal companion for reading along with a recording or the performance itself. Introduction. List of characters. Plot summary. 121pp. 5¼ x 8½. 24944-1 Pa. $2.95

TECHNICAL MANUAL AND DICTIONARY OF CLASSICAL BALLET, Gail Grant. Defines, explains, comments on steps, movements, poses and concepts. 15-page pictorial section. Basic book for student, viewer. 127pp. 5⅜ x 8½. 21843-0 Pa. $4.95

AUTOBIOGRAPHY: The Story of My Experiments with Truth, Mohandas K. Gandhi. Boyhood, legal studies, purification, the growth of the Satyagraha (nonviolent protest) movement. Critical, inspiring work of the man responsible for the freedom of India. 480pp. 5⅜ x 8½. (USO) 24593-4 Pa. $8.95

CELTIC MYTHS AND LEGENDS, T. W. Rolleston. Masterful retelling of Irish and Welsh stories and tales. Cuchulain, King Arthur, Deirdre, the Grail, many more. First paperback edition. 58 full-page illustrations. 512pp. 5⅜ x 8½. 26507-2 Pa. $9.95

THE PRINCIPLES OF PSYCHOLOGY, William James. Famous long course complete, unabridged. Stream of thought, time perception, memory, experimental methods; great work decades ahead of its time. 94 figures. 1,391pp. 5⅜ x 8½. 2-vol. set.
Vol. I: 20381-6 Pa. $12.95
Vol. II: 20382-4 Pa. $12.95

THE WORLD AS WILL AND REPRESENTATION, Arthur Schopenhauer. Definitive English translation of Schopenhauer's life work, correcting more than 1,000 errors, omissions in earlier translations. Translated by E. F. J. Payne. Total of 1,269pp. 5⅜ x 8½. 2-vol. set.
Vol. 1: 21761-2 Pa. $11.95
Vol. 2: 21762-0 Pa. $12.95

MAGIC AND MYSTERY IN TIBET, Madame Alexandra David-Neel. Experiences among lamas, magicians, sages, sorcerers, Bonpa wizards. A true psychic discovery. 32 illustrations. 321pp. 5⅜ x 8½. (USO) 22682-4 Pa. $8.95

THE EGYPTIAN BOOK OF THE DEAD, E. A. Wallis Budge. Complete reproduction of Ani's papyrus, finest ever found. Full hieroglyphic text, interlinear transliteration, word-for-word translation, smooth translation. 533pp. 6½ x 9¼. 21866-X Pa. $10.95

MATHEMATICS FOR THE NONMATHEMATICIAN, Morris Kline. Detailed, college-level treatment of mathematics in cultural and historical context, with numerous exercises. Recommended Reading Lists. Tables. Numerous figures. 641pp. 5⅜ x 8½. 24823-2 Pa. $11.95

THEORY OF WING SECTIONS: Including a Summary of Airfoil Data, Ira H. Abbott and A. E. von Doenhoff. Concise compilation of subsonic aerodynamic characteristics of NACA wing sections, plus description of theory. 350pp. of tables. 693pp. 5⅜ x 8½. 60586-8 Pa. $14.95

THE RIME OF THE ANCIENT MARINER, Gustave Doré, S. T. Coleridge. Doré's finest work; 34 plates capture moods, subtleties of poem. Flawless full-size reproductions printed on facing pages with authoritative text of poem. "Beautiful. Simply beautiful."—*Publisher's Weekly.* 77pp. 9¼ x 12. 22305-1 Pa. $6.95

NORTH AMERICAN INDIAN DESIGNS FOR ARTISTS AND CRAFTSPEOPLE, Eva Wilson. Over 360 authentic copyright-free designs adapted from Navajo blankets, Hopi pottery, Sioux buffalo hides, more. Geometrics, symbolic figures, plant and animal motifs, etc. 128pp. 8⅜ x 11. (EUK) 25341-4 Pa. $8.95

SCULPTURE: Principles and Practice, Louis Slobodkin. Step-by-step approach to clay, plaster, metals, stone; classical and modern. 253 drawings, photos. 255pp. 8⅛ x 11. 22960-2 Pa. $11.95

THE INFLUENCE OF SEA POWER UPON HISTORY, 1660–1783, A. T. Mahan. Influential classic of naval history and tactics still used as text in war colleges. First paperback edition. 4 maps. 24 battle plans. 640pp. 5⅜ x 8½. 25509-3 Pa. $12.95

THE STORY OF THE TITANIC AS TOLD BY ITS SURVIVORS, Jack Winocour (ed.). What it was really like. Panic, despair, shocking inefficiency, and a little heroism. More thrilling than any fictional account. 26 illustrations. 320pp. 5⅜ x 8½. 20610-6 Pa. $8.95

FAIRY AND FOLK TALES OF THE IRISH PEASANTRY, William Butler Yeats (ed.). Treasury of 64 tales from the twilight world of Celtic myth and legend: "The Soul Cages," "The Kildare Pooka," "King O'Toole and his Goose," many more. Introduction and Notes by W. B. Yeats. 352pp. 5⅜ x 8½. 26941-8 Pa. $8.95

BUDDHIST MAHAYANA TEXTS, E. B. Cowell and Others (eds.). Superb, accurate translations of basic documents in Mahayana Buddhism, highly important in history of religions. The Buddha-karita of Asvaghosha, Larger Sukhavativyuha, more. 448pp. 5⅜ x 8½. 25552-2 Pa. $12.95

ONE TWO THREE . . . INFINITY: Facts and Speculations of Science, George Gamow. Great physicist's fascinating, readable overview of contemporary science: number theory, relativity, fourth dimension, entropy, genes, atomic structure, much more. 128 illustrations. Index. 352pp. 5⅜ x 8½. 25664-2 Pa. $8.95

ENGINEERING IN HISTORY, Richard Shelton Kirby, et al. Broad, nontechnical survey of history's major technological advances: birth of Greek science, industrial revolution, electricity and applied science, 20th-century automation, much more. 181 illustrations. ". . . excellent . . ."–*Isis*. Bibliography. vii + 530pp. 5⅜ x 8¼. 26412-2 Pa. $14.95

DALÍ ON MODERN ART: The Cuckolds of Antiquated Modern Art, Salvador Dalí. Influential painter skewers modern art and its practitioners. Outrageous evaluations of Picasso, Cézanne, Turner, more. 15 renderings of paintings discussed. 44 calligraphic decorations by Dalí. 96pp. 5⅜ x 8½. (USO) 29220-7 Pa. $4.95

ANTIQUE PLAYING CARDS: A Pictorial History, Henry René D'Allemagne. Over 900 elaborate, decorative images from rare playing cards (14th–20th centuries): Bacchus, death, dancing dogs, hunting scenes, royal coats of arms, players cheating, much more. 96pp. 9¼ x 12¼. 29265-7 Pa. $11.95

MAKING FURNITURE MASTERPIECES: 30 Projects with Measured Drawings, Franklin H. Gottshall. Step-by-step instructions, illustrations for constructing handsome, useful pieces, among them a Sheraton desk, Chippendale chair, Spanish desk, Queen Anne table and a William and Mary dressing mirror. 224pp. 8⅛ x 11¼. 29338-6 Pa. $13.95

THE FOSSIL BOOK: A Record of Prehistoric Life, Patricia V. Rich et al. Profusely illustrated definitive guide covers everything from single-celled organisms and dinosaurs to birds and mammals and the interplay between climate and man. Over 1,500 illustrations. 760pp. 7½ x 10⅛. 29371-8 Pa. $29.95

Prices subject to change without notice.

Available at your book dealer or write for free catalog to Dept. GI, Dover Publications, Inc., 31 East 2nd St., Mineola, N.Y. 11501. Dover publishes more than 500 books each year on science, elementary and advanced mathematics, biology, music, art, literary history, social sciences and other areas.